Labor in Twentieth Century America

LUMBER AND LABOR

By

VERNON H. JENSEN

FARRAR & RINEHART, INC.
NEW YORK   ::   TORONTO

DEDICATED TO
CHARLES A. GULICK

EDITORS' FOREWORD

A DEFINITIVE history of the men and women who have worked for a living in the nation's major fields of production since the United States has been industrialized still remains to be written. The Labor in Twentieth Century America Series has been undertaken to facilitate the fulfillment of this task for the period of the present century.

By the close of the nineteenth century, the dominant patterns which American life has since assumed were already taking form. The labor movement, having shed its earlier middle-class reformist characteristics, had become primarily committed to the more limited but enormously important purpose of securing higher wages, shorter hours and better working conditions through economic means. This purpose and method still distinguish the American labor movement. But significant differences set off the scope, orientation, membership, financial resources, and relationship to government of organized labor today from that of the turn of the century.

American labor has been on the march in recent years. Its ultimate destination is still somewhat obscure, and the war—in the outcome of which labor has so much at stake—is critically affecting the speed and direction of its movement. Before the advent of world conflict, the impact of the depression and New Deal legislation contributed to the abandonment of outworn concepts and behavior patterns and the appearance of a new vitality in labor circles. In the last dozen years, organized labor has experienced its sharpest internal conflicts; the American Federation of Labor met its first full-scale challenge in the Congress of Industrial Organization; membership figures have sky-rocketed to new heights; strongholds of anti-unionism have been breached; the principle of collective bargaining has been decisively recognized; and the right to organize has been effectively protected.

The story of those who constitute the labor force in industry cannot be told alone through the rise and fall of trade unions, developments in industrial relations and bitterly contested labor conflicts. Equally essential are an analysis of the industrial structure and of the composition of the workers; treatment of the conditions of labor, living standards, and opportunities for education and recreation; and consideration of changing attitudes of behavior on the part of government and the public. These views conditioned the planning and contents of the Labor in Twentieth Century America Series.

Dr. Vernon H. Jensen's volume is the first full and scholarly account of twentieth century labor in a field which, for all its fascination, has been little studied. The primary concern of *Lumber and Labor* are the tough, hardworking men who have made possible America's most distinctive migratory, frontier industry. Here is an industry which has marched across the continent devouring both forests and men, creating problems in human and economic adjustment in the cut-over regions it has left behind. Dr. Jensen deals objectively and sympathetically with its lumberjacks, lumbermen and sawmill workers who constitute a unique group among the nation's workers. Facing constant hazards in a harsh environment, they created their own way of life in and outside the logging camps and gave American folklore a legendary hero in Paul Bunyan. Only in recent years has the lumbering industry been organized. Dr. Jensen's treatment of the complex story of unionization and of interunion conflicts, of bitter industrial struggles, and of the impact of the war upon the industry is authoritative. The war economy's limitless appetite for lumber combined with an acute manpower shortage to produce one of the most critical labor problems in the country. The author's exceptional treatment of this problem stems in part from his extensive first-hand knowledge of both the industry and its workers.

THE EDITORS

December, 1944

ACKNOWLEDGMENT

IT IS impossible for the author to express his thanks individually to all the people who so kindly assisted him at various times while he was conducting his research and while he was preparing the manuscript for publication. A few individuals and organizations deserve special mention. Dr. Charles A. Gulick stimulated the research in the first instance and made many helpful criticisms. Ernest S. Marsh, U.S. labor commissioner, has made very helpful suggestions and has given much of his time and knowledge of the lumber industry, as well as having read, at one time, most of the manuscript.

A wealth of material was made available in the files of the 4L, the Loyal Legion of Loggers and Lumbermen, and the Industrial Employees Union, successor to the 4L, through the assistance of W. C. Ruegnitz, one-time president of the 4L. Likewise, J. B. Fitzgerald, secretary of the Lumbermen's Industrial Relations Committee, has provided valuable information in certain literature and records which he made available. The Southern Pine Association, through its secretary H. C. Berckes, also provided reports which were of value in appraising the conditions of labor in the southern lumber industry. Many union men and leaders have given of their time and experience; among them have been Worth Lowery, president of the IWA, and Peter Terzick, editor of the *Union Register*. In addition, the editors of the *Timberworker*, the *Woodworker*, the Duluth *Timber Worker* and *Midwest Labor* were gracious in making available file copies of their respective publications. Both the Northwest Council of Sawmill and Timber Workers and the International Woodworkers of America have provided convention reports. And the Federation of Woodworkers, before them, did likewise. Various governmental agencies have been very co-operative, especially the Forest Service and the Forest Experiment Station offices of the U.S. Department of Agriculture, which gave freely of their literature and advice whenever called upon. Besides the individuals mentioned above, thanks must be extended to Raphael Zon, H. Gilbert White, R. K. Miller, I. F. Eldredge, Frederick A. Bushee, and Nephi Jensen, who read and criticized parts

ix

of the manuscript. Space will not permit the enumeration of all the other individuals, organizations, and government agencies that have given assistance. Nevertheless, the author is deeply grateful to all of them. The author, of course, takes sole responsibility for the selection and interpretation of all materials used.

The author is deeply grateful to the Graduate Research Council of the University of Colorado and to the Social Science Research Council for grants-in-aid of research which they made available to him, and without which this study could not have been so extensively carried on.

Finally, the author wishes to express his deep appreciation for the assistance given by the editors of the Labor in Twentieth Century America Series. Their criticisms and co-operation have improved the work immeasurably.

VERNON H. JENSEN

Department of Economics
University of Colorado
Boulder, Colorado

CONTENTS

PAGE

EDITORS' FOREWORD vii

ACKNOWLEDGMENT ix

CHAPTER
1. THE INDUSTRY 3

2. MIGRATION, MEN, AND ECONOMICS 20

3. THE NORTHEASTERN REGION 33

4. THE GREAT LAKES REGION 45

5. SOUTHERN PINE 71

6. THE WEST 99

7. EARLY ORGANIZATIONS IN THE WEST 114

8. DEPRESSION AND THE NRA 151

9. THE GREAT STRIKE OF 1935 164

10. A PERIOD OF NEW UNIONISM 187

11. BIRTH OF THE IWA 203

12. INTERNAL CONFLICTS AND JURISDICTIONAL DISPUTES 225

13. EMPLOYER-UNION RELATIONS 246

14. WAR YEARS AND PROSPECTS 273

BIBLIOGRAPHICAL NOTE 292

INDEX 309

LUMBER AND LABOR

1 *THE INDUSTRY*

THE LUMBER industry throughout most of its life has been an aggressive, ingenious, unstable migrant. Hard labor, romance of enterprise, and rough, wholesome, and sordid living are found in the chapter in American history which tells of the lumber industry. The spirit of Paul Bunyan and the exploits of this legendary hero ring true in the industry if one goes behind the gloss of exaggeration in the stories which proclaim his prowess in lumbering. Always on the go, pausing only temporarily, the lumber industry strode from a tiny beginning on the Atlantic seaboard, notably in the Northeast, as it devoured the forests where it found them, moving westward and southward across the length and breadth of the country. There is no wonder that lumbermen and lumberjacks have left a rich and fascinating history. Yet, even though the story is full of exploits of real he-men, it is not a romantic history. It is a history of down-to-earth people struggling and toiling in a harsh environment in order to make a living.

Life in the lumber industry has been varied. Lumberjacks in the early logging camps were almost a distinctive breed, who were quite appropriately described as "womanless, homeless, voteless" workers. But the isolated camp was not typical everywhere and when logging camps were made more accessible, by means of improved highways, the circumstances of life were somewhat altered. Predominantly native-born, although an unduly large number of Scandinavians and French Canadians and other immigrants have worked in the woods in certain areas, the workers have typified the conglomerate American stock with an average number of foreign-born workers. In the South, although isolated logging camps were common at one time throughout broad areas where lumbering was intensively carried on, the lives of the lumber industry workers have blended into living in the South, with its basic differences. In fact, there has always been much shifting back and forth between agriculture and lumbering in broad areas of the South—but this has been true to a certain extent in many other

3

regions. The widespread use of Negroes in the South has given rise to a different type of labor supply and to distinctive labor problems.

Sawmill workers, everywhere throughout the industry, have made up a portion of the vast army of manufacturing industry workers of America, and often have been psychologically and socially distinct from men engaged solely in logging work. Conditions in sawmilling, however, are as varied as those in logging, depending upon whether the sawmills are large, highly mechanized ones or small, locally established or temporary ones.

Whenever the industry has moved, complex problems of human and economic readjustment have been created. Problems in the "cut-over" regions have resulted in much hardship and, particularly in depression times, relief burdens have been heavy.

Employers, almost without exception, have been rugged individualists; self-made men who have won out in the difficult competitive struggle because of hard work and superior ability. Nevertheless, trade associations have a long history and employers have acted concertedly in order to influence favorably railroads or governmental agencies or to oppose unionization of workers—and more recently to bargain with labor unions. The workingmen in the industry also have been individualists to a large degree. Independence has been a characteristic of the lumberjack, and those men who have been part-time farmers have carried the typical view of independence so characteristic of the traditional American family farmer. Organization of labor has always been beset with obstacles. Of course, a large measure of the difficulty has come from a firm, almost religious, opposition to unionism on the part of operators who were thinking in terms of typical American nineteenth century thought.

The history of labor relations in the lumber industry is a story of the reactions and adjustments to problems peculiar to a huge, sometimes highly capitalized, industry on the fringe of the frontier, or operating under frontierlike conditions. It is a story of workmen in an oftentimes unnatural, restricted social environment. That many workers were exploited or taken advantage of by those who operated under relentless forces in an industry which has always been vulnerable to an ever-devouring, ruthless cutthroat competition has been, perhaps, inevitable. The heroic struggle of men to rise to higher planes of living is revealed in the attempts to form unions and improve conditions. Labor has played a characteristically turbulent and rigorous role. The lumber workers have experienced some of the glamour of the frontier environment, together with much of the frontier's ceaseless struggle, hardship, and uncertainty. The history of labor in the industry reveals life under varied and changing conditions.

Labor unionism, except of late years, has made little or no headway in certain sectors of the industry and has been carried on in all regions under extreme difficulties. Immaturity of labor organization in the country as a whole was reflected in the lumber industry in the fact that no labor unions appeared until the late seventies. Only some time afterward was there a real movement toward organization. In the Lake States, during the "boom era" of the eighties, there was a growth of unionism but it was sporadic because individualistically minded workers, immigrants, and part-time agriculturists could not be successfully organized. On the other hand, intense opposition from employers, schooled in individualism, was one of the greatest obstacles to unionism. Later, when the industry was in eclipse in the Lake States and was migrating to the South and the West, it was impossible to bargain successfully under the weakening circumstances of a declining labor market. Working and living conditions, which were always simple and often rather harsh, deteriorated noticeably. The Lake States cut-over region became one of America's important national problem areas.

In the South labor has been so closely associated with an impoverished agriculture that workers have never enjoyed any substantial economic strength or security. Living standards have often been on, or close to, subsistence levels, with only a few exceptions. What could be done to extend unionism in such an environment when, at the same time, there existed strong traditional attitudes of paternalism and strong feelings about "liberty" and "rights" which presumably were thought to be destroyed if workers were allowed to organize? The few attempts to establish collective bargaining in the South were vigorously suppressed. The universal condition, however, has been one of indifference and inability of workers to organize. Wages have continued low, and, because of the tendency for sawmills to become smaller and smaller and to work on undersized, second-growth timber, there is little hope for them to improve except under governmental assistance. The wage and hour legislation of the Roosevelt administration was proving its beneficial effect when the war broke out. After the war is over it will be needed more than ever if long-run improvement is intended for operators and workers alike. The southern lumber industry cannot be healthfully stabilized until wage competition is eliminated and living standards are improved. It will never be stabilized, moreover, until a controlled use of the forest resource is worked out, because promiscuous and unwise cutting of immature trees results in future, as well as present, economic demoralization. Labor legislation and unionism, chiefly the former, may improve working and living conditions. The employers and the government will most likely have to solve the problem of timber use. Almost everywhere the crying need is to recognize timber as a "crop" and not a "mine." Until the time when such recognition is established, any chance at future stabilization and economic improvement is slight.

The only place where unionism developed with any degree of continuity in organization was in the West. By the time the industry developed on a large scale there, the spirit of unionism was more definitely in the air throughout the country as a whole. A militant unionism had already developed in the mining regions of the West, and intolerable living conditions in the lumber camps and poor working conditions carried men into the organized groups. Again, in true lumber industry fashion, unions were vigorously opposed and harshly dealt with.

This intense opposition to unionism in the major lumber-producing areas should not be interpreted as a careless disregard for human welfare. Most lumbermen engaged in labor controversies were not without conscience, and may be said to have pursued a course that seemed to them proper and best calculated to promote the interests and welfare of all concerned. The spirit under which the lumber operators moved was, in part, a reflection of the times and the existing social conscience. Law and custom did not require the employer to grant recognition, while it did give him the right to suppress organizations of workers if he could. The great lesson in the history of labor relations in lumbering, reaching into the twentieth century, is that opposition to unionism, because it forces a trial of strength, results in open warfare. One party may be victorious, but refusal to recognize the other party is certainly not the wisest approach to the problems giving rise to disputes. The violation of civil rights in the course of these disputes leads to retaliation when no other redress is available.

The spectacular history of the Industrial Workers of the World, the I.W.W., in the lumber industry in the South, in the Lake States, and in the West is a case in point. The prevailing attitudes toward the I.W.W. and the frequent lawless treatment of the members of the organization instilled a great hatred and resentment in the men against the "system" which they held was responsible for their suppression. For the most part, the movement was indigenous. Its membership was composed of migratory loggers who had no home ties or voting rights because the industry kept them on the move, and they lived and worked under miserable circumstances. I.W.W. members were certainly victims of the constant buffeting of the prevailing economic and social forces which always appeared unfriendly to them; consequently, they sought redress. The only tactic likely to bring results to these voteless, economically weak workers was direct action. Having little to lose and much to gain, and meeting a tough foe, they resorted to militant tactics.

Without a knowledge of its structure, regional developments and characteristics, processes, living conditions and labor force, and, not least, its economic problems, the history of labor in the lumber industry cannot be fully understood or appreciated. It is essential, therefore, to consider in some detail the leading characteristics of the industry.

Felling trees and cutting them into logs, getting the logs to the mills, and sawing them into lumber have been important activities of pioneers and men of industry from the founding of the country to the present day. For the past fifty years the lumber industry has provided employment for approximately a half million workers. In addition, the wood-using and wood-processing industries have given work to another half million men. Thousands more, of course, draw their wages from the related supply industries.[1] Lumbering is carried on today in over forty states and is an important industry in half of them. Prior to the war it was actually the dominant industry in terms of employment provided in at least nine states, and ranked second in numbers employed in ten others.[2] The war has altered these relationships only slightly. Lumbering has been and is one of America's giant industries.

Within the scope of the lumber industry are found all the activities involved in producing and preparing the raw forest material employed in the secondary wood-using and wood-processing industries. Logging and sawmilling are the primary activities of the industry, but seasoning and planing of lumber as well as shingle, veneer, box, and cooperage production fall within its sphere.[3] There are persons who, possessing only timber land, sell stumpage from time to time to others who cut the logs. Then there are those who are engaged solely in logging, although an open log market on a large scale exists only in the Northwest. In that region logging and sawmilling activities are frequently carried on by separate units. Elsewhere the sale of logs from farm wood lots has increased in recent years and has influenced labor conditions appreciably. The most common industrial unit, however, combines the ownership of timber with logging and sawmilling.

The wood-processing and wood-using industries are not included in the lumber industry. For the most part these industries are distinguished by different characteristics and problems, and they are related only in so far as the raw material used in the processing and wood-using plants originates in the lumber industry. In several instances, however, a very close relationship does exist. In some places, for example, pulp logging is carried on jointly with logging saw timber and involves the same general type of work. Here the two industries cannot be logically divorced from each other. Moreover, where the workers in the pulp-logging camps and lumber-logging camps are organized, they belong to the same unions. There are also some instances where the production of doors, sashes, and even furniture is carried on by lumber producers, although this is not common.

There are four major regions of the lumber industry as well as a number of subregions.[4] Chronologically considered, the first of the major regions is the Northeastern. This comprises an area which begins in Maine, sweeps across other parts of New England of lesser importance in lumbering, and extends over the Middle Atlantic States into parts of New York and Pennsylvania. During the greater part of the nineteenth century this region was the most important producing area.[5] From this part of the United States the industry moved in two directions, southward and westward. To the west were the pine forests of the Lake States, and it is this region which has produced much of the "romance" that has grown up in connection with lumbering. In the closing decades of the nineteenth century the Lake States were the leading producers.

The Southern Pine region, the most sprawling of all, extends through nearly all of the coastal plain and rolling hill areas from Virginia southward over the Carolinas into Florida, and thence westward across Georgia, Alabama, Mississippi, Louisiana, and into Texas. It also spreads northward into Arkansas and part of Oklahoma. In this vast territory certain sections were of greater importance than others, and at least three main subregions are distinguishable. These are the pine uplands, the coastal plain pine areas along the Atlantic fringe, but more extensive along the Gulf, and the hardwood and cypress areas. The last subregion is not a compact one, and its parts are not contiguous. Hardwoods and cypress are found mainly in the broad river bottoms and swampy areas all through the South. Production and labor problems have varied greatly from one subregion to the other, and have changed markedly within specific subregions as the industry has expanded and declined.

The fourth major region is found in the West. It consists of a number of subregions, one of which has a claim to greatest importance. This subregion, running through both Washington and Oregon west of the Cascade Range, has been blessed with the best stand of fir timber that the world has ever known and is commonly referred to as the Douglas Fir region. It has made Washington and Oregon leading producers, and it is the latest stronghold of the industry.[6] An important pine belt extends along the eastern slope of the Cascade Range from northern Washington, through Oregon, and thence into northern California, branching along the Sierra Nevada Mountains almost the length of the state and to the west throughout the coastal area. Pine lumbering is also carried on in western Montana, northern Idaho, and eastern Washington and Oregon. These two large and sprawling subregions are separated by a treeless stretch of land running throughout central Washington and Oregon into Nevada. In California there are, in addition to the pine, the gigantic redwoods, which make up another important subregion.

Three other regions of lesser importance are the Central Hardwood region, the Appalachian region, and the Rocky Mountain region. The first two are located in the eastern half of the United States and shade into the major regions. The Central Hardwood area begins in western Pennsylvania and spreads broadly in a southwesterly direction. It takes in the area from southern Michigan and southern Wisconsin to northern Alabama and Mississippi, and reaches in a narrowing prong as far west as Texas. The Appalachian region stands, with no definite lines of demarcation, surrounded by the Southern Pine region, the Northeastern region, and the Central Hardwood region. The Rocky Mountain region is composed of pockets of forested areas throughout Wyoming, Utah, Colorado, New Mexico, and Arizona.

The four major regions are unequal in importance today. But each was at one time a leading producer (see Chart I). At present the Northeast and the Lake States play a comparatively light role. Both the Northeast and the Great Lakes regions passed their peaks before the turn of the century. The Southern Pine region reached its peak in the prewar years, but has continued as a significant producer. The West attained its greatest production during the mid-twenties.

Another insight into the changing significance of the various regions is found in the fluctuations in total employment of each (see Chart II). A noticeable but not precipitous decline in employment had occurred in Maine and New York by 1879, although the Northeastern region continued to hold its own. In 1889 there were some

CHART I

Lumber Production in the United States by Regions, 1870-1943
(Major Changes Only)

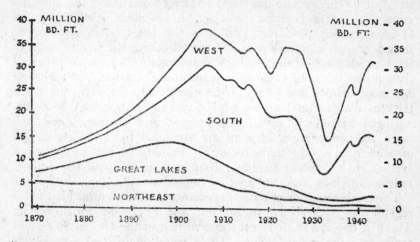

(Sources:

1870-1930, U.S. Department of Agriculture, *A National Plan for American Forestry.*
73rd Congress, 1st Session, Senate Document No. 12. Washington:
Government Printing Office, 1933, I: 216;
1931-1937, *Biennial Census of Manufactures, 1937,* Pt. I, p. 506;
1939-1942, U. S. Department of Commerce, Bureau of Census, *Census of Forest
Products: 1942.* Washington: Government Printing Office, 1944, p. 11.
1943, Estimated.)

65,000 men employed in lumbering in all of the states of the Northeast, 112,000 in the Lake States, 53,000 in the South, and 18,000 in
the West. Following 1890 the decline in employment continued
gradual in the Northeast, but a rapid decline occurred in the Lake
States, where ten years later the number employed had dropped to
63,000, a decline of 44 per cent. For a decade or more after 1900
employment in the Lake States remained almost stable, owing to the
development of hardwood lumbering which offset the decline in pine
lumbering activity. Since then employment has been falling off decidedly and at the same time has been very unstable. In the South,
employment picked up rapidly from 1889 to 1909, when it reached
262,000, and then remained at a high level until the mid-twenties.
Then a downward trend appeared which has since cut the total em-

CHART II

Lumber Industry Employment in the United States by Regions, 1879-1943
(Major Changes Only)

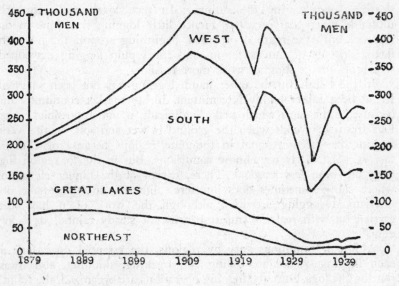

(Sources:

1879-1899, Twelfth Census of the United States, 1900, Vol. IX, *Manufactures,*
Part 3, pp. 807-810;

1899-1937, Work Projects Administration, *Mechanization in the Lumber Industry,*
by A. J. van Tassell and D. W. Bluestone. National Research Project
Report No. M-5, Philadelphia: Work Projects Administration, 1940,
p. 118;

1937-1943, Estimated.)

ployment almost in half. In the West employment rose from 1889 to
1929, to reach 115,000. The years after 1930 have been marked by a
drop in total employment in western lumbering,[7] which even the war
has not markedly increased.

The primary activity in the production of lumber is, of course,
logging, upon which the other activities follow. Logging involves
work in the open and in many cases under harsh or unfavorable
conditions. In the north woods it was essentially a wintertime activity,[8]
because the available means of transportation made it impracticable
to move the logs at other times. When the ground was frozen the logs

could be "snaked," or skidded, to the sleds which could then be moved over the snow to the rivers. Wheeled vehicles were hardly feasible in either winter or summer, and it cost too much to build improved roads. In addition, the pine logs made better lumber if they did not lie in the woods during the summer. In fact, logs were frequently unusable when that occurred. Hence little logging was done in the summer until the railroad provided, beginning around 1875, a more flexible means of transportation, and until pulp logging developed, which also made summer work more feasible.

In the South, on the other hand, logging has not been seasonal. It has been rather highly intermittent due to market conditions and because of the rains which make it difficult, if not impossible, to get logs from the woods when the ground is wet and soft. In the West logging has been seasonal in the pine regions because of climatic factors, particularly deep snow conditions. But in the fir region logging has been less seasonal. There, except at the higher elevations where snow sometimes does interfere, climatic conditions have not interrupted logging activities, although the work often has been carried on with real discomfort because of steady rainfall or heavy dew.[9]

Although conditions vary by regions, the essential operations at each logging chance are felling and bucking, skidding, and transporting the logs. Once the logging operations are organized, the felling of the standing timber is the first task in the job of getting the logs on their way to the sawmills. Important variations in tasks occur between regions and between various sized operations. Likewise, the terminology used varies somewhat. The men who fell the trees are most commonly referred to as "fallers," although they also have been known as "choppers" or "sawyers." The fallers work in pairs with the use of axes and saws, and wedges where the trees are large. Mechanical appliances have not been very successful in this work, although some are in use. Felling trees is hard and strenuous toil and husky, physically impressive men are generally found at it.

After the tree is felled, it is cut into log lengths by the "bucker" or "cutter," while in some regions "limbers" or "knotters" remove the branches. Where operations are large, especially in the West, the person in charge of these workers is commonly referred to as the "bull of the woods," or "strawboss." The logs are "yarded," or assembled, at loading places for the longer trip to the mill. If necessary, the "swamper" clears the way for skidding, or the movement, of the logs to the yarding places. Here draft animals, oxen, horses, or mules, alone or with wagons or big-wheeled log carts, or mechanical equipment such as cable yarders, tractors, and motor trucks have been used. Mechanical equipment has only been employed at big operations and where the trees have been large, notably in the yellow pine area and cypress swamps of the South, and in the West. In some cases the logs are hauled directly to the mills by trucks, or by animals if the distances are not too great. In early times in the Northeastern and Great Lakes regions, the logs were hauled to the rivers on sleds where they were held until they could be floated to the mills on the spring runoff. While the log drive provides one of America's distinctive and exciting spectacles,[10] the railroad provides a more flexible means of transportation. It superseded the log drive some time before the turn of the century as the chief means of getting the logs to the mills, except where small portable mills kept moving to the trees. In the South the railroad has been conspicuous at the larger operations and almost absent at the small ones. Except for very early times when three to four yoke of oxen were commonly used, the railroad has always been dominant in most parts of the West.[11] The motor truck is now used extensively everywhere. It is utilized almost exclusively on small operations and supplements the railroad on the larger ones.

Obviously, the techniques and the degree of specialization in tasks have depended upon the size of the logging unit. Very specialized crews of from two hundred to three hundred men may be found with the larger operations on the West Coast. Sometimes several crews of this size are stationed at a single camp. On the other hand, very small crews of three or four men have been employed, usually in "cleaning-up" operations in the areas not completely cut out by the larger-scale operations, and especially with the small units in the South where men shift back and forth from logging to sawmilling.

Sawmills usually are found in, or near, permanent settlements, although there are many exceptions in the case of small mills. In recent years the motor truck literally has been pulling the small mill out of the woods. Many sawmill communities, however, are comprised of only the lumber company's employees and are frequently quite isolated.

In sawmilling there are great variations between different sized units. Some mills are highly mechanized, with power appliances and rollers for handling and moving timber from the time it leaves the log pond until the lumber is stacked and ready for market. Other mills are less highly mechanized. The smallest ones consist of nothing more than a flimsy carriage and a circular saw. There is no simple way of picturing the extent of mechanization, although it is possible to relate the degree of mechanization to the number of mills of a given size. This involves making somewhat arbitrary distinctions and may obscure the fact that size provides a somewhat inaccurate measure of mechanization. In general, however, mills as small as those in classes 1, 2, and 3 in the accompanying table have only simple and crude machinery and much hand labor is involved. It is equally clear that the large mills are highly mechanized. A rough measure of mechanization may, therefore, be gleaned from the following table:

NUMBER AND PRODUCTION OF MILLS CLASSIFIED ACCORDING TO QUANTITY OF LUMBER CUT, 1929 [12]

Class	Capacity M. Feet		Mills		Quantity Cut	
			Number	Per Cent	M Feet	Per Cent
All			20,037	100.0	36,886,032	100.0
8	50,000	- Over	120	0.6	9,525,088	26.1
7	25,000 to	49,999	213	1.1	7,512,675	20.3
6	15,000 to	24,999	211	1.0	4,092,859	11.1
5	10,000 to	14,999	209	1.0	2,542,604	6.9
4	5,000 to	9,999	414	2.1	2,995,048	8.0
3	1,000 to	4,999	3,100	15.5	5,523,167	15.0
2	500 to	999	3,585	17.9	2,421,990	6.5
1	50 to	499	12,185	60.8	2,272,601	6.1

M means thousand board feet.

Because of the vast differences in level of mechanization, the ratio of hand labor (man-hours) per thousand feet of lumber cut varies considerably. It is very difficult to describe the various job activities briefly or to compare labor costs. In small plants practically all of the work, except that of the sawyer, is of an unskilled nature. Elsewhere it ranges in character from that requiring high technical and mechanical skills down through that performed by completely untrained common labor.[13]

The processes involved in sawmilling, in the larger units, begin with the storing of the logs in the log pond, where they are sorted by the "boomman" who prepares them for the trip to the saw. In the medium-sized and larger mills the logs enter the mill by way of an endless chain arrangement which pulls the logs up an incline to the log deck, from which they are shifted to the carriage as needed. In the small mills logs are not kept in a pond at all and are simply rolled to the carriage from the log deck. The carriage travels on rails and carries the log past the headsaw. In the larger mills the mechanical handling of the heavy timber from this point on is almost uncanny. In the smaller mills, however, frequently the logs are rolled onto the carriage, where the "dogs" are set by hand, and when the boards are cut from the logs they are in turn moved by hand. In the bigger units, the logs are shifted to the carriage with power equipment and the dogs are set mechanically. The sawyer, who controls the sawing of the logs, gives his signals to the carriageman, who, riding upon the carriage, shifts the log before it moves past the speeding bandsaw to produce the proper cut. When it is desired to cut from another side, the log on the carriage is turned mechanically. As the "cants" (large-dimension "stuff") are cut from the log, they fall on live rollers which carry them to the resaw, or gang saws, which reduces them to boards, planks, or other timber forms. By other systems of rollers the boards are carried to the edgers and trimmers where they are trimmed into proper lengths, squared, and the defective parts cut out. Other series of rollers carry the boards to the sorting tables where they are marked by graders, and then they pass on to be stacked by the yardmen. The stacks often are moved mechanically to the kilns, or to the piles, for drying. After drying, the lumber may be surfaced, or planed, on one or more sides. It is then ready for market. Except in the pine regions of the North and the West, sawmilling is a year-round activity, but, of course, production tends to be erratic because of market conditions.

Within the lumber industry sharp variations exist. On a comparable basis, such as output, only a few fairly large mills ever existed in the Northeastern and Great Lakes regions as compared with the mills in the yellow pine area in the South and with the mills in the West. After peak production has been reached, the mills normally tend to become smaller. Today, for example, only little mills are found in the Northeastern and Great Lakes regions. Within each area diversities in the size and number of producing units make for marked heterogeneity. The number of producing units is much greater in the South, and, on the average, the mills are much smaller. Differences in acquisition and ownership of timber lands help to explain why there are many small mills. The fact that stand per acre was much thinner and the actual volume of trees within an operable area was much smaller than in the West also has made for smaller mills in the South. Important, too, has been the cycle of production by which small units followed after the major operations and cut the isolated, left-over stands, or, after a lapse of a few years, cut the small second-growth trees. In the West the logging and sawmilling methods had, of necessity, to be modified. The logs were massive things which required heavy and expensive equipment to handle—especially because the terrain was more rugged. The overhead costs ran much above what they were in most other places. The small unit was not always workable, and large mills, based upon large tracts of forest land, became common. Not all mills, however, were large.

The number of lumber and timber products establishments reported by the Bureau of the Census stood at 25,758 for 1879, increased to 33,090 in 1909, but decreased to 26,119 in 1919, and to 20,037 in 1929.[14] This decrease in number was not wholly due to economic changes in the industry. It was partly a result of a change in reporting which led to the exclusion of all those mills with an annual cut of less than $5,000 worth of lumber in 1919 and less than 50 M feet of lumber in 1929. At least 3,818 mills were not counted in 1929 because their annual production was less than the amount specified. There were 20,037 mills reported for the country at large in 1929, but since then the number of active mills has declined. In the depth of the depression the number of active mills was less than 5,000. The aggregate reported in 1937 was 13,916. The Census figures for 1937 exclude many small mills, and, therefore, are not reliable. For instance, the Census reported 7,089 mills for that year in ten southern states, while the Southern Forest Experiment Station listed "more than 8,000 mills of all sizes, both portable and stationary," for the same year in the states of the Lower South alone.[15] In the last figure the mills in Virginia and North and South Carolina are excluded. They are included in the Census figure, however, and account for 3,226 of the total number reported. All the evidence indicates that the total number of mills in the country of all sizes stood close to 20,000 in the last years of the thirties.

The war boom has had a marked effect on lumbering and has greatly increased the number and the activity of operating mills. In the South the number of small mills has increased greatly because of the higher prices obtainable for lumber. In the West also the number of mills has increased because of the war, but even more important has been the volume of production within mills which have not operated at full capacity over a considerable period of time.

Over 55 per cent of the mills enumerated in 1929 were in ten southern states, and a good number of the excluded small mills were also in that region. The preponderance of large mills was in the West. For instance, of the 120 Class 8 mills, cutting 50,000 M feet of lumber or more annually, 10 were in the South and 103 were in the West. The ratio of Class 7 mills, cutting from 25,000 to 49,999 M feet annually, was 88 in the South to 102 in the West. But the South had

5,944 of the Class 1 mills, cutting from 50 to 499 M feet per year, while the West had only 622 of this small size.[16]

For over twenty years the South has been losing many of its larger units. Of the 263 largest mills in the South in 1934, only 75 had access to a sufficiently large body of trees to permit lasting operation. It was then estimated that 65 of the 263 would terminate activities by 1940, that 60 would close down by 1945, and that another 65 would cease operations by 1950.[17] The estimate for 1940 cannot be readily checked against the facts, but the approaching depletion of the large tracts of essential raw materials makes the disappearance of most of the remaining large southern mills inevitable. The dismantling of large mills and their displacement by "peckerwood" mills which operate upon the isolated stands or oncoming second growth, has been characteristic in the South for two decades. It should be observed, however, that some large mills, as they cut out their own timber holdings, continue to operate as concentration plants, buying logs and rough green lumber from others, and production has remained at a relatively high level. In the West, the large mills are still feasible since there are huge blocks of virgin forest to maintain them.

Because trees grow over broad areas, it has been impossible for the large companies effectively to control the market. Further, the weight lost in manufacture makes it unprofitable to transport logs if they can be as efficiently sawed near their source. Although small mills are usually inefficient, a good medium-sized mill is just as efficient as a good large one, and the large mills do not enjoy any significant advantage in terms of productive efficiency.[18] Because of these factors, production is not concentrated at the point where appreciable control of the industry in relatively few hands is possible. In fact, many attempts to control the industry have not succeeded. There has been a marked degree of concentration in the ownership of timber lands—notably on the West Coast—but this was economically unwise in some instances and has produced difficulties and instability in the industry due to excessive overhead. Conditions of lumber production place a limit upon the size of individual plants. In 1935, only one lumber company was classified among the 200 largest nonfinancial corporations—just barely getting into the group. This corporation embraced several large units operating independently. Concentration, where it has developed, has usually taken the form of single ownership control operating several producing units. This development, however, has been motivated by purposes other than simple control of the market. It is noteworthy that the four largest companies in 1935 cut lumber which amounted to only 4.7 per cent of the total value of all lumber produced.[19]

Concentration has not been as pronounced as in many other industries, but the 1929 Census figures, nevertheless, reveal that the 333 largest mills produced 46 per cent, and 544 largest mills produced 57 per cent of the lumber cut.[20] The number of units not included in this grouping was still large, however, comprising approximately 20,000 other mills. They produced a large enough proportion of the total lumber output to be competitively significant, and militated against any attempts to control the industry by a small number of large producers.

The structure of ownership of the lumber industry has conformed to older patterns than has been the case in many other industries. Individual ownership has been widespread. The broad areas throughout which commercial trees were found, the methods of land acquisition, and the frontierlike conditions which accentuated individualism all help to account for this situation. Considering all units, the corporate form of business organization has been utilized by a relatively small number. It certainly has not prevailed to as great an extent as in the great mass production industries. However, in the regions of large mill concentration the corporate form has been conspicuous, although it is significant that ownership and control in these areas have remained largely in the same hands. But it should be noted that corporate units have ordinarily produced over half of all lumber and timber products since about 1900.[21] From this, however, no effective control has emerged.

The individualistic, ruthless, and courageous spirit normally viewed as a product of the frontier, which infused the economic conquest of this continent, and which viewed with complacency the exploitations of natural and human resources, has been present in each successive advance of the lumberman and the lumberjack into our virgin forests. With a few exceptions, men in the industry, both employers and employees, have been extreme individualists. The play of individualism created numerous difficulties and made it impossible to solve intelligently many of the problems which have in the past, and do now, beset the industry. At the same time, it has helped give lumbering a picturesque history marked by exploits of the traditional "he-man." Located in more or less isolated places, the lumber industry has been neglected in the economic histories of the United States. Yet, nowhere in our broad diversified economy can an industry be found that has been any more "American." [22]

NOTES TO CHAPTER

[1] Eleventh Census of the United States, 1890, *Reports On Manufacturing Industries*. Part 3, pp. 593 ff.; U.S. Department of Commerce, Bureau of Domestic and Foreign Commerce, *The Lumber Industry*. Market Research Series No. 105. Washington: Government Printing Office, 1936, p. 1; National Resources Planning Board, *Forest Land Resources, Requirements, Problems, and Policy*. Washington: Government Printing Office, 1935, p. 3.

[2] Fifteenth Census of the United States, 1929, *Manufactures*, Vol. II, p. 442; National Lumber Manufacturers Association, *Lumber Industry Facts*. Washington: National Lumber Manufacturers Association, 1939, p. 15.

[3] *Biennial Census of Manufactures, 1937*, Part I, p. 499.

[4] U.S. Department of Agriculture, *Forest Trees and Forest Regions of the United States*. Miscellaneous Publication No. 217. Washington: Government Printing Office, 1936, pp. 33-35.

[5] *1905 Census of Manufactures*, Part I, p. clxii.

[6] U.S. Department of Agriculture, Pacific Northwest Experiment Station, *Forest Resources of the Douglas Fir Region*. Forest Research Notes No. 13. Washington: Government Printing Office, 1934, p. 1.

[7] Work Projects Administration, *op. cit.*, p. 118; cf. National Recovery Administration, Research and Planning Division, "Economic Status and Trends of the Lumber and Timber Products Industry," by T. P. Ahrens and V. G. Armstrong, 1934, p. 25 (manuscript).

[8] See below, p. 35.

[9] See below, p. 103.

[10] See below, p. 33.

[11] Twelfth Census of the United States, 1900, Vol. IX, *Manufactures*, Part 3, p. 818; Work Projects Administration, *op. cit.*, pp. 6-7. *See also* p. 45.

[12] Fifteenth Census of the United States, 1929, *Manufactures*, Vol. II, p. 448.

[13] Federal Board for Vocational Education, in co-operation with others, *The Lumber Industry—Logging, Sawmilling*. Opportunity Monograph, Vocational Rehabilitation Series No. 19. Washington: Government Printing Office, 1919, p. 4; U.S. Department of Labor, Bureau of Labor Statistics, *Job Descriptions for the Lumber and Timber Products Industries*. Job Analysis and Information Service, Division of Standards and Research. Washington: Government Printing Office, 1939, *passim*.

[14] Fourteenth Census of the United States, 1919, Vol. X, *Manufactures*, p. 422; Fifteenth Census of the United States, 1929, *Manufactures*, Vol. II, p. 449.

[15] Fifteenth Census of the United States, 1929, *Manufactures*, Vol. II, pp. 442, 449; *Biennial Census of Manufactures, 1937*, Part I, p. 514; U.S. Department of Agriculture, Southern Forest Experiment Station, *Primary Wood-Products Industries in the Lower South*, by H. F. Smith. Forest Survey Release No. 51. New Orleans: Southern Forest Experiment Station, 1940, p. 3.

[16] Fifteenth Census of the United States, 1929, *Manufactures*, Vol. II, p. 449.

[17] Work Projects Administration, *op. cit.*, pp. 120, 186-187.

[18] U.S. Department of Commerce and Labor, Bureau of Corporations, *The Lumber Industry*. Washington: Government Printing Office, 1913, pp. 3-4.

[19] National Resources Committee, *Structure of the American Economy*. Washington: Government Printing Office, 1939, p. 102.

[20] Fifteenth Census of the United States, 1929, *Manufactures*, Vol. II, p. 449.

[21] Twelfth Census of the United States, 1900, Vol. IX, *Manufactures*, Part 3, p. 810; Fourteenth Census of the United States, 1919, Vol. X, *Manufactures*, pp. 429-431.

[22] U.S. Department of Agriculture, *Some Public and Economic Aspects of the Lumber Industry*, by W. B. Greeley. Report No. 114. Washington: Government Printing Office, 1917, p. 60.

2 MIGRATION, MEN, AND ECONOMICS

E VEN TODAY the lumber industry still retains many of its frontier qualities, and an awareness of the environmental characteristics which markedly influence its activities is indispensable for an understanding of its development and problems. It has already been pointed out that the lumber industry has been a great migrant in the course of its dynamic life. The industry has hurried greedily from forest to forest in reckless haste to exploit the "limitless" resource, and has left behind, in most instances, a none too healthy group of small units. These either complete the work of forest destruction and finally are displaced or they struggle for survival against almost insurmountable obstacles—hanging on in impoverishment.

Camps and towns flourished for a day only to be left behind as stragglers in the wake of the relentless advance. When "daylight came to the swamp" calked boots were no longer heard, because the industry migrated and rarely returned. The story is similar everywhere. The "solid and interminable" and "immeasurable" forest seemingly stretched on indefinitely.[1] Almost everyone believed that the forests would last forever. But within two or three decades after the Civil War, daylight had practically come to the Maine woods and was rapidly appearing in the other two great early producing states, New York and Pennsylvania. Continuing the relentless westward drive, the "timber wolves" rushed greedily to Saginaw, Michigan, from whence there spread northward and westward the greatest white pine forest known to man. Surely, here was a forest that could not be cut out in a day—there was no end to these trees—and lumbering boomed from Saginaw to Muskegon and north to Mackinac, across most of Wisconsin and up into Minnesota. The Midwest was growing, and those who settled on the trackless prairies needed more lumber. Rapid cutting was the order of the day. The pattern of speculative timber acquisition and of the policy "cut out and get out" held sway.

The end did not come when the vanguard had passed on. The migration of the industry, following the cutting-out of the raw materials, always left tremendously important economic and social problems behind. These problems, however, never seemed to be the concern of the industry—except that occasionally lumber workers were encouraged, often enticed, into becoming farmers upon the cut-over lands, only to discover that the lands were often unsuitable to agriculture and unproductive. The operators' eyes were on the forests ahead; they refused to see the many problems which they left behind them. Many individuals adjusted quickly through migration, but others not so quickly. Stranded communities and workers were always commonplace in the lumber industry. In the Lake States clean-cutting methods brought lumbering to an abrupt end. For the workers it was "move on or farm." Even now, postlumber-industry impoverishment is conspicuous in the form of depopulated towns, destitute farmers and workers—usually of an older age group—and impoverished local governments and school districts.[2] In the South, cutting was not so "clean" and the industry often hung on in small units, although, likewise, with increasing impoverishment. Even though the industry activities did not terminate abruptly, the human, the social, and the economic problems were still acute. The fast-growing trees of the South reclothed the stump fields left by the exploiters of the original forests and a new young forest of pine and hardwood now supports a large and increasing number of mills. Neither was the West spared. In the state of Washington important production centers such as Aberdeen, on Grays Harbor, are faced with a very real problem. Sufficient available trees to support all the mills, and all the people, no longer exist.[3] Longer and longer log hauls are making it difficult for these mills to meet competition (an aggravating short-term problem of these mills has been the loss of export markets). The Douglas fir industry is moving more and more into Oregon to get nearer to the remaining trees. In all regions, examples of the menace of short-lived, shifting lumber activities are numerous.[4]

A migrant itself, the lumber industry turned many of its workers into migratory laborers.[5] Further, the manner of its organization and operation was responsible for producing a "homeless," "womanless" type of man in certain major sectors. It was in the eastern states, particularly in Maine, where was set the pattern which, with only a few notable exceptions, was to go with the industry across the continent. In the South the "traditional" lumberjack was seldom, if ever, found. An entirely different type of labor supplied the industry there, and the labor supply has been more stationary. In large areas labor has not been wholly dependent upon work in lumbering because of the close association of workers with agriculture. But the northern and western lumberjack was distinctive in dress, language, and mannerisms, and for a long time these characteristics were sufficient to mark him off from other workers.

Recognition of the lumberjack's unique characteristics came early. He was varyingly described, and praised and condemned, depending upon the viewpoint of the particular writer. One of the earliest descriptions, dating from the first part of the nineteenth century, depicted him as a debauched fellow, indolent, intemperate, and dishonest, living a life of vice and misery which resulted from the hard, unsteady work and scanty wages. Another early writer, with greater accuracy, pictured lumberjacks as a "powerfully built race of men," who "though rude in manner, and intemperate, are quite intelligent," with "a passion for their wild and toilsome life." [6] A later writer found that "as a class they are brave, honest, and industrious." [7] Perhaps no more powerful men were ever assembled in a group than those in the lumber industry. It has always been a man's industry, involving heroic work. Weaklings could not stand the "gaff" and consequently did not stay or last long. The rigors of life and work in the open required a brawny, wiry type of fellow who "could take it." The men were proud that they could. Physical prowess and sheer recklessness in its dexterous use was a trait of every respected lumberjack. Of course, this style of life left its mark. The jacks were coarse and rough and extreme individualists, taking great pride in their accomplishments; but they were genuine men with hearts as big as "barrels" when the need for help arose. True, many of them often times boisterously celebrated their return to town, as did cowboys and miners, but not all of them engaged in riotous living on such occasions. Certain aspects of their spontaneous rowdyism have often been overdrawn and certainly little understood.

The lumberjack was a picturesque individual all the while lumbering boomed in the Great Lakes region. When the industry developed in the West, he was there in the early years. Of course, not all workers in the industry were lumberjacks. There were many farmer lads who sought work in the woods during the winter months. And there were the sawmill workers who were more fixed because sawmills were usually in towns—ramshackle affairs though they sometimes were.

Social leeches preyed on the carefree lumberjack in the "boom town" when he emerged from a monotonous winter in the isolated camp.[8] Emotionally starved, he sought satisfaction for long-inhibited desires, and there were many who served his needs—at a price—and took advantage of him. Countless were the cases when the lumberjack was relieved of his hard-earned cash in the course of a few hilarious days, the events of which he could little remember once he was dropped as being no longer useful to his "friends." Some lumberjacks, who for the most part were unattached, lived only from one "binge" to the next. But this was not typical. Most of them were steady if rough fellows.

The nature of their work caused them to live as they did. Apart from the atrocious living conditions and lack of normal emotional and psychological outlets, there was the fact that death was always ready to claim its victims with falling branches and trees, rolling and pitching logs, churning rapids encountered on the log drives, or whirring saws and speeding, powerful machinery in the mills. If death was lurking so close—and it has taken a terrific toll in the lumber industry [9]—why not yell for another drink? If a man was soon to be penned up again in the distant woods all winter until the spring and the log drive, why not have a fling with the bottle and the women? Where the log drive was not used, conditions of virtual or actual isolation in rude, temporary camps located miles back in the woods made for the same general conditions. There has been no spectacular event calling for wholesale celebration excepting, perhaps, the Fourth of July "holidays" in the Northwest when most camps have been customarily closed down while the men have spent a "week" in town.

In contrast to logging for the spring drive, logging with more modern methods of transport and continuous shipment of logs has not presented any special opportunity for leaving the woods. As a result there has been, at times, a more or less continual flow of men moving between town and camp. Of course, a shutdown for whatever cause—seasonal factors or market conditions—is occasion for a trip to town. In the Great Lakes region focal points for assemblage of timber workers were Saginaw, Muskegon, Milwaukee, Minneapolis, and Duluth. In the West there were Seattle, Portland, Spokane, and San Francisco, and many smaller centers such as Aberdeen and Eureka.[10]

Gradually, after the industry moved west, the lumberjack gave way to conditioning forces which changed his life, making him merely a timber worker. It has been observed that

The reckless men, the legendary American lumberjacks, passionate, vigorous, impetuous daredevils who have given the picturesque color to the old-time lumber camp, are now almost a vanished race. The steadiness of a sober and methodical machine age has settled down upon the lumber and wood-using industries as they are seeking to perpetuate themselves in the forest areas of the North, the South, and the West. The gaudy bucka-roo, with his picturesque profanity, his goad stick and his five yoke of bellowing oxen, has been replaced by the prosaic donkey engine. The ubiquitous double-breasted red-flannel undershirt of the old-time lumber jack has vanished.[11]

The industry has moved, it has changed, it has adapted itself to variations in environment. The characteristics of its labor force in its various parts have taken on a modified and, in some cases, a greatly changed pattern. In shifting from region to region lumbering was forced to adjust to new and different physical and economic circum-stances. Besides leaving behind a heritage of complex problems it was always facing new ones. In many ways individual resourcefulness has been a prominent characteristic but, at the same time, many of the industry's major problems were never solved, and many of them were hardly approached because of the need for concerted, co-operative action. Without doubt, the lumber industry's greatest weakness and its greatest problem has always been ineffectual organization.

Concerted action on common problems has not been adequately developed due to psychological, geographic, economic, and legal reasons. Because the industry shifted with the westward-moving fron-tier, the spirit of individualism remained strong within it. Lumber-men have been self-made men who succeeded because of sheer hard work, ingenuity, and often ruthlessness. Those who kept climbing in the industry always were found standing on their own feet. At the same time, however, it must be remembered that the greatest for-tunes have been accumulated through dealing in forest lands. Few men became rich simply through sawing lumber. And once the ques-tion of land ownership and values had been settled, an intense com-petition to liquidate investments often resulted in overproduction, erratic market conditions, instability, and, oftentimes, losses in invest-ment instead of profits. It has been in the lumber production end of the industry that the results of unbridled individualism and "self-interest" have been most noticeable.

The problems of the industry have been made difficult of solution because of geographic factors. In the first place, as has been shown, the center of economic gravity in the industry has continually shifted as the sawmills gobbled up the raw materials. This in itself has been unstabilizing. But when an industry is scattered over such broad areas as are encompassed by our northern, southern, and western forests, and is divided into such heterogeneous producing units as the lumber industry is, any attempt at organization for a concerted attack on common problems is made extremely difficult. Thousands of producing units manufacturing hundreds of different grades and sizes of a multiplicity of products—ranging through all sizes, types, and grades of lumber and timber products, shingles, plywood, and cooperage products—obviously have presented difficult problems of control in this widespread, scattered industry.

Economic structure and problems present, by far, the most difficult and complex phases of the industry organization dilemma. Here, too, while the number of producing units is important, the nature of costs is more crucial. Within the medium to large units overhead costs are considerable and, by nature, require certain minimum competitive standards for the industry as a requisite of stability. At the same time, there are thousands of small producers with relatively negligible overhead costs who move into, or out of, productive activity as changes in the market occur. Their influence is a decisive factor in competition. Because of these conditions, cutthroat competition within the industry has frequently proved tragic for practically everyone concerned—investors, employers, workers, and the public. Another important economic factor has been the long-run decline in the consumption of lumber, due in large part to the cessation of agricultural expansion and the subsequent stagnation of agriculture, as well as to modification of building practices and codes which have reduced wood use. The market for lumber has been on the wane since about 1906—the time of greatest total production and highest per capita consumption.[12] The widespread shift to stone, brick, and reinforced concrete buildings; the partial displacement of wooden trim by plaster trimming and the simplification of trim under the impact of modern architecture; the use of steel sashes and doors, concrete floors with a composition covering—all these have worked to the detriment of volume in lumber production. The decline in total consumption of lumber has been a factor of considerable importance to the instability of the industry.

It will remain to be seen whether the boom in lumbering during the war will be of benefit, and what the postwar years will bring, and whether the ever-growing intensification of competition of substitute materials, which has been so disturbing to the industry, will continue. Very likely changes can be expected. Furthermore, lumber production is necessarily tied to the cycle of building construction, which has always been decidedly erratic in the past, and this has added to the economic difficulties of the industry. Whether building activity in the postwar period will suffice to maintain lumber production at a high level remains to be seen.

Numerous trade association attempts at industry regularization and stabilization have been made. These have appeared in all regions, and some associations have become important institutions in their respective fields. Sometimes they have run afoul of the antitrust laws. In most instances, however, the economic obstacles have been so great that legal obstacles to control have really been inconsequential. Standardization of grades, and even prices, publication of industry information, and other accomplishments of the trade associations have not been sufficient to reach down to the basic problems of excess capacity and cutthroat competition.

The South and the West have been the great producers for a number of years. They are strong competitors for the same market—the Midwest, the Ohio Valley, and the Middle Atlantic States. As may be expected, the economic problems arising from intense competition in the industry center primarily in these two great producing regions.

The lumber industry is very vulnerable to the ravages of unchecked competition. Besides South-West regional competition, there are two other types, intraregional and interindustry. The interindustry competition, or competition of substitutes, has been characterized as the "new competition." [13] Substitute building materials did not provide serious competition until a quarter of a century ago. Formerly lumber "sold itself"—the operator cut it and someone ordered and bought it.[14] The new competition would probably not have been so destructive had the industry not been so dominated by individualism and peculiar overhead costs that it was seriously hampered in developing a cooperative approach to the problem of publicizing the value of its product. Under the circumstances, the competition was not always met intelligently. The fact that there was a lack of advertising must not be taken to mean that there was a seller's market. Far from it. Intense interregional and intraregional competition, and overproduction which often ruined prices, made it difficult to meet the situation.

These latter types of competition, in so far as they are really injurious, are products of burdensome overhead costs and excess capacity. The cost structure in the lumber industry presents a strong case against unrestricted competition. With a considerable excess capacity and a large overhead cost structure, producers having heavy fixed costs are inclined to continue producing even on a declining market although they are cutting at a current loss. At the same time, numerous producers on the opposite extreme of the production structure, with negligible fixed costs, may go in and out of the industry almost at will in accordance with the existing market. In either case there is the most intense pressure to reduce costs, particularly labor costs, and hence the existence of relatively inferior labor conditions. Likewise, there has been a wasteful use of the natural resource and, because of it, the public has lost what it seems to have gained through lower prices. The resource has been "mined" and the "social investment" has shrunk, not only in terms of a timber resource but in all the other values of the forest, such as erosion and flood control, water supply, recreation, and the like. The type of competition which has prevailed in the lumber industry has resulted in what is tantamount to consumption of investment where society was entitled only to the yield.[15] Interregional and intraregional competition shows how the total industry problems are closely interwoven, and how conditions in one sector cannot be appreciated or explained without an understanding of the existent relationships.[16]

The pattern of forest land ownership and management has contributed to the plight of the lumber industry and has an important bearing upon the economic problems which beset it. It has accounted in large measure for the instability of the industry and has been an important factor, in many cases, in explaining the existence of an excess productive capacity.[17] Without attempting an exhaustive analysis of the problems of forest acquisition and management, some of the important aspects of the forest situation which serve as essential background for the structure of industrial relations must be made clear. In testimony before the Federal Trade Commission, the National Lumber Manufacturers Association contended, among other things, that "due to inherent conditions involved in stumpage . . . labor carries an unjust burden . . ." [18]

The transfer of forest resources from public to private ownership is tied up with the land history of the whole country. It is a product of pressures instituted by agriculturists and speculators who possessed an insatiable "land hunger," dating from the earliest colonial times. This land hunger, supported by arguments favoring rapid economic development of new states and territories, and accompanied by the acceptance of the policy of land grants to transportation companies, led to a liberal policy of disposal of forest lands. That the land laws were misused, that they were defective, and that they were loosely administered,[19] is well-known. It was relatively easy to obtain forest lands, and this led to the creation of many large and also many small and diversified holdings, and to the rapid exploitation of the timber resource. So vast was the market for lumber, and so cheap were the forest lands, that lumbering almost literally spread like a "crown fire." Profits were very great. Actually, however, there were more profits from land acquisition than from income from lumbering.[20]

In the South much of the forest region was acquired originally by people interested primarily in agriculture. For a long time ownership was widely distributed and has remained so throughout wide areas. However, large forested areas in southern Alabama and Mississippi and throughout Louisiana and southern Arkansas, as well as in eastern Texas, were the scenes of active timber acquisition in the late nineties and in the first decade of the twentieth century as the Lake States lumbermen left the wrecked forests of the North in search of new timber to exploit. As a result, large holdings did appear, but forest land ownership in the South has always been considerably less concentrated than in the West.

The profits realized in the Lake States region had a profound influence also on the forest history of the West. Without making allowances for important differences, timber acquisition was consummated with great zeal and with the expectation of early returns. Speculation in cheaply acquired lands, with the thought of early development, carried stumpage values high. The result was an abnormal condition of timber ownership.[21] However, the problem of holding forest land has been an important one in many other parts of the country. Excessive speculation in timber resources and the consequent overloading of investment were present in the South as well as in the West, but occurred at a slower pace and with less striking results.

Other factors have contributed to instability of forest ownership. Besides interest on investment, other carrying charges, such as taxes and cost of fire protection, have been onerous. This has produced a pressure to liquidate holdings, with resulting adverse effects on the workers, the community, and the government.

Instability of forest land ownership has been a factor of considerable importance for many years. It is not a recent development, but reaches back to the period of declining lumber consumption and the failure of stumpage prices to increase as anticipated. When timber lands were acquired by private owners, stumpage values were rising. Timber lands are no longer the good investments they once were.

Timber history has been one of almost unbroken value increases. Timber tradition had it that values doubled each ten years. Often they did vastly more than that and great fortunes resulted. During the past decade, however, timber values have become stagnant or they declined. Timber investments are no longer carrying themselves. The vast reserve timber holdings have become a net financial burden upon the operating lumber industry.[22]

The money value of timber holdings increased until about 1921. From 1921 until 1929 such values were relatively stable, but a decided drop occurred during the depression years following. If real values are considered, the rate of appreciation slackened about 1910. Only slight increases were made in the following decade and afterward there were none.[23]

Before it was realized that stumpage values were not going to continue to rise there was an overdevelopment of sawmilling plants in the industry. Since then overdevelopment has been accentuated by the desire to liquidate timber investments. Particularly in the West, the excessive timber holdings are responsible in part for excessive capital investments. These excessive capital investments are in the form of the lands themselves, in logging equipment, and in manufacturing plants. The excess represents a decided burden on the operating industry. It has no little bearing upon the ability of the industry to make ends meet, to say nothing of the way it impinges on labor problems.

The plight of the lumber industry is due largely to its chronic inability to solve the problem of overproduction. This is a problem faced by other natural resource industries. In lumbering an excess production capacity has been built up, which has meant not only a poor general investment policy but has had a disastrous effect upon the market for lumber. It has been claimed that one-half of the existing facilities would supply all requirements of the market. Mills have been built solely to make it possible to pay taxes and interest on stumpage, which could not be carried otherwise. They have even been built in recent years for such a purpose in spite of the recognized existing overcapacity.[24] Excess productive capacity keeps the market chronically overstocked. This, in the absence of control, results in cost cutting and further depressed prices. There are many marginal firms, carrying only a small investment, which cease to be active when the market becomes too depressed, but which come to life rapidly enough whenever prices increase sufficiently to warrant it. These conditions make control well-nigh impossible, make for waste of the timber resource, increase the insecurity of the worker, and imperil the industry.

So far as the worker is directly concerned, it is the intermittent employment—resulting from a disordered, unstable market and irregular production—that is the most injurious. In some sectors wage rates tend to be unbelievably low; in other sectors, if rates are comparable with those in other industries, earnings have been inadequate because of the irregularity of employment.

The lumber industry, notable for the individualism of its members, has not been well-organized in terms of either labor or capital. Its labor force has been classified as only "moderately" organized,[25] and as a matter of fact, workers have had only sporadic organization, and in many sectors none at all. Unionism has been, and is, strongest in the West Coast area. But even there it has had rough sledding. Unionism has always been noticeably weak, or decidedly lacking, in both the Great Lakes area and the South. Opposition to labor organization has been strong, although the opposition has expressed itself through formal organizations only occasionally. Employers have organized trade associations from time to time in order to achieve a degree of orderliness and co-operativeness in the industry.[26] Many of these failed, others were able to carry on. Only a few employer associations, groups organized to oppose or deal with labor organizations, have existed. Traditional opposition to unionism has led to the use of militant tactics and, in many cases, to tacit understanding among employers to ignore or destroy labor unionism wherever and whenever it appeared.

The lumber industry not only has an interesting history in its own right, but is peculiarly valuable for the study of its labor relations. Economic, geographic, and psychological factors have interacted to create its acute problems. A heterogeneity of producing units, with great variations in overhead costs, existing in an industry with a declining market, has contributed to chronic overproduction and intense competition. The industry's economic problems have borne heavily on labor, which has experienced, as a result, lower wages and conditions inferior to those which might otherwise have been provided. The industry's geographic shifts have been continual and the problems of readjustment have been perplexing. Impoverishment has been left behind when the industry has gone on to new areas of production. Men who followed the industry often became migratory workers— "homeless," "womanless," and "voteless"—suffering all the disadvantages of such lives. The industry has been widely scattered over a broad area chronically unorganized due to the economic difficulties and to the strong individualistic attitudes which resulted from frontierlike conditions. Employers could not develop a co-operative approach to industry problems and, for the most part, would not allow their workers to approach their problems co-operatively. The result has been a history of more or less sporadic, but bitter, labor struggles. In recent years, however, a new outlook on labor-employer relations has been appearing in certain parts of the industry.

NOTES TO CHAPTER

[1] H. D. Thoreau, *The Maine Woods.* New York: Thomas Y. Crowell and Company, 1906, pp. 19, 72, 90.

[2] See below, p. 63.

[3] U.S. Department of Agriculture, *A National Plan for American Forestry,* 73rd Congress, 1st Session, Senate Document No. 12. Washington: Government Printing Office, 1933, pp. 106-111; U.S. Department of Agriculture, Forest Service, North Pacific Region, *Industrial Development of Olympic Peninsula Counties.* Portland, Ore., 1937, p. 9.

[4] U.S. Department of Agriculture, Forest Service, Southern Forest Experiment Station, "Reports on Abandoned Sawmill Towns and Sustained Yield Forest Communities in the South, 1935" (typewritten, no pagination); U.S. Department of Agriculture, "Timber: Mine or Crop," *U.S. Department of Agriculture Yearbook,* 1922. Washington: Government Printing Office, 1923, pp. 96-97; U.S. Department of Agriculture, *The Economic Aspects of Forest Destruction in Northern Michigan,* by W. N. Sparhawk and W. D. Brush. Technical Bulletin No. 92. Washington: Government Printing Office, 1929, pp. 15, 35, 45, 58-59; T. W. Smith and M. R. Fry, *The Population of a Selected Cut-Over Area in Louisiana.* Louisiana State University and Agricultural and Mechanical College, Bulletin No. 268, 1936, p. 4.

[5] C. Parker, *The Casual Laborer and Other Essays.* New York: Harcourt, Brace, and Howe, 1920, pp. 651-662; B. P. Kirkland, "Effects of Destructive Lumbering on Labor," *Journal of Forestry,* XVIII, No. 4 (April, 1920), 318-320.

[6] E. A. Kendall, *Travels Through the Northern Parts of the United States.* New York: 1809, Vol. III, pp. 75-79; C. Lanman, *Adventures in the Wilds of the United States.* Philadelphia: 1856, Vol. II, p. 236; cf. R. G. Wood, *A History of Lumbering in Maine, 1820-1861.* Orono, Me.: University of Maine Studies, 1935, Vol. XXXVII, No. 7, pp. 185-186.

[7] U.S. Department of Agriculture, Bureau of Forestry, *A History of the Lumber Industry in the State of New York,* by W. F. Fox. Bulletin No. 34. Washington: Government Printing Office, 1902, p. 37.

[8] Rev. J. H. Geohegen, "Exploitation of the Migratory Worker." Unpublished Master's Thesis, University of Washington, Seattle, Washington, 1923, *passim;* S. H. Holbrook, *Holy Old Mackinaw.* New York: The Macmillan Company, 1938, pp. 107-118, *passim.*

[9] D. D. Leschoier, "Lumbermen's Hazards," *Survey,* XXVI (August 5, 1911), 639-646; National Safety Council, Inc., *Accident Rates in the Woodworking and Lumbering Industries.* Chicago: National Safety Council, 1936, *passim;* M. D. Kossoris and S. Kjaer, "Causes and Prevention of Accidents in Lumber Manufacture, 1939," *Monthly Labor Review,* LI, No. 3 (September, 1940), 663-679.

[10] S. H. Holbrook, *op. cit., passim.*

[11] W. Compton, "Recent Developments in the Lumber Industry," *Journal of Forestry,* XXX, No. 4 (April, 1932), 442.

[12] U.S. Department of Agriculture, Forest Service, Division of Forest Economics, *Lumber Production, 1869-1934.* Washington: Government Printing Office, 1936, p. 75.

[13] C. H. Cheney, *New Competition in the Lumber Industry.* Report before the Annual Convention of the National Association of Manufacturers, Chicago, Illinois, April 28, 1927 (circular); W. Compton, "Lumber: An Old Industry and a New

Competition," *Harvard Business Review*, X, No. 26 (January, 1932), 162; P. A. Bloomer, *Economic Conditions in the Southern Pine Industry as Affected by Code Wage and Hour Provisions*. Statement and brief in behalf of the Southern Pine Association before the National Recovery Administration, February 2, 1935. New Orleans: Southern Pine Association, 1935, pp. 18-21.

[14] U.S. Department of Agriculture, *Some Public and Economic Aspects of the Lumber Industry*, by W. B. Greeley. Report No. 114. Washington: Government Printing Office, 1917, p. 60.

[15] L. C. Boyle, *Argument Before the Federal Trade Commission*. New Orleans: Southern Pine Association, 1916, p. 33.

[16] V. H. Jensen, "Labor Relations in the Northwest Lumber Industry." Unpublished Ph.D. Thesis, University of California, 1939, pp. 17-19; *In the Supreme Court of the United States, The United States of America vs. F. W. Darby Lumber Company. Brief for the United States*, p. 36.

[17] U.S. Department of Agriculture, *A National Plan for American Forestry*, p. 898; C. S. Keith, *Conditions in the Lumber Industry*. Address before a special meeting of the Southern Pine Association, December 15, 1921. New Orleans: Southern Pine Association, 1921, p. 2.

[18] National Lumber Manufacturers Association, *Before the Federal Trade Commission, Brief on Behalf of the National Lumber Manufacturers Association*. Vol. I, "Problems of the Industry." Washington: National Lumber Manufacturers Association, 1916, p. 14.

[19] T. Donaldson, *The Public Domain*. 47th Congress, 2nd Session, House of Representatives, Miscellaneous Document 45, Part 4. Washington: Government Printing Office, 1884, pp. 214-216, 332-356, 543; *Report of the Public Land Commission, 1905*. Washington: Government Printing Office, 1905, pp. 67, 72, 73; W. Compton, *The Organization of the Lumber Industry*. Chicago: American Lumberman, 1916, p. 60; W. W. Folwell, *A History of Minnesota*. St. Paul: Minnesota Historical Society, 1926, Vol. III, pp. 207, 208, 500-515, Vol. IV, pp. 224, 235-249, 261-283; P. W. Gates, "Federal Land Policy in the South, 1866-1888," *The Journal of Southern History*, VI, No. 3 (August, 1940), 303-330.

[20] U.S. Department of Commerce and Labor, Bureau of Corporations, *op. cit.*, p. 38; U.S. Department of Agriculture, *Forestry and Community Development*. Bulletin No. 638. Washington: Government Printing Office, 1918, p. 10.

[21] U.S. Department of Agriculture, *Some Public and Economic Aspects of the Lumber Industry*, pp. 10-11; W. Compton, "The Lumber Industry Stands at Bay," *American Lumberman*, No. 2934 (August, 1931), p. 460.

[22] W. Compton, "Recent Developments in the Lumber Industry," pp. 440-441; U.S. Department of Agriculture, *A National Plan for American Forestry*, pp. 913-915.

[23] National Resources Committee, *Forest Resources of the Pacific Northwest*. Washington: Government Printing Office, 1938, p. 40.

[24] U.S. Department of Agriculture, *A National Plan for American Forestry*, p. 915; H. E. Hardtner, "The Economic Status of Southern Pine," *American Lumberman*, No. 2944 (October, 1931), 596-598; W. Compton, *op. cit.*, p. 443; Southern Pine Association, *Economic Conditions in the Southern Pine Industry*. New Orleans: Southern Pine Association, 1931, p. 30; U.S. Department of Agriculture, *Some Public and Economic Aspects of the Lumber Industry*, p. 59; W. B. Greeley, "Address Before a Meeting of the United States Chamber of Commerce at Portland," *West Coast Lumberman*, LVIII, No. 1 (January, 1931), 30.

[25] National Resources Committee, *Structure of the American Economy*, Washington: Government Printing Office, 1939, p. 119.

[26] J. H. Cox, "Organization of the Lumber Industry in the Pacific Northwest, 1889-1914." Unpublished Ph.D. Thesis, Department of History, University of California, 1933, *passim;* R. F. Fries, "A History of the Lumber Industry in Wisconsin." Unpublished Ph.D. Thesis, University of Wisconsin, 1939, pp. 198-211; W. Compton, *The Organization of the Lumber Industry, passim;* Southern Pine Association, *op. cit.*, p. 2.

3   THE NORTHEASTERN REGION

THE Northeastern region was at one time the leading producing
area. It was, moreover, the region in which the pattern of characteristic lumbering activities, practices, and conditions was initially
established, and which was reproduced elsewhere when the industry
moved on.

Of the states in this region, Maine, New York, and Pennsylvania
had the most important producing centers. Maine is sometimes
referred to as the first and most important early lumbering state.
While its supremacy, in terms of either the number of sawmills or
the volume of lumber cut, can be disputed,[1] Maine does reveal most
faithfully the characteristics of the industry in its early days.

Through migration, practices in lumbering were carried westward
into the regions which developed later. Men from Maine, operators
as well as workers, were frequently found in all successively developed
areas—in New York, in Pennsylvania, and in the Great Lakes states
of Michigan, Wisconsin, and Minnesota. A few went to the South.
Some even reached California, Oregon, and Washington during a
third major migration following what proved to be a "temporary"
location in the Lake States.[2] Operators and men from both New York
and Pennsylvania also migrated westward in large numbers. Everywhere the lumbermen moved with the industry.

Early lumbering activities were similar in all places. In particular
areas, however, the first part of the nineteenth century witnessed the
development of commercial production on a larger scale. Mills could
no longer depend satisfactorily upon the local supply of logs; nor
was this situation remedied by the customary removal of the sawmill
to the raw material. Instead, the logs were driven down the natural
water courses to the mills. With this development the dramatic log
drive became a spectacle of the industry. The Androscoggin, Kennebec, and Penobscot rivers were the major arteries in Maine. In New
York the upper Hudson and other streams in the Adirondacks were
used. The Allegheny and Susquehanna rivers, originating in New

33

York but flowing into Pennsylvania, were major log-driving streams in their upper courses. The leading producing center of the whole lumber industry was located for a long time on the west branch of the Susquehanna at Williamsport. In addition, the Susquehanna had many tributaries which were actively used, perhaps the most notable being the Sinnamahoning. Besides log driving, the rafting of sawed lumber was an important activity on the large streams.[3] The rivers were the first highways, but, in spite of the prevalence of log driving, toward the end of the nineteenth century the railroad was used increasingly for both log and lumber hauling, particularly in New York and Pennsylvania.[4]

With the growth of commercial production on a larger scale, incident upon the economic expansion in the United States during the decades of the 1820's and 1830's and after, the drive to secure large tracts of virgin timber increased, and much speculation in timber lands resulted. Without going into detail concerning the manner of land acquisition and control within the Northeastern region, it is enough to observe that easy, and in some cases questionable, sales were made. This, of course, conformed to the general pattern of our land history—"Agriculture could not develop until the trees were removed anyway." Conditions on the eastern frontier in Maine in the first half of the nineteenth century were typical of later developments in the westward areas. In Maine, more speculation and larger timber holdings appeared than in either New York or Pennsylvania, where private land acquisition had more or less run its course before large-scale commercial lumbering developed. The eastern frontier in Maine witnessed the same speculative fever, shadowy deals, and outright trespass which were common elsewhere. Even prior to 1820, when Maine was made a state, the pattern had been set with some large tracts having been sold, the largest being the "two million" acres purchased by William Bingham—one half on the Kennebec and the other on the Penobscot.[5]

While large holdings were common enough, there was nothing approaching a monopolistic control of the forest. Lumbermen were numerous and, in fact, the conflicting interests of the various log owners had created so many difficulties in the way of controlling the water to suit the needs of many drivers that log-driving companies were formed before 1850 to handle the drives and to deliver the logs at their destination. Incessant controversy resulted in the formation of companies to do the work of sorting the logs at the end of the drive.[6] To facilitate identification, a brand had, of necessity, to be stamped legibly on each log in a manner similar to branding practice in the cattle industry. The great variety of registered brands attests the multiplicity of log ownership. So numerous were the brands that only experts could correctly read this sign language.[7] Further evidence of the lack of monopolistic control is found in the fact that in 1870 there were almost 1,000 sawmill establishments in Maine, 3,700 in Pennsylvania, 3,500 in New York, and many additional ones in the other states in the region. Afterward, the number declined rapidly in New York and Pennsylvania, but not because of consolidation or growth in size of individual units. The decline of the industry was responsible for this, and the evidence points to widespread ownership and the general absence of monopoly.[8]

The initial activities in lumbering naturally centered in the forests, where camps for the woods workers were established as the focal points for the work of getting the logs ready for movement to the sawmills. Logging, at first a highly seasonal activity, became somewhat less so in later years. In earlier days, in Maine, the lumberman could depend on a logging season of no more than four months, but by 1900 a season lasting twenty-six weeks was not uncommon.[9] Because the weather is the decisive factor in determining when the workers could get into the woods and when the logs could be run out, geographic and climatic variations play a role in the seasonality of logging activities. In the whole Northeastern region, for example, logging was always a wintertime activity.[10]

Climate was decisive in making for the short season because the rivers and lakes were the great highways—there were hardly any others. Because the rivers were difficult to navigate upstream, the famous "bateaux" could be used only for carrying limited supplies into the woods for the small crew of those engaged in preparations for the winter's work. The vanguard of camp builders commonly moved into the woods in the early fall. Then the woods were less wet, more comfortable, and there were fewer mosquitoes and other insects. They were, in consequence, more satisfactory for organizing the essential operations. The reference to the woods as the "swamp" had a solid basis in fact, and the difficulties of logging before freezing weather set in often precluded a long cutting season. The vanguard of a few workers built the camp and made their preparations, such as cutting the "tote" road as well as perhaps the main logging roads, and even gathered wild hay for the livestock, if necessary. Before supplies for the camps could be carried in quantities sufficiently large for the main crew, the ice had to form on the rivers and lakes, making it possible to use them as highways. This occurred in late November or early December. In addition, the snow was an essential factor in skidding and transporting the logs to the streams.[11] Of course, when better roads were built and when the railroad penetrated the woods, longer cutting seasons became possible. Further, increased work on the roads gave more "off-season" employment to workers who otherwise would have had to shift elsewhere. Nowhere, however, was there general all-year work in the woods.[12]

Climatic factors made for variations. Activity in the woods in parts of New York and in Pennsylvania was carried on more continuously throughout the year. There the accessibility of the woods made possible a longer logging season and, moreover, logging activities were dovetailed with peeling hemlock bark for the tanning industry. The latter activity had, of necessity, to be carried on from about mid-May until mid-August while the sap was flowing. When hemlock peeling was no longer feasible, the lumberman turned his attention to cutting lumber logs and preparing them for skidding. The skidding, however, usually was not begun until snowfall, at which time the sled was used. In any case, work in the woods was highly seasonal.[13]

The logging and skidding season lasted until the ice went out in March or April, carrying on the spring run-off the logs of the winter's cutting. The logs were sent pell-mell down the rivers with the drivers literally astride them, the main drive—barring catastrophe—running from two to three weeks. The river work was not completed until some time after the log drive because of the necessity of rounding up the stragglers lodged on the riverbanks or found floating aimlessly in lakes and eddies, or stuck in the marshes near the river. During this short period, employment was given to a large number of men.

Work in the lumber industry always has been accompanied by frequent injuries, many of which have been severe. There is, of course, no part of the work that is not attendant with accidents. No other labor required such reckless daring as river work. It was arduous and dangerous. One false step, a faltering nerve, a miscalculation of the eye was enough to send the driver into the water to be drowned or bruised and ground beyond recognition by the churning logs.[14]

Work in the woods is always carried on away from settlements, and it is necessary to provide accommodations for the men. The camps for the men and the hovels for the cattle were built of logs. Obviously, they were crude affairs, and in early times, according to Thoreau, the two were "hardly distinguishable, except that the latter had no chimney."[15] The early camps were much more crude than later ones, but improvements came slowly.[16]

There are a number of vivid accounts of the early lumber camps but they cannot readily be accepted at face value as accurate. The camps varied in size, depending upon the "operation" and the number in the crew. A small camp had one building about twenty feet long and fifteen feet wide for the men. In the earliest ones, up to the 1850's, the chimney was simply a hole in the middle of the roof, three or four feet in diameter, directly under which was the open fireplace built to hold a huge fire kept burning night and day. Later, stoves were used and real chimneys were constructed. Around the fireplace or stove were split logs on pegs, serving as benches. Above were facilities for hanging wet clothing to dry against the morrow's work. Extending around under the eaves were the bunks mattressed with padded arbor vitae leaves, hay, straw, or other substance that would give a mattress effect. The camp building was kept comfortably warm by the huge fire, but it was "drear and savage enough," situated as it was within a clearing no larger than was made necessary by the cutting of the trees with which to build and warm it. The prime, and very likely the only, considerations were whether it was well-sheltered and convenient to the work.[17]

Although camps were crude affairs, gradual improvements were introduced. Larger camps, which became more common during the seventies, could afford to spend more for conveniences. Boards or flattened logs instead of earth floors, separation of cooking and living quarters, and improvements in food were all noticeable.[18] Around 1900 it was a common thing in New York for the camp building to include two floors. The ground floor contained the cook room and dining hall combined, fitted up with long board tables on which meals were served. One end of the ground floor frequently was partitioned off for a "men's room" where the workers whiled away their evenings before climbing to bed in the second-floor room, which was lined with tiers of bunks.[19] The men's room was occasioned by the fact that women were introduced into some of the camps as cooks whereas the customary practice, in earlier times or other places, had been to employ men for this work. In most early camps bunks were built in tiers in such a fashion that the men slept with their feet to the stove— "muzzle-loaders." This construction was without a doubt copied from the early practice of simply sleeping around the fire with feet toward it. Two blankets to help keep him warm and comfortable were generally lent to each man.[20] These things literally gave "solid comfort."

The fare, rigorously simple and, in early days, as monotonous as camp life itself, usually consisted of beans, pork, and bread—the great trinity—garnished with molasses and accompanied by tea flavored with the same. These were the great staple items, and no luxuries provided variation. Later, more variety and better prepared food were recognized as good business. Stoves, professional cooks, greater variety in foods, with fresh meats and vegetables, gradually became more common.[21]

A typical institution at most camps was the "wangin" (also spelled "wangan," "wangun," and "wanegan"). The term is synonymous with what we now call a "company store." On the log drive the bateau, or the wagon, which accompanied the drivers, was the wangin, being filled with equipment and food so that the men might be fed and their needs cared for. The workers engaged in rafting lumber, or logs, ordinarily carried their own supplies. At the wangin, whether in camps or on the drive, the worker bought his tobacco, mittens, and other clothing, the price being deducted from his wages. However, woods workers spent their wages sparingly while in camp, saving their earnings so that they might have a sizable account to draw at the end of the season when paid off. It is not certain that prices were excessive, but it is not out of the range of probability that a dishonest employer would have padded the accounts.[22]

The crew varied in size, depending upon the particular layout. In the early days the crew ranged from ten to fifty men, and included the "boss," choppers, swampers, barkers, ox-teamsters, and the cook. During the 1870's and 1880's crews running up to one hundred and fifty and occasionally to three hundred and fifty men were common. Activities were speeded up considerably and larger scale operations appeared as the demand for lumber increased.[23]

In the early period the labor supply consisted mainly of native sons to whom were added Canadians, in Maine and upper New York, and an occasional Indian. The Canadians were particularly apt in the woods and on the rivers. Some men did nothing but work in the industry, dividing their time between the winter logging work, the spring drive, preparations for the next logging season, and the mills. The mills, which did not operate in the winter at all, had a season that dovetailed with logging. A good part of the industry's labor supply also came from small farms whose owners desired employment for themselves and their oxen or horses during the winter months. Many times such employment was to the detriment of farming, but it was a source of cash income.[24]

In 1890 an increased proportion of the labor force in both Maine and New York was made up of foreign-born workers, but they by no means predominated. Speaking roughly, a little less than one-third of the woods workers and about one-fourth of the sawmill workers in both Maine and New York were foreign-born. In Pennsylvania the foreign-born workers in the industry only averaged one-eighth of the total in both woods and sawmills. In Maine three-fifths of the woods workers were from Canada, the majority being English and not French, and one-fourth were Scandinavians. Nine-tenths of the foreign-born sawmill workers were from Canada. In New York, among the sawmill workers, one-fourth of the foreign-born were English or French Canadians, while one-third were German and one-fourth Irish. Among the woods workers over one-half of the foreign-born were German, with a fair representation of Irish, English, and Scandinavians—not more than one in ten of each named nationality being found. In Pennsylvania the much smaller proportion of foreign-born workers in the industry was made up, to a large extent, of Canadians, Scandinavians, and Germans, with Irish, English, and other nationalities present in smaller numbers.[25] By 1900 production had declined considerably in both New York and Pennsylvania and to a lesser extent in Maine. At the same time, the labor force had changed somewhat. In Maine it was made up more of "imported" workers. The rise of lumbering elsewhere had drawn off much of the native supply of men. The working force at this date consisted of the native sons and Candians who had not followed the lumbering developments westward into Canada or to the Lake States and of "Boston men," comprising Poles, Finns, Russians, Swedes, and Irish.[26]

Sawing the lumber was a distinct phase of the work in the industry. The sawmill was always situated at a place where the logs could be easily received. Before the era of steam-driven mills, they had to be located near the source of water power. Later that was not important, but the mills were still located on the streams where the logs were accessible. The sawing season was limited to the late spring, summer, and autumn months, because when the rivers were frozen there was no power or else the logs were held solid. Because of the limited season, many sawmills operated two shifts—when the market was good—running continuously through the night.[27]

Only fragmentary information about wages is available, and it is dangerous to generalize concerning them. Until after the Civil War, wages ranged from $10 to $20 per month and board for the woods workers, and more for those on the drive. By the 1870's, if the average man could show $50 clear at the end of the logging season he did well. In the whole region teamsters with four-horse teams received from $40 to $45 a month and board, but often they had to provide certain equipment. Almost everywhere actual payment for logging work was made at the end of the season when the men emerged from the woods, and in some cases only part payment was made before the logs were in the booms.[28] Even for sawmill work wages were frequently held back, and men had to take credit at the company store until the time when they were paid. Later, wages rose. At all times, however, the extent of seasonality needs to be kept in mind to get the full import of the income picture. At the close of the nineteenth century the average number of months of employment provided in the woods was 4.16 in Maine, 5.95 in New York, and 7.35 in Pennsylvania. Average monthly wages were $30.36, $32.94, and $38.28, respectively. For sawmills at that time the average duration of employment per year was 7.73 months in Maine, 7.40 in New York, and 7.12 in Pennsylvania, at average monthly wages of $34.71, $35.37, and $38.89, respectively[29]

This rough picture of the situation does not, of course, show the direct overlapping of jobs. The extent to which workers engaged in both branches of the industry, or shifted from the woods to farming, is known only by reference to general statements of such movements. From the Census we discover that annual earnings for logging and sawmilling labor averaged somewhat less than $300 from 1870 to 1890, but increased to around $400 by 1900, in the states of Maine, New York, and Pennsylvania.[30] The average sawmill worker received a higher monthly wage than the average woods worker, although there were more lower-paid workers in sawmills—for instance, those receiving less than $25 a month. A large majority of both woods and sawmill workers received between $25 and $40 a month, most of the workers falling in the $30 to $35 classification. There was a noticeably larger number of sawmill workers in the $40 to $50 classification than woods workers.

Hours of labor were always long, the rule being from daylight to dark in the woods. This meant that breakfast had to be eaten before daybreak—usually an hour before—so that the men could be in the woods at the designated place as soon as it was light enough to begin work.[31] No reduction in the length of the working day occurred until after the turn of the century, and even then work in the woods was for excessively long hours compared to the situation in other industries.[32] In sawmills the hours worked were correspondingly long and remained at twelve a day even after 1900.

That other conditions were not wholesome is revealed in various reports. Employment agents often obtained men in Boston or other places by misrepresenting conditions and the nature of the work to them. Inasmuch as many of the men thus drawn into the woods were without funds, transportation expenses, clothing, and other supplies were often advanced. Because of the misrepresentation of conditions, the men sometimes left the job before having worked long enough to pay the costs involved. Lumbermen appealed to the legislature and in 1907 a law was passed giving protection to the employers. But the law was administered in such a way as to cause forced labor because it was made a criminal offense to break a contract, and the situation was not altered until after a federal investigation and the application of federal authority in the matter.[33]

Reference to labor disputes in this early lumber region are seldom found, and contemporary observations make the point that strikes were unknown.[34] The absence of labor disputes does not mean that relations were ideal and that there was no cause for unrest. On the contrary, there were unrest and discontent. But they did not take form in concerted labor activity. The men cursed and grumbled about their lot and treatment, but they seldom, if ever, thought of an organization. They were too individualistic to believe they could not stand on their own feet and fight their own battles. Although they could not get their wages until spring, they could leave the camp if the boss was too intractable. The men were likely to live or work in a different place every year, and the whole milieu was not conducive to organization. One notable "rebellion" occurred, however, in the early seventies among sawmill workers at Williamsport. This episode has been referred to as "the riots of 1872" by a prominent historian of the industry.[35] The "riots" were symptomatic of the strife existing in other industries in Pennsylvania at the time and were a product of the poor labor conditions in the industry.

Lumbering was active at the time and nearly all the mills were running long shifts. Some of them were operating twelve to fourteen hours a day.[36] The boom was full of logs and the capacity of the mills was scarcely equal to the demand for lumber. To the long shifts was added the "speed-up," and, with the other labor groups being active and the spirit of labor organization being in the air, the men formed an organization. They made a demand for the ten-hour day but it was refused. Consequently, a strike was called, and on June 29, 1872, some 3,000 men quit work. The union's proposal to compromise the issue was rejected, and the strike dragged on for three weeks until several mills succeeded in resuming operations with the employment of strikebreakers and with workers who left the ranks of the strikers. With this development, the operating mills were attacked by the strikers who drove off the scabs and closed the mills. The lumberjacks were rough and tough men who were not reluctant to resort to fighting when there seemed to be no other recourse, and considerable violence ensued. If the operator was unwilling to recognize the men's organization, perhaps the only alternative was to resist his tactics with physical force. This resistance was no solution, for the operators, in early Pennsylvania custom, called for troops, which were dispatched immediately and succeeded in quieting the trouble. The strike leaders were arrested, tried, convicted, and sentenced to the penitentiary. Nevertheless, because of the widespread protests against such harsh treatment, the governor granted the men a full pardon as soon as they reached the prison, and they were immediately released.[37] The strike was broken; but it was a forerunner of labor strife that was to be very violent in other regions of the industry.

NOTES TO CHAPTER

[1] R. G. Wood, *A History of Lumbering in Maine, 1820-1861,* University of Maine Studies, Second Series, No. 33 (Orono, Me.: University Press, 1935), pp. 30-31.

[2] R. G. Wood, *op. cit.,* pp. 226-236; cf. C. L. Goodrich and Others, *Migration and Economic Opportunity,* Philadelphia: University of Pennsylvania Press, 1936, p. 275.

[3] R. G. Wood, *op. cit.,* pp. 12, 99 *et passim;* U.S. Department of Agriculture, *A History of the Lumber Industry in the State of New York,* by W. F. Fox, Bulletin No. 34. Washington: Government Printing Office, 1902, pp. 17-26; J. H. Walker (ed.), *Rafting Days in Pennsylvania.* Altoona, Pa.: Times-Tribune Co., 1922, pp. 29-39; G. W. Huntley, *A Story of the Sinnamahone.* Williamsport, Pa.: The Williamsport Printing and Binding Company, 1936; D. F. Magee, "Rafting on the Susquehanna," Paper read before the *Lancaster County Historical Society,* XXIV, No. 9 (1920), 193-202.

[4] U.S. Department of Agriculture, *A History of the Lumber Industry in the State of New York,* p. 28.

[5] R. G. Wood, *op. cit.,* pp. 48-82.

[6] A. G. Hempstead, *The Penobscot Boom,* Orono, Me.: University of Maine Studies, 1931, Vol. XXXIII, No. 11, pp. 15, 28, 30, *passim;* U.S. Department of Agriculture, p. 22.

[7] R. G. Wood, *op. cit.,* pp. 112, 124-127; H. D. Thoreau, *The Maine Woods.* New York: Thomas Y. Crowell and Co., 1906, p. 46; U.S. Department of Agriculture, *A History of the Lumber Industry in the State of New York,* pp. 26-28.

[8] Twelfth Census of the United States, 1900, Vol. IX, *Manufactures,* Part 3, pp. 807-810.

[9] R. G. Wood, *op. cit.,* p. 17; *Thirteenth Annual Report of the Bureau of Industrial and Labor Statistics for the State of Maine, 1899.* Waterville, Me., 1900, pp. 68-70.

[10] Tenth Census of the United States, 1880, *Report on the Statistics of Wages in Manufacturing Industries,* p. 461; J. H. Walker, *op. cit.,* p. 24.

[11] *Thirteenth Annual Report of the Bureau of Industrial and Labor Statistics for*

the State of Maine, 1899, p. 70; U.S. Department of Agriculture, *A History of the Lumber Industry in the State of New York*, pp. 35-37.

12 *Thirteenth Annual Report of the Bureau of Industrial and Labor Statistics for the State of Maine, 1899*, pp. 68, 84; *First Biennial Report of the Department of Labor and Industry of the State of Maine, 1911-12*, "Industrial Conditions in the Maine Woods," by J. P. Flanagan, Waterville, Me., 1913, p. 207.

13 Twelfth Census of the United States, 1900, Vol. IX, *Manufactures*, Part 3, pp. 863-66; cf. U.S. Department of Agriculture, *A History of the Lumber Industry in the State of New York*, pp. 35-37; *Thirteenth Annual Report of the Bureau of Industrial and Labor Statistics for the State of Maine, 1899*, p. 69.

14 R. G. Wood, *op. cit.*, pp. 99-103; U.S. Department of Agriculture, *A History of the Lumber Industry in the State of New York*, pp. 16, 38; *First Biennial Report of the Department of Labor and Industry of the State of Maine, 1911-12*, p. 218.

15 H. D. Thoreau, *op. cit.*, p. 20.

16 *Thirteenth Annual Report of the Bureau of Industrial and Labor Statistics for the State of Maine, 1899*, p. 69.

17 H. D. Thoreau, *op. cit.*, pp. 20-21; J. H. Walker, *op. cit.*, p. 21; "The Spectator in an Adirondack Lumber Camp," *Outlook*, LXX, No. 1 (January 4, 1902), 18-19.

18 U.S. Department of Agriculture, *Studies of the Food of Maine Lumbermen*, by C. D. Woods and E. R. Mansfield. Bulletin No. 149. Washington: Government Printing Office, 1904, pp. 7-9.

19 U.S. Department of Agriculture, *A History of the Lumber Industry in the State of New York*, p. 34.

20 U.S. Department of Agriculture, *Studies of the Food of Maine Lumbermen*, p. 9.

21 R. G. Wood, *op. cit.*, pp. 91-94; U. S. Department of Agriculture, *A History of the Lumber Industry in the State of New York*, pp. 7, 8, *et passim; First Biennial Report of the Department of Labor and Industry of the State of Maine, 1911-12*, p. 210; J. H. Walker, *op. cit.*, p. 21.

22 R. G. Wood, *op. cit.*, pp. 99, 196.

23 *Thirteenth Annual Report of the Bureau of Industrial and Labor Statistics for the State of Maine, 1899*, pp. 69-71.

24 R. G. Wood, *op. cit.*, pp. 191, 196-197.

25 Eleventh Census of the United States, 1890, *Population*, Part 2, pp. 564-565, 590-591, 602-603.

26 *Thirteenth Annual Report of the Bureau of Industrial and Labor Statistics for the State of Maine, 1899*, p. 68; *First Biennial Report of the Department of Labor and Industry of the State of Maine, 1911-12*, p. 220.

27 R. G. Wood, *op. cit.*, pp. 162-171.

28 R. G. Wood, *op. cit.*, pp. 190-191; *Thirteenth Annual Report of the Bureau of Industrial and Labor Statistics for the State of Maine, 1899*, p. 71; *Annual Report of the Secretary of Internal Affairs of the Commonwealth of Pennsylvania, 1879-80*, Vol. VII, "Industrial Statistics," Part 3. Harrisburg, Pa.: 1881, p. 217.

29 Eleventh Census of the United States, 1890, *Report of Manufacturing Industries*, Part 3, pp. 624-625.

30 Twelfth Census of the United States, 1900, Vol. IX, *Manufactures*, Part 3, pp. 807-810.

31 U.S. Department of Agriculture, *A History of the Lumber Industry in the State of New York*, p. 11.

32 *First Biennial Report for the Department of Labor and Industry of the State of Maine, 1911-12*, p. 207.

33 U.S. Immigration Commission, *Abstract of Reports, 1911*, Vol. II, "Peonage." Washington: Government Printing Office, 1912, pp. 443-449; *First Biennial Report of the Department of Labor and Industry of the State of Maine, 1911-12*, pp. 224-225.

34 *First Biennial Report of the Department of Labor and Industry of the State of Maine, 1911-12*, p. 220; cf. R. G. Woods, *op. cit.*, p. 195.

35 J. E. Defebaugh, *History of the Lumber Industry in America*. Chicago: American Lumbermen, 1907, p. 601.

36 *Annual Reports of the Secretary of Internal Affairs of the Commonwealth of Pennsylvania, 1880-1881*, Vol. IX, "Industrial Statistics," Part 3. Harrisburg, Pa.: 1882, p. 301; *Third Annual Report of the Commissioner of Labor, 1887, Strikes and Lockouts*. Washington: Government Printing Office, 1888, p. 1059.

37 J. E. Defebaugh, *op. cit.*, p. 601.

4   *THE GREAT LAKES REGION*

THE mass attack on the forests of the Lake States did not get under way until after the Civil War. When it did, lumbering was carried out on a larger scale and with greater vigor than before. It was also distinguished by the appearance of large-scale industrial organizations within a frontier environment. The first onslaught in the Great Lakes region was upon the Michigan woods. These were ideally situated for supplying parts of the eastern market by way of the Erie Canal after the most accessible stands of white pine in New York and Pennsylvania had been rapidly cut.[1] The spread of the industry into Wisconsin and Minnesota was based upon the growth of the prairie states' market for lumber, a consequence of the spread of the railroad and its introduction into lumbering. After 1870 several railroad lines were projected northward into the pine region. These lines, stimulated by extensive grants of valuable timber lands, rapidly came to supply an essential service to the lumbermen in the hauling of logs and lumber.[2]

About fifty-seven million original acres of old-growth saw timber in this region—a magnificent stand of white pine—was rapidly opened. The industry enjoyed a mushroomlike growth during the seventies and eighties, and there has never been such a complete and rapid cutting of a forest of this size. The region reached its peak of production about 1900—Michigan's being between 1880 and 1890, Wisconsin's about a decade later, and Minnesota's shortly after 1900.[3]

The railroad was an important causal factor in the growth of the industry, but it was the rivers which at first provided the only means of carrying logs down to the mills. Nor was the use of the river suddenly discontinued. As a matter of fact, practically all the producing centers were associated with famous log-driving streams. Beginning in the eastern part of Michigan, the Saginaw Valley was an early center, having as many as eighty mills by 1882. The whole stretch of twenty miles along the river from Saginaw to Bay City was almost one continuous pile of lumber at the close of each summer sawing season.[4]

Other notable centers of production were in the Muskegon River district on the west side of the lower peninsula in Michigan; on Green Bay in Wisconsin across Lake Michigan, the logs coming from the Oconto and Menominee rivers; and at La Crosse, Wisconsin, on the Mississippi at the junction of the Black River. In addition, there were numerous other places such as Oshkosh, Wisconsin, on Lake Winnebago, which utilized logs from the Wolf and Fox River pineries, Grand Rapids on the Wisconsin River, and Fairchild on the Chippewa. In Minnesota the principal centers of production were at Minneapolis on the Mississippi, along the St. Croix River, and at Duluth near the mouth of the St. Louis River.[5] The growth of all these centers followed the same general course.

Besides the region's excellent timber, the depletion of the most accessible forest in the older Northeastern centers, and the changes in transportation, notable improvements in processes and machinery also contributed to the rapid growth of the industry. In the first half of the nineteenth century some improvements were made, such as the introduction of the muley saw—a more powerful single-blade saw—the circular saw, and the gang saw which, by the addition of a number of saw blades, made it possible to cut several boards through one operation. Also, the carriage for transporting the log past the saw was introduced. In these were the mechanical prerequisites for a great saving of labor and an increased rate of production.[6]

These changes, however, were small in comparison with those which accompanied the application of steam power, which provided half the mechanical power employed in the industry by 1869, and within two decades supplied over 90 per cent of it. The use of the steam engine simplified the problem of location and made possible the utilization of larger, heavier, and more productive machinery. Mills consequently increased in size. In 1889 the band saw was introduced, and thereafter achieved widespread use. Of equal, if not greater, importance was the mechanization of the operations involved in handling logs on the carriage, accompanied by improvements which speeded the movement of the carriage past the headsaw. By the end of the century, steam-actuated mechanical devices were used for turning the log on the carriage and for setting the log for the thickness of the cut.[7] In addition, mechanical conveyance of lumber was introduced into the more advanced mills. Other developments rounded out what is today the general structure of production (although refinements have been made since then): the edger for squaring the edges of boards, the trimmer for cutting out defective parts, dry kilns for seasoning lumber, and planers for finishing it. During this time the great motivating force behind mechanization was the growing demand for lumber, which could not be successfully met through use of the old techniques. The industry was eagerly searching for ways and means of rapidly transforming logs into lumber.

Many mechanical aids, meanwhile, were introduced into logging activities in addition to the use of the railroad. Only the tasks of felling trees and cutting them into log lengths were not successfully mechanized, because the felling of each tree presents individual problems caused by the lean of the tree or the nature of the terrain. From the point in logging where the trees are cut into log lengths, improvements were introduced in all the tasks of handling and transporting logs. At first, as trees were cut farther and farther from the riverbanks, it was necessary to build better roads. In some instances the skid road—built of logs laid crosswise in a corduroy pattern—facilitated operations. This expedient did not really solve the problem, and so the "big wheels" were developed. Huge wheels, eight, ten, or twelve feet in diameter, were mounted on a broad axle. This contraption could be moved astride a log which was lifted at one end and fastened to the axle. It was easy then to drag the log to the landing. Eventually, mechanical equipment was introduced. The donkey engine found its way into the logging camps in the 1880's and was used as the source of power for yarding devices. These consisted of cables wound on drums to drag the logs from the stump to the engine, where they were loaded mechanically for movement to the mill.

The late nineteenth century improvements in lumber production necessitated larger initial investments, which were practical only when there was access to sufficient timber to support a mill over a reasonable period of time. It was, therefore, necessary to acquire larger tracts of timber than had previously been necessary to maintain sawmilling activities.

At the time the widespread mass attack upon the forests of this region developed a great deal of the timber was still in public hands.[8] Within a relatively short period the great bulk of it passed into private ownership. This took place through land grants to various transportation companies; through direct sales by the federal and state governments; and through certain federal and state public land laws which, although designed primarily to create small agricultural holdings, resulted in the "illegal" assemblage of large tracts of forest land. Public timber lands were acquired by private owners with amazing rapidity and in questionable ways. Ill-framed laws, coupled with poor or dishonest administration, permitted land speculation in its most distasteful forms, as well as widespread corruption, extensive fraud, and downright thievery.[9]

Individuals bought thousands of acres of heavily timbered land at nominal prices—in many cases well below the market price—and obtained timber through the land settlement laws by acquisition of the pre-emption right of "settlers" who secretly intended to make such transfer at the time of entry. They also obtained access to timber by securing the power of attorney from Indians and others who held scrip, which then permitted them to locate valuable lands. Many other devious devices were used, and many brazen forms of land speculation were common.[10] Complete information as to the extent of early holdings and the degree of concentration is not available. About 1910, however, in the three Lake States together, four holders apparently had 12 per cent of the timber, seventeen holders had 23 per cent, forty-four holders had 37 per cent, and two hundred and fifteen holders had 65 per cent.[11]

Concentration of holdings, however, was less important as a means of extensive economic control over the industry than as a factor in stimulating excessively rapid exploitation, in facilitating the growth of individual fortunes, and in the shaping of the course of state politics by lumber operators. The accumulated fortunes can generally be traced, either directly or indirectly, to the rise in value of timber lands which had been acquired early.[12] Large timber owners were never sufficiently powerful to build up effective control over the industry as a whole. The forests were too extensive and there was too much flexibility in production to make that possible. Furthermore, the peculiar nature of the overhead cost structure coupled with extreme individualism also were influential. Early attempts to control the industry were generally without success.[13] Although there were many producers and a competitive market, fortunes accrued to those who came into possession of valuable forest lands obtained at nominal prices. It was difficult to lose much money on timberland bought at $1.25 an acre.

Organization of production in this region was dictated by the pressure of an expanding market. With the development of new mechanical devices and production techniques, the aim was to cut out as rapidly as possible—to liquidate forest holdings and move on. As a result, the industry became a great migrant, reaching out farther and farther as the forest receded.

Logging, because there was a continuous "gobbling" of the forest, was always on the move. Sawmilling has been relatively more stable. When a large mill was constructed it was placed at a strategic point, because the life and size of a sawmill depended greatly on the transportation facilities and the area of the forest hinterland. But there were also many small temporary mills, and after their ravenous saws had cut all the available timber they had to move elsewhere.

In 1870 there were over 2,400 sawmilling establishments in the Lake States region, more than 1,500 of them in Michigan. Twenty years later the figure rose to over 3,700, with more than 2,200 of them in Michigan, over 1,100 in Wisconsin, and slightly less than 400 in Minnesota. The average size of the mills in 1890 also was larger than it had been twenty years earlier. The mills in Minnesota were developed later and had, on the average, twice the capital invested in them and used about twice the number of employees per mill as did those in Michigan. The average mill in Wisconsin tended to be larger than those in Michigan, but not so large as the mills in Minnesota. This situation reflects the time and stage of development within the respective areas. By 1900, although the peak of production had been passed in Michigan and Wisconsin, the number of establishments was still over 3,300. They were also smaller than they had been. Minnesota had experienced a growth to 438, the large mill still occupying a prominent position. Shortly after 1900, however, Minnesota too had passed its peak, and the region as a whole had been definitely displaced as the leading producing area. Ten states ranked ahead of the Lake States as producers by 1910. From then on abandoned communities were conspicuous throughout the region.

In addition to being a migrant, the industry was highly seasonal both in sawmilling and in logging. A longer logging season was possible, however, when the logging railroad was used because operations were not tied so definitely to the weather as was the case when the logs were run to the mills on the spring freshets. Likewise, the steam-driven sawmill need not shut down because of want of power as did the water-driven mill. Weather continued to exert some influence, however; logging was easier in winter and logs frozen in the pond could not be taken into the mill. Both activities, therefore, remained seasonal to a great degree.

In logging employment opportunities increased a little in late August or early September, and picked up rapidly through October and November, reaching a peak in January. Employment was maintained through February, but in March a reduction of 25 per cent was not uncommon. In April and May the low point was reached, and

logging employment was less than a third of the January peak. The
number of employees then remained, roughly, the same through the
summer months. In sawmilling the seasonal peak was in the summer
during June, July, and August, and the low point was in December
and January. The fluctuation was not so great in sawmilling, however,
and the number of employees at the low point of employment was
only one-third below the top number. While the peaks of employment
in both branches of the industry were about the same, the trough in
the employment level in logging was twice as deep as in sawmilling.
This meant that there existed a possibility of some dovetailing of employment, because as employment declined in logging, during the
early part of the year, it increased in the sawmilling branch of the
industry. This, however, could provide room for only a third of the
displaced workers.[14]

This situation was not quite so serious for the workers as it might
appear because of the source of part of the labor. Thousands of men
from the farming region to the south of the timber belt in the three
Lake States—as well as farmers from the Ohio Valley—went into the
north woods camps every winter. They thus secured a wage income
to supplement the return from their farms. The circumstances under
which this type of labor entered the industry was injurious to the
standards of those who worked continuously in it. Another source
of labor was somewhat analogous to the type of agricultural labor
just mentioned. Logging camps and sawmill villages required large
quantities of food for the men and fodder for the animals, and farms
were established in the cut-over region to supply these needs. Individuals from such farms were available for work in the woods during
the October to March logging season, but found it more profitable to
go back to farming in the summer.[15]

Before the Civil War, the lumberjacks and workers in the Lake
States area were mostly of native American stock. The New England
States had furnished many men with previous logging and sawmilling
experience.[16] During the seventies and eighties, as the industry expanded rapidly in this region, a strong admixture of Europeans was
noticeable. The 1870 Census lumps all the lumber industry workers
together and does not break down the statistics on nativity by states.
The over-all picture shows that more than 86 per cent of the workers
were of American or Canadian origin and that an additional 5.7
per cent came from other English-speaking groups. Of the small group
of German-born workers, approximately 75 per cent were in sawmill
jobs located primarily in Pennsylvania and New York with a few in

the Lake States region.[17] Although the 1880 Census information on the composition of the logging and sawmilling labor forces is neither entirely accurate nor reliable, it seems clear enough that less than half the lumber industry labor force of the Great Lakes region was native American. There had been a great influx of Canadians—both English and French—and a goodly number of both Germans and Scandinavians. Germans made up 12.4 per cent and 9.4 per cent, respectively, of the workers in Wisconsin and Michigan. Canadians made up a large portion of the working force in each of the three states but were relatively more numerous in Michigan, which was slightly more accessible to them. It is noteworthy that the newly arriving Scandinavians were passing by the waning Northeastern area and the Michigan lumber region and were going on to Wisconsin and Minnesota.[18] The situation in 1890, with a few exceptions, roughly paralleled that of 1880. There was, however, an increase in the total labor force of some 66 per cent, or from about 75,000 to around 125,000 men. Relatively fewer Canadians were found in all three states, while the immigration of Scandinavians made for notable increases in each. This was especially so in Minnesota, where they comprised 27.5 per cent of the working force, and in Wisconsin, where they comprised 21.7 per cent of the workers. A net migration of 7,000 Scandinavian workers into the Lake States lumber industry occurred between 1880 and 1890.[19]

In this sector of the lumber industry there was hardly any child labor and the nature of the work tended to keep a relatively large proportion of the men single, especially those who went into the woods. Because of the lumbering industry there was always a pronounced surplus of males in the total population of the region. In 1890 two-thirds of the woods workers and more than half the sawmill workers were unmarried. In 1900 the same proportions prevailed among the loggers, but slightly better than 50 per cent of the sawmill workers were married. One important variation in the logging labor situation in Michigan was that the proportion of unmarried men was greatly reduced. The industry was on the wane, and the single jacks, free of family ties, could move more readily to Wisconsin or Minnesota.[20]

Information on the living conditions in the earlier logging camps of the Great Lakes region is fragmentary and colored by romantic treatment. Many kinds of camps with varied characteristics existed, and among them there were great differences. Marked variations also occurred through the years as fundamental changes were made in the

size of the lumbering units. In the late nineteenth century there were
year-round camps—some in existence as many as five or six years—
and temporary single-winter camps. Some were operated by the lumber
companies themselves, with their own superintendents and foremen
to direct the work. There were jobbers' (or contractors') camps, which
were operated by those who contracted to cut certain tracts or certain
amounts of logs, the contractor furnishing and paying his own men
and placing the logs at the specified landing. The camps varied in
size from big ones, with as many as two hundred men, to those of
the small contractors, who employed from twelve to fifteen men
housed in simple shanties. The average camp in the eighties and
nineties consisted of from sixty to eighty workers.[21] Not all small
camps were jobbers' camps. Nor were all the large ones operated
directly by the lumber companies. It is true, however, that jobbers'
camps usually tended to be smaller and certainly more temporary
because a contract most frequently covered only one season.

It may be misleading to speak of a pioneer stage of logging, because even in recent times logging has been carried on under conditions which people conceive of as pioneer. It must always be carried
on under more or less rigorous circumstances. Improvements in camps
occurred gradually. The one-room shanty—containing both the cooking facilities and the sleeping quarters—tended to disappear. The
larger camps were generally more substantially constructed and were
supplied with more ample accommodations than the smaller ones.
More niceties of life were introduced into the camps. They varied in
their conditions, however, and in many places a low standard of
comfort continued. When conditions became too bad, it was difficult
to maintain a crew, and poor camps had to get along with a lower
class of labor.[22]

As large-size camps became more common, the buildings continued
to be made of logs but windows were now more frequently found.[23]
The structures, almost without exception, were substantial enough but
usually badly ventilated. This was not because lumberjacks disliked
fresh air or imbibed enough of it in the daytime. It was largely
because it took time and was expensive to cut an adequate number
of windows and because the bunks were built along the side walls,
leaving only the ends of the buildings clear for such openings. Another factor was that of the cold, against which it was absolutely
essential to be protected in the rigorous winter of the north woods.
It was often necessary to maintain a temperature of around a hundred
or more degrees inside over and above that which prevailed on the

outside. It was not difficult to choose between fresher air and more snugness. The problem of ventilation was made still more difficult by the fact that the men lived and slept in the same large room. The evening puff on the pipe filled the air until it was blue with smoke. To this was added the steam and odor from drying, unwashed socks, mittens, and clothes hung around and above the central stove out of reach of the burning heat.[24]

In the center of the bunkhouse a frame was commonly found, about eight by ten feet, built up about six inches from the floor and filled with sand. In it was set the heater which kept the quarters warm. Around the bunkhouse, in front of the bunks ran the "deacon" seat upon which the men "lounged" during the always brief period between the evening meal and the set time to turn in for the night. Life in the lumber camp followed a definite routine and rigorous discipline was maintained.[25]

In the bunkhouse, or shanty, under the deacon seat was stored what little baggage the men had. The lumberjack traveled relatively light and was always able to purchase at the wangin the various articles he needed. Many a lumberjack carried his "turkey" or his "balloon," in which alone was contained most, if not all, of his worldly belongings. Whether this was true or not depended upon where he hailed from. In general, lumberjacks were not hoboes, although a handful doubtless were. Some of them worked only for a "stake," and could not be held once they had enough cash to carry them for a time. But this was not true of most lumber workers, who ranked quite high as laborers and were distinguished by their sense of independence.[26]

Except for the larger camps and those kept active during the whole year, little attention was paid to matters of sanitation outside the cookhouse. As a general rule, the cook shanties were kept cleaner than the bunkhouses, and often even showed signs of scrubbing. While the men insisted that the food preparation be clean, they did not concern themselves equally with the cleanliness of the bunkhouses. Often the men and the employer were both at fault in causing unsanitary conditions. In a bunkhouse that was not swept and cleaned frequently the floor became littered with matches and spittle and the room became ill-smelling.[27]

The men were surprisingly healthy in spite of these conditions. Climatic conditions kept disease germs at a minimum, and during winter months sanitation problems offered few difficulties. Early observers specifically noted the lack of illness, and epidemics were few.

The men were exceptionally robust to begin with, and their hard and simple life close to nature built up great endurance. In later years, however, conditions became worse in respect to the amount of illness. Moreover, the apparent absence of illness in the camps was sometimes misleading, because cases of sickness showed up in the towns to which the men went for treatment.[28]

Sleeping facilities comprised simple wooden bunks, which were uniformly continued in use until quite recently. Iron beds were not introduced until just before the turn of the century and did not become common for some years thereafter. Bunks were usually built in double and sometimes triple tiers with no air space between them, the bottom tier often being on the floor.[29] Conditions were much the same as in the Northeastern region, and revealing is the report of a superintendent of a lumber company, whose camps were above the average in cleanliness, who said that "blankets are washed once a year, in the spring, when they begin to get lousy." "There's more or less lice in every camp," remarked one jobber.[30] It was perhaps fortunate for the men that they were inured to the severest things in life and that they toiled almost to the point of exhaustion each day. Otherwise, sound sleep under such circumstances would have been rare.

The cookhouse was an important establishment. Breakfast was always served about an hour before daylight so that the men could be at their posts when it became light enough to start work. In truth, the loggers' saying that "The day began in a logging camp any time after midnight" was almost based on fact.

A walk, sometimes part of it on snowshoes, of anywhere from half a mile to two miles might be necessary before the place of work was reached. This was no picnic jaunt on a bleak and crisp December or January morning. The creaking, crunching snow underfoot was evidence enough of that; but occasionally a tree which could no longer stand the strain of the intense cold would crack with a sound like a small cannon shot and, with decisive punctuation, give further evidence that this was toil under grim circumstances.

About eleven o'clock in the morning, the noon meal would be delivered to the woods on a sleigh, unless the men were working adjacent to the camp, in which case they ate at the cookhouse. A crackling good fire would be burning when the hungry men gathered. Nevertheless, the beans would sometimes freeze to the tin plates in spite of the roaring fire. The slabs of pork and the biscuits, on the point of freezing before they were devoured, gave warmth and energy within anyway. Afterward, it was on the job again until dusk. Then came the night meal back in camp.

Food was probably always substantial and in most cases there was no skimping. The most frequent criticism was that the fare was monotonous.[31] Even with a tendency to increase the number of different foods offered, adequate variety was frequently lacking. The traditional foods—beans, pork, bread, molasses, and tea—were gradually supplemented with such things as dried fruits, certain vegetables, and fresh meats. By the turn of the century, largely because it was easier than before to get things into the camps, more variety was afforded. One writer with firsthand experience in a camp reports that in addition to the traditional staples including potatoes, there were available "rutabagas, sauerkraut, corned beef, fresh beef, dried apples, prunes, currants, raisins, syrup, sugar, salt, rice, lard, all in large quantities; also a line of spices." Tea, however, "was the only drink, being served in tin basins without milk." [32] Once in a while a camp possessed a cow.

Meals were always eaten in silence and without hats. The foreman, or bull o' the woods, ruled the camp outside the walls of the cookhouse; within, the cook was the "law." He was always considered one of the most important individuals in every camp. Cooks could slap a man down by right if he did not conform to the rules at the dinner table; and they did not allow raised voices. The origin of mealtime silence is not known, but it was practically universal.

Following the evening meal there was a short period of relaxation until the hour of nine, when it was a hard and fast rule that everyone "turn in." Nothing was permitted to interfere with the proper and prompt beginning of the next day's work. During the brief period of relaxation the men conversed about matters of current interest or seeming importance, or retold and passed on their favorite stories of Paul Bunyan or lesser characters. Perhaps, if there were songsters in the group, a ballad might be sung.

Some of the ballads were buoyant in spirit, full of daring and glamour. Others contained the story of tragedy, which was common in the industry.[33] A spirit of unrest and disillusionment often colored the songs and ballads. According to some people, this was more common toward the close of the century. Whether one can trace a changing spirit in the ballads is questionable. It is difficult to date them. It appears that the earliest of them, as well as some of the later ones, are interspersed with dissapointment and disillusionment. This is, perhaps, simply indicative of the fact that all was not romance in lumbering. "Michigan-I-O" was one of the most commonly sung complaints. Its title was often changed to fit the locality.

> The grub the dogs would laugh at
> Our beds were on the snow
> God send us to no worse than hell
> Or Michigan—I—O.

> Along yon glissening river
> No more shall we be found
> We'll see our wives and sweethearts,
> And tell them not to go,
> To the God-forsaken country
> Called Michigan—I—O.[34]

Another song of disillusionment warned:

> You had better work upon a farm
> For half a dollar a day
> Than to drive saw-logs on the Plaver
> And you'll never get your pay.[34]

The teamsters were the first ones out in the morning and were always considered important men. Their wages compared favorably with those of the cook. Other workers, in addition to those already referred to,[35] such as choppers, swampers, buckers, or sawyers, and skidders, were "wood-butchers," or carpenters, who had a place in each camp making and repairing logging sleds, making ox yokes and ax handles, as well as doing general repair work; and blacksmiths, who did the iron work on the sleds, shod the horses, and did the repair work in this line. There were "road monkeys," who kept the sled trails in shape by sprinkling them with water and filling holes that it might freeze over and make the roadbed smooth. They also kept the grooves in repair so that the sleds would keep the track and put sand or straw on the hills to hold the loads of logs back on the downgrade. Then there was the scaler, who measured and recorded the board feet in each log (some workers were paid by the piece). The clerk took charge of the wangin, checked the freight and made the respective charges to the men who procured goods, and kept the time of the men. In some camps this task fell to the foreman.[36]

It is impossible to speak with precision about the wage and income situation in the early period of lumbering in the Lake States. Complete statistical records of provable reliability are not available. The extreme seasonality of all types of work in the industry, the possibility of partial dovetailing of jobs, and the movements in and out of the industry of farmers who never expected anything but seasonal "fill-in" work, all color the wage picture. Total wage payments by states for various years and rates of pay for various types of work are known. The length of the season for various activities likewise has been recorded. However, only general statements as to the actual extent of shifts within, as well as shifts in and out of, the industry can be made with safety.

Evidence exists that the per capita wage in the lumber industry was lower than in other industries.[37] This was due to the seasonality of employment. In the woods, during the 1880's, common laborers received around $15 a month and board. Wages of skilled workers ranged upward around $30 to $40 a month and board. Usually, the men were hired by the month and paid by the day. A practice of wage calculation was to set up a scale of daily wages for various monthly rates, i.e., 61 cents a day when the monthly rate was $16, or 85 cents a day when the monthly rate was $22. An example of how the system worked was recorded by a clerk in a camp around 1890.

If a man worked 72 days at $22 per month he would receive 72 times 85 cents per day or $61.20. From this was deducted the wanegan account of possibly $12, the man receiving a check for $49.20.[38]

Common labor in the sawmills received from $1 to $1.50 a day, variations between mills being accounted for by differences in the number of hours worked per day and by such "gratuities" as free wood, "lower" rents—if living in company houses, and so forth. The customary wage was $1.25 for an eleven-hour day. Skilled workmen received proportionately more. Sawyers received around $4 a day.[39]

Monthly or daily rates of pay are of little significance without some relation to the total time worked. Annual earnings give a better picture of economic well-being. The various factors already mentioned make it impossible to attempt precision in statement with the figures available. One estimate places the annual per capita income in the lumber industry in Wisconsin for 1897 at $386.09.[40] Census information covering the Lake States lumber industry for the year 1890 shows that the average annual wage for all branches of the industry was only approximately $250. But this figure is a simple average without any consideration of overlapping in jobs. Woods workers averaged only approximately $185 for the season, with some variations between the states being explained largely on the basis of the length of seasons. Sawmill workers fared somewhat better, the average annual income being $100 greater.[41] Taking all things into consideration, the average annual income should have approximated $375 to $400 for workers who were more or less continuously employed in the industry. Unskilled workers with year-round work probably earned no more than $300. Those who worked only in logging or sawmilling earned proportionately less.

Workers, for many years, were not paid in cash, or at least not entirely in cash. As a rule, cash was scarce and the workers received due bills payable in the fall or spring at the close of the logging or sawmilling season. In many places, also, the sawmill workers were given "store orders" or took part of their pay in kind from the company store. The method of wage payment was the source of considerable discontent in early times. In many cases sawmill workers were forced to trade at the company stores and, in this practice, were often exploited. There were cases in which, as a condition of employment, employees were required to sign written agreements that they would buy everything they needed at the company store.[42] Frequently, liberal credit was extended in order to capture future earnings. If due bills were not used, workers had to wait until the "end of the season" to collect their wages. Those employers who paid with due bills often used the system as a source of profit. When workers had to have some cash, employers stood ready to discount the due bills for 10 per cent or more.[43] Not until 1890, when the Wisconsin legislature made the due bills negotiable and gave the buyer a labor lien on the logs or lumber, could the worker cash his due bills at any place except with his employer. The change in the law, however, still did not prevent the workman from losing from 10 to 20 per cent when he sold his time check, because such charges were levied by those who did cash them. There existed a Wisconsin law which required weekly or bimonthly payment of wages in cash, but it did not include the lumber industry. In time, lumber companies were required to furnish evidence of indebtedness to workingmen in the form of negotiable paper which was payable at the main office of the company or at any bank in the state.[44]

Strikes in the industry were always more or less localized affairs. Although there were grievances, unionism was slow to take hold. The absence of a trade union psychology, the strength of individualism, the seasonality of the industry, the isolation of groups of workers in camps miles back in the woods, and the customary complete employer town control in the sawmilling centers were all obstacles to co-operative action by workingmen. Farmers who sought temporary cash income in lumbering, of course, had no interest in labor organization. If unions were lacking, industrial conflicts were not, even though the "absence" of strikes was often referred to in order to prove a generally wholesome condition. Actually, however, local strikes or "riots"—the two often being synonymous in the minds of many operators—were frequent.[45] Vigorous measures to thwart and destroy labor activities were applied whenever necessary. The use of blacklists, strikebreakers, "law and order," and strong disciplinary measures, supported by the deferred wage payment system, were common.

It can hardly be said that the lumber workers were successfully organized anywhere in the region at any time. Woods workers were rarely unionized. Sawmill workers, however, did organize occasionally or, without being formally organized, engaged in spontaneous revolt. Many local disputes over hours and the system of wage payment occurred. In 1879 perhaps the earliest attempt at regional organization was made. The Chippewa Valley Workingmen's Association was formed in that year to protest against long hours and payment of wages other than by cash.[46]

Early strikes were often accompanied by much violence. Harsh treatment of lumber workers on strike was quickly met by the use of force. In Michigan, in 1881, strikes at Au Sable and Oscada, and at Muskegon, were successful in achieving a reduction in hours, but a strike at Muskegon the following year failed.[47] In Wisconsin, in 1881, a bitter strike over hours of work occurred at Eau Claire. When scabs were hired, the striking men reacted violently, drove the new men from the mill, extinguished the fires in the boilers, and stopped the plants. The strikers then "took over" the town, defied the city authorities, and handled the sheriff's posse without restraint. An appeal by the mayor to the governor, followed by a personal examination of the situation, resulted in the dispatch of troops. An attack by the 2,000 striking, "large, horny-handed and resolute fellows," was averted and the militia took control. Afterward, however, the mills worked only eleven hours a day.[48]

The peak of labor disputes in this region came in the early eighties with a wave of local strikes which culminated in a series of larger disputes between 1884 and 1886. In Michigan, at Oscada and Au Sable, in June of 1884, all the workers in the sawmill operations, the dock hands, and the boommen at both towns went out on strike. The dispute originated with the dock hands, who on May 1 had demanded and obtained an increase in pay. But on Monday, June 16, the employers reduced the hourly rates to the old level and the dock hands refused to work. The boommen, lumber pilers, and mill workers soon joined with them. These workers were ready for a strike call. Half the men had had no work for five months and, when some of the mills were opened in the latter part of April, no definite arrangements had been made with many of the workers about wages. At some of the mills the men had been at work seven weeks when the first payday came, although, in the meantime, they had been given store orders payable in merchandise at the company-owned stores whenever they sought them. Two of the involved companies owned stores and had adopted the practice of monthly paydays, but had reserved fifteen days' pay. Other companies which did not have their own stores had made arrangements to issue store orders on those stores owned by the two companies. However, only one other company had the same wage payment system. In addition, one paid by the month, another every two weeks, and a third paid weekly. If the men wanted cash for their store orders they were obliged to accept a discount of from 8 to 15 per cent. In the interim before the delayed monthly payday rumors had circulated that wages were to be less than for the previous season.

On June 16 some of the involved companies sent notices similar to the following to the employees working at the rate of $2 a day and less:

Oscada, June 15, 1884.

Your wages are one dollar thirty-seven and a half cents per day. If you work until the close of the season and do satisfactory work you will receive twelve and a half cents per day more. If you do not agree to the above report to the office at once.

The rate of wages differed in the notices and in some cases the amount retained was 25 cents per day. In addition, by a concert of action among the operators, all wages were reduced 25 cents per day below those paid in the previous season. The men retaliated with a printed notice to the mill owners in which they demanded that the same wage rates be paid as for the last season; that no money be kept back by mill owners; and that there be weekly paydays every Saturday.

As soon as the strike started, a number of Pinkerton men were obtained from Chicago. Although there was no violence, the mill owners and the sheriff called for the state militia and two companies were sent to the scene. The investigators sent out by the Michigan

Bureau of Labor and Industrial Statistics discovered only one instance of violence, which was caused when a mill proprietor turned the mill hose upon strikers approaching one of the mills. The men rushed for the hose and in the ensuing melee the operator was struck on the head with the nozzle. Every public speaker among the strikers counseled moderation but firmness, and abstinence from intemperance and violence. The citizens of the two towns heartily supported the strikers. Among the operators there were great differences of opinion. The majority willingly acceded to the workers' demands, but two protested against all of them. All except two mills opened within ten days and the other two were allowed to open only after a two weeks' shutdown. The strike was won when the men obtained the old wage scale. Cash payments of wages was accepted by all the mills, two agreeing to pay cash weekly, and the others in full at the end of the month.[49]

Many strikes occurred in both Michigan and Wisconsin during 1885. All were somewhat localized and, except for one, none was of long duration. These conflicts were symptomatic of a prevailing unrest which broke out in demands for improved wage and hour conditions as well as changes in many practices.[50] Local organizations appeared, but were for the most part very short-lived. In 1885 the Knights of Labor penetrated the area and some of the existing local unions in the Menominee River area affiliated with it.

In Michigan, a brief three-day strike by rivermen, at Cheboygan, for higher wages was lost when the men returned to work at the old wage scale. The largest strike of all occurred at Bay City and Saginaw, lasting from July 6 to September 1. It was a dispute over hours and was precipitated, in part at least, by a misunderstanding among the men about a newly passed Michigan law which looked forward to a statutory ten-hour day. Many of the men thought the law went into effect on July 1, whereas, in reality, it did not become effective until September 23.[51] When hours were not reduced to ten per day after July 1, the men called the strike on July 6, and soon it became general throughout the whole Saginaw Valley. During the period of the strike, 150 Pinkerton "special police" were on duty, as well as ten companies of state troops. Some operators, asserting that these would not have been needed if "this had been a regular strike" and "if our sheriff had been sustained by other authorities," insisted that the strike was the work of "agitators and political demagogues." The strike was finally broken and hours were not reduced until the ten-hour law became effective. Some of the mills did not reopen at all that year because of the shortness of the sawing season remaining.[52]

The traditional attitude which prevailed among many of the operators is revealed by a statement of one of them, who declared: "I like my men but will never submit to have any Committee or anybody else dictate how long my mill should run or what wages I shall pay." [53]

The Michigan ten-hour law precipitated another controversy at Menominee, Michigan, which also involved the workers in Marinette, Wisconsin, across the Menominee River. The day before the law was to become effective, the mill operators on the Michigan side of the river presented to their men the following:

Whereas, The ——— are about to employ me to work for them in their lumbering operations and about their yards, and in various ways connected with their lumbering operations, now, therefore I agree that, in consideration of such employment, and as one of the conditions thereof, I do hereby waive the provisions of the act of the legislature of the State of Michigan, passed in 1885, making ten hours a day's labor, and agree that a day's labor shall be eleven hours, and this agreement shall be in force so long as I am in the employ of the ——— lumber company. [54]

The men, of course, refused to sign it. Anticipating trouble, the Kirby-Carpenter Company began to pick up non-union men and to fetch in outsiders to run the mill. The union men who had affiliated with the Knights of Labor became aroused and all union men from both sides of the river were ordered to go to Menominee to picket the Kirby-Carpenter mill. This resulted in a closure of the mills in Marinette, although the men there were not at the time protesting against the customary eleven-hour day.

Following this action, the mill owners of the district met, called a general lockout, and drew up the following resolution:

Whereas, A large portion of the crews from all the mills on the river, left their positions, and joined together for the express purpose of intimidating certain men from performing labor for which they were legally hired, and to stop work which was being legally prosecuted; therefore

Resolved, That a proper regard for our own interests and for the welfare of society, makes it incumbent upon us to take measures to prevent the recurrence of such unwarrantable proceedings.

Resolved, That it is advisable to close all the mills on both sides of the Menominee as soon as practicable, to remain closed until such time as business can be resumed upon a satisfactory basis. [55]

Immediately, a group of "loyal" employees circulated a petition which the operators agreed to recognize as soon as enough signatures could be obtained to warrant opening of the mills. The lockout continued for two weeks. Then some of the mills resumed work, but others remained closed for the season. Many men left to work on the new railroad lines to the south or went into the woods with contractors to get ready for winter logging. The outcome of the dispute was not defeat for the union because, with the assistance of the Knights of Labor, the men had resisted signing of the employers' hours contracts. They secured, moreover, the ten-hour day (to which they were entitled under the law), ample time for dinner, and cash payment of wages for both sides of the river—in Wisconsin as well as in Michigan.[56]

By 1886 the ten-hour day was more or less universal. Many other grievances, such as cash payment of wages, had been rectified. As a result, the number of strikes declined definitely during the ensuing years. The unions did not spread, and later, when the industry began to decline, no continuous organization of workers was found. Only a few sporadic labor struggles are recorded.

One of the most interesting and significant spectacles of the industry is revealed in the economic and social maladjustments which followed upon the migration and decline of lumbering in the Lake States. It has been indicated above that the peak of production was reached by 1900, and that thereafter a steady decline set in which was as sharp as the rise had been spectacular. That the migration of the lumber industry, partly to the South and partly to the West, was catastrophic is not to be denied. Showing its far-reaching effects are the profound changes in the pattern of land use, as well as in the economic and social structure of the communities left behind. No other region illustrates so well the relation between migration and economic opportunity. Left in the wake of the lumber industry migration were depleted timber resources, unused railroads, and stranded towns and people, because even subsistence agriculture was hardly feasible in the short growing season on the poor, stony soil. Evidence of heroic, but unfruitful, effort to make readjustment by turning to agriculture is everywhere to be seen throughout the region. Stranded communities with the concomitant problems of tax delinquency, land abandonment, and deterioration of many essential public services have been common. The most pronounced manifestations of all these developments were human unrest, poverty, and perplexing relief problems. The result has been economic depletion and impoverishment of a vast area, and the veritable decay of many hard-working people. Problems of gigantic size and extreme complexity have continued unsolved for several decades. Among them were new and different, but just as troublesome, labor problems whose existence was only slightly realized for a long time. But the long-existing and serious social and economic maladjustments were bound ultimately to call attention to themselves.

The rapidity with which the forests were cut out with little, if any, thought for the future was disastrous. The resulting problems were enormous. The condition in which the land was left to suffer the ravages of fire made the situation much worse and diminished the chances of a return of the forest cover. But the encouragement of people by land promoters, representing railroad and logging companies and other large landholders, as well as by the states, to settle on the cut-over lands heaped tragedy on tragedy. Land promotion and settlement schemes were fostered with unjustifiable optimism. "Local boosters were always ready to sacrifice man for the sake of the land."[57] Railroad companies encouraged settlement to recoup the loss of timber tariffs by substituting agricultural produce.

Obviously, parts of the Lake States cut-over area could be used for agriculture, particularly in the southern reaches of the three states where hardwoods had been more common than pine. In fact, lumbering was often only a secondary industry there. In the pine belt settlers scarcely penetrated until lumbering commenced on a large scale and, as a rule, agricultural settlement was exceedingly slow. Few settlers established themselves in the pine region except those who had come to work in the woods. Forests were cut for their lumber, not just to clear the land. However, the workers in the lumber camps had to be fed, and the need for provisioning the camps had created a market which gave rise to settlement of considerable areas near the production centers. When the lumber industry had finished its work, the justification for these agriculturel settlements disappeared. A double tragedy befell the agriculturists when the industry moved; they lost not only their markets but their off-season employment in the industry as well.[58]

One factor offsetting the immediate effect of the lumber industry migration was the development of wood-using industries—notably pulp and paper, and furniture industries—which utilized larger amounts of labor per unit of raw material. Increased employment in them partly made up for the employment lost in the decline of lumbering. But the absolute drop in employment in the lumber industry was sharp in spite of the new industries, and the employment in the secondary industry has declined noticeably through the years and has been unsteady. Employment in lumbering reached the low level of 12,000 workers in 1933, and not all of these were on a full-time basis.[59]

The absolute decline in the number of establishments, and the reduction in size of the remaining ones, was inevitable under the circumstances. As the timber holdings were cut out, the large establishments had to curtail activities. Finally they had to be abandoned. Usually this meant the end of lumbering. Smaller mills could not follow, as is the case in the South, because clean-cutting methods left little timber for the smaller units to work on. In certain areas, however, some hardwood lumbering on a small scale, and a little pine lumbering, is still carried on—notably on the upper peninsula in Michigan and in northern Wisconsin. Logging for pine pulpwood is carried on more extensively in Minnesota. In contrast with earlier times, most of the logging is done through small units. Lumber companies which still have considerable holdings have more or less abandoned logging with large camps and, instead, obtain their logs from small operators. In fact, recent labor legislation has accentuated this trend because of the desire to avoid the restrictions imposed. By buying logs from farmers, who cut from farm wood lots, or from small contractors, the operators may avoid the laws.[60] The tendency to small units, however, was inevitable and had appeared long before the legislation.

With the progressive depletion of the timber there was a gradual substitution of smaller contract camps for the larger camps of the earlier period. The result was an inevitable deterioration of camp conditions, and annual wages have been decidedly inadequate. Lumberjacks, settlers, and "gyppos" receive comparatively low wages and are employed for only a fraction of the year.

Customarily, lumberjacks have been destitute when they have gone out to a camp to work. It often has taken a month's labor to get out of debt to the company for clothes purchased at the camp store and for medical fees, or to clear the debt to the employment agency for fees or transportation to the job. Small scattered trees, cut on a piece-rate basis, have resulted in low earnings. Many of the lumberjacks, owing to years of hard work and unhealthful living conditions, have not been fit to work strenuously in all sorts of weather, and this has contributed to small earnings. Actually, there has been a predominance of older men, those who did not migrate, who have worn themselves out in the long, hard struggle in the woods.[61]

The types of logging operations which have prevailed in the region during the past two decades or more may be grouped, for convenience, into three classes.[62] There are the small "family" operators, the medium-sized "haywire" operators, and the "larger" operators. In a typical family operation might be found a father, a son, and possibly a neighbor working in a partnership. Usually they obtain only a part of their income from logging, either having recourse to farming or the recreation industry for additional income. They often possess horses for skidding or else pay to have the skidding done, and they may or may not own a truck. If not, the hauling is let out under contract. Among the truckers competition is keen and earnings are uncertain.

This type of logging activity obviously is a product of lack of adjustment in the shift to agriculture. The men cut from their own wood lots or contract to cut from someone's land. At least half, perhaps more, of the farmers in the cut-over area are in need of supplemental income, and the family operator badly needs whatever cash income he can get from logging. His average income has been calculated around $450, with about one-third coming from his work in the woods. In recent years many of them were on WPA rolls or someone in the family was maintained by the WPA. After WPA quotas had been reduced, many were forced to work in the woods.

A good majority of the family operators commute to and from the job. Others are "shackers," who put up in ramshackle huts or shacks and live under unfavorable conditions. Shacking has become more and more common in recent years. This trend obviously has been the result of the desire to escape the direct burden of the expenses involved in logging. The contractor or jobber establishes his headquarters camp, from which he sublets "forties" or such portions of timber as two or four men can cut in a season. In most instances, the shackers build their own shacks, although in some instances the materials are furnished by the contractor. At the headquarters camp tools and supplies are provided, and the shackers may have them charged against their earnings. Most shackers are not covered by the protection of social legislation. The conditions under which they live are of the rudest sort. State camp sanitation laws have forced only the simplest of standards.[63]

The haywire operator is, perhaps, one step above the family operator. He usually employs from four to seven men, but this is not the outstanding characteristic. The name itself has an important connotation. The term "haywire" originated in the lumber industry back in the days when baled hay was used in large quantities. A supply of wire accumulated and when, in a run-down camp, quick repairs were required, haywire came in handy. Hence, the term "haywire" outfit meant, and still describes, any run-down camp or concern. The haywire operator probably has been a successful family operator who expanded his activities enough to cease being a part-time farmer. The men he employs are usually not farmers, but men who can work for him as the opportunity arises. He always operates on a narrow margin and tries to effect operating economies wherever possible. He does not always carry workmen's compensation, although it is required by law. Under the Wage-Hour Law he has usually been able to meet the minimum wage, but there have been many violations of the law within the industry.

The large operator usually employs twelve or more men, and has a definite tie-up with a mill or an independent timber broker, which enables him to offer more continuous employment than other operators. As a result, the men he employs are usually not forest farmers but depend entirely on the woods. Working conditions frequently are better. The number of these operators has decreased in recent years.

The relief problem in the cut-over area during the decade of the thirties was the most acute in any of the three Lake States. This is definitely a result of unsolved problems of a decadent industry. The recent—and in many cases ill-advised—settlement, the relative cultural heterogeneity of the region, the isolation, and the depletion of the natural resources are all factors which helped to produce the extremely high relief rate and the meager standard of living. The relief problem has been "an agricultural one only in that many of those usually employed in non-agricultural industry had turned to agriculture after losing jobs. . . ." More than one-fifth of all the households on relief in June, 1935, consisted of persons living alone. "These were cases of former woodsmen or of isolated individuals who had settled on a piece of land or in a village in the Cut-Over Area when the timber had been cut." In addition, unemployability has been more serious in this region than in other parts of these states. "The area contains an usually high proportion of elderly unattached men, former lumberjacks. . . ."[64] The depression simply revealed the effects of the long-declining lumber industry and the failure to do anything sufficiently constructive to solve the many problems it left behind.

Lumbering in the Lake States developed rapidly into a lusty youth, took on some modern ways in its frontier environment, and produced great but unevenly distributed wealth. Lumbering in the Lake States was carefree, reckless and ruthless, matured quickly, and left perplexing problems when it migrated bodily, partly to the South and partly to the West.

NOTES TO CHAPTER

[1] U.S. Department of Interior, Census Office, *Report on the Forests of North America*, by C. S. Sargent. Washington: Government Printing Office, 1884, p. 532; U.S. Department of Agriculture, *The Economic Aspects of Forest Destruction in*

Northern Michigan, by W. N. Sparhawk and W. D. Brush, Technical Bulletin, No. 92. Washington: Government Printing Office, 1929, p. 7.

[2] U.S. Department of Agriculture, *The Economic Aspects of Forest Destruction in Northern Michigan,* pp. 7-8; W. F. Raney, "Pine Lumbering in Wisconsin," *Wisconsin Magazine of History,* XIX, No. 1 (September, 1935), 72.

[3] National Resources Committee, *Regional Planning,* Part VIII, *Northern Lake States.* Washington: Government Printing Office, 1939, pp. ix, 10-11.

[4] U.S. Department of Agriculture, *The Economic Aspects of Forest Destruction in Northern Michigan,* p. 7.

[5] U.S. Department of Interior, *op. cit.,* pp. 556-559.

[6] *1905 Census of Manufactures,* Part 3, p. 620; cf. U.S. Department of Agriculture, *The Economic Aspects of Forest Destruction in Northern Michigan,* p. 7; Work Projects Administration, *Mechanization in the Lumber Industry,* by A. J. Van Tassell and D. W. Bluestone. National Research Project Report No. M-5. Philadelphia: Work Projects Administration, 1940, pp. 7-11.

[7] *1905 Census of Manufactures,* Part 3, p. 620; Work Projects Administration, *op. cit.,* pp. 8-12.

[8] T. Donaldson, *The Public Domain,* 47th Congress, Second Session, House of Representatives, Miscellaneous Documents 45, Part 4. Washington: Government Printing Office, 1884, notation at bottom of map, p. 1052.

[9] U.S. Department of Commerce and Labor, Bureau of Corporations, *The Lumber Industry.* Washington: Government Printing Office, 1913, *History of Minnesota.* St. Paul: Minnesota Historical Society, 1926, Vol. 3, pp. 500-515.

[10] M. N. Orfield, *op. cit.,* pp. 168-218; U.S. Department of Agriculture, *The Economic Aspects of Forest Destruction in Northern Michigan,* p. 73; R. F. Fries, *op. cit.,* pp. 271-285; *Annual Report of the Commissioner of the General Land Office, 1888.* Washington: Government Printing Office, 1888, p. 63; C. E. Russell, "The Mysterious Octopus," *World Today,* xxi, Nos. 8, 9, 10 (February, March, April, 1912), 1735-1750, 1960-1972, 2074-2085, 2200.

[11] U.S. Bureau of Corporations, *op. cit.,* pp. 21-23.

[12] R. F. Fries, "Some Economic Aspects of the Lumber Industry," *La Crosse County Historical Sketches.* Series 3. La Crosse, Wis.: La Crosse Historical Society, 1937, p. 17.

[13] R. F. Fries, "A History of the Lumber Industry in Wisconsin," pp. 198-211.

[14] Twelfth Census of the United States, 1900, Vol. IX, *Manufactures,* Part 3, pp. 836-866.

[15] U.S. Department of Agriculture, *The Economic Aspects of Forest Destruction in Northern Michigan,* p. 14.

[16] W. F. Raney, *op. cit.,* p. 85.

[17] Ninth Census of the United States, 1870, Vol. III, *The Statistics of the Wealth and Industry of the United States,* pp. 840-843.

[18] Tenth Census of the United States, 1880, *Statistics of the Population of the United States,* pp. 929, 830, 853.

[19] Eleventh Census of the United States, 1890, *Report of the Population of the United States,* Part 2, pp. 570-573, 624-625.

[20] R. W. Murchie and M. E. Jarchow, *Population Trends in Minnesota.* University of Minnesota Agricultural Experiment Station, Bulletin No. 327, 1937, p. 65; Eleventh Census of the United States, 1890, *Report of Population of the United States,* pp. 570-573, 624-625.

[21] Industrial Commission of Wisconsin, *Labor Camps in Wisconsin,* by W. M. Leiserson. Madison, Wisc.: 1913, p. 2; A. S. Draper, "Reminiscences of the Lumber Camp," *Michigan Historical Review,* XIV, No. 2 (July, 1930), 441.

[22] Industrial Commission of Wisconsin, *op. cit.,* pp. 15-16.

[23] A. M. Larson, "On the Trail of the Woodsman in Minnesota," *Minnesota History,* XIII, No. 4 (December, 1932), 358; A. S. Draper, *op. cit.,* p. 443; L. Davenport, "Logging Camps in the Northern Woods," *World Today,* IX, No. 5 (November, 1905), 1206.

²⁴ F. P. Bohn, "This Was the Forest Primeval," *Michigan History Magazine*, XX (Spring, 1937), 179; J. C. Mills, *History of Saginaw County, Michigan*. Saginaw, Mich.: Seemans and Peters, 1918, Vol. I, p. 406.

²⁵ R. F. Fries, "A History of the Lumber Industry in Wisconsin," p. 44; A. W. Miles, "End of the Drive," *Michigan History Magazine*, XX (Spring and Summer, 1936), 228.

²⁶ A. M. Larson, *op. cit.*, p. 358; Industrial Commission of Wisconsin, *op. cit.*, p. 15.

²⁷ Industrial Commission of Wisconsin, *op. cit.*, pp. 18-20.

²⁸ F. P. Bohn, *op. cit.*, p. 189; I. Stephenson, *Recollection of a Long Life, 1829-1915*. Chicago: Privately Published, 1915, *passim;* Industrial Commission of Wisconsin, *op. cit.*, p. 23.

²⁹ A. M. Larson, *op. cit.*, p. 358; L. Davenport, *op. cit.*, p. 1208; A. S. Draper, *op. cit.*, p. 443; Industrial Commission of Wisconsin, *op. cit.*, pp. 19-20.

³⁰ Industrial Commission of Wisconsin, *op. cit.*, p. 22.

³¹ R. F. Fries, "A History of the Lumber Industry in Wisconsin," p. 44.

³² F. Hartman, "Life in a Lumber Camp," *La Crosse County Historical Sketches*. Series 3. La Crosse, Wisc.: La Crosse County Historical Society, 1937, p. 20; cf. A. W. Miles, *op. cit.*, p. 229; R. F. Fries, "Some Economic Aspects of the Lumber Industry," p. 16.

³³ See F. C. Rickaby, *Ballads and Songs of the Shanty-Boy*. Cambridge, Mass.: Harvard University Press, 1926, *passim;* cf. J. C. Bowman, "Lumberjack Ballads," *Michigan History Magazine*, XX (Spring and Summer), 1936, 231-241.

³⁴ J. C. Bowman, *op. cit.*, pp. 240-241.

³⁵ See below, p. 14.

³⁶ F. Hartman, *op. cit.*, pp. 20-21; R. F. Fries, *op. cit.*, pp. 15-16.

³⁷ R. F. Fries, "A History of the Lumber Industry in Wisconsin," p. 353.

³⁸ F. Hartman, *op. cit.*, pp. 21-23; cf. R. F. Fries, *op. cit.*, p. 353; Eleventh Census of the United States, 1890, *Report on Manufacturing Industries*, Part 3, pp. 626-629.

³⁹ R. F. Fries, "Some Economic Aspects of the Lumber Industry," p. 16; Tenth Census of the United States, 1880, *Report on the Statistics of Wages in Manufacturing Industries*, pp. 473-479, 493-497.

⁴⁰ R. F. Fries, "A History of the Lumber Industry in Wisconsin," p. 353.

⁴¹ Computations based on Eleventh Census of the United States, 1890, *Reports on Manufacturing Industries*, Part 3, pp. 624-625; *Tenth Annual Report of the Bureau of Labor and Industrial Statistics of Michigan, 1893*, pp. 907-908.

⁴² *Third Biennial Report of the Bureau of Labor and Industrial Statistics of Wisconsin, 1887-1888*, Madison, Wisc., pp. 111-112.

⁴³ *Second Annual Report of the Bureau of Labor Statistics, Michigan, 1885*, pp. 34-37.

⁴⁴ R. F. Fries, *op. cit.*, pp. 354-355.

⁴⁵ Third Annual Report of the Commissioner of Labor, 1887, *Strikes and Lockouts*. Washington: Government Printing Office, 1888, *passim*, by states for the lumber industry; Sixteenth Report of the Commissioner of Labor, 1901, *Strikes and Lockouts*. Washington: Government Printing Office, 1902, pp. 296-299.

⁴⁶ R. F. Fries, *op. cit.*, p. 363; Tenth Census of the United States, 1880, *Report on the Statistics of Wages in Manufacturing Industries*, pp. 474-476, 478.

⁴⁷ *Fifth Annual Report of the Bureau of Labor Statistics, Michigan, 1888*, pp. 398, 402; Third Annual Report of Commissioner of Labor, *op. cit.*, *passim*.

⁴⁸ *First Biennial Report of the Bureau of Labor and Industrial Statistics, Wisconsin, 1883-84*, pp. 151-153; R. F. Fries, *op. cit.*, p. 364.

⁴⁹ *Second Annual Report of the Bureau of Labor Statistics, Michigan, 1885*, pp. 34-37; *Fifth Annual Report of the Bureau of Labor Statistics, Michigan, 1888*, p. 406.

⁵⁰ *Third Annual Report of the Bureau of Labor and Industrial Statistics, Michigan, 1886*, pp. 85, 92, 93, 102-104, 109, 125-126; *Fifth Annual Report of the Bureau of Labor Statistics, Michigan, 1888*, p. 410; *Second Biennial Report of the Bureau of Labor and Industrial Statistics, Wisconsin, 1885-1886*, p. 310.

[51] *Third Annual Report of the Bureau of Labor Statistics, Michigan, 1886*, pp. 92-93; *Second Biennial Report of the Bureau of Labor and Industrial Statistics, Wisconsin, 1885-1886*, p. 238.

[52] *Third Annual Report of the Bureau of Labor Statistics, Michigan, 1886*, pp. 92-99, 104; *Fifth Annual Report of the Bureau of Labor Statistics, Michigan, 1888*, p. 410.

[53] *Third Annual Report of the Bureau of Labor Statistics, Michigan, 1886*, p. 102.

[54] *Second Biennial Report of the Bureau of Labor and Industrial Statistics, Wisconsin, 1885-1886*, p. 238.

[55] *Ibid.*, p. 240.

[56] *Ibid.*, p. 245; *Fifth Annual Report of the Bureau of Labor Statistics, Michigan, 1888*, p. 410.

[57] G. S. Wehrwein, "A Social and Economic Program for the Submarginal Areas of the Lake States," *Journal of Forestry*, XXIX, No. 10 (October, 1931), 915; L. D. Coffman, *Land Utilization in Minnesota*. Minneapolis: University of Minnesota Press, 1934, p. 56; U.S. Department of Agriculture, pp. 73-74.

[58] L. D. Coffman, *op. cit.*, p. 56; U.S. Department of Agriculture, *The Economic Aspects of Forest Destruction in Northern Michigan*, pp. 73-74; Federal Emergency Relief Administration, *Six Rural Problem Areas*, by P. G. Beck and M. C. Forester. Research Monograph No. 1. Washington: Government Printing Office, 1935, p. 11.

[59] R. Zon, "The Cut-Over Region—Breeding Place of Migrants." Statement before the Federal Congressional Hearing on Interstate Migration of Destitute Citizens, August 5, 1940. Files of the Lake States Forest Experiment Station (typewritten).

[60] R. W. Watson, "Forest Devastation in Michigan," *Journal of Forestry*, XXI, No. 5 (May, 1923), 433; E. A. Benson, "Conservation and the Lumberjack," *American Forests*, XLIII, No. 8 (August, 1937), 381.

[61] G. S. Wehrwein, *op. cit.*, p. 919; E. A. Benson, *op. cit.*, p. 382.

[62] G. B. Fox, "Some Economic, Social and Administrative Aspects of Small Timber Sales of Public Forests in the Lake States." Manuscript in the files of the Lake States Forest Experiment Station, p. 5.

[63] Duluth, *Midwest Laborer*, March 18, 22, 1938; Duluth *Timberworker*, May 7, 1937.

[64] Works Progress Administration, Division of Social Research, *Rural Families on Relief*, by C. C. Zimmerman and N. L. Whetten. Research Monograph XVII. Washington: Government Printing Office, 1935, p. 38.

5   *SOUTHERN PINE*

THE development of lumbering in the Southern Pine region followed upon the inevitable decline of the industry in the Lake
States. Except along the Atlantic Coast, where an export trade in
lumber had long existed, the forests were logged mainly for local
consumption until the late seventies. What was, at first, a gradual
development took on impetus when many northern lumbermen, recognizing the rich possibilities in the South, spread their interests to the
yellow pine of that region. For thirty years, from about 1876, great
areas of virgin forest were purchased by timber land speculators and
lumbermen, laying the foundation for a rapid, large-scale, mechanized
exploitation.[1]

As in other regions, speculators—as distinct from lumbermen,
although the distinction cannot always be maintained—were active
first. Then came the lumbermen. Both northern and southern men
were involved in the speculative and lumbering activities. A few
northern lumbermen arrived before 1880, more came in the following
decade, but the great influx was between 1890 and 1900. The rapid
extension of railroad facilities after 1880, which opened the northern
market, also played a part in the growth of the industry.[2] In contra-
distinction to other more recent industrial developments in the South,
the cheapness of labor was not a primary cause of the shift of lumbering to that region. It has, however, been both an important causal and
a resultant factor in the competitive picture in the course of the
industry's history.

So closely was the initial development of southern pine lumbering
tied to land speculation in some parts of the South, and so influential
was the nature of land ownership upon the industry's characteristics
and activities, that an examination of the manner in which the forest
lands were acquired is imperative.

Land acquisition in the South had a twofold motivation. Until
some time after the Civil War, land was secured essentially for agricultural purposes. One result of this was the diversification of owner-

ship of relatively small tracts of land. In a wide area of the Southern
Pine belt, for example, large timber holdings have never been conspicuous. In large sectors of the five federal public-land states, on the
other hand—Florida, Alabama, Arkansas, Louisiana, and Mississippi—
as well as in East Texas and South Georgia, land acquisition was
motivated by the desire to possess timber lands. When these lands were
opened for sale, there was a mad dash to gobble up the available
timber. The history of these areas, thus, closely parallels developments
in the Lake States and the West.

For a period of time after the Civil War, when the prospects of
future lumber activity were becoming brighter, the desirable lands in
the five public-land states were effectively locked up from sale because
of the Southern Homestead Act of 1866. Under this act, the land was
subject to entry only by homesteaders. This restricted the development
of the lumber industry. While the act was in force, units of land in the
choice yellow pine region big enough for large-scale lumbering, if
obtained, had to be acquired fraudulently. The act was a part of the
"Reconstruction" program, and it came to be looked upon as discriminatory on the ground that the lands involved were not suitable
for agriculture and that, consequently, the measure's only effect was to
hinder the development of the lumber industry in the South.[3] A move
to repeal the act came to a head in 1876, and was opposed by lumber
interests in the North and West who feared that repeal of the law
would bring increased competition. When restrictions upon the sale
of public lands in the five states were removed, however, the northern
men joined those of the South in flocking to the land offices to acquire
the choice timber. The greatest speculative activities were in Mississippi, Louisiana, and Texas. Through opening the lands to unrestricted
entry, absentee ownership was established over great tracts of timber.[4]
As a result, concentration of ownership of timber lands was marked
in the yellow pine area, and large-scale exploitation was characteristic.

Lumbering in the South comprises the production of pine, cypress,
and hardwood lumber. In most sectors one type will predominate
although there is a wide intermixture of varieties. Pine is the most
common, the long leaf (or yellow) and slash pine being found
throughout the coastal plain, with loblolly and shortleaf pine covering
the hilly and piedmont regions. The cypress is found in the swampy
areas throughout the coastal plain. The hardwoods predominate in the
river bottoms, primarily along the Mississippi, and north of the "piney
woods" area and throughout the Appalachians.

The first commercial development of lumbering on a large scale in the South was in the yellow pine region. Here occurred almost a repetition of lumbering history in the Lake States. Rapid cutting was the order of the day. Inevitably, there followed rapid depletion and a shift to less valuable pines in the upland regions. The tremendous increase of production began during the 1870's. By 1880 it stood at approximately 2,500,000,000 board feet. Thereafter, it doubled every ten years, reaching its peak in 1909 when it stood at slightly less than 20,000,000,000 board feet. Production for the region as a whole did not fall off abruptly, as in the Lake States; for it averaged almost 80 per cent of the 1909 peak, or 16,000,000,000 board feet, during the next two decades.[5] This was due to the huge size of the forest area and to the rapidity with which trees mature in this area so that second-growth trees quickly attained saw-log size. Important in maintaining the industry in the face of the necessity of using poorer logs has been the proximity to market. The Southern Pine region continues to this day to be a great lumber-producing area.

As a general rule, the large mills have been restricted to the Gulf Coast area, particularly in Mississippi, Louisiana, and Texas. A few large establishments have operated in Florida and southern Alabama, and in Arkansas. Small mills have always predominated in the northern reaches of the Gulf States and throughout the states along the Atlantic Coast. Over a period of two decades or more, important structural changes have been taking place. The large mills have been disappearing rapidly. Small peckerwood mills, which literally peck at the woods here and there, have followed to work on the residual stands and the oncoming second growth. Consequently, small mills are now everywhere the characteristic type.[6]

In 1919 large mills sawed 67 per cent of the total lumber cut, while small ones cut only 33 per cent. Since then there has been a complete reversal in the relationship.[7] In the lower South, just prior to the War, approximately only 1 per cent of the mills had a capacity of at least 80 M board feet per ten-hour day, 2 per cent had a capacity of from 40 to 79 M board feet, and 5 per cent had a capacity of from 20 to 39 M board feet. The remainder, 92 per cent, were small units with a daily capacity of less than 20 M board feet. Small mills are just as conspicuous in North and South Carolina and Virginia as in northern Georgia and Alabama. In North Carolina, 95 per cent of the lumber cut comes from mills with a daily capacity of less than 10 M board feet. Throughout the pine region where small units operate, the lumber sawed by the small mills is usually sold to planing mills or concentration yards where it is seasoned, surfaced, and graded and made ready for the wholesale market. Five hundred concentration yards operate in the lower South, seventy operate in North Carolina, and elsewhere the picture is roughly similar.[8]

The degree to which mechanization was introduced into the southern lumber industry depended largely upon the type of producing unit. In the case of the larger units, which dominated in production until the early twenties, all the helpful mechanical developments of the times were found. The big mills were made possible by the widespread utilization of mechanical transportation facilities. The railroad was the backbone of the large-scale logging activities. In addition, steam cable yarders were used to ground skid logs in the clear-cut logging of the early period, although animals supplemented cable yarders by being used frequently in the bunching of logs. High-lead and sky-line yarding were employed to a limited extent on the larger operations, particularly in the logging of swamps. They are much more widely used in the West. High-lead yarding differs from ground yarding in that a tall spar tree is used to support the block and cables high above the ground in order to raise one end of the log while in transit. Sky-line yarding utilizes two spar trees, one near the donkey engine and the other at some distance away. Logs are picked up between them and carried to the landing. By these two methods it is possible to yard several logs at one haul and at greater speed. Gasoline cable yarders, which are lighter and more maneuverable, have had more recent use. Tractors, too, have proved more mobile than steam cable skidders.

Small operations were never so highly mechanized. Major changes in logging practice have come about through the introduction of the truck; this has made economically available timber stands which were either too sparse or of insufficient total volume to warrant the use of highly mechanical methods. They can haul almost directly from the stump. With the smaller operations, animals are always extensively used in the woods. They are always used for bunching logs, being just as efficient with small timber as are any of the mechanical devices.[9]

For many years there has been an increased tendency for large southern mills to supplement cutting from their own holdings by their own crews with logs purchased from independent contractors cutting small bodies of timber.

Large sawmills in the South were highly mechanized and took advantage of all new developments until around 1920. Since then advances in design and construction of mechinery has had little effect upon the South because the large mill has been on the way out. There is little incentive for extensive replacement or for considerable investment in newer equipment. The principal recent changes center in the introduction of electricity and techniques of kiln drying. Half the large pine mills use resaws for further reduction of lumber produced on the headsaw and less than half use gang saws. Such mills usually turn out a much better product than the small mills in which, in many cases, there is no edger, and in some instances not even a cut-off saw. Mechanization in the small mill is summed up in the use of the circular saw. In all, the few technological developments which have taken place in the southern lumber industry since about 1920 have been slight compared to the advances made in Pacific Coast lumbering.

Southern logging and sawmilling are irregular rather than seasonal. On the whole, they have provided more days of employment throughout the year there than in the Lake States. According to the Census of 1890, work in the woods, in transportation, and in the mills averaged from 8.5 to 10 months per year in the various southern states.[10] This is still roughly true today for the more or less permanent operations. With the small units, operations are almost unpredictable. It is difficult, and at times impossible, to carry on logging in most parts of the South during extended periods of the year because of the heavy rains which make the ground soft.[11] Because the rains do not have a definite seasonal pattern, there can be no definite seasonal pattern in production of logs. There are, therefore, many idle days. The large mills usually have tried to keep a supply of logs on hand. With them, market conditions have been the decisive factor in determining continuity of production. With the small mills it has not been practical to build up a supply of logs much in advance of the sawing, and the result is much intermittent employment at those times when it is difficult to get logs out of the woods. Likewise, market conditions have been important with the small units because it does not cost much to suspend lumbering operations if the market is bad. Sawmilling usually is more continuous than work in the woods. For the industry as a whole, both production and employment have been decidedly irregular.

It is notable that the working force in the Great Lakes lumber industry did not move to the South when the industry shifted its center of gravity there. Few immigrants, likewise, have been found in lumbering occupations in that region, and for the same reasons. The labor traditions did not encourage workers to migrate to that region, especially when they could go to the West under conditions more to their liking. While cheap labor did not attract the industry to the South, there was a plentiful supply.

Compared with that in the West and in the Lake States, the labor force in the southern lumber industry is strikingly different in one major respect. It has been made up of both whites and Negroes, and, if not drawn from an agricultural background, the men have been strongly influenced by it. The lumber industry has been for years the largest employer of Negro labor in the South outside of agriculture.[12] Significantly enough, the white worker in Southern lumbering has not yet been adequately studied, while the Negro worker has been almost entirely ignored.

The total labor force in southern lumbering apparently doubled from 1880 to 1909. In the latter year it reached 262,000 but shrank to around 235,000 in 1914, at which level it stood, except in the depression year of 1921, until about 1925. In the mid-twenties employment began to decline, and during the depression year of 1933 it stood at 90,000. In 1937 it had risen again to around 149,000.[13]

In 1910 over half the labor force was composed of Negroes and they still are in the majority. Many more Negroes have worked in the sawmills than in the woods. Generally speaking, the Negroes have outnumbered the whites in the sawmills about six to four in the unskilled jobs, while the whites have outnumbered the Negroes two to one in the skilled classifications. The situation, however, varies from state to state. The Gulf States have used proportionately more Negro unskilled labor in the sawmills. In the woods the Negroes have about equaled the whites for the region as a whole. In Arkansas, the whites in the woods work have definitely outnumbered the Negroes three to one, and in Texas two to one. But in Florida, Georgia, and South Carolina the Negroes have outnumbered the whites both in the woods and in the sawmills. In the other states the two groups have been about equally divided.[14]

The great variations among states are due to differences in the lumber industry itself. In the large-scale operations, as a rule, relatively more Negroes have been used all around. In the small operations, which usually have been scattered through farming territory, whites, often shifting back and forth from farming to woods work and to the sawmills, have predominated. The hill folk have been more natural woodsmen, and in the uplands the Negroes have, therefore, been less conspicuous. Everywhere throughout the industry's history, the Negroes have been assigned to unskilled work. There is an average of nine unskilled Negro workers to every two skilled ones in the sawmills. Among the whites the division of skilled and unskilled has been roughly equal. A report for the year 1934 shows that common labor is made up roughly of approximately 73 per cent Negroes and that skilled labor is 55 per cent white. The over-all average is approximately 40 per cent white and 60 per cent Negro.[15]

Another conspicuous difference in the labor force in the southern lumber industry, in contrast to the West or the Great Lakes, has been the predominance of family men. For the southern labor force in 1900 the ratio of single men to married men was 42 to 49, not including widowed or divorced persons. In the West and in the Lake States in 1900 the ratio was slightly less than two single men to each married one. In 1933 percentages of 64 married and 36 single in logging and 69 married and 31 single in sawmilling prevailed.[16] The changes in percentages may be due to the depression and the tendency to keep married men so that the single men suffered more unemploymnt.

The southern lumber industry did not produce a homeless migratory class. The working force was relatively stable so long as the work lasted. It is true, of course, that lumbering in the South followed the pattern of the industry and cut out the trees rapidly. When the trees were cut out the industry moved, and the problems of human adjustment were just as, if not more, difficult than they had been in the Lake States. Solution of the problems was perhaps made even more difficult because fewer people who were left stranded were able to adjust through migration.

An adequate comprehension of the character of the labor force in southern lumbering demands an understanding of its relationships to agriculture and the southern traditions. In the first place, the southern worker's background has been nonindustrial and distinguished by a large potential supply of unskilled, undisciplined workers. The opportunities for work in the lumber industry offered to southern men, both Negroes and whites, better money incomes than they had ever known in agriculture, and they flocked to it. In addition, the paternalism of the "Old South," which stemmed from slavery days, has strongly influenced the labor picture.[17] Many wage earners worked only part time in the industry, shifting back and forth between agriculture and work in the woods.[18] These workers, self-contented and strongly individualistic, cherished a sense of independence. Their wants were simple, and as long as these were cared for they did not press for much more. Rather than hold themselves down to continuous routine work, they preferred their independence.[19]

Part-time work has always been common in southern lumbering. It is bound to become more and more important because of the basic trend to increasingly smaller operating units. Especially is part-time farming part-time logging important in northern Mississippi, northern Georgia, South Carolina, and northward. In the peckerwood mills, however, the workers are most often "buck" Negroes who are "permanently" attached to the industry and who live in bunkhouses, or rather small shacks, and do their own cooking. The area in which the small units predominate is a specialized lumber subregion, being made up of farms and forests and is primarily agricultural. The lumber industry is a much less important source of employment than is agriculture, but it is the only important manufacturing industry in much of the area. After the principal virgin forests were removed, lumbering was carried on only in a limited way, although it has been coming back in the past decade as numerous small mills work on the maturing second-growth trees. The major part of the cash income of the part-time farm families in this lumber subregion is earned not on the farm but in the lumber and woodworking industries. Wages have been low and hours long because the labor force has been drawn from the redundant farm population, which has been notoriously a low income group.[20]

Living conditions of workers in the southern industry vary sharply from one area to another. In the company-owned sawmill town and the company-operated logging camp conditions are quite different from those found where the workers live in independent towns or on farms. In the latter two, the workers' conditions merge into the general picture of living in the South. This does not mean, of course, that the company towns have not been affected by the general environment. Wide variations and differences between regions prevailed.

The company town, the "mill village," in the southern lumber industry did not grow out of a desire to control the lives of the workers. The company town was created out of the necessity of providing places of abode where none existed previously.[21] In addition, the absence of discipline in community living among the newly recruited labor force threw a great responsibility upon the employer. The southern traditions of paternalism naturally carried into the lumber towns.

The lumber manufacturer . . . in the South, knows that his workmen are dependent entirely upon the continued operation of the mills for food and shelter. They are "his" people. He is usually the mayor of the mill town, and the arbiter of the differences that arise between the men. The relationship between management and plant employees is entirely different from that found in industry generally.[22]

"I'm just like a father," said one employer. "I care for them while sick. I get them out of jail. I have doctors deliver their babies."

Crude as most temporary company towns were, they often gave the worker more in actual conveniences than he had previously known. It is important to note, however, that the lack of sanitation facilities is not so serious on an isolated farm. The economic and social isolation had kept the living standards low and the people uneducated, and, consequently, living standards continued low.

Company stores, which appeared for the same reasons that company towns did, showed wide variations in conduct. They were, of course, used as a means of control by the lumber companies and in many cases constituted important sources of profit.

Differences in company towns are often explicable in terms of the operating life of the sawmill. They were short-lived, except in a few special cases, and this meant that certain limits existed to the volume of investment in the structures built. You could find almost what you looked for from towns with a variety of interests, hardly distinguishable from any other southern towns, to small villages composed only of unpainted shacks and a commissary,[28] having little or no salvage value once lumbering in the area was finished.

One of the most comprehensive early reports of conditions in the lumber industry, within a specific sector, offers a revealing picture. "We found," declared the report, "conditions of employment at a very low ebb and practically every labor law on the statutes being violated." Among the most widespread evils were the company stores and the wage payment practices, which existed in spite of the semimonthly payday law. In some places—where the semimonthly payday law was being ignored—workers who were in need of cash were forced to borrow from their employer or an outsider, "whom [sic] we have reason to believe was a stool pigeon for the employer. . . . In practically every case usury rates of interest were being charged," so that the involved worker was actually paying interest on his wages being illegally withheld. Besides discounting of wages, "commissary books, coupons, metallic checks, and other substitutes for cash" were being used and seemed "to have been deep rooted." It was not unlawful to issue coupons or other nonmonetary means of payment. It was illegal, however, to refuse to redeem them at full face value and to compel workers to trade at a designated place. Of the 200 companies investigated, in Louisiana, 120 directly operated commissaries. How many of the others who had entered into agreements with local storekeepers was not revealed, but it was common throughout the South for the lumber operator who operated no commissary of his own to make arrangements with a local storekeeper and then require all employees to trade there. It was also revealed that 119 companies issued substitutes for cash—although this is not to be construed to mean that this proportion were violators of the law.[24]

Throughout the South, some lumber towns were closed, that is, the company reserved to itself all rights to furnish the requisites of life. A few companies leased rights to others, and some even permitted workers to go outside to other towns to make purchases if they wished to do so. Evidence of control within the company towns and the use of company stores for profit exists over a wide area and over many years.[25]

A recent report on scrip payment shows that over 90 per cent of the company stores in the lumber industry, the large majority of which are in the South, are owned by the parent department and are not subsidiaries. Only 8.2 per cent of the stores did over 50 per cent of their business in cash, 29.1 per cent did between 20.1 and 50.0 per cent, 31.0 per cent did between 10.1 and 20.0 per cent, and 21.7 per cent did less than 10.0 per cent. Either scrip or book accounts were used for the other sales, and 39 per cent of the lumber industry company stores reported use of scrip.[26] Another recent report reveals that 69 per cent of the large companies and 41 per cent of the small companies operate commissaries.[27] Prices in the commissaries have been said to "run through all variations from chain store prices to gouging." [28] The commissary ranges, therefore, from a real service and convenience to employees to an unconscionable device for recovering a substantial part of the wages paid.

Company housing is still provided nearly everywhere. A survey in 1939, to which reports were voluntarily submitted and which, consequently, may not be entirely representative, showed that 60 per cent of the wage earners were furnished dwellings.[29] Another recent report covering 132 companies showed 12,717 houses owned and rented to both white and Negro workmen. The former most commonly rented dwellings with from three to five rooms and the latter averaged one room less. The monthly rentals averaged approximately $2 and $1.50 per room, respectively, for the whites and Negroes.[30] It is reported that rents charged to Negro workmen often only average about half those charged to whites, but in many cases "half is too much for what they get." [31] As a rule, however, rents have conformed to no standard, nor could they with the existent variety of conditions. Certainly the average operator has expected to collect enough to repay him for his investment, but the investment often has been slight and housing conditions wretched.[32] In East Texas in 1927, for example, it was discovered that as a rule the houses provided were "inadequate to the needs of a normal family. . . . Very poor provision is made for sanitation and conveniences are limited." Of 825 homes visited in 16 camps and communities, 312 were without electric lights, 510 were without running water, and "no adequate sewage facilities were found in any of the camps." [33] Random visits by the author to lumber communities in the South, plus testimony of various individuals, revealed that such conditions have been, and are, common throughout the lumber region. On the other hand, there have been instances of more tolerable conditions.

The Southern Pine Association has cited more widespread existence of various utilities with garden plots being furnished the majority of those renting houses from the company, and in some cases free fuel being provided. In one instance, however, it was reported that "such conveniences as water, light and power are usually furnished by the larger mills," [34] with the implication that not even all the large ones do so, and that the smaller ones probably do not furnish them. This approximates the existing facts.

Statistical description of wages in the southern lumber industry is open to serious qualification. In the first place, the available data does not reveal the sharp variations from section to section and within sections. It is easier to develop a general picture of money rates than of real wages. In the main, the broad distinction between the Gulf Coast area and the uplands pine region needs to be kept in mind. Not that the money wage differentials have been so pronounced, but workers who carry on part-time farming are not completely dependent on the lumber industry for their livelihood.

According to the Census of 1890, the average monthly earnings for woods workers varied from approximately $20.00 in Virginia and in North and South Carolina to an average of around $39.00 in Louisiana and Texas. Very few woods workers received more than $35.00, except in Louisiana, Texas, and Arkansas. In sawmilling, the range in monthly incomes was not quite so great—running from an average of approximately $22.00, in the first above-mentioned states, to an average of around $38.00 in Louisiana and Texas.[35]

The Louisiana Bureau of Statistics of Labor reported in 1901 that in twenty-seven mills of various sizes, lowest weekly wages paid varied from $3.00 to $9.00. The highest weekly wages paid varied from $6.00 in the smallest mills—although some of the smallest mills also made

minimum weekly payments of $18.00—to $30.00 a week. It was notable
that in each type of mill, employing from 7 and 8 men to 175 and
200 men, that the lowest weekly wages were around $3.00, although
some mills did not pay less than $6.00 or $7.50. The maximum wages
paid were much higher in the mills employing more than 50 men,
although there was no strict uniformity. Some large mills paid rates
similar to the worst low rates, and some of the largest mills did not
pay more than $12.00 to $15.00.[36] Another Louisiana report for 1904-
1905 gives average weekly wages in the lumber industry for unskilled
workers as $8.22, and the average for the sawyers $15.93.[37] Wages in
Louisiana have generally compared with the best paid in the southern
lumber industry, and, therefore, represent optimum average earnings.

At this point, it is important to make clear that such differences in
earnings as have existed between the South and other leading lumber-
producing regions are not in any real sense justified by differences in
cost of living.[38] Nor can they be justified on the basis of nonwage
items which, it is often claimed, are provided the southern worker.
"The average southern sawmill gives a man very little in addition to
his wages." The low rentals cannot be considered as donations, and
"welfare work in the lumber camps and sawmill towns is practically
non-existent . . . an expensive" luxury. It must be concluded, therefore, that "the money wage of the sawmill worker is practically his
actual wage." [39]

According to the United States Bureau of Labor Statistics, wages
for laborers in sawmills in 1907 in Alabama, Florida, and South Carolina, as examples, averaged 13.1, 15.0, and 10.9 cents per hour, respectively. In 1910, the average wage for laborers in ten states ranged from
10.9 to 16.9 cents per hour. Average wages for carriage men, doggers,
and edgermen, taken as examples, ranged, within the three states
mentioned above, from 14.3 to 20.0, 12.9 to 18.3, and 15.6 to 25.9 cents
per hour, respectively.[40] During the period 1912-1928, laborers' wages
increased from about 14.0 cents to 23.0 cents per hour. Doggers' wages
increased from about 18.0 cents per hour to about 27.0 cents, while
edgermen's wages increased from about 23.0 cents per hour to around
37.5 cents. These rates were from 15 to 25 per cent below the national
average for the lumber industry. Weekly earnings in the South lagged
behind in comparison with the national averages to a comparable
degree. Laborers' earnings averaged around $9.00 a week in 1912 and
about $14.00 in 1928. Doggers earned around $10.00 a week in 1912
and about $16.00 in 1928; while edgermen earned about $14.00 per
week in 1912 and about $22.00 in 1928. These averages, however, do

not tell the whole story. In 1913, laborers in ten southern states received average weekly wages of from $7.00 to $10.00, with Arkansas, Louisiana, and Texas the only ones averaging more than $9.00. Doggers averaged about one dollar more as a rule, while edgermen's weekly earnings in the same states ranged between $12.00 and $17.00.[41]

By 1921 average hourly rates had increased markedly. Laborers were receiving, in the various states, from 15.5 to 23.2 cents per hour, doggers from 15.9 to 27.0 cents, and edgermen from 26.4 to 36.3 cents. In 1928 average hourly rates in the various states for laborers ranged from 16.5 to 24.3 cents and their average actual weekly earnings ranged from $8.48 to $11.90 in the various states. Edgermen's average hourly rates ranged from 32.6 to 40.5 cents and their average actual weekly earnings ranged from $18.11 to $21.20.[42] Wages in logging were roughly the same. The average of hourly earnings for classified labor was 31.8 cents, for common labor 24.2 cents, in 1927.[43]

Wage rates have been low in the lumber industry of the South because of the agricultural background from which most of the workers stem. Most of them, consequently, had long been accustomed to the simplest sort of life. Wage rates have been so low and employment often so irregular that even unusually long hours of work have not added materially to earnings. The wage increases during the war years did not change the relative picture, because prices too had increased, and southern lumber industry workers continued to live on a very low plane.

Until the passage of the National Industrial Recovery Act and the Fair Labor Standards Act, hours of labor were nearly always ten a day, or more, in the southern lumber industry,[44] although in some areas a nine-hour day was not uncommon. In 1910 only 9 per cent of the workers were employed less than sixty hours a week. Approximately 63 per cent were employed sixty hours a week, six days for ten hours a day. The remainder, 28 per cent, worked over sixty hours a week, either eleven or twelve hours a day for six days a week.[45] From 1911 to 1913 a number of strikes occurred in Louisiana and Texas, and the ten-hour day became more common. After 1913 slight change in hours of labor was made, until less than a decade ago.

Accidents in the lumber industry are of frequent occurrence. Historically, the situation in the South has been one of "apathy and indifference. . . . If there has been ruthless material waste on the one hand, the waste in life and limb has been equally appalling on the other. . . ."[46] Most southern states were notoriously slow in adopting workmen's compensation laws, although there were important exceptions. They have given little attention to considerations of social and industrial welfare. Although Texas and Louisiana had workmen's compensation laws by 1914, only Alabama, Georgia, and Virginia had enacted laws by 1921. At the same time, the provisions of these laws were, in the main, less liberal than those found outside of the South. North Carolina did not establish a workmen's compensation system until 1929, and Florida and South Carolina not until 1935. Mississippi still relies on the law of employer's liability.

The fact that work often was done in isolated places in the woods meant that unless the employer made some provision for medical care none was available. Out of this situation developed the practice of charging a medical fee and in some cases a hospital fee. A monthly charge of from $1 to $1.50 for medical service was made. The employer either contracted with a local physician to care for injured men, or hired one outright if his lumbering activities were on a large enough scale. While most of the medical service rendered was better than that which other rural and small-town working people received, the system was really inadequate, and that it was grossly abused in many cases was known almost from the beginning, and there were many complaints.[47]

In the late thirties 64 per cent of the employers provided medical service, with an additional 11 per cent providing it for accidents only. Hospitalization was provided by 29 per cent, with an additional 17 per cent providing hospitalization for accidents only. The average monthly charge for medical attention varied from 75 cents to two dollars, and the hospitalization charge ranged from one to two dollars per month.[48]

Reports of peonage in the southern lumber industry have trickled out at various times. Individuals guilty of establishing peonage have been prosecuted and convicted. Strictly speaking, however, a system of peonage has never existed on any real scale in southern lumbering. Peonage was apparently eliminated at the close of the century when United States laws against it were enacted and subsequently upheld in the United States Supreme Court in 1904. Later when an Alabama statute, which actually worked to enforce involuntary service in liquidation of a debt, was tested it was held invalid.[49] Nevertheless, occasional cases of peonage were still found. It was difficult to secure convictions in such cases, owing to antecedents and surroundings of the victims and witnesses, and the frequent existence of strong local sympathy for the defendants. In the annual report of the attorney general of the United States for 1907, a recommendation was made for clarification of the federal laws so as to eliminate all chance of dispute as to the meaning of peonage, because state laws were being used in various ways to uphold peonage and other kinds of involuntary servitude.[50]

Abuses of the vagrancy laws were common in the South. Both Negro and white laborers were sometimes arrested and fined and imprisoned for no offense at all, or simply for being out of a job. Afterward, an employer would appear and pay the fine on condition that the debt would be worked out. As late as 1925-1930, a number of prosecutions of lumber camp operators occurred, particularly in Florida. A law had been passed in 1919 that made arrest for simple debt the basis for involuntary servitude, and it was claimed that lumber operators were influential in its passage. Under this law, whenever it was taken advantage of by an occasional unscrupulous individual, it was almost impossible for Negroes legally to protect themselves because of the difficulty of upholding their cases in the local courts.[51]

During the mid-twenties it appeared that excessive drain of logs from the forests had brought about the exhaustion of timber resources in many localities in the South. Abandoned mills and dying communities had been left behind. Cut-over lands and stranded population were the obvious results.[52] The common approach to the problem of stranded workers in the lumber industry was to get them onto the land. Many people tried to farm. During the mid-twenties, the Southern Settlement and Development Organization, which was a federation of land owners in the states stretching from Florida to Texas, was given support by the Cut-Over Land Department of the Southern Pine Association to encourage the development of agricultural communities.[53] This scheme provided no solution because much of the land was not suitable for agriculture. People were stranded on unproductive lands in many areas and their plight was conspicuous during the depression period.[54] However, the southern trees are prolific and the forests have rapidly grown up again. The industry is now offered an opportunity to establish more permanent and stable employment and communities than was the case in the past.

Relations between employers and workers in the southern lumber industry have not always been as amicable as might appear on the surface. Formal relationships, given expression through collective bargaining, have seldom developed. Labor organization has been sporadic and almost negligible. This has been due to the scattered and isolated nature of the industry units and the close relationship to agriculture, and to the peculiar social conditions in a region which has been traditionally unsympathetic to labor organization. The truth is that the combination of social, economic, and physical conditions has never allowed men to organize freely in the lumber industry of the South.

Southern employers have organized in various ways over a period of many years. Trade association activities have had a fairly long history, reaching back to the latter part of the nineteenth century when group co-operation first appeared. Although there have been a number of different associations, some localized to special areas, there has been a definite continuity. In the pine industry the Southern Pine Association has been dominant since its organization in 1914. It gradually incorporated a substantial portion of the membership of other associations, and at one time it represented about 75 per cent of the annual production of southern pine lumber,[55] although the displacement of large companies by small ones, which do not subscribe to the association, has reduced the membership coverage to about 40 per cent of total production at the present time. The Southern Pine Association has not openly opposed labor organization, but it has opposed various forms of labor legislation.

The organization and activities of "employer associations"—groups specifically organized to meet or deal with labor—are more obscure. It is known, of course, that southern employers have strongly opposed unionization of workers. One of the first trade associations in the southern lumber industry—subsequently known as the Yellow Pine Manufacturers Association—was originally organized to increase prices, but pursued activities inimical to organized labor. If any labor organization was developed in any part of the yellow pine region, information was immediately sent to the different members of that association. While it worked to lift lumber prices, it opposed organization for maintenance or increase of wages.[56] In 1907 the Southern Lumber Operators Association was organized specifically to combat unionism.[57] This association operated quietly, and little is definitely known of its activities. During the labor troubles in Louisiana and Texas between 1911 and 1913 it was, however, widely accused of maintaining a blacklist, forcing acceptance of yellow-dog contracts, and fostering a system of espionage and discrimination.[58]

The Knights of Labor succeeded in establishing a few locals at various spots during the late 1880's. In 1890 a strike among the lumber workers broke out at Ray, Alabama, which ended in defeat for the union. In 1899 the locals established by the Knights in the vicinity of

Pensacola, Florida, demanded shorter hours and abolition of doctor and hospital fees, but without success.[59]

When the employees of the Ruddock and Louisiana Cypress Saw Mill Company demanded a reduction in the working day from eleven to ten hours and were refused, the 600 hands ceased work on June 14, 1902, and organized a union. A committee was selected to negotiate with the company, but the company held out. A few days later the employees of the Lutcher Sawmill Company, at Lutcher, Louisiana, acted similarly, presenting the same demands. On June 29 the two companies gave in to their employees—although they refused to sign a contract—and the men returned to work.[60] The unions, however, soon ceased to function.

The next labor dispute occurred in 1907. In this instance the strike was more than local. It was a spontaneous walkout of practically all lumber workers in western Louisiana and parts of eastern Texas. The industry was faced with unusually low prices for lumber, and when the operators attempted to cut wages, the workers objected. The walkout was of short duration, however, because everywhere, except in the Lake Charles district, the workers went back to work almost immediately when they were promised wage increases as soon as economic conditions improved. The Lake Charles workers held out slightly longer but gained little more than the others.[61]

It has been claimed that the promise to restore wages was not kept. Certainly no living labor organization emerged, and it is noteworthy that the Southern Lumber Operators Association was formed at this time. As soon as the threat of unionization dissipated, the employer organization became inactive.[62]

Early in 1910 a vigorous labor organization did appear in the same region. This was the Brotherhood of Timber Workers, an indepndent, unaffiliated union inspired by followers of the Industrial Workers of the World. With headquarters in Alexandria, Louisiana, it gained members in Louisiana, Texas, and Arkansas. The union took in Negroes as well as whites, and when its organizing campaign seemed to be gaining momentum, the moribund Southern Lumber Operators Association revived to plan a vigorous attack against it. A leading figure in the employer opposition to the union was John H. Kirby, the largest lumber operator in Texas and one-time president of the National Association of Manufacturers.[63]

As their first move in the fight to destroy the labor organization, the employers decided to curtail operations to four days a week. This did not frighten the unionists. Consequently, on July 19, 1911, a secret session of about 150 members of the Southern Lumber Operators Association met in New Orleans "to plan war against the I.W.W.," and gave the executive committee power to close any of the 300 affiliated mills in Texas, Louisiana, and Arkansas. Eleven Louisiana mills in the "infested area" around De Ridder and in various parts of southwestern Louisiana and Texas, employing 3,000 men, were ordered closed immediately, and many others of the 300 controlled mills were subsequently shut down. The operators stated that they would discharge members of the labor organization as fast as they were discovered. Mississippi operators, however, refused to close their mills. They were having no trouble and saw no reason why they should take such drastic action.[64]

Mr. Kirby denounced the union as being the spawn of the I.W.W., although the Brotherhood of Timber Workers was not then affiliated with it. He attacked the I.W.W. on various occasions as a socialistic, Ishmaelitic organization which was aiming at distruction of the A.F. of L. which, he declared, "was based on the right of property and respect therefor." On other occasions, however, he was outspoken in his condemnation of the American Federation of Labor. He declared that the I.W.W. would "bring disorder and the rule of brute force into every community in America." But aside from these objections, he said, that because of "the soundest principles of public morals and peace and order, the lumber manufacturers cannot stand any present additional burden. . . ." [65]

When the lockout started, the Brotherhood mapped out a series of demands which included a minimum wage of two dollars for a ten-hour day (an increase in wages and a decrease in hours); bi-monthly payment in lawful United States currency; freedom to trade in independent stores; reasonable rents; revision of doctor and hospital fees; improvements in camps and towns; disarming and discharge of company guards; and the rights of free speech and assemblage.[66]

A severe campaign of blacklisting inflicted frightful punishment on most of the active leaders of the workers, Aiding the employers was the fact that the mills were heavily stocked with lumber and the market was down. Hence there was little interest in opening the mills anyway.[67]

Another secret session of the Southern Lumber Operators Association was held in New Orleans on October 31. A committee was appointed to devise plans for the reopening of the mills. Kirby reported that the fight was progressing satisfactorily, and that "the mills seemed to be in better shape, as far as their labor was concerned."

As the mills were reopened, slightly higher wages were offered and the ten-hour day was granted. While no locals of the union were recognized, the union was not completely shelved, and it fought on in spite of the blacklisting and discrimination.[68] The lockout continued for seven months at many of the mills, until February, 1912.

In the early part of May, 1912, the Brotherhood of Timber Workers held a convention in Alexandria and, by a vote of three to one, decided to affiliate with the I.W.W. and to push organization work throughout a greater area.[69] The I.W.W. had been organized at Chicago in 1905 as a national labor organization, dual to the A.F. of L., and was based on the principle of industrial unionism. Some of its leaders were radicals of an American brand who often preached a philosophy of revolution. The rank and file, nevertheless, probably had no such definite ideology, and were simply approaching their job problems in a direct and vigorous way on the economic front because that seemed to be the only way to secure redress. The I.W.W. soon came to be the champion of the unskilled and downtrodden workers.[70]

Bill Haywood, a leader of the I.W.W., attended the convention and expressed great surprise that no Negroes were present. Inquiring about their absence, he was informed that the Negro workers were meeting elsewhere because it was against the law in Louisiana for white and black men to meet together. Haywood declared:

You work in the same mills together. Sometimes a black man and white man chop down the same tree together. You are meeting in convention now to discuss the conditions under which you labor. This can't be done intelligently by passing resolutions here and then sending them out to another room for the black men to act upon. Why not be sensible about this and call the Negroes into this convention? If it is against law, this is one time when the law should be broken.[71]

The Brotherhood's decision to join with the I.W.W. disturbed the operators. The *Lumber Trade Journal* reported that the labor situation "promises to be more serious during the summer and fall than it was . . . last year." It was also asserted "that the lumbermen of the South will not treat with these agitators goes without saying . . . the only policy which the lumbermen can pursue is that followed in the past . . . to fight the question to a finish. . . . The mills will never agree to recognize the union." Later the *Lumber Trade Journal* editorially asserted that "the labor situation, wherever it comes to the front, should be dealt with firmly and in a manner which can leave no doubt as to the intentions of the manufacturers to manage their own businesses without interference from agitators." [72]

The adamant stand of the operators' association, the continued severe treatment of union men, and the militancy of the union leaders led to trouble during the summer. It came to a head in an outbreak of violence at Graybow, Louisiana. On Sunday, July 7, 1912, a group of union men under the leadership of the president of the Brotherhood of Timber Workers, A. L. Emerson, who had been sent into the region from Chicago as an organizer for the I.W.W., arrived in Graybow to hold a meeting. Their arrival was discovered in advance, although the decision to hold a meeting in Graybow was made the same day in a nearby town. M. M. Galloway, of the Galloway Lumber Company, is said to have informed a group of mill employees that the unionists were coming, whereupon John Galloway was reported to have said, "By God, they can't speak here, don't let them speak here." S. B. Buxton, an employee of the company and a resident of Graybow, then said that it was a public road and that they had no right to stop them: "You can all fight that wants to . . . I won't have anything to do with it." It was reported that M. M. Galloway then said, "Buxton, I think that's all right. We have no right to interfere with them. Those who do not want to stay, go home. Those who want to hear the speaking, all right, but don't start any trouble."

Men were reported to have been armed an hour before the union men arrived. It was also reported that some men had been drinking and that some of them had asked the commissary man to open up, to which the latter replied, "Boys, I think I've sold you enough for today." Buxton claimed that M. M. Galloway spoke up and said, "No, go and open up and pour it into them, and let them be feeling good by the time the union boys get here." Others denied that there had been any drinking.

Shortly after the meeting commenced, gunfire broke loose. Who started it was never conclusively determined. Three men—two unionists and one company man—were killed and several more men were wounded. Fifty-eight unionists and sympathizers were arrested and charged with being involved in a conspiracy. Emerson and eight associates were charged with murder. They were all held in jail for three months before the four weeks' trial commenced.

Voluminous, contradictory testimony was recorded. Judge Hunter, for the defense, tried to show that the Galloway Lumber Company was not interested in prosecuting the defendants, "but that it was the Southern Lumbermen's Association [sic.] fight to break the union."

On another occasion he asserted, "They've got the wrong crowd in court." Many witnesses testified for and against the defendants. According to a newspaper report, some of them "plainly disappointed the State." During the trial it was revealed that one of the witnesses was on the payroll of the Kirby Lumber Company as a detective and was also a member of the union. It was revealed that Burns detectives were in the union's inner councils, and that one was a general secretary who managed to get away with the union records.

Finally, on November 3, within an hour after the jury had been given the case, a verdict of not guilty was rendered and the murder and conspiracy charges were dismissed and the prisoners released.[73]

The labor difficulties were not immediately settled, but the union was never so vigorous again. Strikes at Merryville, Louisiana, which broke out in late 1912 and continued for seven months, and at Sweet Home Front, Louisiana, in the autumn of 1913, were the last struggles of the Brotherhood. The union began to crack when some of the most obnoxious causes of dissatisfaction, such as payment in scrip and forced use of company stores and monthly payment of wages, were modified and small wage increases and shorter hours were granted. At the same time, the strain of blacklisting, discrimination, and fomenting of racial conflict had an effect. After three years of struggle, the union had been completely destroyed.[74]

In 1919 union organization among the loggers and sawmill workers again appeared in the South. This time two A.F. of L. unions, the International Timber Workers Union and the United Brotherhood of Carpenters and Joiners of America, carried on the work. The center of activities was at Bogalusa, Louisiana, although the Timber Workers Union was also active at other points. The attempt to organize the workers culminated in an incident at Bogalusa on November 22, 1919, which was as tragic as the Graybow affair.

Bogalusa was the largest lumber center in the world at the time and was the property of the Great Southern Lumber Company. Bogalusa lumber operations began in 1907, and in 1914 Bogalusa was incorporated, with W. H. Sullivan, vice-president and general manager of the company, as mayor, an office which he held until his death.

In the early summer of 1919, a Sawyers and Filers Union was organized as a federal local. Some two months later, William Hutcheson, president of the International Brotherhood of Carpenters and Joiners of America, claimed the workers, who then gave up the federal charter in exchange for one from the Brotherhood of Carpenters and Joiners. There was also a regular Carpenter local in the town. Nevertheless, it was the Timber Workers local, with three-fourths of the members Negroes, that was the greatest affront in this notorious anti-union region.

The various locals were organized into a Central Trades Assembly with Lum Williams, president of the Carpenter local, as president. Williams was a Mississippi country boy who had developed great promise as a leader and was respected by all the people who knew him. Because of his power with the men, Sullivan, who was convinced that Williams was the only man who could hold the unions together, is reported to have offered him $10,000 and a lifetime job if he would quit the union. This Williams refused to do. To organize the Negroes, Williams had set up an office on his own property near a garage which he operated. Within eight weeks the whole plant had been organized. The Negroes were brought into the Timber Workers local through the process of selecting a few trusted Negroes to spread the word around. Sol Dacus, who was one of them and was the leader of the Negro workers, was made vice-president of the local.

Once the organization work became known, many individuals were fired or discriminated against. The company built a high barbed-wire fence around the plant. A gang of "strong-arm men" was recruited. A characteristic citizens' committee, the Self-Preservation and Loyalty League, was formed by all the principal merchants who followed the company's policy, the pretext being that the unionists were radicals. Strong-arm men were taken into the Self-Preservation and Loyalty League, and were also made deputy sheriffs.[75]

Whenever a union committee had approached Sullivan in protest against layoffs, he agreed with the union men and sent orders to have the men rehired. Nevertheless, after the fence was built and the Self-Preservation and Loyalty League was formed, an incident occurred that was of great significance. A powerful steam engine drove a huge belt which pulled the machinery in the mill. It was a common thing for a steel wrist pin, fastened with a nut and cotter key, to work loose occasionally when the key sheered off. Whenever this occurred, the plant was immediately shut down for a few minutes while repair was made. In late September, when this occurred one night, the man in charge of the engine was ordered to keep it running anyway. The engineer then went down the line and warned the men that the engine was going to crack up, which it did. Afterward, the plant was completely shut down. The next day, a few union men were told they could have work repairing the damage and overhauling the plant if they would tear up their union cards. For sixty days the plant continued idle. Many things happened during this period. The "deputies" rambled around town and many Negroes were molested. Sol Dacus had his house ransacked several times, but he managed to keep out of their hands.

In order to relieve the unemployment situation, Williams turned the union headquarters into an employment office and sent about three-fourths of the idle men out on levee work.

On November 19, a mass meeting was held in Bogalusa, which was attended by W. L. Donnels, a United Brotherhood of Carpenters and Joiners organizer. Shortly before traintime, Ed. O'Brien, president of the Sawyers and Filers Union, was dramatically arrested at the union meeting and taken away. This broke up the meeting and Donnels boarded a train for New Orleans. When the train pulled into Rio, about six miles south of Bogalusa, there was the crowd of uniformed men with O'Brien, making an "example" of him. He was plastered all over with painted letters "I.W.W.," and appeared to have been maltreated, purportedly because he had made utterances in sympathy with the Centralia prisoners.[76] Affidavits against the men who took O'Brien from the union meeting were made before the U.S. commissioner in New Orleans on November 21, charging the men with illegally wearing the uniform of United States soldiers. Much indignation was expressed by company sympathizers because of the filing of the affidavits.[77] At the same time an intensive search was made for Sol Dacus, who fled to the swamps. It was later discovered that the O'Brien affair was staged as a part of the plot to disrupt the unions, it having been shown that he was working with the company.

On November 22, following the noon whistle, the siren, calling the "deputies" together, was sounded. This group proceeded to the union headquarters and called Williams out. The assertion which came out in the press that Williams was armed is not well-founded. About fifty shots were fired; when the shooting was over, Williams and two other union men were found dead in the office. A fourth wounded union man was taken to the company hospital where he died. After the volley of shots, Williams's brother, who was also in the office, picked up a .22 rifle, which belonged to Williams's son and had been left in the office by him, and fired at the deputies, wounding one of them in the leg. Williams's brother was saved by jumping a fence and being surrounded by women.

Troops were sent to the scene, but the union could not get the governor to do anything to protect the rights of the organized men.

Three grand jury investigations were made at various times, but there was never a report. Several years afterward, Williams's widow was reported to have won a judgment against the company for damages.

In retrospect, the "Southern Pine" lumber industry, composed of a multitude of heterogeneous units sprawled throughout more than ten states, has conformed to the traditions of lumbering in other regions only in part. Rapid exploitation of the timber resource, of course, has been characteristic, particularly in the yellow pine area. The industry either has been closely associated with southern agriculture or it has been strongly influenced by it. The labor force has been different, being composed of Negroes and whites drawn primarily from agricultural backgrounds. Wages have been lower in the South and living standards more meager than in the Lake States or the West. Company housing, which has been widely provided, and the few welfare activities have not materially changed the basically poor situation of the lives of the workers. Employers have associated for the purpose of controlling their economic conditions and to curb labor organization. Labor unions have been quite inconspicuous, and when, on a few occasions, organization was attempted, it was ruthlessly suppressed. Recent attempts of workers in the southern lumber industry to establish collective bargaining fall in a later chapter. Because of the relative importance of the Southern Pine region and its peculiar labor conditions, producers in the West always have been concerned with the southern lumber industry.

NOTES TO CHAPTER

[1] U.S. Department of Agriculture, Southern Forest Experiment Station, *Primary Wood-Products Industries in the Lower South*, by H. F. Smith. Forest Survey Release No. 51. New Orleans: Southern Forest Experiment Station, 1940, p. 3.

[2] J. Boyd, "Fifty Years in the Southern Pine Industry," reprint from *Southern Lumberman*, CXLIV (December 15, 1931), 59.

[3] J. Ise, *The United States Forest Policy*. New Haven: Yale University Press, 1920, pp. 49, 82; P. W. Gates, "Federal Land Policy in the South, 1866-1888," *Journal of Southern History*, VI, No. 3 (August, 1940), 306-311.

[4] P. W. Gates, *op. cit.*, pp. 303, 321-330; L. H. Haney (ed.), *Studies in the Industrial Resources of Texas*. Bulletin of the University of Texas, No. 3, 1915, pp. 76-77; The Texas Planning Board, *A Review of Texas Forestry and Its Industries*. Austin, Tex., 1937, p. 11.

[5] U.S. Department of Agriculture, *A National Plan for American Forestry*, 73rd Congress, 1st Session, Senate Document No. 12. Washington: Government Printing Office, 1933, I:216. See above p. 10, Chart I.

[6] U.S. Department of Agriculture, Southern Forest Experiment Station, *Primary Wood-Products, Industries in the Lower South*, pp. 3-5; Southern Pine Association, *Economic Conditions in the Southern Pine Industry*. Presented to the U.S. Timber Conservation Board, July 1, 1931. New Orleans: Southern Pine Association, 1931, pp. 32-34, 42-45.

[7] Work Projects Administration, *Mechanization in the Lumber Industry,* by A. J. Van Tassell and D. W. Bluestone. National Research Project Report No. M-5. Philadelphia: Work Projects Administration, 1940, p. 79.

[8] U.S. Department of Agriculture, Southern Forest Experiment Station, *Primary Wood-Products Industries in the Lower South,* p. 5; U.S. Department of Agriculture, Forest Service, *Forest Resources of the Piedmont Region of North Carolina,* by J. W. Cruikshank. Forest Survey Release No. 6. Asheville, N. C.: Appalachian Forest Experiment Station, November 15, 1940, p. 34.

[9] Work Projects Administration, *op. cit.,* pp. 80-82, 85; U.S. Department of Agriculture, Forest Service, *Forest Resources of the North Louisiana Delta.* Miscellaneous Publication No. 309. Washington: Government Printing Office, 1938, p. 28.

[10] Eleventh Census of the United States, 1890, *Reports of Manufacturing Industries,* Part 3, pp. 624-629.

[11] B. R. Morley, *Characteristics of the Labor Market in Alabama.* Bureau of Business Research, Printed Series No. 1, University of Alabama, Tuscaloosa, Ala., 1937, pp. 40-41.

[12] M. N. Work, "Negro Occupations," *Southern Workman,* XLIV (February, 1915), 111; C. S. Johnson, *The Negro in American Civilization.* New York: Henry Holt and Company, 1930, p. 44; C. G. Woodson, *The Rural Negro.* Washington: The Associated Publishers, Inc., 1930, pp. 98-99.

[13] See above, p. 11; cf. Work Projects Administration, *op. cit.,* p. 118; C. L. Goodrich and Others, *Migration and Economic Opportunity.* Philadelphia: University of Pennsylvania Press, 1936, p. 275.

[14] L. J. Greene and C. G. Woodson, *The Negro Wage Earner.* Washington: Associated Publishers, Inc., 1930, pp. 124-127; Thirteenth Census of the United States, 1910, Vol. IV, *Population,* pp. 435-534; U.S. Department of Commerce, Bureau of Census, *Negro Population in the United States, 1790-1915.* Washington: Government Printing Office, 1915, pp. 513-520.

[15] U.S. Department of Commerce, Bureau of Census, *op. cit.,* p. 542; Southern Pine Association, "Labor Conditions in Southern Pine Industry." Compiled by Southern Pine Association, March 3, 1934, p. 1 (mimeographed).

[16] Twelfth Census of the United States, 1900, *Special Reports on Occupations,* pp. 220-422 *et passim;* Southern Pine Association, "Labor Conditions in Southern Pine Industry." Compiled by Southern Pine Association, June 19, 1933, p. 2 (mimeographed).

[17] W. T. Couch (ed.), *Culture of the South.* Chapel Hill: University of North Carolina Press, 1935, pp. 646-647.

[18] Works Progress Administration, Division of Social Research, *Part-Time Farming in the Southeast,* by R. H. Allen and Others, Research Monograph IX. Washington: Government Printing Office, 1937, pp. 178-186; Conversation with R. K. Miller, field inspector, Wage and Hour Administration, Department of Labor, Atlanta, Ga., December 18, 1940.

[19] A. Berglund, G. T. Starnes, and F. T. DeVyver, *Labor in the Industrial South.* The Institute for Research in the Social Sciences, University of Virginia, 1930, Chapter I.

[20] Works Progress Administration, Division of Social Research, *op. cit.,* pp. 169, 173-174; cf. P. A. Bloomer, *Economic Conditions in Southern Pine Industry.* Statement and brief in behalf of the Southern Pine Industry before the National Industrial Recovery Board. New Orleans: Southern Pine Association, 1935, p. 11.

[21] A. Berglund, G. T. Starnes, and F. T. DeVyver, *op. cit.,* p. 54.

[22] Southern Pine Association, *Economic Conditions in the Southern Pine Industry,* p. 40.

[23] A. Berglund, G. T. Starnes, and F. T. DeVyver, *op. cit.,* p. 55.

[24] *Ninth Biennial Report of the Bureau of Statistics of Labor of the State of Louisiana, 1916-1918,* pp. 96, 124-134.

[25] G. Creel, "Feudal Towns of Texas," *Harpers Weekly,* LX, No. 3031 (January 23, 1915), 76.

[26] "Company Stores and the Scrip System," *Monthly Labor Review,* XLI, No. 1 (July, 1935), 44-50.

[27] Southern Pine Association, "Labor Conditions in Southern Pine Industry," p. 6; Southern Pine Association, *Employment Conditions and Living Costs and Conditions in Southern Lumber.* New Orleans: Southern Pine Association, 1937, p. 9.

[28] Conversation with R. K. Miller, December 18, 1940.

[29] Southern Pine Association, "Costs, Employment, Wage and Other Operating Data for 50 Southern Pine Manufacturers." Compiled by Southern Pine Association, October 20, 1939, p. 5 (mimeographed).

[30] Southern Pine Association, *Employment Conditions and Living Costs and Conditions in the Southern Lumber Industry,* p. 13.

[31] A. Berglund, G. T. Starnes, and F. T. DeVyver, *op. cit.*, p. 58; cf. *Eighth Biennial Report of the Bureau of Labor Statistics of the State of Texas, 1923-1924,* p. 12.

[32] U.S. Department of Agriculture, Forest Service, Southern Forest Experiment Station, "Reports on Abandoned Sawmills and Sustained Yield Forest Communities in the South" (typewritten, no pagination); C. Todes, *Labor and Lumber.* New York: International Publishers, 1931, pp. 80-81; *Eighth Biennial Report of the Bureau of Labor Statistics of the State of Texas, 1923-1924,* pp. 13-14.

[33] Texas State Department of Labor, *The Industrial Bulletin,* Vol. I, No. 2. Austin, Tex., February 1, 1928, pp. 30-31.

[34] C. C. Sheppard, *Wages and Hours of Labor in the South.* Statement in behalf of the Southern Lumber Industry before the National Industrial Recovery Administration, July 20, 1933. New Orleans: Southern Pine Association, 1933, p. 11; Southern Pine Association, "Labor Conditions in Southern Pine Industry," *passim;* Southern Pine Association, *Employment Conditions and Living Costs and Conditions in Southern Lumber Industry, passim.*

[35] Eleventh Census of the United States, 1890, *Reports on Manufacturing Industries,* Part 3, pp. 624-629.

[36] *First Annual Report of the Bureau of Statistics of Labor of the State of Louisiana, 1901,* pp. 159-160.

[37] *Third Biennial Report of the Bureau of Statistics of Labor of the State of Louisiana, 1904-05,* p. 56.

[38] W. F. Ogburn, "Does It Cost Less to Live in the South," *Social Forces,* XIV, No. 2 (December, 1935), p. 211; "Differences in Living Costs in Northern and Southern Cities," *Monthly Labor Review,* XLIX, No. 1 (July, 1939), 22-38.

[39] A. Berglund, G. T. Starnes, and F. T. DeVyver, *op. cit.*, pp. 33, 36-37.

[40] U.S. Department of Labor, Bureau of Labor Statistics, *Wages and Hours of Labor in the Lumber, Millwork, and Furniture Industries, 1890 to 1912,* Bulletin No. 129. Washington: Government Printing Office, 1913, pp. 29-33.

[41] A. Berglund, G. T. Starnes, and F. T. DeVyver, *op. cit.*, pp. 39-52; U.S. Department of Labor, Bureau of Labor Statistics, *Wages and Hours of Labor in the Lumber, Millwork and Furniture Industries, 1915,* Bulletin No. 225. Washington: Government Printing Office, 1916, pp. 32-35.

[42] U.S. Department of Labor, Bureau of Labor Statistics, *Wages and Hours of Labor in Lumber Manufacturing, 1921,* Bulletin No. 317. Washington: Government Printing Office, 1923, pp. 15-21; U.S. Department of Labor, Bureau of Labor Statistics, *Wages and Hours of Labor in the Lumber Industry in the United States, 1928,* Bulletin No. 497. Washington: Government Printing Office, 1929, pp. 31, 35.

[43] Southern Pine Association, *Wages and Hours of Labor in the South.* Statement in behalf of the Southern Lumber Industry before the National Industrial Recovery Administration. New Orleans: Southern Pine Association, 1933, p. 7.

[44] *Third Biennial Report of the Bureau of Statistics of Labor of the State of Louisiana, 1904-05,* p. 56; *Eighth Biennial Report of the Bureau of Labor Statistics of the State of Texas, 1923-24,* p. 36; Texas State Department of Labor, *op. cit.*, p. 30.

[45] Thirteenth Census of the United States, 1910, Vol. X, *Manufactures,* p. 498.

[46] F. L. Hoffman, "The Industrial Accident Problem in the Lumber Industry," *Southern Pine and Reconstruction.* Report of the 4th Annual Meeting of the Southern

Pine Association. New Orleans, 1919, pp. 131-32; *Second Biennial Report of the Bureau of Labor Statistics of the State of Texas, 1911-12*, p. 246.

[47] *Ninth Biennial Report of the Bureau of Statistics of Labor of the State of Louisiana, 1916-18*, p. 97; *Eighth Biennial Report of the Bureau of Labor Statistics of the State of Texas, 1923-24*, p. 14.

[48] Southern Pine Association, *Employment Conditions and Living Costs and Conditions in the Southern Lumber Industry*, p. 6.

[49] U.S. Immigration Commission, *Abstract of Reports*. Senate Document No. 747, 61st Congress, 3rd Session. Washington: Government Printing Office, 1911, II: 443-449; M. C. Terrell, "Peonage in the United States," *Nineteenth Century and After*, LXII (1907), 309-311; A. Johnson (ed.), *The New Economic Freedom*. The Chronicles of America Series, Vol. XXI, Part 1, "The New South," by H. Thompson. New Haven: Yale University Press, 1919, pp. 123-124.

[50] U.S. Department of Justice, *Annual Report of the Attorney General, 1907*. Washington: Government Printing Office, 1907, pp. 207, 211.

[51] M. N. Work, *Negro Yearbook, 1931-32*. Tuskegee, Ala.: Negro Yearbook Publishing Company, 1933, pp. 139-140; New York *World*, November 24, 1929.

[52] U.S. Department of Agriculture, Forest Service, Southern Forest Experiment Station, "Reports on Abandoned Sawmill Towns and Sustained Yield Forest Communities in the South, 1935."

[53] H. C. Berckes, *A Decade of Service*. New Orleans: Southern Pine Association, 1925, p. 24; cf. T. L. Smith and M. R. Fry, *The Population of a Selected "Cut-Over" Area in Louisiana*, Louisiana State University and Agricultural and Mechanical College Bulletin No. 268 (January, 1936), p. 31.

[54] Federal Emergency Relief Administration, Division of Research, *Six Rural Problem Areas*, by P. G. Beck and M. C. Forster, Research Monograph No. 1. Washington: Government Printing Office, p. 10.

[55] U.S. Department of Commerce, Bureau of Foreign and Domestic Commerce, *American Southern Pine*, by W. L. Neubrech. Trade Promotion Series No. 191. Washington: Government Printing Office, 1939, p. 29; Southern Pine Association, *Economic Conditions in the Southern Pine Industry*, pp. 2-3, 111-112; J. Boyd, *op. cit.*, pp. 16-17.

[56] U.S. Commission on Industrial Relations, *Final Report and Testimony on Industrial Relations*. Washington: Government Printing Office, 1916, V: 4394, 4412.

[57] W. Compton, *The Organization of the Lumber Industry*. Chicago: American Lumberman, 1916, p. 17.

[58] *Voice of the People*, various issues from October 9, 1913, to July 23, 1914; C. Todes, *op. cit.*, p. 97; S. D. Spero and A. L. Harris, *The Black Worker—The Negro and the Labor Movement*. New York: Columbia University Press, 1931, p. 331; G. Creel, *op. cit.*, p. 77.

[59] F. Myers, "The Knights of Labor in the South," *Southern Economic Journal*, VI, No. 4 (April, 1940), 485; H. T. Warshow (ed.), *Representative Industries in the United States*. New York: Henry Holt and Company, 1928, p. 480.

[60] *Second Biennial Report of the Bureau of Statistics of Labor for the State of Louisiana, 1902-03*, p. 40.

[61] Industrial Workers of the World, *The Lumber Industry and Its Workers*. Chicago: Industrial Workers of the World, 1920(?), p. 76.

[62] C. Todes, *op. cit.*, p. 171; New Orleans *Times-Democrat*, July 20, 1911; G. Creel, *op. cit.*, p. 77.

[63] New Orleans *Times-Democrat*, July 20 to August 8, 1911; J. H. Kirby, *The Perils of Democracy*. New Orleans: Southern Pine Association, 1918, p. 1.

[64] New Orleans *Times-Democrat*, May 17, July 20, 1911; Industrial Workers of the World, *op. cit.*, p. 76.

[65] J. H. Kirby, *op. cit.*, *passim*; New Orleans *Times-Democrat*, July 20, August 8, 1911.

[66] New Orleans *Times-Democrat*, July 20, 1911.

[67] Industrial Workers of the World, *op. cit.,* p. 76; G. Creel, *op. cit.,* pp. 77-78; *Voice of the People,* December 25, 1913.

[68] New Orleans *Times-Democrat,* November 1, 1911; Industrial Workers of the World, *op. cit.,* p. 77; *Voice of the People,* December 25, 1913; C. Todes, *op. cit.,* p. 171.

[69] *Lumber Trade Journal,* May 15, 1912, p. 1; New Orleans *Times-Democrat,* May 17, 1912; S. D. Spero and A. L. Harris, *op. cit.,* p. 331.

[70] See below, p. 114.

[71] W. D. Haywood, *Bill Haywood's Book.* New York: International Publishers, 1929, pp. 241-242.

[72] *Lumber Trade Journal,* May 15, 1912, pp. 1, 13, 34, June 1, 1912, p. 13; New Orleans *Times-Democrat,* May 17, 1912.

[73] For more details, see New Orleans *Times-Democrat,* October 18 to November 3, 1912.

[74] Industrial Workers of the World, *The Lumber Industry and Its Workers,* I.W.W. Publishing Company (not dated, about 1920), pp. 27, 77; *Voice of the People,* January 1, January 29, March 5, 1914.

[75] Conversation with Z. D. Nichols, business agent for the Carpenters Local, New Orleans, La., December 28, 1941; New Orleans *Times-Picayune,* November 23, 1919; C. Todes, *op. cit.,* pp. 174-178.

[76] New Orleans *Times-Picayune,* November 23, 1919; see below, p. 137, for information on the Centralia case.

[77] New Orleans *Times-Picayune,* November 23, 1919.

THE WEST

THE beginnings of the great lumber industry of the West reach back to the third quarter of the nineteenth century. In its early years it supplied the local and California coastal demand, and also provided a little lumber for the Pacific overseas trade. As an important competitor in the national market, however, its history falls almost entirely within the twentieth century. Not until it was realized that the forests of the Great Lakes region would last only a few years, and that they would not supply the continued growing demand for lumber, did the great forests in the West attract attention. Interest in them was aroused simultaneously with the development of interest in the southern forests. Yet the western lumber industry lagged behind that of the South because of the inadequacy and expensiveness of transportation facilities. This situation, however, did not deter speculative activity, which was even more rampant in the West than in the South and duplicated on a larger scale the practices which had been commonplace in the Lake States.[1]

Speculation in timber lands, stimulated in the late eighties, was accelerated as the prospects of the region appeared more favorable. As usual, overoptimism effectively obscured an accurate view of the situation. Speculative activities continued almost without abatement until around 1910, when they became even more frenzied as a result of the ominous warnings of the early twentieth century conservationists who predicted an early total depletion of the nation's forests. From 1910 on, because timber land values failed to appreciate, speculative profits disappeared.

It would not be far from the truth to say that the Lake States lumber industry moved itself bodily into the West once its raw material was practically gone. Although many producers did shift their interests to the Southern Pine region, or at least showed concern over developments there, the movement to the West was much more pronounced. The western lumber industry roster is replete with the names of lumbermen who were prominent in Michigan, Wisconsin,

and Minnesota. Not only did the operators move their capital, but a
large segment of the labor force migrated as well. In contrast, lumberjacks seldom moved to the South.[2]

The West did not loom large in the national lumber market until
transportation developments made it possible to take the timber
products out. Meanwhile, during the 1880's, with an anticipated decline in the supply of lumber in conjunction with the continued
building up of the Midwest, lumber prices improved. Because of the
prospect of profits in lumber sales, the northwestern timber owners
eagerly sought to develop transportation facilities. Water shipments of
lumber, although relatively large, especially to the California markets,
had not provided a sufficient outlet to warrant large-scale production,
nor had the water shipments placed the western industry in national
competition. Some other means of transportation was needed.

The transcontinental railroads were great users of timber, but not
until they provided carriage for timber products to the East was
the industry really set free to grow. Within the region, the Oregon
and California Railroad was opened in 1873, and the industry developed along its line. Railroad building was active in Washington
in the early eighties, and in 1883 the Northern Pacific Railway reached
the coast, entering Tacoma by way of Portland. By 1887 this line
opened a direct route over the Cascades to Puget Sound, and branches
were built. A great event for the region occurred when the Great
Northern Railroad reached Puget Sound in 1893. This was followed
by a more rapid expansion of the lumber industry. It was approximately in the last decade of the century that the western lumber
industry became an important factor in the national lumber market.
Later, the Panama Canal added impetus to its development. Washington and Oregon soon took places at the head of the list among
the leading lumber states, although "Southern Pine" still supplied the
greatest total volume.

An understanding of timber land acquisition and the nature of
timber ownership within the region is necessary to comprehend both
the organization and the chronic problems of the western lumber
industry. To a striking extent the manner of timber land acquisition
set the pattern of the lumber industry for many decades.

Early government timber land policies were essentially unsound.
From the vantage point of the present it appears that the intense
speculative fervor with which timber lands were acquired in this
region was not warranted. But when land acquisition was running
its course, it was difficult to see, or realize, that acute problems would

emerge from it. And who would have been strong enough to have stopped the speculation? It was motivated by the fact that stumpage values had been appreciating for a number of years, and that great fortunes had been accumulated through dealings in forest lands.[3] In this region, as in others, timber offered easy wealth. But conditions changed, and stumpage values did not appreciate after about 1910, whereas carrying charges increased considerably. The primary result was the building of an excessive fixed investment which became a burden on the operating industry. The only way out seemed to be to cut the timber as rapidly as possible, and this has resulted in a more or less chronic overproduction, particularly in depressed times.

The largest holdings of timber in this region are accounted for by the land grants to railroad companies—grants to the Southern Pacific and Northern Pacific companies. In addition, the Timber and Stone Act was employed for the purpose of building up huge holdings through the use of dummy entrymen, and the Homestead Act also was used.[4] In 1910 the most striking examples of concentration of timber ownership were in Oregon and Washington. Three owners, the Southern Pacific and Northern Pacific railroads and the Weyerhaeuser Timber Company, controlled 191 billion board feet. In addition, there were 83 owners who had acquired over a billion board feet each. The aggregate holdings of these owners were 411.7 billion board feet, or 59.4 per cent of the privately held stumpage in the two states. The timberlands of California illustrated, in 1910, the same tendencies, although the individual holdings were not so large. Nearly 75 per cent of the privately owned timber in the state was in 39 holdings.[5] Since then part of the Southern Pacific grant has been taken back by the government, and the size of the national forests has been increased. In spite of the tremendously large holdings, it should be emphasized that diversification of ownership has been broad enough to make problems of overproduction chronically serious. Great pressure to reduce expenses has been continually felt because of the nature of the overhead cost structure, and this has exerted great influence on labor relations. In recent years, the situation has become more acute, as the instability of land ownership attests.[6] Industry control has been nigh on to impossible because of the diversity of interests.

Lumbering in the West has been centralized more in Washington and Oregon than elsewhere. Around Puget Sound, on Grays Harbor and Willapa Harbor, and along the Columbia River, particularly around Portland, the western lumber industry has had its greatest development. In California there has been no great concentration of production. Units were scattered and were located primarily to serve the local demands. In the pine region of eastern Oregon and through Idaho and Montana, another area of lumbering activity has been developed, but it has been nowhere equal in importance to that of the Douglas fir region.

The extent of mechanization was notable as soon as the industry developed on a large scale in the Douglas fir region, and it has continued so to the present. The huge trees and the more rugged terrain required high-powered equipment. Here, mechanization and logging engineering have had maximum development.[7] Progressive improvements in powerful stationary ground, high-lead, and sky-line yarders and in forest railroads continued until the mid-twenties. Along with the increased size and power of the machines came more speedy operations. More recently, the flexible crawler tractor and motor truck have increased in importance. With these developments significant changes in labor requirements appeared. Changes in mechanization have reduced man-hour labor requirements progressively for many years.[8] In the pine regions mechanized equipment was never so extensively used. Different woods practices, more akin to those used elsewhere in the industry, were satisfactory. Instead of cable yarders, the big wheels were used.[9] Now, tractors and trucks literally dominate in logging in these pine areas.

Logging operations have varied considerably in size, depending in part upon the locality and the nature of the contractual relationship. Logging has been carried on both by sawmill companies which saw their own logs and by contractors. In addition, there have been many independent logging companies in the Northwest which have produced their own logs and sold them on the open market. In any case, variations in size have ranged from very small gyppo operators, meaning the contractors who cut specified timber with a small crew of workers,[10] to large operators with four or more "sides" (a "side" is a complete yarding and loading crew), using several hundred men.

Sawmills in the Douglas fir region have ranged in size from huge cargo, rail, or combination mills, varying in degree of refinement in manufacturing, to medium-sized, and to very small mills, many of which are located in the Willamette Valley in Oregon, that cut only rough lumber and railroad ties. In the two pine regions the same relative degrees of size have been characteristic too. Many large, highly mechanized mills have operated, but there have also been numerous small ones adjacent to small local market areas throughout the whole region. The industry has been made up of heterogeneous units, many of which exist simply to liquidate excessive investment in timber. The industry has tended chronically toward overcapacity and, with the large number of producing units, to cutthroat competition.

The great fluctuations in production due to market conditions make it difficult to give an accurate statistical count of the number of establishments in the industry. Census figures show more than 1,500 units in Washington, Oregon, and California in 1900. This tabulation includes very small mills which are no longer counted by the Census. Although there are relatively few small mills in the West, as has been indicated, there are quite a number of them in certain localities. In 1937 the number of units reported in the three states was only slightly less than 1,500.[11] This includes the pine area in Washington and Oregon. A few mills should be added to the total if Idaho and Montana are included.

The length of time men have worked in the woods each year has been governed by the methods of logging and the demand for logs or lumber. In the Douglas fir region, market conditions permitting, many operators have been able to carry on logging for the entire year, and in no case less than nine months. Snow and bad, windy weather at the higher elevations in the winter, or dry fire-hazard weather in the summer, have caused seasonal shutdowns. The demand for lumber falls off in the late fall because of the decline in building activity and does not pick up again until about March. The influence of the market often has determined the degree of unemployment during the normally slack periods. In the region as a whole, except in boom times, the men have been fortunate to average more than eight or nine months' work a year.[12] The seasonal pattern runs as follows: Logging and sawmilling activity, roughly, move together, although sawmilling is somewhat more stable. The peak is reached in logging about April, and in sawmilling about May. There is a definite decline in July, with a secondary peak reached in October. During December through February, logging may be anywhere from 25 to 50 per cent below normal for the industry as a whole, and sawmilling from 15 to 25 per cent below normal.[13] In spite of the pronounced seasonality of production and employment, the seasonal problem has not been so acute as the cyclical problem, and much less so than the random fluctuations due to economic conditions peculiar to the industry.

In the pine regions of California, Idaho, and Montana seasonal factors have been more forceful. In Idaho and Montana the cutting season in the woods in early times was confined principally to the winter months. Snow and cold weather were as important there as in the Lake States. In California the reverse was true; there was a markedly dull season for about five months during the winter. The woods crew usually was only about one-fourth of its peak size during the snowy season.[14]

Sawmilling in California has been relatively less seasonal. The sawing season customarily started shortly after the logging was under way and continued for a month or more longer.[15] Likewise, in the interior pine region, sawing has been done during the spring, summer, and autumn months.

Exactly how many Lake States lumber industry workers migrated to the West may never be determined. Perhaps as much as half the labor force in the western lumber industry in the early twenties had worked in the lumber industry of the Lake States.[16] Although it is widely believed that the labor force has been predominantly foreign-born, the Census statistics show that the force, as a whole, has been of American origin. However, there has been a sizable proportion of foreign-born Scandinavian workers, particularly in the logging end of the industry, where they have been in the majority among the foreign-born.

In 1890 about 46 per cent of the sawmill employees in Washington and Oregon were of native parentage, with an additional 12.5 per cent of foreign parentage. Foreign-born whites constituted 40 per cent. In 1900 the foreign-born constituted 30 per cent. In the logging end of the industry, in 1900, approximately 60 per cent of the workers were foreign-born, Scandinavians comprising about 25 per cent of the total, Finns 7 per cent, and South Europeans 5 per cent. The remainder was comprised of over forty races of immigrants. In California more South Europeans always have been found among the workers.[17] In 1910, 47, 54, and 44 per cent of the sawmill laborers in California, Oregon, and Washington, respectively, were native-born, and 49, 40, and 46 per cent, respectively, were foreign-born. In Washington and Oregon, between 1900 and 1910, a number of Japanese and other Orientals were given work in the industry as common laborers, but their number was never large and many of them soon shifted elsewhere. In logging 38, 71, and 55 per cent of the workers in California, Oregon, and Washington, respectively, were native whites; and 56, 27, and 43 per cent, respectively, were foreign-born.[18] The great predominance of native-born loggers in Oregon was due to the early agricultural migration into the Willamette Valley and the Coos Bay regions. There, native sons worked in the industry almost exclusively. In other parts of the western region the influx of men from the southern lumber industry from the close of the second decade as well as some hill folk from the South, has been conspicuous.

Percentages of native-born workers in three western states in 1930 were found to be as follows: [19]

	Loggers	Operatives	Sawmill Laborers
California	55	75	48
Oregon	70	80	80
Washington	66	80	66

Scandinavians still predominated among the foreign-born, with a good representation of Finns in parts of Oregon and Washington. There continued to be a few Japanese in Washington, but their number was small.

Most of the workers look to the industry as a permanent source of livelihood. They are the typical workers in the industry, and they have little else to turn to. Some loggers from the coastal areas, however, customarily go out with the fishing fleets at certain times of the year. In southern Oregon the relationships to agriculture are still close, and the same is quite true in the pine region. Many of these men are "stump" ranchers who are trying to make a farm out of a piece of cut-over land. To them the work in the lumber industry is simply a temporary expedient which turns out to be, however, also a continuous necessity.

During the past two decades the working force has changed its characteristics considerably. Formerly, many of the workers, particularly in the logging end of the industry, were homeless, migratory men. These migratory workers were of two types: those who moved within the industry from job to job because of the irregularity of employment and those who moved up and down the coast, and sometimes inland even to the wheat belt in the Dakotas, taking whatever work could be found. The first type of migratory worker has always been the more important, and loggers have seldom even shifted from fir logging, the "long-log country," to pine logging, the "short-log country." The men in the second class generally have been only common laborers. The "hobo," the professional tramp, seldom has been found because the men in the industry have not liked the "camp inspector" or "boomer," the man who just moves casually from camp to camp seeking a few days' work here and a day there. The I.W.W.

saw to it that the "bindles," rolls of blankets which the men nearly always carried, were dispensed with by the early twenties.

The plight of the homeless, womanless, voteless, migratory worker in the West was given much publicity prior to and during the war because of the rise of the I.W.W. It is true that the majority of lumber industry workers in the West, at one time, were single men. In 1900, according to the Census returns, more than two-thirds of the workers in the lumber industry in Washington, Oregon, and California were unmarried. This may be a conservative figure inasmuch as it is very likely that many of the migrant lumberjacks were never approached by the census takers. Reliable estimates, a decade later, place the number of unmarried loggers in lumber camps at about 90 per cent.[20] Seldom were there any family houses provided in the camps—operators did not like to be bothered with married men.

Workers are no longer as migratory as they once were. Improved camps, the automobile, and hard-surfaced roads have brought about this change.[21] More family men and a more stable group now work in the industry. Among the loggers, however, employment is less steady and turnover is still an important problem. Men still move from camp to camp but there is less movement up and down the region and hardly any movement in and out of the industry, except in those sections where the industry is related to agriculture.

Living conditions help to explain the attitudes of men. Lumber camps in the earlier days in the West, until the war period, were notoriously bad. Structures were temporary affairs and, in many cases, not well-built. Conditions were such that they were hardly comprehensible to those who did not have a firsthand view of the situation.[22] Men carried their blankets and slept in wooden, vermin-infested bunks in overcrowded bunkhouses. They had no bathing facilities and were offered slight chance for recreation.[23] Dr. Norman Coleman, one-time president of the 4L, the common designation of the Loyal Legion of Loggers and Lumbermen, an organization established during World War I to deal with labor relations,[24] told of a conversation with an old friend who had had an intimate acquaintanceship with camp conditions prior to the war period. The latter spoke of "crowded bunkhouses, wooden bunks in tiers, dirty straw, vermin, wet clothes steaming and stinking about the central stove, men pigging together without ventilation, privacy, or means of cleanliness. . . ."[25] It was testified that "Men have to carry their own bedding . . . some bunks are just wooden affairs filled with straw. . . . Most camps have no caretaker . . . the men have no chance, or care or desire to improve their conditions. They just come in and sleep. Nearly all camps are infested with bedbugs, some have fleas, and some are lousy." [26] An impartial student said, "The chief complaints of the men concerning the bunkhouses is with regard to cleanliness and provision for drying clothes. The bunk houses are usually poorly built and at best are hard to keep clean . . . perhaps a third of the time, the men come in covered with mud and thoroughly wet. They have to clean up in the bunk house, and usually get it fairly dirty in so doing. Clothes need frequent washing, and if there is no suitable place to dry clothes they must be dried in the men's living room." [27] A pithy characterization of conditions was given by a government commission. "We are dealing with an industry still determined by pioneer conditions of life. Hardy contacts with nature make certain rigors of life inevitable, but the rigors of nature have been reinforced by the neglects of men. . . . The unlivable condition of many camps has long demanded attention. . . . There has been a failure to make of these camps communities." [28]

The chances for normal social life were scant. The men took their recreation and experienced their social life outside the camp, on the "skidroad." The skidroad was the road over which the logs were dragged in the days when oxen were used. For years the term has referred to the common meeting place for loggers, such as Second Avenue from Yesler Way to Main Street in Seattle, or Burnside Street around Erickson's Saloon and the area to the north in Portland. Seattle, Tacoma, Portland, Spokane, Eureka, and San Francisco have been famous as assembly points and clearinghouses for the migratory lumber workers. [29] Fleeing the monotony of the isolated logging camp with its lack of outlet for natural human desires, the men found their relaxation and recreation in an environment provided by all those agencies which are in the business of profiting out of the peculiar needs of the homeless worker. The situation that existed for many of the men was succinctly portrayed by one of them, when he said, "Have you ever thought of how we, the workers in the woods . . . are really approached and 'entertained' when we visit our present centers of 'civilization' and 'culture'? What is the first thing we meet? The cheap lodging house, the dark and dirty restaurant, the saloon or the blind pig, the prostitutes operating in all the hotels, the moving picture and cheap vaudeville shows with their still cheaper, sensational programs, the freaks of all descriptions who operate on the street corners. . . ." [30]

The leading of unnatural lives in such abnormal surroundings, with no way of avoiding them, was bound to have definite effects on the workers. Protest against the type of life in which the lumberjack found himself first came in an organized way from the I.W.W. with a radical philosophy which was a product of the environment. One operator spoke for many when he asserted that "The movement of the I.W.W. is merely the cry of the oppressed. . . . It is misery become articulate. . . ." [31] These conditions were not peculiar to the Douglas fir region alone. They prevailed throughout the western lumber industry with but minor variations. [32]

The I.W.W. centered its attention on widespread camp reform during World War I period. The labor disputes which followed seemed to be interfering with production of lumber essential to the war effort. The Spruce Production Corporation, a unit under the authority of the War Department, was established to increase lumber production, and an army corps was sent into the region to assist with the work in the camps. Wherever soldier labor was at work army standards had to be maintained. [33] Later, under the authority of the Spruce Production Corporation, 4L inspectors visited camps and gave attention to matters of sanitation and the rudimentary comforts which the men were entitled to, and which were necessary if the men were to have the proper morale. These occurrences led to rapid improvement. Fairly satisfactory living quarters have become the general rule. The best camps are well-constructed of dressed lumber and equipped with individual beds, private lockers for clothing, hot and cold water, steam heat, and other accommodations. The general appearance of the camps has become more pleasing. The same is true in California, although the 4L did not get into the picture there until later. The California State Immigration Commission early became concerned with housing conditions, and legislation was passed which improved the situation measurably. [34]

Wages in the West Coast lumber industry have always averaged higher than in either the South or the Lake States lumber region. In 1890, according to the Census, they averaged $10 a month higher than in the Lake States, and $20 a month higher than in the South, both in the woods and in the sawmills. [35] Average annual earnings, however, have not been proportionately greater, because workers in the South have averaged at least a month more of employment during the year than those in the West. By 1910 wage rates in the West, except in very highly skilled jobs, were practically double those in the South. Thereafter, the differential in wages increased only slightly. At the same time, wages in the lumber industry have not compared

favorably with wages in other industries in the West, and earnings
have always been erratic.[36]

Complaints about wage payment practices were common before
World War I period. No uniform system has ever prevailed, but it
has been customary to compute wages on an hourly basis and to pay
by the month. It also has been customary to have a "draw day" during
the interval between paydays, at which time workers could get a substantial portion of the money then due them. Some work has been
done under contract, and piece rates have been used in certain occupations, notably in falling and bucking of timber in the woods and in
stacking lumber in the sawmills. The early complaints centered mainly
in the fact that time checks, memoranda or evidence of indebtedness,
were not negotiable and workers were often put to great inconvenience
and even loss in getting their earned wages.[37] In the main, these
grievances have been cleared up. Wage payment, except when there is
fraud, is not a problem because each of the states early passed laws
to protect workers in the collection of wages.[38]

Generally, hiring has been done either at the plant or logging
camp, by superintendents or foremen, or through commercial employment agencies, such as the Western Operators Association in Seattle,
and smaller agencies there and at other places. In most cases it has
been necessary to hire loggers in town rather than at the camp.
Camps have been located so far back in the woods that one needed
assurance of a job before undertaking the journey out. Complaints
against employment abuses have been, and still are, frequent, although
most of the early abuses have been eliminated. Fee-splitting practices,
giving of false information about jobs or working conditions, forfeiture of fees paid even though no job existed upon arrival at sawmill
or logging camp, and sending men unfit for the work, which en-
dangers the lives of other workers, were common complaints.

The lumber industry has been a peculiarly fertile field for private
employment agents because of the inconstancy of employment. Unscrupulous agents, if they chose, were able to exploit workers rather
easily. So aroused was public indignation toward the practices and
evils which prevailed in this region that early laws to regulate, and
even to abolish, commercial employment agencies were enacted. Popular protest was voiced in 1914 in the state of Washington by the
passage of an initiative measure prohibiting the collection of fees
from workers by employment agents. It was claimed that lumber companies were active opponents of the bill. Nevertheless, it was passed
but later was declared unconstitutional. Regulation of employment

agencies, however, was obtained in Washington, Oregon, and California by 1915.[39] During the twenties complaints were less frequent and agitation in the past decade for union hiring halls has been more for organization purposes than to eliminate abuses.

Although both logging and sawmilling always have been extremely hazardous occupations, particularly logging, accident frequency and severity rates have been higher in the West than elsewhere. The loss of life and limb has been appalling. While improvement has been made through laws, regulation, inspection, education of workers, and general safety compaigns, the losses still continue to be enormous. It is not possible to give a precise statistical picture except for recent years. Accident statistics, except for the past decade, are fragmentary. For the industry as a whole since 1926, when the United States Bureau of Labor Statistics began to compile industrial injury rates for manufacturing industries, logging has consistently had the highest number of injuries per million employee-hours worked. The 1939 frequency rate was 105.39, with 173 disabling injuries, for every thousand workers. The severity rate, showing the number of days of disability charged per thousand hours worked, also was relatively high, 17.95. Sawmills, too, have a noticeably high injury experience, with a frequency rate of 48.78 and a severity rate of 4.70. In 1939 the frequency and severity rates for all manufacturing in the United States were respectively 15.43 and 1.64, while workers in fabricated structural steel, notorious for its work hazards and having the highest rates in the iron and steel products industries, had rates of 34.85 and 4.80, respectively. The rates for the western lumber industry have been higher than in the South or Lake States lumber industries. For 1939 the frequency rate in logging in the West was 109.58, in the South 102.32, and in the Lake States 96.67.[40] The causes which have contributed most to the higher rates in the West have been rough terrain, high-powered equipment, and the contempt for danger which seems to develop among loggers. For the ten-year period from 1924 to 1933, inclusive, compensation paid by the Department of Labor and Industries of Washington, for both fatal and nonfatal injuries in the lumber industries, amounted to $18,049,878.[41] This would average at least $30 per year per workman; and the bill in Oregon has been roughly comparable. It should be noted that the figures for the pine regions in the two states are included as well, whereas the accident hazards have not been so great in the pine regions whether in Washington, Oregon, or California.

Because injuries have been frequent and because the work has been carried on in more or less isolated places, it is but natural that some sort of scheme should have been developed to give the men medical and hospital care. Following the practice in the Lake States and in the South, the men commonly have been charged medical and hospital fees, ranging from one to two dollars a month. But this was never popular with the workers because they disliked certain administrative aspects of the system, such as the company selection of the physician and hospital.[42] Workmen's compensation laws were adopted rather early in all the western states. Washington and California adopted compulsory systems for certain classes of employees, and the lumber industry was included. Oregon adopted an elective system but denied legal defenses to those who did not insure in the state system.

The lumber industry moved into the West as a strapping youngster looking for fortune. Here was a timbered region that would test the mettle of the young giant who had leaped from the Lake States into the West in a stride. The trees were larger and the terrain rougher than had been known elsewhere. In typical, rugged fashion the industry went rapidly to work. Newly designed and more powerful equipment was secured for logging. Larger and speedier saws were installed. But the market for lumber was erratic and overproduction early became a chronic problem. Producers formed associations to standardize types of lumber and to control prices in order to regulate production, but were never really successful. Employment was not steady and many workers were forced to move about frequently in search of it. Living conditions in hastily built, temporary camps, situated miles back in the woods, were disagreeable and men tried to escape them by moving to camp after camp. The hazard of accident was increased with the high-speed equipment. The industry needed organization.

NOTES TO CHAPTER

[1] S. A. D. Puter, *Looters of the Public Domain*. Portland, Ore.: The Portland Printing House, 1908, *passim;* U.S. Department of Commerce and Labor, Bureau of Corporations, *The Lumber Industry*. Washington: Government Printing Office, 1913, pp. 17, 228-229.

[2] C. L. Goodrich and Others. *Migration and Economic Opportunity,* Philadelphia: University of Pennsylvania Press, 1936, p. 275.

[0] U.S. Department of Commerce and Labor, Bureau of Corporations, *op. cit.,* p. 38; J. Ise, *The United States Forest Policy.* New Haven: Yale University Press, 1920, p. 48.

[4] U.S. Department of Commerce and Labor, Bureau of Corporations, *op. cit.,* pp. xx, 17, 219-221, 236, 263; J. Ise, *op. cit.,* p. 53.

[5] U.S. Department of Agriculture, Forest Service, *Timber Depletion, Lumber Prices, Lumber Exports, and Concentration of Timber Ownership.* Washington: Government

Printing Office, 1920, pp. 63-64; cf. U.S. Department of Commerce and Labor, Bureau of Corporations, *op. cit.*, Part 2, pp. 1-114.

⁶ U.S. Department of Agriculture, Forest Service, Pacific Northwest Experiment Station, *Facts Bearing Upon the Instability of Forest Land Ownership in Western Washington*, by S. A. Wilson. Portland, Ore.: Pacific Northwest Experiment Station, 1934, *passim* (similar one for Oregon).

⁷ A. J. F. Brandstrom, *Analysis of Logging Costs and Operating Methods in the Douglas Fir Region*. Seattle, Wash.: Charles Lathrop Pack Forestry Foundation, 1933, *passim*.

⁸ Work Projects Administration, *Mechanization in the Lumber Industry*, pp. 34-58.

⁹ U.S. Department of Agriculture, *Lumbering in the Sugar and Yellow Pine Region of California*. Bulletin No. 440. Washington: Government Printing Office, 1917, p. 5. For explanation of "big wheels," see above, pp. 12-13.

¹⁰ E. B. Mittleman, "The Gyppo System," *Journal of Political Economy*, XXXI, No. 9 (December, 1923), 840-851.

¹¹ Twelfth Census of the United States, 1900, Vol. IX, *Manufactures*, Part 3, pp. 807-810; *Biennial Census of Manufactures, 1937*, Part 1, p. 502.

¹² U.S. Department of Agriculture, *Logging in the Douglas Fir Region*, Bulletin No. 711. Washington: Government Printing Office, 1918, pp. 8-9.

¹³ W. S. Hopkins, *Seasonal Unemployment in the State of Washington*. University of Washington Publications in the Social Sciences, 1936, Vol. VIII, No. 3, pp. 124-25; cf. Thirteenth Census of the United States, 1910, Vol. IX, *Manufactures*, pp. 496-497.

¹⁴ *Third Biennial Report of the Department of Labor and Industry of the State of Montana, 1916-18*, pp. 46-47; *Sixteenth Biennial Report of the Bureau of Labor of the State of California, 1913-14*. California State Printing Office, 1914, p. 55; U.S. Department of Labor, *Labor Laws and Their Administration in the Pacific States*. Bulletin No. 211. Washington: Government Printing Office, 1917, pp. 46-47.

¹⁵ U.S. Department of Agriculture, *Lumbering in the Sugar and Yellow Pine Region of California*, p. 5.

¹⁶ C. L. Goodrich and Others, *op. cit.*, p. 275; cf. R. W. Murchie and M. E. Jarchow, *Population Trends in Minnesota*. University of Minnesota Agricultural Experiment Station Bulletin 327 (February, 1937), p. 86.

¹⁷ Reports of the Immigration Commission, *Immigrants in Industry*. 61st Congress, 2nd Session, Senate Document 633. Washington: Government Printing Office, 1911, III: 343-346; *Sixteenth Biennial Report of the Bureau of Labor of the State of California, 1913-14*, p. 74.

¹⁸ Thirteenth Census of the United States, 1910, Vol. IV, *Population*, pp. 435-534; *Abstract of Reports of Immigration Commission*. 61st Congress, 3rd Session, Senate Document 747. Washington: Government Printing Office, 1911, 1: 664; Thirteenth Census of the United States, 1910, Vol. IX, *Manufactures*, pp. 496-97.

¹⁹ Fifteenth Census of the United States, 1929, Vol. IV, *Population*, pp. 193-195, 1367-1369, 1706-1708.

²⁰ C. Parker, *The Casual Laborer and Other Essays*. New York: Harcourt, Brace and Howe, 1920, p. 113; Rev. J. H. Geohegen, "Exploitation of the Migratory Worker." University of Washington, Seattle, Wash., 1923, p. 23.

²¹ Works Progress Administration, Division of Social Research, *The Migratory-Casual Worker*, by J. N. Webb. Monograph No. VII. Washington: Government Printing Office, 1937, p. 75.

²² C. Parker, *op. cit.*, pp. 91-124; C. Parker, "The I.W.W.," *Atlantic Monthly*, CXX, No. 5 (November, 1917), 621-622; R. G. Tugwell, "The Casual of the Woods," *Survey*, XLIV, No. 14 (July 3, 1920), 472-474; *Report of the President's Mediation Commission to the President of the United States—Unrest in the Lumber Industry*. Washington: Government Printing Office, 1918, pp. 13-15; E. D. Thompson, "The Case of the Lumberjack," *World Outlook*, June, 1920, p. 22.

²³ *Four L Bulletin*, May, June, July, August, November, 1918, June, 1920.

²⁴ See below, p. 129.

[25] *Four L Bulletin,* September, 1920; cf. U.S. Commission on Industrial Relations, p. 4212.

[26] U.S. Commission on Industrial Relations, *op. cit.,* p. 4212 *et passim,* pp. 4185-4191, 4207-4223, 4382-4383.

[27] U.S. Department of Labor, Bureau of Labor Statistics, *Industrial Relations in the West Coast Lumber Industry,* by C. R. Howd. Bulletin No. 349. Washington: Government Printing Office, 1924, p. 42.

[28] *Report of the President's Mediation Commission to the President of the United States—Unrest in the Lumber Industry,* pp. 13, 14.

[29] Rev. J. H. Geohegen, *op. cit.,* p. 9 *et passim;* U.S. Commission on Industrial Relations, *op. cit.,* pp. 4121, 4187; S. H. Holbrook, *Holy Old Mackinaw—A Natural History of the American Lumberjack.* New York: The Macmillan Company, 1939, pp. 194-207.

[30] "Why I Am A Member of the I.W.W.," *Four L Bulletin,* IV, No. 10 (October, 1922), 9.

[31] U.S. Commission on Industrial Relations, *op. cit.,* p. 4319; cf. C. Parker, *op. cit.,* pp. 91-124; F. A. Silcox, *Report of the President's Mediation Commission to the President of the United States—Unrest in the Lumber Industry,* pp. 14, 15.

[32] D. T. Mason, *Timber Ownership and Lumber Production in the Inland Empire.* Portland, Ore.: The Western Pine Manufacturers Association, 1920, p. 81; *Eighth Report of the Bureau of Agriculture, Labor, and Industry of the State of Montana, 1902,* pp. 212-213; U.S. Department of Agriculture, *Lumbering in the Sugar and Yellow Pine Region of California,* pp. 5, 8, 9; U.S. Department of Agriculture, *Logging in the Douglas Fir Region,* pp. 8, 11; C. R. Griffin, "The Short Log Country," *International Socialist Review,* XVII, No. 7 (January, 1917), 422-423.

[33] See below, p. 131.

[34] *Sixteenth Biennial Report of the Bureau of Labor of the State of California, 1913-14,* p. 51.

[35] Eleventh Census of the United States, 1890, *Report on Manufacturing Industries,* Part 3, pp. 624-629.

[36] U.S. Department of Labor, Bureau of Labor Statistics, *Wages and Hours of Labor in the Lumber, Millwork, and Furniture Industries, 1890-1912.* Bulletin No. 129. Washington: Government Printing Office, 1913, p. 26 *et passim;* U.S. Department of Labor, Bureau of Labor Statistics, *Wages and Hours of Labor in the Lumber Industry in the United States, 1928.* Bulletin No. 497. Washington: Government Printing Office, 1929, p. 35 *et passim;* cf. A. Berglund, G. T. Starnes, and F. T. DeVyver, *op. cit.,* pp. 46-47; *Monthly Labor Review,* LXI, No. 3 (September, 1935), 657.

[37] U.S. Department of Agriculture, *Logging in the Douglas Fir Region,* p. 9; *Sixteenth Biennial Report of the Bureau of Labor of the State of California, 1913-14,* pp. 74, 76, 80; *Sixth Biennial Report of the Bureau of Labor Statistics and Factory Inspection of the State of Washington, 1907-08,* p. 5.

[38] U. S. Department of Labor, Bureau of Labor Statistics, *Labor Laws and Their Administration in the Pacific States,* pp. 24-28.

[39] U.S. Department of Labor, Bureau of Labor Statistics, *op. cit.,* pp. 17-19; U.S. Commission on Industrial Relations, *op. cit.,* pp. 4127, 4222; *Sixteenth Biennial Report of the Bureau of Labor of the State of California, 1913-14,* pp. 62, 136; *Seventh Biennial Report of the Bureau of Labor Statistics and Factory Inspection of the State of Washington, 1909-10,* p. 14.

[40] M. D. Kossoris and S. Kjaer, "Causes and Prevention of Accidents in Lumber Manufacture, 1939," *Monthly Labor Review,* LI, No. 3 (September, 1940), 663, 668; M. D. Kossoris and S. Kjaer, "Industrial Injuries in the United States During 1939," *Monthly Labor Review,* LI, No. 1 (July, 1940), 92.

[41] E. P. Kelly, "Costs of Accidents, A Heavy Drain," *West Coast Lumberman,* LXI, No. 5 (May, 1934), p. 24.

[42] U.S. Department of Labor, Bureau of Labor Statistics, *op. cit.,* p. 104; *Sixteenth Biennial Report of the Bureau of Labor of the State of California, 1913-14,* p. 139.

7 *EARLY ORGANIZATIONS IN THE WEST*

Labor relations in the West Coast lumber industry have been marked by many bitterly fought disputes and much ill will and discontentment which did not break out in open struggle. Organization was not always looked to as a solution for the many problems. Irregularity of the work had accustomed the lumberjacks to shifts in employment. An individualistic worker who had grievances simply asked for his time and moved on. The turnover rate for the industry was unusually high. The scattered mills and camps and the constant flux in the labor force in practically all localities militated against permanent organization. Nevertheless, in contrast with other lumbering sections, the West Coast developed a tradition of labor organization. Unions appeared and struggled for life. They were fought ruthlessly by individual employers and by employers' associations, and sometimes succumbed to force or perished for other reasons. Unions have sparred with each other over issues of principle and jurisdiction. They seldom gained a firm foothold on working conditions. Yet, however great the difficulties, the tradition of organization once having taken root has never been eradicated.

Of all the labor organizations, the Industrial Workers of the World was, without doubt, the best-known. Other unions which figured prominently in the earlier years were two A.F. of L. affiliates, the Shingle Weavers and the International Union of Timber Workers. In the minds of many operators any labor organization was I.W.W. but, apart from the ideology of revolution preached by I.W.W. soapbox orators, there was slight difference in the demands of I.W.W. and A.F. of L. unions. There never has been a better illustration of the extent to which the labor movement is a response to environment. The I.W.W. was neither an importation from abroad nor merely the creation of the mind of an "intellectual." In the Northwest it was more or less an indigenous movement. It was a searching on the part of oppressed, downtrodden, "outcast" workmen for some of the natural enjoyments of life which were denied them. It grew out of "a bond of groping fellowship," [1] which led men to the organization, although they did not always understand its philisophy. The A.F. of L. had never offered much directly to industrial as opposed to craft workers, and lumberjacks, who fall in the industrial grouping, often refused A.F. of L. leadership and joined the industrially organized I.W.W. On the other hand, there were many craft-minded workers, particularly in the sawmills and shingle mills, who supported the A.F. of L. unions. Consequently, an intense struggle over the structure of organization between the A.F. of L. unions and the I.W.W. prevailed. It should be noted that the activities of both union groups, except for a slight I.W.W. activity in the upper Columbia River drainage basin, known as the Inland Empire, were confined to the Douglas fir region. In the California pine region, however, there was practically no organization.

Like producers in other regions, the employers often attempted organization for purposes of price and production control. This was to be expected in an industry with a cost structure such as the lumber industry has had, But even in the shingle branch of the industry, which was much more centralized than lumber production, such control rarely succeeded for long. By continued endeavor on the part of a few individuals, however, functioning organizations gradually emerged.

The first meeting of lumbermen ever held in the Northwest was in Tacoma on October 6, 1891. Standards for grading lumber were adopted, but the depression of 1893 killed the association which had been formed. In early 1896 the Seattle Lumber Exchange made its appearance and attempted to bring order into the industry. About the same time, the Puget Sound Timberman's Association was organized to determine demand and limit output. The Seattle Lumber Exchange expanded into the Washington Lumber Exchange, but soon disintegrated. Lumbermen, however, were gradually made to realize the importance of association. Negotiations with the railroads for a reduction in rates on shipping lumber had shown them the value of concerted action. At the same time, they had seen the effectiveness of the organized white pine manufacturers who had worked against them in an association in the matter of rate reductions. In 1901, under the leadership of Victor Beckman, the Pacific Lumber Manufacturers Association took form in Seattle.

About this time, the Southwest Washington Manufacturers Association was also organized and worked along with the P.L.M.A. E. C. Griggs, of the St. Paul and Tacoma Lumber Company, was

elected president of the P.L.M.A., an office he held for ten years. He
had been convinced during the depression of the nineties that low
prices and ruthless competition could only be eliminated by imposing
uniform standards of grades and prices. It was extremely difficult to
accomplish this, however, and in 1911 W. B. Mack, of Aberdeen,
at a meeting of the P.L.M.A., underscored the treachery of fellow
members of the organization. "I don't see a ray of hope. . . . Every
time a price is given," he declared, "some other fellow cuts it. . . .
Everybody seems to be fighting everybody else. . . ." The leaders
in the industry became increasingly aware that a more inclusive
organization was desirable. In 1911 a plan for amalgamation of the
existing associations was worked out. The new organization, the West
Coast Lumber Manufacturers Association, now the West Coast Lumbermen's Association, was to include all the lumber operators of the
merging associations.[2] At present it is composed of approximately
200 producers of Douglas fir lumber in western Washington and
Oregon. The membership produces in the neighborhood of 90 per
cent of the production of Douglas fir lumber.

The P.L.M.A. maintained an effective lobby in the Washington
state legislature. It succeeded in passing a bill limiting liability for
personal injuries to workmen, and worked through the House Committee on Labor to defeat certain "vicious labor measures."[3] One of
these was the "fellow servant" bill, which would have made the
employer responsible for accidents; another required the licensing of
stationary engineers, which was considered as a scheme to unionize
the lumber industry; another made it compulsory to pay wages twice
a month and in coin; and, finally, one bill attempted to fix the
amount to be paid for board in mill and logging camp company
houses.[4] The W.C.L.A. has definitely avoided any activity in the
industrial relations field although it is generally believed to have given
informal advice to members and it has tried to influence labor legislation. As the W.C.L.A., it accepted the services of a detective agency
so that its members could be informed about the work and doctrines
of the I.W.W.[5] The W.C.L.A. supported the 4L during the war and
favored its retention afterward. In the field of labor relations, many
lumber industry employers were members of the Employers Association of Washington, an organization which took in members from the
Columbia River to British Columbia, and as far east as the Cascades.
Individual memberships and factory memberships were sought. Outside of Seattle its strongest center of organization was at Grays
Harbor, although it included from 10 to 80 per cent of the employers

in various other districts. The lumber industry was the best-represented of all employer groups. The object and purpose of the association was to act as "an intelligence bureau on industrial matters; to act as advisor and counsel and to assist with all difficulties or troubles" such as labor disputes and labor legislation.[6] As is to be expected, the activities of this organization were carried on quietly and little is known of them, but the organized workers always had to cope with the association. Another organization of great importance at the time was the Lumbermen's Protective League which was organized to fight the labor organizations during the strike of 1917. Besides working through associations, individual employers have been strongly opposed to organized workers and, on the whole, have been able to resist them.

The earliest union in this section of the industry appeared among the "shingle weavers" about 1890. Because of the nature of their work and the manner in which it was done, this group was fitted to take the lead. Shingle production was relatively more centralized than other activities in the lumber industry,[7] and was carried on by a more or less homogeneous group of craftsmen. Identity of interest and more favorable circumstances for organization than prevailed elsewhere in the lumber industry led the shingle weavers to pioneer in organization. Their progress, however, was not uniform, and their early activities fluctuated with the economic status of the industry. When depression came in 1893, a one-cent reduction per thousand for packing shingles was followed by a strike, which the shingle weavers' union lost. The depression and the strike destroyed the union, and wages for packing shingles dropped to three cents per thousand. After the mid-nineties, economic conditions improved and by 1900, as a result of various local strikes, new unions were formed and the level of wages was raised.[8] In January, 1903, the various Shingle Weavers locals met at a convention in Everett, Washington, and formed the International Shingle Weavers Union of America.

Meanwhile, the shingle producers were continuing in their efforts to control production and to regulate prices. The results were most disheartening because of the undermining influence of cutthroat competition which, at the same time exerted a marked downward pull on wage rates. The solution seemed to lie either in stabilization of industry output or in cost reduction. It would have been easier to achieve the latter if there was no union. In January, 1904, a large mill on Puget Sound tried to cut wages, but the union resisted successfully. In April the operators interested in price maintenance through curtailment of production attempted to get the union to call out its members wherever mills refused to close in accordance with their program. The union declined until the Washington commissioner of labor secured an agreement on wages between mill owners and the union with the understanding that when the price of shingles fell below a certain minimum the mills should close or were to be closed by the union if they failed to stay in line.[9] However, it amounted to nothing, because in June a general reduction in wages was announced, accompanied by discrimination against union labor. The employers, being "banded togther," felt they could "easily replace union men at the cut scale." The opposition to the wage cut led to a lockout at Everett on June 27, and the mills were closed five weeks before reopening at the old scale.[10] The general fight with labor, supplemented by a car shortage, resulted in a curtailment of production and improved prices, a condition which the operators themselves had been unable to accomplish. Significantly enough, the operators, in fighting the union, were trying to destroy the one policing agency which they could use in their attempt to place a floor under competition.

A number of strikes occurred during 1905, but the most important of the early shingle weavers' strikes occurred in 1906 at Ballard. Shingle prices had improved but wages had remained stationary. On April 2, fourteen mills were closed when a demand for wage increases was rejected, but the manufacturers shifted the issue to union recognition by refusing to negotiate. The strike assumed industry-wide significance after the shingle manufacturers met in Seattle on April 25. Here a campaign was outlined and a defense fund of $50,000 was raised to be used against the union at the discretion of the executive committee of the Shingle Mills Bureau, an organization which previously had been formed to control prices of shingles at the mills. This fund was to protect any contributing manufacturer involved in labor troubles, and to provide the Ballard mills with workmen. The assistance given the Ballard employers extended the strike. The union officials contended that the strike would have been won except for the aid the Shingle Mills Bureau organized. In retaliation, a general strike against the 365 mills affiliated with the bureau was called for June 21, but the employers decided to let the strike continue for a time with the hope that it would fail. Later, the strategy of the operators was to open one mill in each center with all the mills cooperating to provide the crew. When this proved effective, the employers decided to put an end to the union once and for all. By the end of July, the union accepted defeat and, at a convention in Tacoma, called the strike off. But within six months the union again demanded higher wages and won them without a struggle because the market for shingles had improved. The employers cared not to make an issue of the demand, inasmuch as recognition was not involved.[11]

During this same period logging and sawmill workers were organizing. In 1905 they received a charter from the A.F. of L., and the International Brotherhood of Woodsmen and Sawmill Workers was born. This union, however, was never vigorous or effective. In 1906 the Royal Loggers, an organization of loggers on Puget Sound, made some headway until the organizer absconded with its funds. Notwithstanding the existence of a "general spirit of unrest," low wages, general complaints about working and living conditions, and victimization by "employment sharks," organization among the workers in the camps and mills was more difficult than among the shingle weavers. This occurred because the former were scattered in remote places and there was a constant movement of workers because of the irregularity of employment.[12]

The I.W.W. appeared on the national labor scene in 1905, and shortly afterward became active in the lumber industry. The rise of this movement centered in the problem of organization of the unskilled and in the relative merits of craft and industrial unionism. The industrial principle appealed to many timber workers, and the I.W.W. appeared to them to be the only potent organization they could enter. In addition, timberworkers were skeptical of officialdom, especially that of the A.F. of L. They were afraid of the kind of trade union official whom Mark Hanna described as the "labor lieutenants of the captains of industry." They felt or suspected that such officials might, and probably would, be disloyal.[13] Many lumber workers wanted a vigorous fighting organization befitting their natures. They were not interested in a "coffin society" only, or a unionism which stressed benefit features, as many A.F. of L. craft unions did.

The I.W.W. gained prominence in the northwestern lumber industry when their organizers took over leadership of a sawmill strike in Portland in March, 1907.[14] A walkout had occurred when twenty-eight chute men struck against an increase of hours to eleven a day, and then included among their demands an increase in the daily wage to $3. The strike spread rapidly, with I.W.W. organizers stepping in and signing practically every striker. Only one of the twelve Portland mills remained open. Strikebreakers were imported from the Puget Sound region at $3.75 per day, but quit when they discovered that a strike was in progress. The state commissioner of labor offered to act as mediator. The offer was accepted by the strikers but was rejected by the mill operators. The Western Federation of Miners sent $20,000 for a strike fund, but this assistance was offset when the Central Labor Council of Portland, affiliated with the A.F. of L., denounced the strike as well as the I.W.W. Shortly after, crews were secured and the mills gradually resumed operations. Naturally, the I.W.W. blamed the A.F. of L. for scabbing. Although the struggle was lost, it brought the I.W.W. to the attention of the workers and the public, and, inasmuch as improvement in wages followed, the I.W.W. was given credit by many workers.

On the national scene the lumberjacks played little part in the earliest internal vicissitudes of the I.W.W. Although organizers had been at work in the industry for three years, it was not until the convention of 1908 that the lumberjacks were well-represented. At this convention held in Chicago, a western delegation led by J. H. Walsh, a national organizer for the I.W.W., numbering twenty men and popularly referred to as the "overall brigade," a group of "red-blooded working stiffs," gave the meetings a purely wage-worker complexion. The men in the group had "beat their way" from Portland, holding propaganda meetings en route.[15] These ill-treated men of the western forests placed little trust in the political weapon because, as migrants, they were often denied the vote. Furthermore, organized politics and the law had always been prejudicial to the men. They were suspicious of political action and parties, since they felt that voting and legislating were methods for deluding workers. To them, different techniques were necessary to meet a ruthless opponent who ruled with a hard fist and an independence that almost kept any idea of co-operation or collective bargaining from sprouting, let alone taking root. These men, who supported the Vincent St. John and W. E. Trautmann faction of the I.W.W., influenced the subsequent philosophy of the Wobblies by driving out "intellectuals," such as Daniel De Leon, and shaping the antipolitical philosophy of the organization.

The organizational activities of the I.W.W. often brought the men face to face with municipal authorities. If organizers were denied the right to speak on the streets, a call was sent out to all "foot-loose working stiffs" that a free speech fight was on. They converged on the city by hundreds and almost literally broke into the jails. Their purpose was to speak, be arrested and crowd the jails, making themselves "guests" of the city and a burden on the taxpayers.[16] Free speech struggles occurred at Missoula, Montana, in October, 1909; in Washington: at Spokane, in November, 1909; at Wenatchee, in May, 1910; at Walla Walla, in June, 1910; at Aberdeen, in November, 1911; at Seattle, in July, 1913; and at Everett in 1916.[17]

A notable I.W.W. strike occurred at Grays Harbor, Washington, in 1912.[18] It had its beginning at Hoquiam, on March 14, and spread rapidly to Aberdeen and Raymond, after the operators had rejected a demand for higher wages. Ten days later, the Aberdeen Trades Council, affiliated with the A.F. of L., refused to endorse the strike. On March 27 a "citizens' committee" was established to find a way of settling the strike. Those who were impatient insisted upon immediate action, and vigilantes were organized "to put down the strike by intimidation and force." The I.W.W. headquarters were raided, the leaders were arrested, and as many of the men as could be rounded up were forced to leave Aberdeen, being "escorted" from the city by vigilantes.[19] At Hoquiam, at the same time, 150 strikers were loaded into boxcars for deportation. But, with the mayor opposing the act, the railway company refused to move the cars, and the men were released. At Raymond 460 deputies were sworn in and about 150 Greek and Finnish workers were shipped out of town. After this the vigilantes followed a program of systematic deportations throughout the area. This, however, did not break the strike. It continued, with the men demanding increased wages, reinstatement of all men, and a preferential union shop. The citizens' committee proposed that the strike be settled on the basis of a minimum wage of $2.25 a day, with preference for American labor and exclusion of all I.W.W. members. This was accepted by the operators, and, because crews were secured, the strike was lost in spite of the fact that the I.W.W. attempted to have it spread to all lumber workers in western Washington. Although mid-April found the I.W.W. still holding officially to its demands, the strike was called off on May 7.[20]

During 1912 and 1913 unionism was at a low ebb in the lumber industry on the West Coast. In the first year the I.W.W. locals were consolidated into the National Union of Forest and Lumber Workers, which was already on the decline. At the national convention in September, 1913, only 640 I.W.W. lumber workers were reported as members, and during 1913 and 1914 the consolidated organization went to pieces. Only a few scattered locals with tiny memberships remained.[21]

Meanwhile, a change in the two A.F. of L. unions was effected. Inasmuch as the early attempts to organize the lumber workers had failed and the Shingle Weavers had managed to hold together, the latter asked for and obtained jurisdiction over the entire lumber industry. In 1913 the International Union of Shingle Weavers, Sawmill Workers and Woodsmen was formed, with J. G. Brown as president. In February, 1914, a demand for the eight-hour day, supported by a threat of a strike on May 1 if the demand was not granted, was vigorously opposed by the employers, who made an aggressive attack on the union and succeeded in operating their mills on an "open-shop" basis. A number of locals asked the executive board to hold a referendum on the strike question. In its stead, a special convention was called which decided to try to secure at the Washington polls in November the enactment of the eight-hour initiated measure. The bill was lost, and the action of the union in threatening a strike and then deciding to trust to political action was the turning point in the union's history. The membership began to fall off. The Shingle Weavers had had their fill of attempting to organize the lumber workers, and in 1916 reorganized themselves on their original basis. Concurrently, the sawmill and camp workers organized into a new union, the International Union of Sawmill and Timber Workers, with E. E. Wieland as president.[22]

The decline of the I.W.W. led to "stocktaking" of its organizing plans and tactics. The I.W.W. had operated through organizing meetings and the formation of locals in the towns in which the lumber workers congregated when out of work. It was hoped that the men would become tied to the local and not to the job. But the isolation of the producing centers and the distances to the camps proved a great disadvantage. A new plan of organization was evolved about 1914; it aimed at the establishment of a few permanent central branches, with a secretary in charge and a delegate on each job to sign up members. The job-delegate system proved effective. If the "bull o' the woods" got "Wobbly horrors" and fired the delegate, or if the delegate quit, it was easy for the I.W.W. to replace him and continue its work.[23]

The vigorous campaign during 1916 to revive the organization among the lumber workers developed stiff opposition at many places. A free speech fight at Everett resulted in a bitter tragedy. The fight followed upon an A.F. of L. Shingle Weavers' strike which began on May 1, 1916, after a failure of the operators to raise wages voluntarily according to the terms of an agreement made a year before. A bitter internal quarrel of long standing had kept the union in turmoil. Although the term was not then current, "quickie" strikes called by I.W.W. sympathizers within the Shingle Weaver local were of common occurrence. The operators were so enraged that they would have nothing to do with any union, which meant a refusal to deal with the A.F. of L. Shingle Weavers. As the strike wore on, I.W.W. leaders decided to secure a hold in Everett to "open up the town" to union organization. The Shingle Weavers, under the leadership of E. P. Marsh, had encountered obstinate resistance from the employers but had not invited the assistance of the I.W.W. I.W.W. meetings had been frustrated and many members had been arrested and deported to Seattle, which led to the resolve to carry on the free speech fight. On October 30, forty-one I.W.W. supporters left Seattle by boat for Everett. There they were met at the dock by sheriff-led vigilantes. After being beaten, the men were taken to the outskirts of town, where they were made to run the gantlet between rows of vigilantes who wielded clubs. Although there were no fatal casualties some of the men were beaten until they were bloody. These were the tactics which open-shop leaders up and down the region were advocating to get rid of the unionists.[24]

A second effort to carry men to Everett in order to assert the union's right to hold meetings was attempted by the I.W.W. when the *Verona,* with 260 men aboard and accompanied by another vessel carrying 39 men, set out from Seattle on November 5, 1916. Sheriff McRae, a former shingle weaver but no longer sympathetic to the union, and bitterly opposed to the I.W.W., received advance word from the Pinkerton agency and lined the dock with 200 armed vigilantes. When the *Verona* was made fast McRae demanded that the leaders be pointed out. This was refused, and upon the sheriff's command ten minutes of shooting followed when the men attempted to disembark, after which the boat backed away. In addition to the five I.W.W. members and two vigilantes killed, thirty-one I.W.W. members and nineteen vigilantes were wounded. The I.W.W. contended that all the shooting was done by the vigilantes whose cross fire from three separate groups struck down all the men hit.[25] The charge that the men on board the ship had guns was never adequately proven.

When the boat returned to Seattle all its occupants were placed under arrest by the police of that city, and seventy-four were held on murder charges. Feeling ran high. Mayor Gill courageously denounced the vigilantes as murderers, ordered improved treatment of the prisoners, and held his position under threat of recall. Both the Seattle Labor Council and the State Federation of Labor denounced the Everett authorities and urged all locals to give support to the I.W.W. The trial of the first defendant resulted in acquittal, after which the other prisoners were released.[26]

The I.W.W. also became active and conducted a significant strike in the waning Lake States lumber industry of Minnesota in December, 1916. The strike started when the mill men of the Virginia Rainey Lake Company demanded the eight-hour day and a 25-cent increase in daily wages. Many lumberjacks in the region, following the example of the sawmill workers, demanded a minimum wage of $40 per month, a nine-hour day, an hour for lunch "to be eaten at camp and not in a snowdrift," paydays every two weeks, and the abolition of the hospital fee.[27]

One operator ridiculed the demand for a payday every two weeks, remarking that the men "want to be able to draw pay at any time as in the past." This employer found "The demand that the men go to and from work in daylight . . . preposterous, and at this time applicable to no lumber camp. The men themselves don't ask for it and would never dream of it." The lumber industry workers received shabby treatment at the hands of the local authorities. On the first day of the strike I.W.W. leaflet distributors were arrested, but were released after being warned. On the following day the local newspaper intimated that the strike was petering out and offered as proof of this fact that "Not a man was arrested last night," which implied that such a development was unusual. On January 2 a number of men "of the I.W.W. type" were arrested, although no charge was preferred against them until the following day.[28]

The guardsmen employed by the operators had, for the most part, had experience on the range the previous summer, and were a tough lot. Slowly the operators secured men from the camps and operations were gradually resumed because "drastic measures . . . [had] been successful in handling the rebels in the woods." It was also reported that the "police are making it uncomfortable" for the I.W.W. Two armed guards were stationed at each camp and it was reported that this "had a wholesome effect." [29] The strike was finally decisively broken but brought about a temporary improvement in wages and living conditions.

In the West the labor dispute of 1917 was the most spectacular and all-embracing controversy that had taken place in the lumber industry up to that time. This conflict provides a key to the understanding of the labor problems of the western industry for several years. It was typical of the industry in so far as the handling of union men was concerned, but it was unique in the tactics finally employed and in the eventual outcome. Vigorous organizing work had been carried on by both I.W.W. and A.F. of L. unions. Of the two factions the

I.W.W. was numerically stronger. Neither union, however, had pushed formal organization very far, but support of union principles extended far beyond the actual membership. The I.W.W. had 3,000 members and had in addition an even larger number of supporters. The two A.F. of L. unions, the Shingle Weavers and the Timber Workers, had approximately 2,500 members between them. Because prices of lumber had improved during 1916 and the first part of 1917, leaders in both I.W.W. and A.F. of L. groups thought the time was ripe to make a determined effort to secure improved living conditions and a shorter workday.

The I.W.W. centered its initial efforts in the Inland Empire, while the A.F. of L. unions centered theirs in the fir region. The I.W.W. met in convention in Spokane on March 5 and 6, 1917, and formed the Lumber Workers Industrial Union. A set of demands for the pine region, which the convention drew up, included better living conditions in the camps, the eight-hour day, higher wages, and union recognition. July 1 was the strike date set. In May the Shingle Weavers met in convention and instructed the executive board to endeavor to secure the eight-hour day by conference and, if this failed, to call a special convention for June 30. The employers flatly refused, and the special convention was called, and fixed July 16 as the strike date. The International Union of Timber Workers met in convention on June 6 and drew up a set of demands calling for a minimum wage of $3 for eight hours in the mills and $3.50 for nine hours in the camps, better conditions, union recognition, the closed shop, and greater freedom from employer control at the camps in matters not directly related to the work. The union insisted upon a conference with the employers by July 12, and also set July 16 as the day for the strike if the demands were not granted. The Timber Workers and the Shingle Weavers were planning their activities together.[30]

Instead of meeting with the unions, the employers met in Seattle on July 9, decided to fight, and formed the Lumbermen's Protective Association to resist the union demands. The association agreed to raise a strike fund of $500,000 and to fine any member $500 per day for operating less than ten hours per shift. The new organization resolved "that the establishment of an 8-hour day in the lumber industry at this time when production in all manufacturing industries must be maintained at the maximum is impossible, and that employers therein hereby pledge themselves unequivocally to maintain a 10-hour day for the purpose of maintaining the maximum production in the lumber industry."[31] The operators inconsistently linked their cause with national defense welfare while refusing mediation efforts of federal and state officials. The unions, meanwhile, were willing to accept mediation.

During the spring trouble had broken out on the log drives in Idaho and Montana, and persisted and spread in spite of company interference, suppression by local authorities, and prevention of picketing by state troops. The I.W.W. strike had originally been set for July 1, but the impatience of the men made the strike pretty general before that time. Violence and terrorism were, as might be expected, quite common.[32]

As the A.F. of L. strike plans for the fir region reached maturity, the I.W.W. leaders met and discussed the strike proposition just prior to the customary shutdown over the Fourth of July. They were not inclined to spread their strike to the fir region. In accordance with their conclusions, notices were sent to all members on July 9 to the effect that no strike had been called. The men were cautioned not to "fall for the bunk" of a Timber Workers' strike. Almost immediately afterward this action was rescinded when job delegates arrived in town and revealed the true feelings of the lumber workers. It was obvious that all men in the camps would go out with the Timber Workers on July 16. Jumping the gun, in order to take credit for the strike, the job delegates hurriedly returned to the camps on July 13 and informed the men that a strike was under way. Three days later the A.F. of L. unions struck as planned. The strike spread rapidly, and it is probable that forty to fifty thousand men were idle at the start. By August 1, not more than 15 per cent of the mills on the West Coast were running. The employers claimed that 75 per cent of the men were idle only because of intimidation. This is not true. Membership in the I.W.W. and A.F. of L. unions grew rapidly once the strike was under way, although the precise number of men in the unions is not known. It has been estimated that over twenty thousand men actively supported the strike, and there is little evidence of worker intimidation. As the strike developed, all other demands gave way to that for the eight-hour day, and the struggle was fought out primarily on that issue, with recognition, of course, a subordinate but significant issue.[33]

The strike took on added importance when ship carpenters on Grays Harbor refused to handle lumber from ten-hour mills late in July and when the suspension of production jeopardized the supply of lumber for the Camp Lewis cantonment. Reverberations of the struggle resounded in the halls of Congress when Senators Poindexter of Washington, Myers of Montana, and King of Utah vigorously condemned the I.W.W. and advocated the use of military force to drive them out. Other senators held that, even if the charges were true, it was a matter for the local authorities and not the federal government. Military force was not used largely because Senator Borah opposed it.[34] The government, however, did use troops from Camp Lewis to protect mills which were cutting lumber for the camp. Secretary of War Baker and Governor Lister of Washington urged employers to grant the eight-hour day. The governor even issued a proclamation calling upon employers to concede the eight-hour day. This they refused, most of them bitterly resenting what they regarded as unwarranted interference in the strike. The sentiment of many operators was voiced editorially by the *American Lumberman,* which declared that "it is really pitiable to see the government . . . truckling to a lot of treasonable, anarchistic agitators . . . playing into the hands of our enemy and doing tremendously more harm to the allied cause than the German army is doing. . . . With a little firmness . . . the situation could be relieved."[35] As the strike wore on, a fair number of mills—none members of the Lumbermen's Protective Association—conceded the eight-hour day and resumed operations. Many, however, were almost immediately forced back onto the ten-hour day by the pressure of the Loggers Association, which refused to allow members to supply logs to eight-hour mills.

By the first of September the I.W.W. leaders became worried that there might be a stampede back to work and, following a referendum of the men, transferred their fight to a "strike on the job." Exactly what the referendum revealed is not known, because its results were never made public. The Shingle Weavers and Timber Workers decided not to call the strike off until the eight-hour day was universal, but did permit their men to return to work. After this the two A.F. of L. unions played inconsequential roles.[36]

Carrying the strike to the job was a significant tactical move. The I.W.W. leaders reasoned that it was impossible to finance the strike any longer; that by staying away from the jobs they left them open to scabs; that with the continuance of arrests the most active leaders would all be in jails. On the other hand, by transferring the strike to the job the struggle could be continued. Instead of being hungry on the picket line, the men could draw their pay and have the operators finance the struggle.

Because of the methods used to thwart the strike, a sullen spirit prevailed among the men. Instead of doing a day's work they practiced "conscientious withdrawal of efficiency," shifted frequently from job to job, and in some cases engaged in sabotage. But attempts to run down acts of criminal sabotage on the part of the I.W.W. proved fruitless.[37]

There was evidence, however, that individual members did resort to such practices as driving spikes in logs to break saws, wasting materials through careless work, and the like.[38] The procedures for slowing down production varied. Sometimes a crew would go out to a job, work a few days on a ten-hour basis, and after the boss had gone to some expense in provisioning his mess house and getting started, the men would quit at the end of eight hours. Usually the whole crew would be fired. A new crew might repeat the performance —a foreman thought he had the worst crew in the world until he got the next. In other cases, an operator would have a full crew except for fallers, of which, perhaps, he had only half enough, and the I.W.W. would try to make sure that he did not get more. The employer thus was carrying practically a full crew but was getting only a restricted output. In addition, turnover was tremendous.[39]

The operators were baffled by the problem of meeting these tactics. They found it far easier to take men off the picket line and jail or deport them. The leaders were now difficult to find, and when the workers changed the rules, because they were denied the right to bargain, and carried the strike to the job, the employers did not know how to respond. Senator Borah remarked that

the I.W.W. are about as elusive a proposition as you ever ran up against . . . it is almost impossible to deal with them. . . . You cannot destroy the organization. That is an intangible proposition. It is something that you cannot get at. You cannot reach it. You do not know where it is, it is not in writing. It is not in anything else. It is a simple understanding between men, and they act upon it without any evidence of existence whatever.[40]

In view of the constant charges against the I.W.W. of treasonable conspiracy, President Woodrow Wilson sent his Mediation Commission, composed of W. B. Wilson as chairman, Felix Frankfurter as secretary, J. L. Spangler, E. P. Marsh, and J. H. Walker, to investigate and, if possible, to restore peace in the lumber industry. The chief achievement of the commission lay in the report it submitted. The investigations showed that loyalty or disloyalty to the government was frequently confused with the willingness or unwillingness of workers to accept conditions of employment dictated by employers themselves. The commission revealed that the operators took advantage of the popular prejudice against the I.W.W. as an unpatriotic organization to break not only the strike but all the unions. Of course, the I.W.W. and the operators were unwilling to enter into time agreements, but the A.F. of L. unions were. The failure to remedy the evils of the industry was ascribed to the attitude of the operators by the commission, which declared:

This uncompromising attitude on the part of the employers has reaped for them an organization of destructive rather than constructive radicalism. The I.W.W. is filling the vacuum created by the operators. . . . The hold of the I.W.W. is riveted instead of weakened by unimaginative opposition on the part of employers to the correction of real grievances. . . . The greatest difficulty in the industry is the tenacity of the old habits of individualism.

In similar language the uncompromising stand against the eight-hour day was condemned in view of the fact that the lumber industry was "almost the only industry on the coast" in which it did not prevail. "In truth we cannot escape the conviction that with too many opposition . . . has become a matter of pride instead of judgment, a reluctance to yield after having defeated the strike." [41]

As the autumn wore on, the production situation became a matter of grave concern because of the need for spruce for airplane construction. "Owing to labor conditions in the woods," the shipments of spruce were less than half the required ten million feet per month. Early in October, Colonel Bryce P. Disque was sent to the West to investigate conditions. Out of his visit emerged the 4L, the Loyal Legion of Loggers and Lumbermen. Ostensibly, it was a "creation" of the government through the War Department. The popular view that the plan of organization was originally conceived by Colonel Disque [42] is to be questioned. Some time before the War Department had occasion to step in, plans were devised for controlling both sides of the industry. Labor men always felt that the employers had created the 4L. At a conference of "12 or 15 of the leading employers of the West Coast . . . one of the loggers suggested" to Colonel Disque "that the Government organize a patriotic organization of some kind, a 'loyal legion' to line up the workers behind the Government program," and "this suggestion was enthusiastically received by the other employers and by Colonel Disque." [43] These statements may be true enough, yet, as a matter of fact, they do not tell the whole story, because the plans were formulated by leading lumber operators "long before Colonel Disque had been heard of." [44] The plans were submitted to Secretary of War Newton D. Baker, who approved them.

They were also approved by the Secretary of Labor and Samuel Gompers.[45]

The 4L commonly was referred to as "a fifty-fifty" organization in which employees and employers were equally represented. In its inception it was not really a representative organization, for it was born under the cloak of patriotism with the authority of the War Department giving it the breath of life. All members, employer as well as employee, were required to sign a pledge which was described as "one of Uncle Sam's long-range guns" and as the "weapon" with which Colonel Disque was "bombing pro-Hunism out of the Northwest forests." It read:

I, the undersigned, in consideration of my being made a member of the Loyal Legion of Loggers and Lumbermen, do hereby solemnly pledge my efforts during this war to the United States of America, and will defend and support this country against enemies, both foreign and domestic.

I further agree, by these presents, to faithfully do my duty toward this country by directing my best efforts in every possible way to the production of logs or lumber for the construction of Army Airplanes and Ships to be used against our common enemies. That I will stamp out any sedition or acts of hostility against the United States Government which may come within my knowledge, and I will do every act and thing which will in general aid in carrying this war to a successful conclusion.[46]

In the organizing drive anti-German propaganda literally flooded the woods. "Agitators" who promoted strife were held to be aides of the Kaiser. Stories of how American airplanes constructed of spruce were flying over the Huns were spread to build patriotism and morale. Flagpoles were set up in each camp around which night and morning ceremonies were employed to instill patriotic sentiment. Emphasis was placed upon the development of a feeling that lumbering "though 6,000 miles from the firing line was not inferior soldiering."

. . . And while the rifle and bayonet and the smoke and the shock and the fiery glory of the battle field would be welcome to most of these soldiers in the silent woods, they will have a splendid part in the victory when it comes. And it is coming—with the toot of the spruce locomotive and the crash of the falling trees and the shriek of the saws and the long trains of clean, clear spruce that builds the battle fleets of the air, the war eagles that carry the glad tiding of freedom to all the world.[47]

The first 4L local was organized on November 30, 1917. Organization proved easy. By the end of the year there were ten thousand members in over three hundred locals, and by April there were seventy thousand mmbers. At the request of employers in the Inland Empire, who reasoned that pine was largely a war material, the organization was extended and soon numbered over one hundred thousand members. The lumber industry was divided into districts, with a commissioned officer detailed to each one. At first, the only official in the local was a secretary appointed by the officer in charge. Later, this official was elected from among the workers.[48]

To supplement the labor supply and augment production, soldier labor was brought in, but not intentionally to take the place of civilian workmen. The soldiers were used only on "cost plus" operations, and the soldier labor was not turned over directly to the operators. The Spruce Production Division was formed, through which the soldiers were sent to the mills and camps which had a labor shortage. Many people felt that the presence of the soldier had a beneficial, psychological effect on the civilian logger because "it obfuscated the disloyal and anarchistic tendency, and bolstered up and supported the loyal men."[49] The soldiers in the woods received the going wage, minus their army pay, with an additional deduction for the army ration allowance at the rate of $7.35 a week. This method of payment was maintained in spite of the protest that the "sprucers" were being favored over the men in the trenches. Had this not been done, actual conscription of labor would have existed and the civilian workmen would have complained bitterly against unfair competition. Colonel Disque established a maximum wage which was designed to stop the bargaining for labor which had greatly accentuated an already bad turnover problem.

The mere presence of soldiers, however, was not adequate to settle the "labor problem." Poor working conditions and ill treatment of workers were the problems to be solved. Colonel Disque operated on the assumption that the men would respond to fair treatment coupled with the plea to support the government, which they did. Meanwhile, conditions were immeasurably improved, because military standards had to be met in all camps wherever there were soldiers, and other camps had to follow suit.[50]

Finding a solution to the eight-hour day question posed a difficult problem. Although some employers in the Douglas fir region had granted it, many who might have granted it held back because of fear of disrupting the Lumbermen's Protective Association. The majority, moreover, still believed it was an economic impossibility to operate successfully on an eight-hour basis. In the Inland Empire the lumbermen voted to establish the eight-hour day, but later rescinded their action on the ground that it was an individual matter. At a meeting in Portland with Colonel Disque on February 27, 1918, the employers became deadlocked over the question and decided to leave the matter in his hands. He ruled that the eight-hour day was essential to the settlement of the labor difficulties. Several companies, however, had to be compelled to observe it. At the same meeting a resolution was adopted expressing complete confidence in Colonel Disque and pledging support for any action he might take. At a later meeting with the representatives of the employees on March 4, the same confidence was voted. Similar meetings were held in the Inland Empire. Following this accedence to authority, a set of regulations was issued by Colonel Disque on March 10, in which he stated, "Strict compliance of operators and employees is enjoined." Chief among the regulations was the adoption of the eight-hour day with time and one-half for overtime. In addition, a uniform charge of $7.35 a week for board was established. Also, employers furnishing housing accommodations were required "at the earliest practicable date to supply clean bedding [mattresses, pillows, blankets, sheets, and pillow slips] to all men" with a weekly change of sheets and pillow slips at a charge of $1.00 a week. Strict compliance was to be assured by making it unpatriotic to fail.[51]

Up to the middle of 1918 Colonel Disque and his staff had decided all policies and settled all problems. But the size of the organization imposed too great a burden. It was decided that changes in organization were necessary, and employer and employee conferences were held. The employers, on July 19, endorsed the open shop, the eight-hour day, the method of conference for settling disputes, a permanent body composed of employers and employees to consider all questions, and supreme control for Colonel Disque for the duration of the war. The employees, in convention on August 5, decided to have each local elect a committee of three to confer with the employer on all questions. In addition, districts were marked out and the delegates from each met separately and elected district councils of three members who were to sit with three employers appointed by Colonel Disque. From each of these councils one employer and one employee were selected to sit on the board of directors. Eight districts in the Douglas fir region and four in the Inland Empire made a total of twelve, with a board of twenty-four members.[52]

The newly formed 4L board of directors met on August 19 for its first meeting, adopted a constitution, accepted the existing operating principles. They also provided that all complaints as to violations had to be supported by some tangible evidence, after which an investigation was to be made and the accused given a chance to controvert the findings. The nature and purposes of the organization were set forth in these words of the constitution:

. . . to promote a closer relationship between the employer and the employee . . . to standardize and coordinate working conditions; to improve the living environment in the camps and mills; to infuse a spirit of patriotism in the lumber workers during the present national crisis; to stimulate the production of lumber for war purposes and stamp out sedition and sabotage in the Pacific Northwest.

The Loyal Legion of Loggers and Lumbermen is not a labor union in the common acceptance of that term, but is purely a patriotic association. . . . It has not and will not countenance the use of any of the facilities at its command for either the organization or disruption of legitimate labor unions nor is it to be considered dual or antagonistic to any existing legitimate labor union.[53]

While the 4L was solidifying its position, divergent views on the lumber industry situation came from two A.F. of L. sources. At the annual convention of the A.F. of L., convened in St. Paul in the summer of 1918, the lumber industry situation was referred to without animosity, and partial credit for establishment of the eight-hour day was taken.[54] On the other hand, the Washington State Federation of Labor, rejecting the 4L constitution at its meeting in Aberdeen, June 26, attacked Colonel Disque and the 4L as enemies of labor. In addition, following the Aberdeen convention, the Timber Workers resumed organizational activities. Unionists in the region looked upon the 4L with misgivings. They became alarmed and opposed it when uniformed men broke up meetings of the Timber Workers. Colonel Disque denied responsibility for such acts, but did nothing to stop them except to advise the unionists to suspend organization activities until after the war. Finally, the complaints of the Timber Workers reached the ears of Samuel Gompers, who engaged in a long discussion with the Secretary of War. Before anything materialized from their interchanges the war came to a close.[55]

When hostilities ceased, the question of the future of the 4L was raised. The West Coast Lumbermen's Association urged that it continue, but sentiment among the employers was divided. While a referendum among the 4L locals indicated that only 20 per cent were in opposition to the continuation of the 4L, the Timber Workers claimed the favorable showing resulted from the use of open voting with employer representatives present. To decide the fate of the organization, 4L conventions met in Portland and Spokane on December 6 and 9. Votes were practically "unanimous" for continuance of the 4L, with Colonel Disque being retained as president.[56] The 4L became a unique organization, a "company union" industry-wide in its scope.

A new constitution, preserving the general lines of the old, was framed, except for changes induced by the ending of the war.[57] Its objectives were declared to be the establishment of "the basic principles of the 'square deal'" by providing a common ground for employer and employee; to insure the worker an equitable wage and maximum efficiency to the employer; "to maintain the basic eight-hour day"; to "standardize" conditions; to promote various welfare activities; to "co-operate with legislative bodies"; "to institute and maintain, when feasible, employment service"; and to build patriotism. These were no different from its earlier declared goals. Jurisdiction of the organization was restricted to "the lumber districts of Oregon, Washington, Idaho, and Montana," and it was not extended to California until a later date. Membership was open to any individual in the lumber industry if he were a citizen or had declared his intention of becoming such, provided he had not been a draft evader. Each member had to sign an elaborate pledge:

I, the undersigned, firmly convinced that the best interests of both employer and employee in the lumber industry are conserved by the principles set forth in the constitution and by-laws of the Loyal Legion of Loggers and Lumbermen; and that the great principles of democracy upon which the United States was established and upon which it must continue, are based upon the mutual co-operation which is the foundation of the Loyal Legion of Loggers and Lumbermen; do solemnly promise and vow that I will, to the utmost of my ability, seek to promote a closer relationship between the employers and employees of the industry; to standardize and co-ordinate working conditions; to improve the living environment in camps and mills; to promote the spirit of co-operation and mutual helpfulness among the workers and operators, as a patriotic endeavor looking toward the welfare of all; to build up the efficiency of the industry for the prosperity of every individual connected therewith; and to stamp out anarchy and sabotage wherever I may find it.

Anyone who went on strike or walked off the job without using the facilities of the 4L was subject to a fine. The initiation fee was one dollar and dues were twenty-five cents a month, plus local dues. The employer matched all employee payments. In addition, the operators were required to deposit "a surety bond or certified check for the term of one year, subject to renewal at the expiration of that period, in the sum of $2.50 for each employee, computed on the basis of the average number of employees, no bond to be in amount less than $100." This was to be a guarantee of good faith and compliance subject to forfeiture in the event of failure to comply with any decision of the board, provided ample opportunity for hearing had been given.

The settlement of local disputes was left to a committee of employees meeting in conference with the employer. If they failed to agree, the dispute was taken to the district board, then to the board of directors where the president was permitted to cast the deciding vote in case of a tie. An appeal could be made to arbitration, which was to be final.

Many companies refused to support the peacetime 4L. When the war ended there were 1,001 locals with 79,591 members. By February 28, 1919, according to Colonel Disque, only 17,000 members in 261 locals had paid dues. At the close of 1919 the 4L claimed 33,948 new members for the year, but the average membership was only 16,703. Although 10,572 new members were added during 1920, the average membership during that year came to only 17,733. Then, in the depression year of 1921, the average dropped to 8,777, with a recovery in 1922 to around 10,000, at which figure it was stabilized during the twenties.[58]

Although "the substantial employers" clung to the organization in the hope "to standardize the employment problem in the industry," most employers were indifferent to the 4L and were opposed to any worker association. Colonel Disque pointed out that "the difficulties being experienced . . . are not in securing employee members, but in the securing of employer members. Where we have reached to date the employees have joined in almost every plant 100 per cent, but of approximately 800 operators less than 300 have agreed to join the organization." With the employees, it was the skilled sawmill workers who generally supported the 4L. If the company chose to belong then the workers became members, but if the company chose not to belong there was little chance for the employees to bring it into the organization.[59]

A more direct type of opposition came from the Timber Workers and the I.W.W. Their previously guarded antagonisms came into the open once the war was ended. Both rival organizations made more emphatic attacks on what they considered the enemy of labor. Indicative of worker opposition to the 4L was the I.W.W. revival. In May, 1919, the members in the Lumber Workers Industrial Union amounted to 4,500. By May, 1921, 15,000 were claimed on the basis of convention votes, although the figure was probably padded considerably. The Timber Workers also attempted to revive their organization. In March, 1918, following the disastrous results of the 1917 strike, the Timber Workers and Shingle Weavers amalgamated as the International Union of Timber Workers. At the time of amalgamation, there were only 203 shingle weaver and 2,324 timber worker members. The year 1918 had been a difficult one for this new union, and it was fortunate to be able to maintain an average membership of 2,500. In 1919 the membership increased to over 8,000.[60] Here, then, were two nuclei of opposition to the numerically reduced 4L.

At the same time, what belief there was in Colonel Disque's professed loyalty to labor was largely shattered because of his shortsighted utterances concerning the Seattle "general strike" of 1919. He referred to it as "a knockout blow to one-sided industrial relations organizations" led by "a minority" of "foreign anarchists," who were attempting "to commit a colossal robbery," by engineering "a Bolsheviki reign of terror." As a matter of fact, the Seattle general strike was conducted by "business unions" for business purposes, and was a decidedly orderly, nonrevolutionary affair.[61]

The functioning of the 4L never matched its ideal, formal structure. Professing fairness, the organization, without doubt, made the worker more passive because of the joint membership. On the other hand, it made the employer more dominant and actually possessed many undemocratic features. The ultimate disposition of all important questions resided in the board of directors, and if the employer withdrew, for whatever cause, the local collapsed. Thus the workers had no power to keep the individual employer in line.

Harmony within the 4L was a fiction, and so, too, was the system of peaceably solving industrial disputes. Admittedly, there were fewer strikes, because the 4L did not tolerate them. The few strikes that occurred were not at 4L plants. The unrest, so typical in the industry, was not wholly or wholesomely removed. The workers continued suspicious of the 4L, which even betrayed itself upon occasion. Notable among its failures was its inability to handle the wage problem in the interests of the worker and the industry.

In 4L literature much was said about "the minimum wage scale" and the "going wage." The "maximum wage" set up during the war, something not found in any other industry, had been removed early in 1919. It was the duty of the board of directors to determine the minimum wage for camps and mills. The going wage was a matter for men and management to decide through conference, although in practice it was customary for district boards to set the going wage for their districts. When the war ended, wages had been generally at the maximum, which was 50 cents per hour in the mills and 55 cents per hour in the camps for unskilled workers. In the spring of 1919 there was a general "unofficial" cut of from 5 to 10 cents per hour. The board of directors, however, raised the minimum rates by 5 cents per hour to 45 and 50 cents, respectively, for mills and camps. Later in the year the minimum was made 50 cents in mills as well, while six months later wages were increased 5 cents.

No serious difficulties developed until the full advent of the depression late in 1920. Wages had been reduced to the minimum scales, while action was taken against some companies for violation of the minima. Pressure for wage reduction grew among employers. On December 20, the board of directors made a flat reduction of 10 cents per hour. A further reduction was blocked in March, when employee representatives proved to the employer representatives that lumber industry wage rates had been reduced much more than those in any other industry. But the situation grew acute when many employers gave notice of withdrawal from the 4L. The upshot was another cut in the rate on June 1, approved by the board of directors, leaving the minimum at 37½ cents.[62]

The depression played havoc with the 4L. Its membership fell off and previously loyal workers lost faith in its ability to cure the malicious, senseless wage-cutting evil which had so often plagued the industry. The operators chose the easy way to gain competitive advantage or economic "salvation"—by putting the burden on the worker through cutting wages. Dr. Norman Coleman, who had succeeded Colonel Disque as president of the 4L, emphasized the futility of this approach, but to little avail.[63]

Very damaging to industrial relations in the lumber industry was the tragic Centralia massacre. The causes of this tragedy, the fact that it could occur, and the aftermath constitute a black chapter in the history of the lumber industry. It was largely a product of war hysteria, but it was also a spectacular climax to a long sequence of events which reach back into the roots of labor relations in the industry.[64] As early as the autumn of 1916, in a manner all too typical of many communities in the area, a committee of Centralia townspeople had carried a group of I.W.W. members to the county line, where they were told never to return.[65] Nevertheless, the I.W.W. "brazenly" opened a hall in 1917, which was raided by "a group of businessmen" during a Red Cross parade in May, 1918. The building in which the office was located was practically demolished. In June, 1919, a group of businessmen, in broad daylight, raided a newsstand operated by a blind news agent, Tom Lassiter. His stand and literature were destroyed because it had been his custom while distributing the Seattle *Union Record,* an A.F. of L. publication, to slip I.W.W. literature between the leaves. Lassiter was taken out of town and "warned" against his undesirable activities. The Seattle *Union Record* protested vigorously against the treatment of its agent, but no one was ever prosecuted for this illegal behavior.[66]

In June, 1919, G. F. Russell, secretary of the Washington Employers Association and president of a local lumber company, called a group of businessmen together in the Chamber of Commerce. At this meeting the Citizens Protective League was formed and F. B. Hubbard, president of the Eastern Railway and Lumber Company, was selected to lead the organization. Its declared purpose was to deal with the I.W.W.[67]

In September the I.W.W. had the effrontery to open another hall, which resulted in calling the Citizens Protective League together on the night of October 20 with the newspaper-announced objective of getting rid of the Wobblies. Plans were discussed at length and the leader of the league was reported to have become "highly incensed when the Centralia Chief of Police informed the gathering that the I.W.W. had a legal right to remain in Centralia." The local commander of the American Legion, William Scales, expressed his belief that, while he was opposed to a raid, no jury would convict men who led it. When a trade union representative refused to serve on a committee to oust the I.W.W., a committee could not be appointed in open session, and "it was agreed to appoint a secret committee." Whether this committee was set up is not known.[68]

A raid was expected by the I.W.W., and Mrs. J. G. McAllister, who owned the hotel in which the I.W.W. hall was located, appealed to the police for protection of her property—she knew what had happened to the I.W.W. hall in May, 1918. In addition, Elmer Smith, the I.W.W. attorney, made a trip to Olympia to seek protection from the governor. Moreover, about a week after the meeting of the Citizens Protective League, the I.W.W. distributed leaflets from house to house which declared:

To the Citizens of Centralia We Must Appeal

To the law-abiding citizens of Centralia and to the working class in general.

We beg of you to read and carefully consider the following:

The profiteering class of Centralia have of late been waving the flag of our country in an endeavor to incite the lawless element of our city to raid our hall and club us out of town. For this purpose they have inspired editorials in the Hub, falsely and viciously attacking the I.W.W., hoping to gain public approval for such revolting criminality. These profiteers are holding numerous secret meetings to that end, and covertly inciting returned service men to do their bidding.[69]

On Armistice Day, 1919, a parade was held under the auspices of the American Legion. The line of march was announced. Twice it was to pass the I.W.W. hall. Anticipating a raid and believing they had a right to defend their property, Britt Smith, secretary of the local I.W.W., Wesley Everest, Ray Becker, James McInerny, and others were gathered in the hall. Loren Roberts, Bert Bland, and Ole Hanson were stationed on Seminary Hill to the east. O. C. Bland and John Lamb were in the Arnold Hotel and "John Doe" Davis was in the Avalon Hotel on the opposite side of the street. As the parading Centralia legionnaires reached the hall the second time, they stopped in front of it. Shortly after, shooting began—whether before or after the attack on the hall has been in dispute. Some people testified that the paraders marked time, and others that a rush was made on the hall. In the affray that followed, three legionnaires were killed, W. O. Grimm, A. McElfresh, and B. Casagranda. Others were wounded. Great excitement followed during which the hall and its contents were destroyed, while all the I.W.W. men found were placed under arrest.

One I.W.W. war-veteran member, Wesley Everest, who had done considerable shooting from the hall, escaped through a rear door of the building only to be pursued by legionnaires. Brought to bay on the bank of the Skookumchuck River, he shot Dale Hubbard, the leader of his pursuers. But he was soon overpowered, beaten, and led to jail with a strap around his neck, barely escaping lynching.[70]

That night a lynching did occur. The town lights were turned off while a crowd entered the jail and took a man supposed to be Britt Smith. Near the outskirts of town the man was brutally maltreated and hanged to a bridge over the Chehalis River. The next morning the Centralia papers told of the lynching of Britt Smith. And not until Smith was captured during the day was it discovered that Everest had been the victim. The body hung on the bridge until someone cut the rope the next day, dropping it into the shallow water where it lay for some hours. Afterwards it was taken to the jail and placed in sight of the other prisoners. No undertaker would care for the body, and it was buried at night without services by four jailed I.W.W. members, accompanied by a squad of armed guardsmen.[71]

Suspicion and fear contributed to the tenseness which pervaded the atmosphere of Centralia. Placards were mounted in shop windows:

Have you any information of the whereabouts of an I.W.W.?

Any person or persons having information, no matter of how little importance, concerning the whereabouts of a member of the I.W.W. or any information whatever concerning the outrage on Armistice Day will confer a favor on the city officials if they will call at once at the city hall and give whatever data they have to the chief of police.

All information will be treated strictly confidential.

Office open at 8:30. Come at once.

The American Legion, which was strongly influenced by the lumber interests of the community, took over the law-enforcing function with the justification that it wished to avoid further lawlessness. The Centralia *Chronicle* asserted that, "to even sympathize with the perpetrators of the tragedy is proof evident that the sympathizer is a traitor to his country." A reflection of the current hysteria lay in the arrest of the editor, the president, and the secretary of the board of directors of the Seattle *Union Record,* and the closing of the press on the ground that it published an unpatriotic editorial which violated the Espionage Act. This editorial read:

DON'T SHOOT IN THE DARK
Violence begets violence
Anarchy calls forth anarchy

That is the answer to the Centralia outrage. And the reason for it is found in the constant stream of laudation in the kept press of un-American, illegal and violent physical attacks upon the person of those who disagree with the powers that be.

The rioting which culminated in the death of three or four returned ex-service men at Cer alia last night was the result of a long series of illegal acts by these men themselves—acts which no paper in the state was American enough to criticize except the Union Record. . . .[72]

Contrast the tone of this statement with the frantic assertions in the extra edition of its bulletin which the 4L published. Under the heading "Centralia Affair Makes Issue Clear" was given a rabid account of the tragedy which patriotically lauded the parade and declared:

It chances that their [the company of legionnaires] temporary halt comes opposite the headquarters which bear the significant letters, I.W.W.

There is nothing in the moment to presage an eventuality. . . .

It was not murder. It was not an attack on the American government. It was monumentally worse than either of these crimes. . . . It is rebellion. It is treason. . . . It was an attack upon society. It holds every man who went at his country's bequest to risk his life, in utter contempt. It spits in the face of every mother who gave her son that democracy might be safe. It holds up to derision the American nation and every individual who claims its protection. . . .

It was not simply an attack on the American government. . . . These were not bodies of troops under arms. . . . These were a company of free men, exercising the right of free assemblage for purposes undeniably worthy and noble. It was an attack on American sentiment, American honor, American traditions of right and wrong; on American ideals of freedom, democracy and fair dealings.

In an entirely different tone the lynching was referred to as "the rough and ready justice of the old-time Vigilance Committee. But it was justice." [73]

Eleven members of the I.W.W. were charged with murder—those not accused of the actual shooting being indicted on a charge of conspiracy to kill. The defense sought a change of venue and the trial was moved to Montesano in Grays Harbor County, which, of course, did not satisfy the defense because public feeling ran high there. A request for a second change of venue was denied in spite of evidence of the widespread distribution of a circular which read in part as follows:

No outrage since the World War has so thoroughly aroused public indignation as this ruthless slaughter of four heroes . . . struck down by members of a traitorous organization. . . . If at their trial their guilt is proven beyond doubt, and this guilt is practically admitted by the I.W.W. themselves, it is the duty of every juror, as an American citizen, to cast his ballot for conviction and maximum punishment and thus sever a few heads of a many-headed monster that is eating at the heart and vitals of the nation Centralia's armistice day victims fought to save. For a juror to not so cast his ballot would be as traitorous an act as the Armistice day massacre itself.[74]

The denial of a satisfactory change in venue meant that the trial was held in a community charged with the sharpest prejudice.

The prosecution built its case around the death of W. O. Grimm, whose body was found in the middle of the street following the melee. This was unfortunate for the defense because it frustrated its attempt to introduce evidence to prove the existence of a conspiracy to destroy the I.W.W. in order to justify the argument that the defendants were simply protecting themselves and their property. Judge J. M. Wilson refused to permit the introduction of such evidence until the defense could prove an overt act on Grimm's part. G. F. Vanderveer, attorney for the defense, was not able to prove that Grimm had committed an overt act, and this literally hamstrung the defense. If the defendants had been charged with the murder of A. McElfresh or B. Casagranda, whose bodies were found immediately in front of the I.W.W. hall, proof of an overt act might have been easier.

While the defense could not prove an overt act on Grimm's part, the testimony of Dr. Frank Bickford at the coroner's inquest is interesting. He said that the raid was suggested when the parade halted and that the door of the I.W.W. hall was kicked open before the shooting from inside began. Conflicting statements on the question of aggression are difficult to reconcile, but the evidence points to the likelihood that a rush toward the hall preceded the shooting.[75]

Vanderveer argued that evidence of a conspiracy against the I.W.W. should be accepted by the court to prove apprehension, to show why the I.W.W. had armed themselves, to refute the prosecution's contention that the I.W.W. fear of assault was mere "bunkum" to conceal other motives, and to refute the contention that an I.W.W. conspiracy existed. Vanderveer offered evidence to prove the existence of an intricate state-wide conspiracy to do away with the I.W.W. In addition, he offered to prove that Grimm had cognizance of the plans of the raid and supported them. None of this evidence was allowed by the judge.[76]

Other aspects of the trial were unfavorable to the defense. In spite of Vanderveer's vehement objection, troops were stationed near the courthouse. In addition, Legion men in uniform were paid four dollars a day by the Centralia American Legion to sit in the courtroom throughout the trial. Two defense witnesses whose testimony placed Grimm near the I.W.W. hall when the raid began were arrested for perjury. This was plainly intimidation. State witnesses discredited by their own testimony, however, were not subjected to such treatment.[77]

Ninety-three persons were examined during a two-week period before the twelve jurors and two alternates were chosen. The jury was made up of four farmers, a teamster, two stationary engineers, a real estate agent, a fisherman, a carpenter, and two laborers, and was not unrepresentative. When the trial was concluded, the jury spent a full day in deliberation before reaching a verdict, which the court would not accept. The jury found two of the defendants, E. Barnett and J. Lamb, guilty of only third-degree murder. The judge held that this was inadmissable—that a verdict of first- or second-degree murder or of acquittal had to be rendered. The second verdict, delivered after the jury had been out another two hours, found seven of the men guilty of second-degree murder, two acquitted, and the tenth declared insane.[78]

With the second verdict the jurors submitted to the court this petition, which they had all signed: "We the undersigned jurors respectfully petition the court to extend the [sic] leniency to the defendants whose names appear on the attached verdict." [79] When a sentence of a minimum of twenty-five years and a maximum of forty years was given—the Washington law simply prescribed punishment of not less than ten years—some of the jurors were astonished by the court's complete disregard of their plea for leniency.

The first verdict is especially interesting because Barnett was accused by the prosecution of having fired from the Avalon Hotel the shot that was fatal to Grimm. The defense alleged that it was "John Doe" Davis, escaped, who fired the shot and that Barnett was in the Roderick Hotel. A number of witnesses, and Barnett himself, testified that he was in the Roderick Hotel as a spectator during the affray. The report of the Federal Council of Churches of Christ in America concluded that "The weight of the evidence tends to support his [Barnett's] own contention." [80] The jury evidently thought along similar lines in formulating its more lenient first verdict of third-degree murder against him. A legionnaire, E. P. Coll, "to clear the Legion's name," made a study of the case and concluded that Barnett had been framed.

And why did they frame Barnett? Because he had *been* in the front room of the Roderick Hotel alongside the I.W.W. hall when the raid took place. . . . The prosecution knew that he could prove there had been a raid by legionnaires. So they made him a defendant to keep him from being a witness, and to do that they placed him across the street in the upper window of the Avalon Hotel with a blazing rifle in his hand.[81]

An "unofficial jury," composed of six labor men elected by as many A.F. of L. labor organizations in the Northwest, sat through the trial and reported on the findings. Their presence seemed to give validity to Vanderveer's contention that it was a class trial—that the I.W.W.

was on trial, not the individual defendants whose lives were in jeopardy. Overlooking the point of law raised by the judge, and also mindful of the evidence which the judge would not accept, the labor jury held that the defendants were "not guilty," that there was a "conspiracy by the business interests of Centralia . . . that the hall was unlawfully raided . . ." and, finally, that "the defendants did not get a fair trial." [82]

It has since been revealed that the verdict was a compromise among the jury members, and between justice and hysteria. Even the state and the defense agreed on one point: that the nature of the charges required either a verdict of first-degree murder or acquittal. If there was a conspiracy and murder, the verdict should have been murder in the first degree; if there was no conspiracy to murder, but protection of self and property, then the verdict should have been acquittal.

The Montesano verdict violates both justice and common sense. . . . The men accused were either guilty of premeditated murder—murder in the first degree—or they were innocent. . . . Here is a case of jury incompetence—of a verdict born of compromise or fear of personal consequences, or of plain lack of comprehension, or of reluctance to accept a sworn responsibility. . . . The jury finds that it was murder without premeditation. As well have held that Grimm committed suicide. . . . Fear of personal consequences can only be inferred. . . . Lack of comprehension was revealed in the jury's invidious discrimination between conspirators.[83]

Since the fateful days of the trial, most of the jurors have openly expressed their true feelings. Many signed affidavits admitting that they had believed the defendants to be innocent. They had agreed to the compromise verdict because of the hysteria that prevailed and to protect themselves, and because some members of the jury had been in favor of hanging the defendants regardless of the evidence. P. V. Johnson, one of the jurors, afterward said that "I know I make mistake but it was too much for one man to do. . . . I cannot get it out of my mind these many years; maybe I go back to Sweden . . . no one will say 'There goes Pete Johnson; he helped send innocent men to prison.' . . . You know we took a ballot, and it was four for acquittal. But they would not stick with me. First it was two left me and then three. The other Johnson said, "You must be a God-damn wobbly yourself.' And Sellars kept yelling, 'It is P. V. Johnson who is holding out, it is P. V. Johnson!' I thought the bailiff would hear him; he was a stool pigeon. . . ." Another juror, W. E. Inmon, later said, "I signed the leniency petition the same as the rest. . . . I thought they'd get two to five years. . . . When me and Sweitzer give in to second degree, we figured we was doin' the right thing under the circumstances—but we made a terrible mistake. . . . It's not a good thought to live with, that you've sent innocent men over the road." [84]

Some of the jurors worked tirelessly with other interested persons and sought for the release of the men. J. McInerny died in prison of tuberculosis. L. Roberts was released in 1930, after being declared sane. The two Bland brothers, J. Lamb, B. Smith, and E. Barnett accepted paroles in 1932 and 1933. Ray Becker refused to accept a parole at that time, insisting upon a pardon, but he finally did accept a parole in 1940.

The Centralia incident and the "anti-red" hysteria of the early twenties played havoc with the I.W.W. Late in 1922, however, the organization showed decided signs of life, and trouble developed in certain camps. On May Day, 1923, a strike to effect the release of all political "class war" prisoners was undertaken. An incidental feature was the design to secure bedding in all the camps. Men were still carrying blankets in some cases. Several camps, generally believed to have been 4L, were closed down, 4L "members" having carried Wobbly cards. About one-third of the lumberjacks supported the strike. On May 7, the official order was to "carry the strike to the job," which had little effect. This practically marked the end of the dispute, but as the men made their way to the camps, lumberjacks were busy, wherever it was necessary, seizing and burning bundles of blankets taken from those who were inclined to weaken on the demand for clean sheets. The I.W.W. officials announced that the purpose of focusing public attention again upon the demand for release of all political prisoners had been achieved, and so they claimed success.[85]

Meanwhile, the International Union of Timber and Sawmill Workers was having difficulties. It fought its last valiant battle at Klamath Falls, Oregon, in 1922,[86] where a once-flourishing local had dwindled almost to the vanishing point. The strike, which occurred on February 28, was a spontaneous walkout of unorganized men and women against an increase of hours to nine a day. But within a week practically all the strikers were initiated into the union. To fight the workers the struck mills simply announced an indefinite closing and refused to meet the union representatives.

The mayor of Klamath Falls attempted to get the parties together but failed because of the stand of the operators. Then on March 9, at the suggestion of the workers, he appealed to the United States

Department of Labor and to the State Board of Conciliation for aid. Local sentiment seemed wholly on the side of the strikers. Even the 4L was sympathetic because the union was defending a cardinal principle—the eight-hour day.[87] The State Board of Conciliation, which at first delayed taking action while the federal mediators attempted settlement, finally intervened when the mediators failed to accomplish anything. The board had power to require compulsory arbitration, although its sole weapon to compel acceptance of its decisions was to publicize its findings.

Anxious to use its mediatory powers rather than its mandatory powers, for this was its first case, the board tried conciliation. Composed of two businessmen, Chairman W. E. Woodward and J. K. Flynn, and one labor man, O. R. Hartwig, the board held joint hearings in April. These revealed that the controversy rested entirely upon the question of the nine-hour day, and, although this strike was in the pine region, it had serious ramifications for the entire Northwest lumber industry since the operators in the Inland Empire were seriously considering a return to a longer day.

The operators contended that California "ten-hour day" competition made it incumbent on them to run on a longer basis. The cost data they submitted, however, was held "incomplete and unsatisfactory" by the board. Employees testified that if economies were necessary, they would be willing to accept a reduction in wages, but no increase of the working day.[88]

A final attempt at conciliation followed the hearings, when it was agreed that employers and employees should meet at their respective plants in an endeavor to compose their differences. These meetings failed, and the board handed down a decision on April 27, upholding the position of the unionists. The union accepted, but when the employers rejected it the struggle continued.

The next development was a move to discredit the union leaders among the local businessmen, which was followed by an unsuccessful attempt to introduce strikebreakers. The strike dragged on until June 18, when the union capitulated and voted to allow members to go back to work on the company's terms. As an aftermath of the strike, the International Union of Sawmill and Timber Workers disbanded on March 23, 1923, surrendered its charter to the A.F. of L., and closed its Seattle office. Before the year was out, the Klamath Falls lumber industry had returned to an eight-hour day, but the union was gone.[89]

In the essentially frontierlike conditions in which the lumber industry of the West developed, labor relations were tragic. Industrial and social conditions were unstable and organization would naturally have been difficult. When the obstinate attitude of the employers on recognition is considered, it is surprising that there was any unionism at all. A reason for the militant, uncompromising type of unionism which developed lies in the operators' belligerency. Furthermore, the migratory workers in the industry had no weapons apart from those found in direct economic action. The uncompromising attitude of most employers is revealed in the failure of the 4L, with its employee representation, to maintain itself in the industry in a substantial way. The complete elimination of independent unionism was to delay the development of more wholesome, stable relations for more than two decades.

NOTES TO CHAPTER

[1] *Report of the President's Mediation Commission to the President of the United States—Unrest in the Lumber Industry.* Washington: Government Printing Office, 1918, p. 15.

[2] J. H. Cox, "Organizations of the Lumber Industry in the Pacific Northwest, 1890-1914." Unpublished Ph.D. dissertation, Univer·ity of California, 1937, pp. 17, 63, 221, 230-241 *et passim*.

[3] *Pacific Lumber Trade Journal,* March, 1905, p. 9.

[4] J. H. Cox, *op. cit.,* p. 85.

[5] *American Lumberman,* No. 2003 (October 4, 1913), 60.

[6] U.S. Commission on Industrial Relations, *Final Report and Testimony.* Washington: Government Printing Office, 1916, V, pp. 4136-4137, 4157.

[7] U.S. Commission on Industrial Relations, *op. cit.,* p. 4100.

[8] U.S. Department of Labor, Bureau of Labor Statistics, *Industrial Relations in the West Coast Lumber Industry,* by C. R. Howd. Bulletin No. 349. Washington: Government Printing Office, 1924, p. 55.

[9] J. H. Cox, *op. cit.,* p. 118; U.S. Department of Labor, Bureau of Labor Statistics, *op. cit.,* pp. 55-56.

[10] *American Lumberman,* No. 1518 (June 25, 1904), 25, No. 1522 (July 23, 1904), 29; cf. J. H. Cox, *op. cit.,* p. 118; *Fourth Biennial Report of the Bureau of Labor, Statistics, and Factory Inspection for the State of Washington, 1903-04,* p. 63.

[11] *Fifth Biennial Report of the Bureau of Labor, Statistics, and Factory Inspection for the State of Washington, 1905-06,* pp. 176, 191-196; J. H. Cox, *op. cit.,* pp. 128-132; U.S. Department of Labor, Bureau of Labor Statistics, *op. cit.,* p. 56; *American Lumberman,* No. 1615 (May 5, 1906), 44.

[12] *Ninth Biennial Report of the Bureau of Labor Statistics and Factory Inspection for the State of Washington, 1913-14,* p. 119.

[13] P. Brissenden, *The I.W.W.* Columbia University Studies in History, Economics, and Public Law, No. 83. New York: Columbia University Press, 1919, pp. 85, 87-88.

[14] U.S. Department of Labor, Bureau of Labor Statistics, *op. cit.,* pp. 64-65; P. Brissenden, *op. cit.,* p. 205.

[15] P Brissenden, *op. cit.,* p. 221.

[16] P. Brissenden, *op. cit.,* p. 262; Industrial Workers of the World, *Twenty-Five Years of Industrial Unionism.* Chicago: I.W.W. Publishing Company (not dated), p. 13-20.

[17] See below, p. 122.

[18] U.S. Department of Labor, Bureau of Labor Statistics, *op. cit.,* pp. 65-66.

[19] R. Bruere, "Following the Trail of the I.W.W.," New York *Evening Post,* February 16, 1918. A report of an interview with W. J. Patterson, lumberman and shipbuilder of Grays Harbor.

[20] U. S. Department of Labor, Bureau of Labor Statistics, *op. cit.,* p. 66.

[21] E. B. Mittleman, "The Loyal Legion of Loggers and Lumbermen," *Journal of Political Economy,* XXXI, No. 6 (June, 1923), 324; U.S. Department of Labor, Bureau of Labor Statistics, *op. cit.,* p. 67.

[22] U.S. Department of Labor, Bureau of Labor Statistics, *op. cit.,* pp. 56-61.

[23] *Ibid.,* p. 67.

[24] W. C. Smith, *The Everett Massacre.* Chicago: I.W.W. Publishing Company, 1917, pp. 35-51; B. S. Coleman, "The I.W.W. and the Law: Everett," *Sunset Magazine,* XXXIX, No. 1 (July, 1917), 35, 68-70; Industrial Workers of the World, *op. cit.,* p. 18.

[25] Industrial Workers of the World, *op. cit.,* p. 25; W. C. Smith, *op. cit.,* pp. 84-93.

[26] B. S. Coleman, *op. cit.,* p. 35; cf. U.S. Department of Labor, Bureau of Labor Statistics, *op. cit.,* p. 69.

[27] *Daily Virginian,* December 26, 28, 30, 1916; George Harrison, "Hitting the Trail in the Lumber Camps," *International Socialist Review,* XVII, No 8 (February, 1917), 455.

[28] *Daily Virginian,* December 29, 30, 1916, January 2, 1917.

[29] *Ibid.,* January 3, 5, 6, 1917; cf. G. Harrison, *op. cit.,* p. 466.

[30] *West Coast Lumberman,* XXXII, No. 372 (April 1, 1917), 42; U.S. Department of Labor, Bureau of Labor Statistics, *op. cit.,* p. 69-71; Industrial Workers of the World, *The Lumber Industry and Its Workers.* Chicago: I.W.W. Publishing Company, undated, about 1920, p. 78.

[31] U.S. Department of Labor, Bureau of Labor Statistics, *op. cit.,* p. 71; cf. Portland *Oregonian,* July 10, 1917; C. Merz, "Tying Up Western Lumber," *New Republic,* XII, No. 152 (September 29, 1917), 243.

[32] U.S. Department of Labor, Bureau of Labor Statistics, *op. cit.,* p. 70.

[33] *West Coast Lumberman,* XXXII, No. 380 (August 1, 1917), 26; U.S. Department of Labor, Bureau of Labor Statistics, *op. cit.,* p. 73.

[34] *Congressional Record,* "Activities of the Industrial Workers of the World." 65th Congress, Vol. LV, Part 6, August 11, 1917, pp. 5942-5951.

[35] Quoted by C. Merz, *op. cit.,* p. 244; cf. U.S. Department of Labor, Bureau of Labor Statistics, *op. cit., pp.* 73-74.

[36] *Industrial Worker,* September 19, 1917; U.S. Department of Labor, Bureau of Labor Statistics, *op. cit.,* pp. 74-75.

[37] Industrial Workers of the World, *The Lumber Industry and Its Workers,* pp. 78-81; E. F. Dowell, *A History of Criminal Syndicalism in the United States.* The Johns Hopkins University Studies in Historical and Political Science. Series LVII, No. 1. Baltimore: Johns Hopkins Press, 1939, p. 36.

[38] Conversation with J. H. Cox, Berkeley, Calif., October 10, 1937; U.S. Department of Labor, Bureau of Labor Statistics, *op. cit.,* p. 76; R. Bruere, *op. cit.,* February 16, 1918, p. 1, March 2, 1918, p. 4.

[39] Industrial Workers of the World, *op. cit.,* pp. 79-81; U.S. Spruce Production Corporation, *History of the Spruce Production Division.* Washington: U.S. Army, 1920(?), p. 15.

[40] *Congressional Record,* Vol. 56, Part 4. 65th Congress, 2nd Session, March 21, 1918, p. 3821.

[41] *Report of the President's Mediation Commission to the President of the United States—Unrest in the Lumber Industry,* p. 14; cf. J. S. Gambs, *Decline of the I.W.W.* Columbia University Studies in History, Economics, and Public Law, No. 361. New York: Columbia University Press, 1932, p. 37.

[42] U.S. Spruce Production Corporation, *op. cit.,* pp. 15, 19; U.S. Department of Labor, Bureau of Labor Statistics, *op. cit.,* p. 77; *Four L Monthly Bulletin,* August, 1918.

[43] U.S. Department of Labor, Bureau of Labor Statistics, *op. cit.,* p. 77.

44 V. H. Jensen, "Labor Relations in the Douglas Fir Lumber Industry." Unpublished Ph.D. Thesis, University of California, 1939, p. 63.

45 U.S. Spruce Production Corporation, *op. cit.*, p. 16; cf. *Four L Monthly Bulletin*, March, 1918.

46 *Four L Monthly Bulletin*, May, 1918; cf. U.S. Spruce Production Corporation, *op. cit.*, p. 19; U.S. Department of Labor, Bureau of Labor Statistics, *op. cit.*, p. 78.

47 *Four L Monthly Bulletin*, see all issues January-November, 1918.

48 *Four L Monthly Bulletin*, April, September, 1918; U.S. Department of Labor, Bureau of Labor Statistics, *op. cit.*, p. 81.

49 U.S. Spruce Production Corporation, *op. cit.*, pp. 17-20; *Four L Monthly Bulletin*, March, September, 1918.

50 U.S. Spruce Production Corporation, *op. cit.*, pp. 20, 21, 75, 76; *Four L Monthly Bulletin*, May, July, September, 1918.

51 U.S. Spruce Production Corporation, *op. cit.*, pp. 5, 21; U.S. Department of Labor, Bureau of Labor Statistics, *op. cit.*, pp. 80-81; *Four L Monthly Bulletin*, March, July, 1918.

52 U.S. Department of Labor, Bureau of Labor Statistics, *op. cit.*, pp. 81-82; cf. *West Coast Lumberman*, XXXIV, No. 404 (August 1, 1918), 22; *Four L Monthly Bulletin*, August, 1918.

53 *Four L Monthly Bulletin*, September, 1918.

54 *Report of Proceedings of 38th Annual Convention of the American Federation of Labor*, St. Paul, Minnesota, 1918, pp. 79, 222.

55 U.S. Department of War, *A Report of the Activity of the War Department in the Field of Industrial Relations During the War*. Washington: Government Printing Office, 1919, p. 47; Seattle *Union Record*, June 15, July 13, 27, November 23, 1918.

56 *West Coast Lumberman*, XXXV, No. 412 (December 1, 1918), 24; U.S. Spruce Production Corporation, *op. cit.*, pp. 95-96; U.S. Department of Labor, Bureau of Labor Statistics, *op. cit.*, p. 86.

57 *Constitution and By-Laws of the 4L*, 1919.

58 *Four L Bulletin*, March, November, 1919; U.S. Department of Labor, Bureau of Labor Statistics, *op. cit.*, p. 74; U.S. Spruce Production Corporation, *op. cit.*, p. 26; E. B. Mittleman, *op. cit*, p. 338.

59 *Four L Bulletin*, March, 1919; E. B. Mittleman, *op. cit.*, p. 338.

60 *Proceedings of the Fifteenth Convention of the Industrial Workers of the World, 1919*, p. 4; *Proceedings of the Thirteenth Convention of the Industrial Workers of the World, 1921*, pp. 3-7; cf. U.S. Department of Labor, Bureau of Labor Statistics, *op. cit.*, pp. 97-99, 101-102; *Monthly Labor Review*, XV, No. 1 (July, 1922), 167-168.

61 *Four L Bulletin*, March, 1918; S. Perlman and P. Taft, *A History of Labor in the United States, 1896-1932*. New York: The Macmillan Company, 1935, pp. 439-442.

62 U.S. Department of Labor, Bureau of Labor Statistics, *op. cit.*, pp. 90-91; *Four L Bulletin*, July, 1919, February, July, December, 1920, January, April, May, June, 1921.

63 *Four L Bulletin*, January, 1920, May, 1922.

64 J. W. Lockhart, "The I.W.W. Raid at Centralia," *Current History*, XVII, No. 1 (October, 1922), 55; cf. Federal Council of Churches of Christ in America, *The Centralia Case*. New York: Department of Research and Education, Federal Council of Churches, 1930, pp. 8-10; for an I.W.W. account see, R. Chaplain, *The Centralia Conspiracy*. Chicago: I.W.W. Publishing Company, 1920; for an American Legion account see, B. H. Lampman, *The Centralia Tragedy and Trial*. Published by the American Legion, 1920.

65 T. McMahon, "Centralia and the I.W.W.," *Survey*, XLIII, No. 6 (November 29, 1920), 123.

66 T. McMahon, *op. cit.*, p. 173; Federal Council of Churches of Christ in America, *op. cit.*, p. 9.

67 A. L. Strong, "Centralia, An Unfinished Story," *Nation*, CX, No. 2859 (April 17, 1920), 510.

[68] Federal Council of Churches of Christ in America, *op. cit.,* pp. 9, 10, 45; cf. T. McMahon, *op. cit.,* p. 173.

[69] Federal Council of Churches of Christ in America, *op. cit.,* pp. 10-11.

[70] J. W. Lockhart, *op. cit.,* p. 56; cf. Federal Council of Churches of Christ in America, *op. cit.,* p. 13.

[71] Federal Council of Churches of Christ in America, *op. cit.,* p. 13; cf. J. W. Lockhart, *op. cit.,* pp. 56-57; T. McMahon, *op. cit.,* pp. 173-174.

[72] T. McMahon, *op. cit.,* p. 174.

[73] *Four L Bulletin,* Extra Edition, December, 1919.

[74] *Survey,* XLIII, No. 20 (March 13, 1920), 734.

[75] T. McMahon, *op. cit.,* p. 174; Federal Council of Churches of Christ in America, *op. cit.,* p. 16.

[76] Federal Council of Churches of Christ in America, *op. cit.,* pp. 27-28; *Survey,* XLIII, No. 20 (March 13, 1920), 735.

[77] Federal Council of Churches of Christ in America, *op. cit.,* pp. 29-30, 43.

[78] Federal Council of Churches of Christ in America, *op. cit.,* pp. 25, 30; *Nation,* CX, No. 2859 (April 17, 1920), 508.

[79] Federal Council of Churches of Christ in America, *op. cit.,* p. 30.

[80] Federal Council of Churches of Christ in America, *op. cit.,* p. 36; cf. E. Barnett, "From a Centralia Prisoner," *Christian Century,* XLVI, No. 18 (May 8, 1928), 619.

[81] C. E. Payne, "Captain Coll-Legionnaire," *Nation,* CXXIX, No. 3340 (July 10, 1929), 38.

[82] A. L. Strong, *op. cit.,* pp. 508-9; cf. *Survey,* XLIV, No. 3 (April 17, 1920), 115.

[83] Portland *Oregonian,* March 15, 1920; Seattle *Post-Intelligencer,* March 16, 1920.

[84] *Timberworker,* December 25, 1936.

[85] Seattle *Union Record,* April 26, 27, 28, May 7, 1923; *Four L Bulletin,* January, April, May, June, 1923.

[86] V. H. Jensen, *op. cit.,* pp. 122-131; Oregon State Board of Counciliation, "Findings of the State Board of Conciliation—In the matter of a controversy between Big Lakes Box Company, et al . . . and their Employees." Dated April 26, 1922 (typewritten).

[87] *Four L Bulletin,* June, July, 1922.

[88] Oregon State Board of Conciliation, *loc. cit.*

[89] *Four L Bulletin,* July, 1922, January, April, 1923; cf. *Oregon Labor Press,* April 13, 1923.

8 DEPRESSION AND THE NRA

D<small>EPRESSION</small> began to afflict the lumber industry as early as 1925, when there were numerous requests and demands for curtailment of production to preserve prices.[1] Because the lumber market was erratic, the insecurity of the individual operator increased. This intensified his drive for self-preservation, which led to "cost cutting" or to greater liquidation of investment, neither of which improved the market situation. The great threats of overproduction and unemployment bore more and more heavily as the industry passed into a period of stagnation and decline. Workers were brought face to face with the stark reality of unemployment long before it was apparent in an acute form in other industries.

No organization existed that was able to cope with the problems effectively. Apart from the economic stagnation of the industry, the years from the mid-twenties to the depth of the depression in 1933 were uneventful. Industrial relations, on the surface, appeared peaceful, but actually they were not. The 4L had become quite lackadaisical and ineffectual. It did not develop enough constructive activities to keep vigorous.[2]

By the middle of 1928 conditions in the lumber industry were causing noticeable concern. Unemployment was increasing rapidly. W. C. Ruegnitz, president of the 4L, warned of the dangers, saying, "The industry is heading straight for trouble if something is not done to secure . . . steady annual employment for the greatest number of men." [3] By 1929 the depression had advanced rapidly making chronic problems acute. By June of 1930 fir logging and milling were at the lowest ebb in seventeen years. But production was to be cut half again before the bottom was reached. During 1932 less than 20 per cent of the industry capacity was being utilized. Only half the workers were employed and most of these on short time. Wage cutting became prevalent and the 4L minimum wage was lowered time and again, until it reached $2.60 a day in the spring of 1932. At the same time, wages were as low as $1.50 in some non-4L plants. Finally, the 4L minimum wage was suspended in November, 1932.[4]

A revealing statement of the desperate situation the industry was in was made by Vice-President Malarkey of the M. and M. Plywood Corporation.

. . . fir manufacturers are competing among themselves rather than with other industries and these further price reductions are coming out of labor and out of labor only. . . . Some of the factories in our line of business have cut wages to $1.80 or $2.00 a day. Now we hear of a factory starting off with $1.35 base wage and putting its men on a profit sharing plan when they know in advance there aren't going to be any profits. . . . The M. and M. people want to establish a $3 minimum wage. . . . I want the plywood manufacturers to get together and post a $25,000 cash bond as a guarantee that they won't cut wages below $3.00 for an eight-hour day. . . . Each manufacturer will know that . . . he is competitive on labor with the other manufacturers.[5]

Others also recognized that wage cuts are not a help to the industry, but a hindrance, because low wages help to drive the price of lumber down with them.

A comparable situation existed in the rest of the industry. When average wages per hour in 1933 had reached the low levels of 36.6 cents in the West, they had dropped in the South to 15.0 cents. When in the same year weekly earnings in the West averaged $13.40, they averaged $6.80 in the South. Apart from the general business depression, there were many causes of the industry's predicament. The period of agricultural expansion had passed. The postwar agricultural depression had had an important effect on lumber sales for repair and replacement. Competition of substitutes had been relentless.[6] There had been a pronounced downward trend in lumber consumption from 1906. Alongside of this, the tax system, which forced liquidation of standing timber, problems of private ownership of timber, and other conditions had resulted in establishment of excess capacity and the piling up of overhead costs. The effects of chronic illness in the industry had been felt long before 1929, and the depression only served to make them worse. Capital and labor had little security in the industry.[7]

The complaint often was made that the antitrust laws held the industry from applying the necessary correctives.[8] To a certain extent this was true, but merely to wipe out the laws which prevented price and production control could not have solved the problems of the lumber industry. If statutory barriers to production and price control were removed, economic (as distinguished from legal) factors still would remain an effective obstacle to the control of production. The antitrust laws, to a certain extent, must carry some blame for the excess production capacity, but the economics of the lumber industry are such that control is well-nigh impossible unless other important problems are solved. Lumber manufacturers have tried for years to violate the antitrust laws but never have been able to do so.[9]

Competition has been cutthroat whenever a declining market has existed. Consequently, control of competition often has been sought. Ownership mergers have been possible, but never were effected on a large scale because of the economic outlook for the industry. Consolidation of control of production units is not practicable in the lumber industry as long as the tendency to overexpand has not been eliminated. Mergers are not likely to be large enough to establish effective control. Nevertheless, requests for suspension of the antitrust laws have been made to the end that "cooperation between competitors for the purpose of controlling production, stabilizing markets, maintaining employment opportunities, and conserving natural resources," [10] might be attained.

As soon as it was realized that the National Industrial Recovery Act was likely to become law, the secretaries and managers of the regional lumber associations were called together under the auspices of the National Lumber Manufacturers Association.[11] Following preliminary informal discussions, a meeting was held on May 23, 1933, in Chicago, at which a provisional code was drawn up. The provisional code then was considered by each of the regional lumber associations. On the approval of the plan that was drawn up, the regional lumber associations selected representatives, who met in Chicago on June 29 and resolved themselves into the "Emergency National Committee." After more than a week's continuous work, the committee prepared a draft of its code.

Drafting of the code required strenuous efforts to harmonize the varied interests created by the industry's wide scope from the standpoint of location, products, markets, and labor. The code was full of compromises. Especially is this true of the labor provisions, although there was little labor participation in its formulation.

There were no labor unions to demand participation, and the 4L was at a low ebb. The wages and hours provisions of the code brought sharp conflict between western and southern industry representatives. Much time was spent in arguing about hours, a discussion unintelligible to workers who had been lucky to average around three hours per day in the previous three depression years and who, in normal times, did not average six hours per day for the entire year.[12]

Toward the close of the period of formulation, many meetings and conferences were held in the various districts, at which the tentative code provisions were scrutinized. All operators were invited to public meetings to discuss the provisions submitted and to vote on them. On July 10 a copy of a proposed code was handed to General Hugh S. Johnson, administrator of the National Industrial Recovery Act, who set a public hearing for July 20. A final draft was submitted July 28, and was supported by forty-seven lumber and timber products associations. Then there followed a long series of negotiations between the committee and representatives of the NRA, during which much of the code was rewritten. On August 19 an agreement was reached and the President signed the code, the declared purpose of which was "to reduce and relieve unemployment . . . ; to improve the standards of labor . . . ; to maintain a reasonable balance between the production and consumption of lumber and timber products; to restore the prices thereof to levels which will avoid the further depletion and destruction of capital assets; and to conserve forest resources and bring about the sustained production thereof." Immediately after approval of the code, the various groups in the industry organized a corporation, the Lumber Code Authority, to administer it.[13]

Except in the West, where the 4L was present, no labor organizations were in existence. In the West, the Western Pine Association and the West Coast Lumbermen's Association decided that the labor aspects of the industry control program should be conducted through the 4L. Articles V, VI, and VII, covering Labor Provisions, Hours of Labor, and Minimum Wages, contain the essential items pertaining to labor. Article V of the lumber industry code contained Section 7 of the NIRA. Article VI set up maximum hours of employment at forty per week for each workman, with certain exceptions. It is quite apparent that the reduced hours were for "production control" and not to "spread the work," as contemplated in the NIRA, because employees had not worked that many hours in some time. No restrictions on daily working hours were made. Certain salaried officials were exempt, as were such ordinary workmen as watchmen, firemen, and repair crews, whose work requires the exemption. But such workmen were not to constitute more than 10 per cent of all employees. Temporary emergency work was expected along with seasonal work.

Logging camps, "which on account of elevation or other physical conditions or dependence upon climatic factors are ordinarily limited to a period of ten months or less of the calendar year," were classed as seasonal operations. Seasonal operations were permitted to work more than forty hours a week so long as the average for the year was not more than forty hours per week.

Article VII, which contained minimum wage provisions, is where the greatest compromise was made. The great differential between the South and the West had to be considered. Finally, it was decided that minimum wages should not be less than 40 cents per hour, unless in any division or subdivision of the industry the prevailing hourly rates for the same class of employees on July 15, 1929, as determined by the administrator on the basis of statistical evidence, was less than 40 cents per hour. In such cases the rate was not to be less than the rate then prevailing, plus 15 per cent if the hourly rate was less than 30 cents. Through the work of the 4L, the minimum wage in the West was set at 42½ cents. The southern lumber industry, "with considerable courage," proposed a minimum wage of 22½ cents and a forty-eight-hour week, "volunteering to undertake a great adventure." The administrators, however, raised the minimum to 24 cents per hour in the South and established the work week at forty hours.[14]

On the insistence of the 4L, demands for increased minimum wages under the code were considered during the early part of February, 1934. The demand for a 7½ cents an hour increase was not granted because there was intense southern opposition, and the Lumber Code Authority held "the wage scales as provided in the code were predicated upon a contemplated increased demand . . . which has so far not materialized. Any general raise in wages must be deferred until other competing industries raise their wages." [15]

There were three other significant portions of the code: Article VIII, Control of Production, which made provision for production quotas; Article IX, Cost Protection, which gave power to the Code Authority under emergency conditions to establish "reasonable cost" for any or all items, with rules and regulations for the application thereof; and Article X, Conservation and Sustained Production of Forest Resources, which, together with Schedule C, Forest Conservation for the Lumber and Timber Products Industries, set up a long-range program of forest rehabilitation, conservation, and forestry control.

General enforcement was left up to the Compliance Division of the NRA, but, under the authority of an order issued April 7, 1934, a

"National Labor Complaints Committee" for the lumber industry with eight "Regional Labor Complaints Committees" were supposed to be set up. These committees were to handle all complaints alleging violation of Article V, VI, and VII. The National Labor Complaints Committee was to have consisted of not less than four nor more than eight members, one-half of which was to represent employers and to be appointed by the Lumber Code Authority; the other half to represent employees and to be appointed by the President upon recommendation of the Labor Advisory Board of the NRA. The employer members were duly appointed, but trouble was encountered in attempting to name the employee members of the committee. Deputy Administrator A. C. Dixon was at one time verbally notified that William Green and Jett Lauck had been appointed. Later, Arthur Sturgis, of the Labor Advisory Board in the National Recovery Administration, handed Dixon a memorandum that embodied a revision of both the National and Regional Labor Complaints Committees which would be necessary before Green would approve of them and consent to serve.

No action was ever taken on the suggested changes and the committees were not created. Nevertheless, a labor complaints committee functioned on the West Coast from August 31, 1933, to the late period of the code's life. This was the semiofficial "joint committee on labor" representing the 4L and the various code agencies. These agencies were the West Coast Lumbermen's Association, Pacific Northwest Loggers Association, Douglas Fir Plywood Association, Douglas Fir Door Manufacturers Association, Washington and Oregon Shingle Association, Pacific Northwest Box-Association, Pacific Veneer Package Association, and the Douglas Fir Subdivision of the Pole and Piling Division. The "joint committee on labor" was set up to handle applications for seasonal classification, to provide hearings for employees or their representatives in case of alleged violations, to deal with alleged code violations arising through field audits, and to prepare rules and regulations covering labor matters for employers under the committee's jurisdiction. During 1934 this committee handled 360 cases which were considered of sufficient seriousness to be mentioned to the Lumber Code Authority, of which it disposed of 349. The remaining eleven cases were referred to NRA compliance offices in either Seattle or Portland.[16]

Nationally, the Compliance Division of the NRA handled alleged violations of the labor provisions of the code. Its record is not imposing, and the failure of enforcement contributed materially to the eventual group abandonment of the code. The cases involving violation of labor provisions docketed by the Compliance Division increased from 276 in the period from November 18, 1933, to January 1, 1934, to 808 in the second quarter of 1934. Thereafter a decided drop in the number of cases occurred, there being relatively few cases in the last quarter of the code's life. The drop in cases docketed, beginning with the third quarter of 1934, coincides with the time when the industry began to lose faith in enforcement promises, with the result that violations were not so religiously reported.[17] Most of the cases involving code violations originated in the South, because of the relatively great changes required by the wages and hours provisions and the large number of producing units.

The price-fixing and production quota features of the code gave considerable trouble and caused many complaints. Perhaps the failure of many operators to live up to the price and production requirements contributed to the collapse of the code more than violation of the labor provisions. In the light of nonenforcement, those who were honest were being penalized. One unfortunate accompaniment of the price-fixing activities was that demand did not increase, because building activity lagged, even though the minimum prices under the code were approximately at the market level and from 15 to 25 per cent below the level of 1929. Hard-pressed establishments sought ways through which minimum prices might be evaded without apparent violation of the code. All manner of subterfuge was perpetrated, such as cash refunds or unusually large losses at "poker games." To make matters worse, it was discovered that as a result of a technical oversight wholesale distributors were not legally subject to the code. Wholesalers were known to have purchased lumber at code prices and then to have sold it at lower prices and made money. Obviously, they must have engaged in some sort of secret cash transaction with the mill operator involved.[18]

The operators' reactions to the code were not uniform, and this fact caused difficulties in its administration and reduced its effectiveness. There were those operators who recognized the advantages of applying the code and wanted the industry controlled systematically for the interest of all. Some of them, naturally enough, found the restrictions uncomfortable, but production and price control are necessary in the lumber industry to keep it from dissipating its working capital.

A crisis developed in November, 1934, in regard to the price-fixing provisions. The legality of price fixing in all the codes was uncertain in view of conflicting court decisions and, with the increase in violations, a definite move for suspension developed. A public hearing was called during which support of and opposition to suspension were evenly matched. In late December the National Industrial Recovery Board officially suspended all minimum prices under the code.[10]

The Lumber and Timber Products Industry Code was dead before the Schecter decision nullified the NRA. It was very ill before the Belcher case, which involved flagrant violations of wages and hours provisions by an Alabama manufacturer whose indictment in the spring of 1934 was dropped. A district judge sustained a demurrer to the indictment of the Belcher Lumber Company on the ground that the National Industrial Recovery Act was unconstitutional. The case was selected as an ideal test case by the NRA authorities and the Department of Justice. An appeal was taken directly to the Supreme Court. It was stated and generally understood that the validity of wage and hour regulations was to be established. After such a decision, enforcement could go forward vigorously. But, following months of preparation, the case was suddenly dropped on March 26, 1935, because the Lumber and Timber Products Code contained administrative provisions peculiar to itself with respect to the extension of discretionary powers to nongovernmental agencies. Revision of this feature was being considered then as a subject for further legislation. It also was held that better test cases were being pressed. The decision to drop the Belcher case gave rise to confusion, as well as to despair concerning the Lumber Code, which was further intensified when the Department of Justice announced that "meanwhile and pending desirable amendments to the Lumber and Timber Products Code, there will be no relaxation in enforcement of other codes." [20] The inference was that the Lumber Code in its existing form would not be enforced. The industry code agencies sent telegrams to officials of the National Recovery Administration stating that in the absence of enforcement support the code was intolerable and should be suspended.

The dismissal of the Belcher case emphasized the voluntary nature of the code. The Schecter decision, later, changed this situation only technically. The lumber industry was thus the first great industry to discard its code.[21]

The application of the NRA code, though short-lived, was an interesting attempt in the direction of industry control. Its inception was enthusiastically supported by many lumber operators and workers. Hostility gradually developed when enforcement provisions proved ineffective and code violations were not punished. It can hardly be called a thoroughgoing experiment in control of the industry, because the apparatus was only partly set up and the "plan" was never carried out in accordance with the specifications. The experience under the code, however, offers a lesson in the difficulty of control in the lumber industry.

The most important development arising out of the code labor provisions was the stimulus given to union organization in the West. The 4L had been recognized in the code administration by the western lumber operators, and because of the collective bargaining provision required in the code the 4L gained many members. But the claims [22] that the 4L embraced a majority of the lumber industry workers in the Pacific Northwest need qualification. It was strongest in the pine area and increased its following there, but its membership in the Douglas fir region was relatively slight. With an established and "authoritative" clearinghouse for industry data, and being the only organization in a position to claim representation for the workers, the 4L felt optimistic. Yet it did not meet the challenge of labor unrest, which was notably present during the code years. The 4L had included only a small percentage of the workers in the industry, and not even these were vigorously represented.

The workers did not take to the 4L, and the A.F. of L. and the National Lumber Workers Union, a Communist organization which had come into existence back in 1929 as an affiliate of the Trade Union Unity League, both made efforts to gain members. The National Lumber Workers Union attempted to gain support by presenting its own labor provisions of a code. These called for a minimum wage of 55 cents an hour and $3.30 per day with adjustments to meet any rise in the cost of commodities, a guaranteed five-day work week for thirty-eight weeks per year; and the elimination of the speed-up, the 4L and "all other company unions," and all private hiring agencies.[23] The A.F. of L. had had no organization in the lumber industry for ten years, except some feeble Shingle Weaver locals at a few places. Suddenly, interest was aroused. Workers, motivated by the promises of the National Industrial Recovery Act, formed their own independent unions and federal charters were granted to them. Mass meetings were held and locals sprung into existence with surprising activity in both sawmilling and logging branches of the industry. State Federation officials in both Oregon and Washington swung into action. Enough locals were formed to hold a conference at Enumclaw, Washington, in July, 1933, at which the Northwest Council of Sawmill and Timber Workers Unions was formed.[24] The 4L found itself facing active union competition. Rivalry manifested itself in many places, and many workers in the 4L carried A.F. of L. cards. The spontaneity with which organization of workers was effected is to be explained in light of the appalling depression conditions. They possessed strong feelings of frustration and helplessness. Organization offered them a "new deal," and they flocked to it.

It is common for labor disputes to occur in the early stages of organization, and it is not surprising that a number of small strikes broke out in the lumber industry in 1934. On March 30 loggers at Vernonia, Oregon, demanded increased wages of the Clark-Wilson Company, which shut down its camps and refused to meet with the federal local, affiliated with the A.F. of L. Although there was some fear that the strike would become general, it did not, and the men returned to work after two weeks, when small pay increases were granted. Recognition of the local had not been demanded.[25] A somewhat larger strike occurred on Vancouver Island during the same spring. Here the employers offered small wage increases and partial recognition through camp committees, but the men held out for their full demands and eventually lost the strike.[26]

During May, June, and July, 1934, logging and lumber operations were seriously affected by the West Coast longshore strike. Many mills and camps were forced to close because lumber could not be shipped by water. By June about 17,000 lumber industry workers were idle. At Longview, Washington, on June 19, sawmill workers struck in sympathy with the longshoremen and the mills were closed for four days. Following the strike action, which had been carried out by a minority group, the 4L local of the Weyerhaeuser Company voted to ask all men who were members of the A.F. of L. to resign from the 4L. Several men were dropped from membership because of picketing during the sympathetic strike. At Longview the controversy between the A.F. of L. and the 4L was acute.[27]

The A.F. of L. local, as a result of the struggle, filed charges against the Long-Bell and the Weyerhaeuser Timber Company for violation of Section 7a of the NIRA. Early in September the Seattle officers of the Regional Labor Board held a hearing at Kelso, Washington, to take testimony regarding the complaints which alleged violation of the code on three counts. The charges were that employers had interfered with, coerced, and intimidated employees in collective bargaining; that they had assisted an employees' organization; and, finally, that they had refused to make an agreement with the union.[28]

On November 6 the Regional Labor Board released an opinion at

Seattle which held that the Long-Bell and Weyerhaeuser companies at Longview were violating Section 7a of the NIRA. The board observed that "it appears to be the contention of the Company that it is not required to comply with the provisions of Section 7a. . . ." The companies were told that "if it is at all possible to do so, that these men [A.F. of L.] be placed on a preferred list." The companies objected to the decision and to the manner in which it was given publicity, stating that the matter should have been referred to the National Labor Relations Board for action through the federal courts if justified. The companies claimed that the board had failed to find evidence of discrimination against A.F. of L. men.[29]

The 4L meanwhile bitterly denounced the "malicious newspaper propaganda sent out by an A.F. of L. member of the Regional Labor Board," denying that the evidence established the charges of the union. It also condemned the "publicity" as "premature" and "libelous" on the ground that the hearing was simply an investigation, and in other respects supported the position taken by the two lumber companies.[30] Nothing further came of this case.

The instability, unrest, and weakness in the lumber industry from the mid-twenties to the mid-thirties were symptomatic of the plight of an industry with unsolved, chronic economic problems. Employers failed to earn profits and lost capital, while workers lost employment and suffered large reductions in their standards of living. Meanwhile the attempt to organize the industry under the National Industrial Recovery Act failed because it was undertaken without sufficient planning or balanced authority from all the groups which should have participated.

NOTES TO CHAPTER

[1] *Four L Bulletin*, May, June, 1925; cf. *Thirteenth Semi-Annual Report for the 4L Board of Directors, May, 1925*, p. 1.

[2] V. H. Jensen, "Labor Relations in the Douglas Fir Industry." Unpublished Ph.D. Thesis, University of California, 1939, pp. 132-156.

[3] *Twentieth Semi-Annual Report for the 4L Board of Directors, November, 1928*, p. 3.

[4] West Coast Lumbermen's Association, *West Coast Lumber Facts*. Seattle, Wash.: West Coast Lumbermen's Association, 1937, p. 15; *Four L Lumber News*, April 1, 1932.

[5] *Four L Lumber News*, September 15, 1931; March 15, 1932; see also *West Coast Lumberman*, LIX, No. 3 (March, 1932), 11.

[6] See above, p. 26.

[7] National Recovery Administration, Division of Research and Planning, "History of the Code of Fair Competition for the Lumber and Timber Products Industries" (official history, typewritten), pp. 292, 323.

[8] National Lumber Manufacturers Association, *Before the Federal Trade Commission, Brief on Behalf of the National Lumber Manufacturers Association*, p. 143;

W. Compton, *The Lumber Industry and the Anti-Trust Laws*. Speech before the National Conference on the Relation of Law and Business at New York University, October 26, 1931, p. 4 (leaflet); *West Coast Lumberman*, LVIII, No. 1 (January, 1931), 30.

[9] National Recovery Administration, Division of Review, *Economic Problems of the Lumber and Timber Products Industries*. Work Materials No. 79, Industries Studies Section, March, 1936 (mimeographed), p. 259.

[10] W. Compton, *op. cit.*, p. 4.

[11] National Recovery Administration, Division of Research and Planning, "History of the Code of Fair Competition for the Lumber and Timber Products Industries," p. 42; D. T. Mason, *The Lumber Code*. Yale University, School of Forestry, Lumber Industry Series XI. New Haven, Conn.: 1935, p. 8.

[12] National Recovery Administration, Division of Research and Planning, *op. cit.*, p. 1; cf. C. W. Bahr, "A Brief Survey of the Provisions of the Lumber and Timber Products Code," *Journal of Forestry*, XXXIII, No. 3 (March, 1935), 222; *Washington State Labor News*, July 28, 1933.

[13] *Lumber Code Authority*, Washington, D.C., Vol. I, Bulletin 1; National Recovery Administration, Division of Research and Planning, *op. cit.*, p. 58; D. T. Mason, *op. cit.*, pp. 8-9; Southern Pine Association, *Administration of the Lumber Code in the Southern Pine Division*. New Orleans: Southern Pine Association, 1934, p. 3.

[14] *Lumber Code Authority*, Vol. I, Bulletin 1, Vol. II, Bulletin 62; *West Coast Lumberman*, LX, No. 7 (July, 1933), 3, LX, No. 8 (August, 1933), 16; Southern Pine Association, *Administration of the Lumber Code in the Southern Pine Division*, p. 15; F. Reed, "The National Lumber Code," *Journal of Forestry*, XXXI, No. 10 (October, 1933), 644-648.

[15] *Four L Lumber News*, February 1, 1934; *Southern Pine Division Code Bulletin*, I, No. 22 (February 23, 1934), 1.

[16] National Recovery Administration, Division of Research, "History of the Code of Fair Competition for the Lumber and Timber Products Industries," pp. 242-248; cf. *Lumber Code Authority*, Vol. I, Bulletin No. 99, pp. 2, 3; *Four L Lumber News*, March 1, April 15, October 15, 1934.

[17] National Recovery Administration, Division of Research, *op. cit.*, pp. 294, 295, 296, 300.

[18] C. W. Bahr, *op. cit.*, pp. 221-222; cf. *Four L Lumber News*, October, 1934; F. A. Silcox, "Forestry—A Public and Private Responsibility." Address before the National Control Committee of the Lumber Code Authority at New Orleans, March 13, 1935 (typewritten), p. 3; Conversations with A. C. Dixon, Eugene, Ore., August 20, 1938, and F. H. Ransom, Portland, Ore., August 26, 1938.

[19] C. W. Bahr, *op. cit.*, p. 221; cf. C. Southworth, "Planning in the Lumber Industry," *Plan Age*, I, No. 5 (May, 1935), 12; *Four L Lumber News*, June 15, December 15, 1934, January 1, 1935.

[20] *Monthly Labor Review*, XXXIII, No. 3 (September, 1935), 657; J. B. Woods, "The Lumber Code Situation," *Journal of Forestry*, XXXIII, No. 6 (June, 1935), 579; *Southern Pine Division Code Bulletin*, I, No. 66 (April 13, 1935), 3; cf. *Business Week* (June 29, 1935), 17.

[21] *Lumber Code Authority*, Vol. II, Bulletin No. 74; *West Coast Lumberman*, LXII, No. 4 (April, 1935), 28; *Business Week*, No. 304 (June 29, 1935), 17.

[22] *Four L Lumber News*, June 15, November 1, 1933.

[23] *Voice of Action*, August 7, 1933.

[24] *American Federationist*, XLI, No. 9 (September, 1934), 965; cf. *Washington State Labor News*, June 30, 1933, February 23, July 27, 1934; V. H. Jensen, *op. cit.*, note p. 177, for a list of locals and the date of formation.

[25] Portland *Oregonian*, March 31, 1934.

[26] L. T. Smythe, "Organization of Timberworkers on Vancouver Island." Unpublished Master's Thesis, University of Washington, Seattle, Wash., 1937, pp. 5-6.

²⁷ *Four L Lumber News,* May 15, June 15, July 1, August 1, 1934. *American Federationist,* XLI, No. 9 (September, 1934), 962-966; *Washington State Labor News,* February 23, 1934.

²⁸ *Four L Lumber News,* September 15, 1934; cf. *Voice of Action,* September 21, 1934.

²⁹ *Four L Lumber News,* November 15, 1934.

³⁰ *Thirty-second Semi-Annual Report for the 4L Board of Directors,* November 9, 1934, pp. 10, 11.

THE GREAT strike of 1935 is the outstanding landmark in the history of industrial relations in the lumber industry. The vigorous, militant tactics of the unionists and the strong counter activities of the employers were characteristic of the industry. The absence of a unified, effectively directed approach on either side was as much an industry characteristic as it was a consequence of newness in organization. Divisions and schisms in the ranks of the opposing sides were common. The 1935 strike was no less spectacular than that of 1917. When the 1935 strike was over, however, unionism was definitely established in the industry. The dispute provides an essential key to many of the subsequent developments in industrial relations in lumbering.

Strike talk was prevalent in the camps and mills in Washington and Oregon early in 1935. Several local job strikes had occurred throughout 1934 and some A.F. of L. locals had assisted the longshoremen in their famous coastwise strike of that year, creating a close liaison between them. There were struggles over the right to organize and it was obvious that unions were growing. But no strong coordinated leadership had developed.

On March 23, 1935, a convention of the Northwest Council of Sawmill and Timber Workers Unions met in Aberdeen. The Executive Board of the A.F. of L. had just previously given jurisdiction over the workers in the lumber industry to the United Brotherhood of Carpenters and Joiners of America. Surprisingly, the Sawmill and Timber Workers Union delegates, without any pronounced objection, approved the action and accepted the leadership of A. W. Muir, executive board member of the United Brotherhood of Carpenters and Joiners of America, who had been sent out to take charge of the lumber industry unions. At the same time, Fred Lumm, president of the Vernonia local, was made president of the Northwest Council of Sawmill and Timber Workers Unions, Norman Lange, president of the Tacoma local, was made vice-president, and Edgar Hall, of

Westport, Oregon, was made secretary. Demands were drawn up in the form of a uniform working agreement to be presented to the industry, with May 6 set as the date for a strike unless they were met. The proposed working agreement asked that the union be the sole collective bargaining agency in each plant or camp; that the hours of labor be six per day and thirty per week; that there be overtime and holiday pay provisions; that no strikes or lockouts occur during the life of the agreement until all mediation and conciliation had failed; that a system of modified seniority be established; that vacations with pay according to the length of service be introduced; that a base wage of 75 cents per hour and proportionate increases to higher classifications be set; and that thirty days' written notice of desire to terminate the agreement be given.[1]

In mid-April, notice of the long-looked-for strike was made public. An Associated Press dispatch from Olympia announced that formal demands had been served on six Olympia lumber and plywood companies. At this time the forthcoming strike also was revealed in Portland by Charles Hope, regional director for the National Labor Relations Board. He declared that all attempts to put a damper on the general strike movement had failed. The 4L complained that "part of the Northwest press unwittingly played into the hands of the lumber unionizers . . . by giving prominence to a threatened strike in logging camps and sawmills." Certainly, the publicity made groups which were hesitant about striking alone anxious to go along with the crowd, and unprecedented requests came from the men in the woods to be enrolled in the unions. Workers were organized and ready to move at any time, in the direction of either negotiation or strike.

At the same time, high 4L officials announced the results of a two weeks' survey, claiming that "90 per cent of the men did not want to strike," and emphasized that such a move would produce nothing but hatred and suffering for the employer, employee, and the public. This was the usual 4L cry, but to the worker only a strike seemed likely to bring results.[2]

Most operators were not willing to negotiate. They asserted that they were not able to meet the union demands and would close and stay closed. Although the employers were worried over the absorption of the Sawmill and Timber Workers Unions by the Carpenters, most of them were for "riding the storm out" by playing a waiting game because of the meager resources of the strikers. Obviously, this was a better tactic than resistance through use of strikebreakers, which always creates excitement. But the assistance obtained from the Federal

Emergency Relief Administration and the support of the Carpenters, Longshoremen, and other labor groups gave the workers unsuspected power to engage in a prolonged struggle.

In the midst of the strike threats and countercharges that the men did not want to strike, the Longview local balloted to determine the wishes of the men. This vote represented one of the largest organized groups. Longview, moreover, formerly had been an important center of 4L activity. The vote was overwhelmingly for the strike, provided the demands were not met by May 6. The union then submitted its proposed uniform working agreement to the management of both Long-Bell and Weyerhaeuser companies, promising that if actual negotiations were started sufficient time would be given to complete them before an actual walkout would be precipitated. Locals throughout the Douglas fir region placed similar demands in the hands of employers.[3]

Preparations for negotiations were going on in a businesslike manner in many localities, but some men were restless and unwilling to wait until May 6. The first actual break came at Vernonia, where there had been a two weeks' stoppage the year before. The Vernonia loggers of the Clark-Wilson Company voted to strike on April 19, declaring that fifty union men had been replaced by non-union men. Some declared that the early action was designed to prevent the timber already cut in the woods from being moved. Also playing a part in hastening developments was the existence of an old Wobbly tradition of direct, vigorous action among these men. This was the case elsewhere in the lower Columbia River area, where the men also would not hold back. A week later a second early walkout occurred at Bellingham when 1,000 men left their jobs because of alleged discharge of union men.

Things began to move fast as both sides sparred for advantage. Hopes of inducing the opposing factions to get together dimmed as the West Coast Lumbermen's Association announced that it would resist the ruling of the National Labor Relations Board, in the case involving the Long-Bell and Weyerhaeuser companies at Longview, that the majority labor group, as determined in elections, should represent all the workers for collective bargaining. "At no time and under no circumstances will the west coast lumber industry submit to rulings based upon the principle involving denial of representation of any minority groups of employees in collective bargaining." In general, the operators sought to diminish the power that the board might bring to bear in establishing peace. A. W. Muir, Carpenter-appointed leader and spokesman for the lumber industry workers, attempted to make capital of the attitude expressed by the operators toward the board by saying, "This calls for an amendment and it is this: We'll take any board. We want to negotiate." [5]

Although Muir was playing for public support, it is also true that he really did desire a speedy settlement. Muir branded the Vernonia and Bellingham incidents as lockouts on the ground that the companies had brought in non-union men and then discharged union men without cause. Muir was using all the strategy at his command. He knew full well the task of holding in check such a large group of "green" union men who were, for the most part, undisciplined. There is reason to believe that he did not want the strike at all, but the men were determined and he was bound not to turn back without securing material concessions such as wage increases or direct union recognition.

On April 23, E. S. Marsh, United States labor conciliator, was ordered by H. L. Kerwin, director of the Conciliation Service for the Department of Labor, to survey the situation and endeavor to secure meetings between employer and worker representatives. Marsh went to work immediately and met important lumber operators and Muir. The latter was asked to prevent walkouts, such as had occurred at Vernonia and Bellingham, until an attempt was made to reach an agreement.

The Long-Bell and Weyerhaeuser companies at Longview seemed to offer a key to the whole situation, because they were willing to negotiate and were large enough to wield considerable influence in the industry. Muir felt that if an agreement could be reached with these two large companies the rest of the industry would probably be forced to follow suit, and, therefore, he worked hard on this possibility. Meanwhile, other camps and mills were being closed by local action ahead of the date set for the strike. On May 3 there were out on strike 2,000 mill workers and 1,500 logging camp workers in Washington and 1,775 mill workers and 850 logging camp workers in Oregon.[6]

On May 6, when the strike got under way in earnest, hopes for peace were not entirely gone. The large mills at Longview were running, with negotiations in progress. So, too, were the large McCormick mills at St. Helens, Port Gamble, and Port Ludlow, and the same was true at Aberdeen where a number of mills continued to operate. By the close of May 6 an estimated 10,000 men were on strike. Of 20,000 working, half were on the job only because negotiations were in progress. Elsewhere pickets took their posts and the strike got under way without disorder. But negotiations at Aberdeen were broken off, and on May 7 between 4,000 and 5,000 additional workers did not report for work. This pushed the total out on strike to 15,000, slightly less than 50 per cent of the men then employed in the lumber industry in the Douglas fir belt. Numerous small mills, especially in southern Oregon, were not closed.[7]

Commissioner Marsh attempted to get the disputing parties to use the conciliation service of the United States Department of Labor, but failed in large part because of employer unwillingness. The West Coast Lumbermen's Association explained publicly that "the industry is not organized to deal with its workers as a whole." Nevertheless, the West Coast Lumbermen's Association could have performed a valuable service if it had been able, or willing, to act for the industry. Prolongation of the strike was caused by the fact that the employers were so poorly organized for labor negotiations. Operators who were amenable to negotiation were afraid to make independent settlements because of fear of being out of line with the ultimate industry settlement.[8]

The Oregon Emergency Relief Administration announced that workmen on strike would be eligible, on the basis of a federal ruling, to benefits if they were destitute. A similar rule applied in Washington. This was bitterly resented by many lumbermen. C. C. Crow, publisher of *Crow's Pacific Coast Lumber Digest,* who represented the most rabid anti-union thought in the industry, declared:

> This makes it clear that Roosevelt intends to finance the A. F. of L. in its fight to force the lumber industry into a closed shop. . . .
> Lumber manufacturers are determined that they will not submit to this communistic move. . . . A prominent lumber man is supposed to have said, "It is bad enough to have to fight an organization like the A. F. of L. but when you have your own government assisting in putting a strangle hold on you the problem is a serious one." [9]

Commissioner Marsh succeeded in getting some, but not all, Portland operators to convene in a peace parley on May 7. The general feeling manifested was that the great impediment to settlement was the "closed-shop" issue, alongside of which the wage issue paled into insignificance. On that question the operators would not give ground. The next day Seattle felt the strike when ten out of twelve mills went down. Then the first Willamette Valley mill closed as the strike continued to spread. However, the Willamette Valley was scarcely further touched.[10]

On May 9 the negotiations at Longview between Muir and the representatives of the managements of the Long-Bell and Weyerhaeuser companies resulted in an agreement, subject to ratification by the men in secret ballot. The next day, however, 900 employees of the Weyerhaeuser mill at Longview struck before casting their votes and without authorization of the mill workers' strike committee. This action was due partly to restlessness and partly to rumors. But the most important thing in causing the strike was the advance disclosure of the terms of the agreement by loggers who had voted on it the night before.[11] Incidentally, the Communists took credit for the workers' coming out before the sawmill vote was taken. The Communists, after having stirred slightly in the industry for a number of years, were actually caught unprepared for the swift movement of organization which had taken place. They had missed an opportunity to influence the convention at Aberdeen at which the Carpenters took control over the lumber industry workers. Subsequently, at their own conference in Tacoma on April 17, they voted to disband their dual National Lumber Workers Union in favor of "boring from within." Belatedly, they were trying to gain control of the workers. At Portland, the night before the strike broke at Longview, labor leaders had employed strong-arm methods to prevent the convening of a Communist meeting, and to keep "radical influences" from affecting the strike.[12] The strength of the Communists at this time, however, should not be overemphasized. The key to the truth in the situation at Longview was a genuine dislike for Muir's leadership, particularly among the rank-and-file loggers who did not relish an outsider directing them. When the proposed agreement—intended by Muir as a model for further settlements—was revealed to the loggers, providing for a base wage of 50 cents an hour, a forty-hour week, recognition of the union but not the "closed shop," and time and one-half for overtime, it was rejected by a vote of nine to one. The loggers, accusing Muir of having sold them out, informed the sawmill workers, who struck and afterward rejected the proposed agreement eight to one.

The Long-Bell and Weyerhaeuser companies made a second offer for Longview plants and logging camps of an additional 5 cents an hour increase in all brackets, with recognition of the union as the agency for collective bargaining for its members only. This offer was voted on by secret ballot with approximately 2,100 men participating. It was rejected two to one. The companies and union representatives conferred again on May 12 in another effort to find ground for settlement, but failed and broke off negotiations.[13] No effort was made by the managements to operate either of the closed plants.

By May 12, it was estimated that 90 per cent of all operations in the Douglas fir region were at a standstill. Negotiations still were in progress with the McCormick Lumber Company, which had been working in close harmony with the Long-Bell and Weyerhaeuser companies at Longview. These three companies advocated compromising with the union and were able to hold their own in a discussion with the representatives of the balance of the industry at Tacoma on the 14th. On the 16th the McCormick Lumber Company and the local unions of St. Helens, Oregon, Port Gamble and Port Ludlow, Washington, with the aid of E. P. Marsh, United States labor conciliator, reached an agreement similar to the one that was rejected at Longview. The local unions were recognized for collective bargaining. Complaints were to be adjusted through standing committees elected at each plant. The company was allowed preference in hiring unemployed men from other of its own camps and mills, rather than hiring new men. Seniority rights were recognized, although the company retained the right to hire and discharge after giving an acceptable reason. The forty-hour week and 50 cents an hour were agreed to.[14]

In accordance with the union laws, the agreement had to be submitted to the Northwest Council for ratification. This was done on the 18th. Then it was submitted to the workers at the plants and camps for secret ballot. On the 19th the employees at Port Ludlow and Port Gamble voted overwhelmingly for the agreement, but at St. Helens mass picketing by outside men closed the plant before the vote was taken. The insurgents then endeavored, without success, to persuade the men at Port Ludlow and Port Gamble to repudiate their vote and leave the job.[15]

Twice within ten days Muir's leadership had been seriously challenged. Because of the compromise in the proposed agreement at Longview, he was placed under fire and a widespread split in the union ranks occurred. Muir accused Norman Lange, president of the Tacoma local and vice-president of the Northwest Council, with having caused rejection of the Longview agreement. In his struggle with Muir, Lange was supported by the vote of 1,600 members of his local. Muir was again challenged by the insurgents when they succeeded in closing the McCormick mill at St. Helens. A showdown between Muir and the insurgents over control of union policy was imminent with the assembling of the Northwest Council in Longview. Before this took place, Muir used his "authority" to remove Lange from office in the Council. This embarrassed the Tacoma local, which had voted to support Lange. The local either had to repudiate its president or face expulsion from the Brotherhood.

Whether Muir had authority to remove Lange from office was bitterly questioned in the Northwest Council convention. The factional dispute occupied most of the first two days' meetings. When Muir appeared at the convention and emphasized the authority of the Brotherhood to expel individuals or locals, and the Brotherhood's power to withhold assistance, the Council acted to replace Lange. Along with this, the Council reduced its wage demand from 75 to 50 cents as the minimum and accepted the eight-hour day and forty-hour week, although it continued to insist on recognition of the union and time and one-half for overtime. Union recognition, however, did not entail the closed shop. The conservative group thus controlled the Council, but because the insurgents dominated in a number of localities, the interunion fight was not so easily settled. Muir supporters vigorously condemned the leaders of the insurgent group and associated them—in many cases falsely—with Communists.[16]

While the union was being torn internally, various groups were endeavoring to break the strike. A critical situation developed when worried farmers threatened to use vigilante tactics if they were denied ample shipping crates for their ripening berry crop. Sheriff J. W. Connell of Washington County, Oregon, and Governor Martin of Oregon both threatened to take action to protect individuals who would go to work in the mills. Actually, the trouble was settled without difficulty through conferences with farm leaders arranged by Ben Osborne, secretary of the Oregon State Federation of Labor, and the delivery of crates was permitted.[17]

Governor Martin of Oregon was again anxious to intervene when the first violence in the strike occurred at Forest Grove on May 23, after the Stimson Mill was reopened in defiance of the strikers. Pickets had been sent from Portland to reinforce the local union men, and when a state patrolman was treated roughly the pickets were driven with tear gas from the roadway leading to the mill. The pickets were in an ugly mood and a nasty situation was avoided by the timely arrival of C. H. Gram, state labor commissioner. The latter conferred with Bert Hall, leader of the pickets, and informed him of the impending arrival of troops. The union men acquiesced when Gram pleaded with them to stay out of the roadway. In view of the immediate establishment of order, General G. A. White of the Oregon

National Guard, who had been sent to the scene by the governor, advised against the calling of troops.[18]

Governor Martin of Oregon ordered the State Board of Conciliation to investigate the lumber tie-up. Both employers and union leaders who were subpoenaed did not want the board to exercise its mediation services. The chairman, O. M. Plummer, and the labor representative of the board, W. E. Kimsey, submitted a majority report to the governor in which they explained their inability to get the parties either to conciliate or to arbitrate the dispute, adding that without an extended investigation of the industry it was impossible to pass judgment on the wage question. In a minority report, C. M. Ryan, employer representative on the board, emphatically declared that the employers were in no position to pay wage advances. Nevertheless, on May 22 the 4L board of directors, after three days of proposals and counterproposals, decided to increase wages. Even though employer members of the board were at first reluctant to grant wage increases, the employee representatives made it plain that the only way to defeat the men on strike was through higher pay.[19]

The possibility of federal intervention was always present. The governor of Washington, however, did not want a federal mediation board appointed at this time. Nor, moreover, did Muir, who was confident that within a few days other large operators would follow the precedent of the McCormick Lumber Company and make agreements with the union. Employers were also almost unanimously opposed to a federal board because they feared its personnel would likely be unsympathetic to the economic problems of the industry and because it might jockey them into arbitration, which they did not want at all. The operators seemed convinced that such a board would act in accordance with popular sentiment instead of being "sternly practical." These considerations account for the absence of federal intervention in the early period of the strike.

Many operators were anxious to operate their plants provided adequate police protection could be assured. Informal conferences had been held by operators and, in spite of the 4L decision to increase wages, a semiorganized resistance to wage increases or union recognition in "any form" was built up. The situation was complex enough to support the view that "the greatest menace to safe and quick settlement," as the Everett *News* declared in an editorial, lay in "the activities of intemperate radicals among the mill operators as well as among the timber workers." [20]

On May 27 the Supreme Court invalidated the NIRA and helped

make a confused situation still more confused. The action of the court encouraged the operators, while the workers felt weakened. Partly as a result of the NIRA decision and immediately following it, Muir, on May 28, consulted with state labor officials as to the best means of ending the Longview strike. It was decided that a ballot was inadvisable because of the lack of either experience or discipline among the strikers and that the situation called for stern action by Muir. At a long conference with the Longview operators, at which Marsh, Lumm, and a conference committee composed of twenty-five employees of the two companies were present, the managements of the Long-Bell and Weyerhaeuser companies informed Muir and the group that they still stood behind their wage offer but were convinced that the local union was neither strong nor disciplined enough to warrant immediate contractual relations. They let Muir know that they were willing to deal with the union provided the membership could follow the laws and policies of the Brotherhood. Some of the employee representatives were ready to break off negotiations with the companies, but capitulated when Muir faced them with the alternative of being dropped by the Brotherhood if they did not accept the offer. The upshot was that on the night of May 28, at a union meeting attended by about a thousand men, a practically unanimous vote favored the agreement which provided a minimum wage of 50 cents per hour, the eight-hour day with a forty-hour week, and time and one-half for overtime. It is significant that a similar offer had been rejected less than two weeks earlier.[21] The acceptance of the agreement at Longview did not necessarily presage any movement toward general cessation of the strike, and there was evidence that the industry generally would ignore the Longview settlement.

Invalidation of the NIRA encouraged most operators to play a waiting game until the union cracked. This position, however, played into the hands of left-wing leaders at a time when it would have been relatively easy to establish a more or less uniform industry-wide settlement with the more conservative unionists. The hand of the militant unionists was strengthened and dissension in the union was increased. Now that government support of collective bargaining seemed to have been laid aside, it was easy to convince many of the workers that more militant, direct action was necessary. Moreover, the drastic compromise reductions in their original demands, as accepted at Longview, permitted the radicals to charge Muir and his supporters with a sell-out.

Left-wing influences became more vocal and assumed a more open and active role in the strike. The Communists officially announced their claim to leadership. This was an exaggeration, but they were actually assuming a far more important role than ever before. Precisely how strong the Communists were, it is impossible to tell. In Everett, one of the centers of "radicalism," it was the opinion of the usually well-informed editor of the *News* that less than 2 per cent of all the 3,000 strikers were Communists.[22] Other centers of Communist strength were Olympia and Grays Harbor. Wherever possible the Communists did everything they could to discredit the A.F. of L. leadership. There is reason to conclude that they were more concerned with keeping the dispute alive than in securing a reasonable settlement.

Muir, also opposed by non-Communists who rejected his settlement, issued peremptory orders to the locals in various areas to reorganize the strike committees to conform with the Brotherhood policy or to suffer expulsion. The struggle between the intra-union groups grew more intense each day. Violence flared up when, on June 3, Lumm and E. S. Hall, officers of the Northwest Council, were beaten by an unknown body of men who threatened the same treatment to Muir and other union officials.

On June 5 a "rump" convention comprised of representatives of the insurgent group in the unions at Aberdeen, Hoquiam, Shelton, and Olympia met in Aberdeen for the purpose of wresting control of the strike policy from Muir. The four hundred delegates present voted to renew the original strike demands and formed the Northwest Joint Strike Committee. They also adopted a resolution urging the removal of Muir as spokesman and sent it to Bill Hutcheson, president of the Carpenters, and William Green, president of the A.F. of L. Muir lost no time in declaring the meeting unauthorized by the union because it had been called at the instigation of "Communists and other radical groups." [23]

An insurgent group at Longview, by massing a huge throng of pickets, succeeded in preventing employees from going to work and reclosed the mills on June 6. The action of the Grays Harbor locals at Aberdeen had been accepted by the Longview insurgents, and they appointed new strike committees to supersede the Muir leadership, deciding at the same time to stand on their original demands.[24]

While these events were transpiring, the 4L was trying to gain control of the situation at Everett and Tacoma by advocating a secret ballot to determine the desires of the workers. The Sawmill and Timber Workers Union refused to participate and at Everett ordered the workers to turn in any ballot they might receive to union headquarters. Even the Everett employers were lukewarm, holding that they were waiting to meet with the unionists as soon as the "radicals" were ousted.[25] At Tacoma, where the 4L had earlier been very strong, the local group took the initiative in sending out a letter with a postal card ballot to get an opinion on the question of returning to work on the basis of the 4L wage increase. The ballots were sent to 1,752 workers certified to be on the May 3 employment lists of the nine Tacoma sawmill, plywood, and door plants. The ballots had been addressed to a special post-office box, the key of which was in the hands of postal authorities until the committee, composed of Mayor Smitely, the Reverend E. M. Hegge, and the Reverend Sidney James, took the ballots out on June 4 to count them. Of the 1,752 ballots mailed out, 1,068, or 61 per cent, were returned. Of these, four were rejected and 925, or 87 per cent, favored ending the strike in accordance with the terms specified. Although widely heralded as a seven-to-one verdict for return to work, this actually represented the desires of only 52 per cent of those who had been employed on May 3, a majority of 98 out of 1,752 workers. Union officials claimed the balloting was not fair—that men who had not been on the payroll for eight years received ballots—whereas the employers insisted that the payroll lists were correct.[26]

On the basis of this vote, preparations for opening the mills were begun. Police Commissioner Frank Callender and Sheriff Jack Bjorklund were asked point-blank if they would give the plants protection. Callender told the employer-employee committee that over 400 men would be required to police the mills, as compared with the 125 suggested. He frankly admitted that it was beyond the capacity of the public safety department to furnish more than a small fraction of the men needed. The appeal was then carried to the sheriff, a former secretary of the Longshoremen's Union, who replied, "I'll give what protection I can, but you start operations and see what happens. I haven't enough men to meet such demands." E. C. Griggs, II, spokesman for the committee, asked, "Will you or will you not then take the next step and see the governor?" Bjorklund replied, "No, you see him." The sheriff was not inclined to promise what he could not give. Exhorting the operators to recognize the principle of collective bargaining and deal with all the men, he accused them of "going pretty strong . . . when you ask me to prostitute my principles." Callender, who had accompanied the committee, explained: "I told these gentlemen . . . if they opened the mills other unions would go out. I am satisfied if the mills open up under guard we will have a general tie-up." [27]

In spite of this, the operators went ahead with plans to open the mills. As both Governor Martin of Washington and Governor Martin of Oregon guaranteed state protection to men who returned to work, the strike situation became more tense almost everywhere.[28] On June 10 state police ordered pickets to keep clear of the White Star Lumber Company mill at Whites, Washington, and the pickets disbanded. On the next day state police removed all but two pickets at the Coates Lumber Company mill in Tillamook, Oregon. A more spectacular development was the forced eviction of pickets at Bridal Veil and at Forest Grove, Oregon.

A truck driver of the Bridal Veil Lumber Company was stopped by a group of men, was pummeled, and his truck sent over a fifteen-foot embankment. As a consequence, Sheriff Pratt ordered all picketing stopped at the mill, claiming that the pickets "broke their word and failed to picket peacefully." The S.T.W.U. challenged the order of the sheriff, being determined to maintain "the legal right to picket," and claimed that the "beat-up gang" was not from the striking sawmill union workers. Pickets were arrested as fast as they came onto the line. By the evening of June 12 the jail was full and 175 men who had assembled from Portland to help picket were either loaded onto buses or marched down the highway to the outskirts of Portland, where they were told to "keep going" and their arrests were "terminated." The union officials made an attempt to obtain an injunction the next day, but Circuit Judge Crawford refused to grant the request, although he did call for a hearing. B. A. Green, attorney for the union, charged that the governor's office might have had an interest in the attack on the driver because of a desire on the part of the state executive to put an end to picketing in the lumber strike. The union insisted that the pickets had always conducted themselves in a peaceful manner. Deputy District Attorney Frank Sever contended, however, that there was no lawful picketing because there was no dispute between the company and its employees. The unionists accused the state patrolmen of mistreating them and beating some of the pickets. To substantiate their charges, the president of the Portland local, W. F. Wedel, offered his back as an exhibit to the court, and Judge Crawford announced, for the benefit of the court reporter who included it in the record, that he could count six red stripes and several dots on the man's back. Wedel said that the dots were made when deputy sheriffs and state police poked him in the back with the ends of their sticks.

The strikers lost their injunction plea because the judge felt that the sheriff had used reasonable discretion. The judge explained that labor should not suffer for the action of irresponsibles, but "it must suffer for them if its own legitimate activities cannot be carried on without creating a hazard to persons and property generally." He said that, although labor was not responsible for what had happened, it had "furnished the occasion out of which arose the fear of violence and disorder and its unquestioned right to picket lawfully must yield temporarily to the paramount right of community peace." The sheriff then agreed to permit picketing again after one week.[29]

While the Bridal Veil pickets were being dispersed, a hundred or more pickets were driven away from the Stimson mill at Forest Grove on June 13 by state police. The state police were met by a barrage of rocks which injured a small number, and only a few pickets were arrested.

Violence also occurred at Bellingham, Washington, when a group of strong-arm men from Seattle challenged the picket lines and, after engaging in a fight, were incarcerated in the county jail. The arrested men included the head of a strikebreaking agency and four associates, who implicated the management of the leading Bellingham lumber company which, while denying responsibility, agreed to proceed with negotiations with the workers. On June 14 negotiations were opened with the Bloedell-Donovan Company, the third largest producer in the region, with Pat Kelly, of the Washington State Department of Labor and Industries, and Commissioner Marsh acting as intermediaries. At a mass meeting a proposed agreement, recognizing the local of the S.T.W.U. as the collective bargaining agency, was presented to the employees who voted decisively in favor of it. Subsequently the mill opened.[30]

At other places mills were resuming work or preparing to open. A former 4L plant, along with two other lower Columbia River operations, signed union agreements. It was becoming evident that the conservative element among the workers was gaining control at certain places. Even at Longview there was much dissatisfaction with the failure of the insurgent leaders to open negotiations on the original demands. At some places preparations for opening without granting recognition were being made. On June 18 the Portland sawmill companies advertised that all positions were open to applicants. But in view of the longshoremen's refusal to handle lumber, the operators were not very optimistic. Although the employers claimed that over a thousand men responded and employers were given assurance by the police that no more than eight pickets would be present at any one plant, they did not attempt to operate the mills. At Tacoma all but three mills were opened on June 21 as state police and deputy sheriffs gave protection. Seattle mills opened without agreements on June 22.[31]

Mass picketing at Tacoma resulted in the arrival of the National Guard on June 23. The governor asserted that Mayor Smitely had informed him that local authorities were unable to cope with the situation and that Tacoma and Seattle operators had requested him to send troops.[32] The Tacoma Central Labor Council, denying that Mayor Smitely had appealed to the governor, protested on the ground that the troops caused disorder where none had occurred before. A delegation of union leaders from Seattle and Tacoma could not persuade the governor to withdraw the soldiers.

On their first day in Tacoma the state troops went into action to move the pickets back. At seven o'clock in the morning about seventy-five soldiers, carrying rifles with fixed bayonets, were taken by a circuitous route to the east end of the Eleventh Street bridge, the principal point at which pickets had assembled to discourage returning night shift workers. A crowd of two or three hundred was there. Without preliminaries, the soldiers methodically began "walking" the crowd back. The strikers took their time, but the troops were not in a hurry. When the crowd had been cleared from the bridge, the men stood in the street and jeered at the soldiers and were answered by the occasional use of gas. Beyond this no further effort was made to disperse the people.

At a general union meeting—at which every local in the city was represented—it was decided not to call a general strike, but the Longshoremen's Union voted not to work so long as armed troops remained in the city. The next day General Pennington arrived with more troops and immediately issued an order prohibiting picketing so long as the National Guard was in charge of the situation. No more than three persons were permitted to congregate at any one place. Soldiers even entered stores and ordered people who were looking out the windows to make their purchases and leave. There had been no formal declaration of martial law, but citizens were restrained in their liberty of action and there were arrests without charges. The Tacoma *Times* editorially declared that those arrested "have been denied counsel, refused bail and prohibited from notifying family or friends of their predicament. . . . Civil liberties have been flouted. Right of trial, of knowledge of accusers, of information about charges, has been scorned. The right of peaceful picketing has been thrust aside." [33]

Mayor Smitely, with the City Council concurring, offered mediation. The workers accepted, but the operators spurned the offer on the ground that the city officials had previously confessed themselves incapable of offering protection to the men who wished to return to work. They declared that any meeting would only complicate the situation and that the matter was already in the best hands—those of the governor. [34]

On June 26, Governor Martin stated over the radio that the troops would not be withdrawn from Tacoma until industrial peace had been established. "I insist," the governor also declared, "on respect for collective bargaining, for peaceful picketing, for the right to strike, even for the privilege to quit . . . and I don't admire nor support that employer who would take advantage of the situation to beat down wages . . . but also I shall continue to demand respect for the right to work." He then indicated that he was going to give the same protection to other communities, provided a majority of the employers and workers presented sworn petitions showing they had satisfactory wage and hour agreements. [35]

The Seattle branch of the American Civil Liberties Union, which subsequently investigated, reported that "no justification has existed at any time for the extreme measures taken by the Governor of the State in assigning state patrolmen and national guardsmen to Tacoma . . . not a single arrest has been made by either city or county police authorities in connection with the strike activities . . . neither city nor county police authorities requested the use of troops." [36]

The attempts to open the sawmills in various places created a tense situation because only a few of the operators had entered into agreements. Violence had occurred where mills had opened without the sanction of unionists, and additional violence seemed certain inasmuch as preparations were being made to open other mills. The insurgents were still strong, and unionists everywhere were hostile toward the attempt to break the strike and disgruntled over the use of the militia. The fact that the longshoremen, who were sympathetic to the insurgents, were refusing to work wherever troops were on the ground, which, incidentally, was a threat to Pacific Coast maritime peace, made the situation more critical. Because of these conditions, Secretary of Labor Frances Perkins, on June 26, at the request of the United States Conciliation Service, appointed a Federal Mediation Board composed of Superior Judge Roscoe R. Smith of Seattle, Judson Shorett, Seattle attorney, and the Reverend Father George F. Thompson, Church of the Madeline, Portland. An immediate protest was made by lumber operators on the ground that "there is no occasion for a mediation board—there is nothing to mediate." In a telegram the operators declared that "the appointment of a mediation board will only prolong the trouble, postponing the return of the men to the mills, because naturally they will hesitate to go back pending the long process of mediation." F. H. Ransom, president of the Eastern and Western Lumber Company in Portland, placed the blame for the dispute upon "outside interests. If the lumbermen and their employees, who have always been able to adjust their differences in the past, could be left alone, everyone could soon be back to work and happy." [37]

Meanwhile, the struggle between the union factions continued. Muir was endeavoring to break the hold of the insurgents at various places. To the men at Longview he sent a sharp letter, announcing that new locals were being set up separately for employees for the Weyerhaeuser and Long-Bell plants and commanding the men to go back to work. On July 1 the mills at Longview began operations with only 700 men, and the National Guard was ordered to be in readiness to move in if violence occurred. The biggest obstacle to complete settlement here was the intra-union fight. The Central Labor Council had sided with the anti-Muir faction, and Muir consequently requested the A.F. of L. to revoke its charter. The situation was so tense that it was practically impossible for the Federal Mediation Board to intervene. The Central Labor Council, accordingly, sent a telegram to Secretary Perkins asking for the appointment of a special investigator. This was not done because it was apparent that the difficulty was intra-union and had to be dealt with by trade union officials and not the government.

In order to bring recalcitrant bodies into line, C. C. Young, general representative of the A.F. of L., addressed a letter to all Central Labor Councils to the effect that aid given to the Northwest Joint Strike Committee was in violation of Article XI of the A.F. of L. constitution; that those bodies giving aid were subject to revocation of their charters; that the Brotherhood of Carpenters had full jurisdiction; and that an attack upon the strike leadership was an attack on the Brotherhood. Young then called upon all central bodies who were not conforming "to immediately expel the local unions which have been suspended or expelled from the Brotherhood of Carpenters and repudiate the so-called 'Northwest Joint Strike Committee.'" William Green took action to clear the Longview situation by informing Secretary Dyer of the Kelso (Longview) Central Labor Council that the charter of Local 2504, S.T.W.U., the original local, had been officially revoked. He also promised Muir that he would take further action if it was necessary.[38] This paved the way for a gradual resumption of complete operations, and by the end of July the Weyerhaeuser and Long-Bell mills in Longview were operating with a force of 3,700 men.

The same day that the Longview mills reopened, an attempt to open the mills at Aberdeen was frustrated by an enormous picket line of almost 2,000 men. A clash with the police occurred when it was discovered that a gravel thoroughfare near one of the mills had been strewn with roofing nails. Under penalty of immediate ejection if they refused, pickets were forced to gather them up. But when another handful was thrown from the crowd, the street was cleared of workers by the use of gas. The Federal Mediation Board had, in the meantime, established friendly contacts with some Aberdeen operators and was making a little progress. It was handicapped, however, by the non-co-operative attitude of the leading employers. There was continued disorder, and on July 7 National Guardsmen were sent to Grays Harbor for strike guard duty. The governor claimed that the mayors of Aberdeen and Hoquiam and the sheriff of Grays Harbor County had asked for them. The area was not placed under martial law, but guardsmen were stationed around the mills to permit the return of such men as wished to work. Several thousand people—mill workers, wives, children, and sympathizers—marched from Aberdeen to Hoquiam and back to show their unity and to demonstrate against the opening of the mills and the presence of the troops. Aberdeen was the stronghold of the Northwest Joint Strike Committee and workers stood out solidly against the back-to-work movement, with the result that the situation remained deadlocked for a time.[39]

While troops were in Aberdeen, the insurgent storm center tended to veer toward Everett, where extremists on both sides continued to make mediation difficult. Everett, at this time, was the only place where operations were not resumed. The intra-union struggle there was intense. The insurgents were strong. An attempt to open one mill on July 5 was met with mass picketing which gave rise to use of tear gas by state and city police. The operators were convinced that "radical" groups controlled the union to the extent that union recognition in any form was impossible. They continued to exert pressure on the governor to send troops. However, the Weyerhaeuser Company, employing nearly half of the total workers in the Everett area, stated that it would not join in a request for troops or attempt operation under military rule.[40]

To get rid of the insurgent leadership, Muir was considering revocation of the Everett charter and installation of separate locals at the plants of each of the six companies as the only way to bring about a peaceful settlement. On July 13 the Everett Sawmill Workers Union repudiated the Northwest Joint Strike Committee in a secret ballot by a vote of 328 to 272—but there was a normal working force of 2,000—and the Brotherhood of Carpenters issued six plant charters. The situation was further complicated when four mills immediately opened without granting union recognition. The insurgents tried to stop the back-to-work movement. Open-air demonstrations and a march on city hall were started, but the marchers were routed by riot clubs and gas bombs in the hands of state patrolmen. In the evening an insurgent crowd of 2,500 people stormed the Labor Temple and prevented the newly formed conservative unions from meeting. The situation was acute because the presence and aggressive action of the state patrolmen had changed public opinion to favor the insurgent group. Considerable responsibility for the turmoil must rest on the employers who refused to give time for the newly organized conservative unions to begin negotiations and insisted on opening under armed protection.[41]

The situation at Tacoma had continued tense with intermittent acts of violence and disorder. Finally, on July 11, the Tacoma city commissioners wired the Federal Mediation Board and the U.S. Department of Conciliation requesting intervention. Before anything could be done, an outbreak occurred which was the direct aftermath of the breaking up of an attempted parade of the strikers and strike sympathizers who had been dispersed by guardsmen the night before. Strikers had been in an ugly mood all day and shortly before four o'clock in the afternoon trouble started. A large crowd assembled at the federal building and started marching around and around at the intersection of Eleventh and A streets. The leader of each squad carried an American flag. The people marched only on the crossings, believing that this relieved them of the necessity of having a parade permit. Although traffic was blocked, the city police made no attempt to disperse them. The troops made no attempt to interfere but maintained a line of men with fixed bayonets all the way across the bridge. Around four-thirty, when lumber workers began returning across the bridge from the mills, the marchers began jeering at the workers. A few gas bombs were released at intervals, but no determined effort was made to clear the crowd away until about five o'clock when the troops decided to clear the square immediately adjacent to the bridge. A number of heads were cracked as resistance to the guardsmen developed. One man, who attempted to disarm a guardsman, was carried away in an ambulance. The tactics of the guardsmen did not prove successful because the wind was blowing down Eleventh Street toward the bridge and the gas rolled back toward the troops, only a few of whom were wearing gas masks. Exploded gas grenades were picked up and hurled or kicked back among the guardsmen. As the use of gas grenades failed, a military truck was used to expel gas from its exhaust pipe, but the truck caught fire and burned.[42] When the fighting finally ceased, the crowd disappeared.

Following this incident, the Federal Mediation Board began to work in Tacoma. While there were numerous sporadic acts of violence, workers there voted early in August by secret ballot—1,291 to 97—to accept the employers' offer of an agreement which provided for wage increases in all classifications, union recognition, and return of all strikers within thirty days.

During the latter part of July the strike definitely was on the wane at all points, except Aberdeen. The workers at Olympia voted by ballot to accept an agreement recognizing plant committees, wage increases, and return of all strikers. At the same time, the Stimson Lumber Company of Seattle resumed operations under union sanction, as did four Portland mills where agreements had been reached.[43]

Following the Tacoma settlement, the Federal Mediation Board began work at Aberdeen. Muir had revoked the Aberdeen charter and created a new local, when he was relatively free of trouble at other places, but the insurgent influence remained strong. The newly chartered union could claim only 400 members, while the union whose charter had been revoked claimed 3,700. Practically all the operators had agreed in writing to recognize the union authorized by Muir, and so the main obstacle to settlement of the strike revolved around the inter-union struggle. The Muir group asserted that there would be a swing to the regularly chartered union if the workers who wanted to join it were assured adequate protection. But this was not wholly true. The National Guard in Aberdeen was fair, and the situation was handled better there than elsewhere. The workers were standing behind the original local.[44]

The deadlock was pried open a little when the old and the new local met in Aberdeen late in July to consider transfer of membership to the latter. This was arranged, and with less than a third of its

claimed membership voting, the old local decided to accept the jurisdiction of the new local. The bitter intra-union fight then subsided,
and negotiations with the operators were begun.

No sooner had negotiations got under way at Aberdeen than
complications developed. The Bay City Lumber Company, operating
under an agreement with the Muir local, had been picketed by members of the outlaw union, with the result that the longshoremen
refused to load ships tied up at the mill docks. Following the vote to
merge the two locals, both factions agreed to remove the pickets at
the Bay City mill and declared an armistice, pending final negotiations. Longshoremen thus were allowed to load the ship. Then on
July 29 a large crowd, including Communist sympathizers, assembled
at the plant entrance. Following a parley with the mill manager, the
sawmill workers withdrew their objections to loading the ship, but
the longshoremen officials then took upon themselves the task of dic-
tating to the manager what sawmill workers he should retain and
let go. The negotiations at Aberdeen centered on this plant, and the
unwarranted interference of the longshoremen promptly upset them.
The Washington state labor officials and the Federal Mediation Board
worked hard in the face of serious obstacles to clear this situation.
Communists, working under cover, contributed to the obstructionist
tactics of radical sawmill workers and longshoremen. The employers
were unwilling to meet the wage situation constructively. Moreover,
the operators wanted assurance that there would be no further inter-
ruption from the longshoremen before they agreed to reopen. Finally,
on August 14 a settlement was reached. The new local was recognized
for collective bargaining purposes, but the operators reserved the right
"to negotiate with any individual, committee, or committees of our
employees for collective bargaining purposes for the employees whom
they represent." Any change in base pay or hours, however, was to
apply to all employees. The eight-hour day and forty-hour week with
a base rate of 50 cents per hour were accepted. The original demands drawn up in Aberdeen were cut down to the Longview agreement negotiated by Muir, over which the strike mainly had been
prolonged. The terms were accepted out of necessity.[45]

While the strike was over, peace had not been achieved. During the
ensuing months, minor skirmishes with employers broke out sporad-
ically. Within the unions dissension and unrest still continued. The
memory of internal union conflict which marked the strike could not
be easily erased.

For a number of reasons the strike of 1935 has unusual significance in the history of labor in the lumber industry. The rapid, genuine response to the call to organize and the almost complete support of the strike were surprising. The workers gained unionization, although unity was damaged and they failed to get a standard agreement. For the latter the operators were largely responsible. If the majority of the employers in the industry had had the foresight to go along with the early Longview settlement, standardization might almost have been achieved at a stroke, and the painful weeks of continuation of the strike could have been avoided. By holding out against any settlement with the union the employers opened the way for left-wing elements to enter the industry labor scene. The militant opposition of most employers and the resort to state police and the militia, in some cases, in opening the mills was also shortsighted and contributed greatly to ill will in the industry. The intense dislike of outside leadership among the workers contributed to insurgency, but the problem of leadership could have been solved peaceably in time, once stable relations were established. The course of events, and the bitterness which developed, seriously jeopardized worker unity for many years, and gave an unhappy direction to labor-employer relations in the industry.

NOTES TO CHAPTER

[1] *Report of Proceedings of the Fifty-Fifth Annual Convention of the A. F. of L., 1935,* p. 366; *Washington State Labor News,* March 29, 1935; *Timberworker,* September 7, 1936.

[2] Portland *Oregonian,* April 16, 1935; *Four L News Service,* April 24, 1935.

[3] Portland *Oregonian,* April 18, 1936.

[5] Portland *Oregonian,* April 20, 1935; Portland *News Telegram,* April 20, 1935.

[6] Portland *News Telegram,* April 30, May 3, 4, 1935; Portland *Oregonian,* May 1, 1935.

[7] Portland *Oregonian,* May 6, 7, 8, 1935; N. Sparks, "The Northwest General Lumber Strike," *The Communist,* XIV, No. 7 (September, 1935), 814; *Timberworker,* September 7, 1936.

[8] *West Coast Lumberman,* LXII, No. 6 (June, 1935), 26; Seattle *Post-Intelligencer,* May 6, 1935; Portland *Oregonian,* May 16, 1935; interview with Jay Ollinger, head of the Department of Labor and Industries, Washington, June 22, 1937.

[9] *Crow's Pacific Coast Lumber Digest,* May 13, 1935, pp. 1, 4, 20.

[10] Portland *News Telegram,* May 7, 1935; Portland *Oregonian,* May 7, 9, 1935; *Four L Staff Letter,* May 9, 1935.

[11] Portland *News Telegram,* May 9, 1935; Portland *Oregonian,* May 11, 1935.

[12] Portland *News Telegram,* May 10, 1935; *Voice of Action,* May 14, 1935.

[13] Portland *Oregonian,* May 13, 1935.

[14] Agreement, dated May 16, 1935 (typewritten).

[15] Portland *Oregonian,* May 21, 22, 1935.

[16] Portland *Oregonian,* May 13, 25, 26, 27, 1935; Everett *News,* May 26, 1935; Seattle *Post-Intelligencer,* May 23, 1935; *Washington State Labor News,* May 21, 1935.

[17] Portland *Oregonian,* May 19, 20, 1935; Portland *News Telegram,* May 18, 21, 1935; *Oregon State Federation of Labor Yearbook, 1935,* p. 10.

[18] Portland *Oregonian,* May 23, 24, 1935; Portland *News Telegram,* May 23, 1935.

[19] Portland *Oregonian,* May 23, 28, June 15, 1935; *Thirty-third Semi-Annual Report for the 4L Board of Directors, May 20-22, 1935,* pp. 1-4.

[20] Everett *News,* May 24, 1935.

[21] V. H. Jensen, "Labor Relations in the Douglas Fir Industry." Unpublished Ph.D. Thesis, University of California, 1939, pp. 221-222; Portland *Oregonian,* May 30, 1935; see above, p. 169.

[22] Everett *News,* June 3, 1935; cf. *Daily Worker,* June 1, 1935.

[23] Portland *Oregonian,* June 5, 6, 1935.

[24] Portland *Oregonian,* June 6, 8, 1935.

[25] Everett *News,* June 1, 1935.

[26] Tacoma *Daily Ledger,* June 5, 1935; *Four L News Letter,* June 4, 1935; Tacoma *Times,* June 7, 1935.

[27] Tacoma *Times,* June 7, 1935.

[28] Portland *Oregonian,* June 8, 10, 1935.

[29] Portland *Oregonian,* June 11-18, 1935; *Oregon Voter,* June 15, 1935.

[30] *Four L Lumber News,* July 1, 1935; V. H. Jensen, *op. cit.,* p. 240.

[31] Seattle *Post-Intelligencer,* June 22-25, 1935.

[32] Seattle *Post-Intelligencer,* June 24, 1935.

[33] Tacoma *Times,* June 28, 1935.

[34] Tacoma *News,* June 27, 28, 1935.

[35] Seattle *Post-Intelligencer,* June 27, 1935.

[36] Seattle *Star,* July 1, 1935.

[37] Seattle *Post-Intelligencer,* June 27, 1935.

[38] V. H. Jensen, *op. cit.,* p. 252; Seattle *Post-Intelligencer,* July 18, 1935.

[39] Seattle *Post-Intelligencer,* July 3, 8, 9, 1935; *Timberworker,* September 7, 1935.

[40] Seattle *Post-Intelligencer,* July 5, 6, 1935.

[41] Everett *News,* July 4, 17, 21, 1935.

[42] Tacoma *Labor Advocate,* July 13, 1935; Seattle *Post-Intelligencer,* July 13, 1935.

[43] Seattle *Post-Intelligencer,* July 25, 1935.

[44] Seattle *Post-Intelligencer,* July 26, 1935.

[45] V. H. Jensen, *op. cit.,* p. 261.

10 *A PERIOD OF NEW UNIONISM*

THE ENDING of the great strike of 1935, it has been observed, did not mean the advent of peace. To the 20,000 to 30,000 unionized men, organization was new, and dissension smoldered within their ranks. Employers, too, lacked experience in collective bargaining and many of them learned only with difficulty. Among both groups there seemed to be a dearth of restraint and judgment. Misunderstandings and inexperience made for numerous breaks in peaceful relations and work stoppages. The greatest single obstacle to continued peace was the heterogeneity of agreements. For this the employers, excepting a few unusual ones, and the insurgents were largely responsible.

To chronicle all the minor disputes incident to interpretation and application of the diverse agreements would be an impossible and tedious task. But it is no exaggeration to say that they were of daily occurrence, and a more or less continuous ferment was noticeable everywhere. Not even all of the numerous local strikes and work stoppages warrant attention. Only a few of the most important events occurring in the West need consideration, but certain events, particularly those occurring in the Lake States and in the South, need to be fitted into the picture of new and expanding unionism.

Because unionism was assured in the industry in Oregon and Washington, loggers in British Columbia, who had made little headway while organized as the Lumber Workers Industrial Union, having affiliation with the Workers Unity League, entered into negotiations with the Brotherhood of Carpenters and Joiners for the purpose of changing affiliation and reached an agreement to transfer membership in February, 1936. Before long recognition was wrested from the employers, but not without a stiff struggle colored by strike activity.[1] Organization was also spread more extensively and intensively throughout Oregon and Washington and was definitely improved. Some areas in the fir belt, however, remained difficult to organize and the pine region remained substantially in the hands of the 4L.

An incident illustrative of the immaturity of collective bargaining occurred early in 1936 when a movement for wage increases began throughout the western industry. Improved market conditions made employers more or less willing to pay a moderate increase. And so, in spite of the chronic bickering during the previous months, wage adjustments through peaceful negotiations were obtained throughout the Puget Sound and Grays Harbor districts. In the Columbia River District, however, the situation was entirely different, and there a strike and lockout of considerable proportions occurred. Inadequate machinery for handling disputes, and inexperience and stubbornness in negotiations, contributed heavily to the developments.

Sawmill workers in Portland presented lengthy and complicated demands to their employers, and such an impasse was reached in the negotiations that a simple flat 5-cent per hour increase in wages, without any change in working conditions, was granted and accepted. No formal agreement was entered into because an old Wobbly tradition of "no signed agreements" was strong among the men and the employers did not wish to sign an agreement either.

With the loggers the story was different. Following the strike of 1935 an employers' association, the Columbia Basin Loggers Association, after having been in a moribund state for many years, was revived to deal with the unions in a collective bargaining capacity for all logging operators in the region. This was the operators' answer to the union tactic, probably also inherited from Wobbly strategy, of "picking off one camp at a time." Obstinacy and a nonciliatory attitude on both sides led to a deadlock in negotiations. The militant unionists resorted to direct pressure by calling strikes at three camps on May 4. The operators retaliated by ordering the unionists to restore all operations, by May 11, to the conditions preceding the strike or all the camps would be shut down. On May 12 thirty logging operations were closed, causing some mills to shut down because of a shortage of logs.[2] At this point, C. R. Gram, labor commissioner for Oregon, assisted by B. W. Sleeman, business representative of the Portland District Council of Carpenters, and E. P. Marsh, federal labor conciliator, stepped in and called conferences between the two parties. Negotiations were resumed and with the understanding assistance of Gram and Marsh an agreement was finally drawn up for submission to a referendum vote of the membership of the union without recommendation. The intention of Gram and Marsh was to leave the proposition solely to a vote of the loggers, as the terms would affect only them directly. But the Columbia River District Council was following a policy in which it signed all agreements instead of allowing the locals to do so. Because of this the sawmill workers, who were members of the Council the same as were the loggers, could not be denied the right to vote, and, to be sure, the Council would not consider allowing a part of the membership to be split off to vote separately on any issue. The count of the loggers' vote showed that they had voted to accept the agreement, while the sawmill workers—who thought they were voting as the loggers desired—voted against it. However, the election was thrown out on June 7 because of an alleged technical irregularity in the voting in two Portland plants. A second election was ordered immediately with the same machinery, and every precaution was taken to avoid the charge of fraud. The agreement, known as the "Gram-Marsh Agreement" was at this time approved.[3] Newness in bargaining had led to unnecessary strife and ill feeling.

The pitfalls into which the bargainers stumbled in 1936 and from which they emerged bruised and unfriendly were not avoided in 1937. Uncompromising attitudes and inability to give and take, on both sides, led to strikes and lockouts. This time Charles Hope, regional director of the National Labor Relations Board, intervened and proposed a settlement by which the employees were to resume work immediately with a wage increase of 10 per cent and all other issues to be submitted to arbitration. Both parties agreed to accept this procedure for settlement and Father George Thompson of the Madeline Parish, Portland, was appointed arbitrator. Consequently, 13,000 Columbia River loggers and sawmill workers resumed work in the camps and mills while arbitration was undertaken.[4] The settlement finally reached was obtained largely through negotiations rather than as an award of the arbitrator. Apparently all that was needed was someone to keep the negotiations proceeding in the proper direction. Again immaturity of labor relations had kept the parties from a settlement of their difficulties, which were, for the most part, of their own making.[5]

Elsewhere in the industry, in the Lake States and in parts of the South, the encouragement afforded in "New Deal" legislation, implemented by the success of the strike of 1935 in the West and the spread of unionism there, led the workers to organize. Bitterness and violence seemed natural concomitants. In the industry everywhere this was a period of new unionism.

In Minnesota, in the fall of 1935, unionism reappeared among the lumberjacks after an absence of over twelve years. The men in three logging camps presented demands for recognition, wage increases, and improved working conditions. An incipient strike failed but the men struggled on. After some delay, an A.F. of L. charter was obtained in April, 1936, and by the end of the year the union was in a relatively strong position. When demands were almost universally ignored, a strike was called for January 1, 1937, which spread throughout northern Minnesota. With the help of the Farmer-Labor party relief kitchens were established and the men were fed and sheltered in Duluth, Gheen, and Grover Conzet Camp.[6]

On the surface a threefold struggle seemed in progress, involving the union, the farmers and small contract loggers, and timber interests. This was not true, many of the farmers were also loggers and were sympathetic with the aims of the workers. The strike took on some political coloring when Frank Ronkainen, a small contract logger, posed as spokesman for the farmers, while actually he was representing the timber interests. He attempted to discredit the jacks and, at the same time, criticized Governor Benson and the Farmer-Labor party for helping them. After three weeks the strike was settled through the efforts of a committee appointed by the governor, and the 4,000 Minnesota lumberjacks scored a victory.[7]

Ronkainen, nevertheless, continued his attacks on the union by denouncing the governor for the assistance given to "a handful of outside agitators." Denouncing him for "helping a bunch of non-voting, floating racketeers who do not own property in this state. . . ." In answer, the union leaders condemned Ronkainen for his antilabor activities. Admitting that the members of the union had no property, they served notice that they intended to remedy the situation by forcing "more of your profits from you . . . so that we lumberjacks also can live like human beings." Said the union spokesman: "That we are 'floaters' is also correct. . . . But not through choice." Governor Benson later pointed out: "The general strike of woods workers has justly called attention to the plight of a neglected group of workers. The strike was only a natural consequence of working conditions and a depressed wage scale characteristic of an unhealthy industry."[8]

Labor organization in the South was only stimulated slightly by the guarantee of protection of organization under the NIRA. Nevertheless, there were sporadic activities at a few points, particularly in Alabama and Arkansas. Under the National Labor Relations Act organization activities became a little more widespread, but with only occasional success. A few cases under the act, which have been investigated and which have gone on to hearings, reveal the harsh way in which men have been handled whenever they expressed themselves through organization. In the face of claims of congenial relations these cases reveal a type of treatment afforded to unions when they appeared that makes a black picture. That such treatment is likely to be typical of a broad cross section of the industry is implied in the activities of the Southern Lumber Operators Association.[9] Many substantial employers, however, have not belonged to this association, and countless small operators have felt no personal need for it.

Labor organization has had little chance for success among the low standard workers with meager economic resources in the South because of the traditions of individualism and paternalism which prevail.

An A.F. of L. Lumber and Sawmill local was formed at the S. E. Belcher Lumber Company operations at Green Pond, Alabama, as early as August, 1933, which local was subsequently given a charter by the Carpenters in April, 1935. Although some success was had through a number of brief strikes, the attitude of the company was uncompromising. An A.F. of L. local was formed at the Nauvoo plant of the Smith Lumber Company, Red Bay, Alabama, in 1935. The company flatly refused to recognize it. The union struggled along until August 3, 1936, when a strike was called which lasted until August 29, at which time the company called the men back on its own terms.

Perhaps the most important early case in Alabama involved the Greenboro Lumber Company. An A.F. of L. local was organized in Greenboro in October, 1935, but the attitude of the company "was, from the beginning, antagonistic to the formation" of the union. The secretary-treasurer of the company said that "anyone who joined the union would be fired immediately," whereupon workers denied their membership, because, as one put it, "he had me scared." On November 7, 1935, Gerald Harris, organizer for the United Brotherhood of Carpenters and Joiners of America, called on the company officials and informed them that he had been chosen by a majority of the company's employees to engage the company in collective bargaining. The plant was ordered immediately shut down and the men were lined up and brought in one at a time to ascertain their desires. To this procedure Harris objected. Even after it was revealed that a majority of the employees supported Harris, the company still refused to bargain collectively. Two days later the plant was shut down for an extended period because of lack of orders. The company, however, had operated double shifts before the closure, and did so upon resuming work about a month later. Although the question of representation was not settled because it could not be decided what the appropriate unit was, the National Labor Relations Board ordered the company to cease and desist from interference with its employees' activities.[10]

In Arkansas there was considerable spontaneous organization during late 1934 and 1935. The activities centered in Warren where sawmills were operated by the Bradley Lumber Company, the Crossett Lumber Company, and the Southern Lumber Company.[11] All three companies followed a policy of discharging men for union activity. Other smaller mills in the locality did likewise. Following complaints, the National Labor Relations Board, because it was short-staffed, concentrated on the Bradley case, but could do nothing. Because of espionage the union leaders—men doing common labor in the mills— knew less and less each time the National Labor Relations Board man met them. The board ran into other difficulties. Bradley secured a temporary restraining order against the board, but it was later dissolved. The board attempted to hold a hearing at Warren, but the court refused to allow it and the board had to resort to an ex parte hearing in New Orleans without the company. In the meantime, the National Labor Relations Act had been held constitutional, whereupon Bradley immediately entered into a compromise settlement. Shortly after, the Southern Lumber Company came in to "get right" with the board, recognized the union, and signed an agreement.

Although all three companies had acted in close unison, the Crossett case continued to give the board its greatest difficulty. The A.F. of L. local had been so successful in its organizing drive that at one time it had fully three-fourths of the employees of the Crossett Lumber Company within its ranks. Shortly after the drive was launched the Southern Lumber Operators Association sent an operative of the Pinkerton Detective Agency to the plant. This association dates back to 1906, but in 1934 it was revived "to deal with the conditions of labor" and consisted of approximately forty lumber companies. It established a benefit trust fund "for the purpose of assisting members of the Association to resist any encroachments" and provided for making payments from the fund to members whose plants were closed because of strikes. The first Pinkerton agent reported that approximately four or five hundred employees were members. Mr. Arnold, manager of the mill, did not believe the report and a second agent was sent in the latter part of June. All this took place before the National Labor Relations Act came into effect. The second Pinkerton agent lost no time in joining the union, and soon had himself elected vice-president. Meanwhile, he made daily reports to the association. On October 10, 1935, the union discovered that the man was a labor spy. When he became useless, he was immediately replaced by another agent, and finally a fourth Pinkerton man was sent to the scene.

On the basis of the information obtained from the agents, many men were discharged. In addition, a form of blacklist was sent to members of the association and men were refused employment in other plants. One man who was twice denied employment with a particular company was readily hired when he gave an assumed name. The board produced evidence proving coercion, intimidation, and interference—also the issuance of circulars designed to discourage union membership.

On August 8 a brief four-day strike had been launched in protest against the discriminatory discharges. When the morale of the strikers began to break, the sheriff of Ashley County became the leading spirit in arousing a back-to-work sentiment and informed Arnold, the manager, that the men were ready to return. A committee was chosen to meet with Arnold, but the union had no part in selecting the members. Nor were the union's approved representatives allowed to meet on the ground that Arnold did not have to meet with anyone not in the employ of the company. The only thing that was offered the men was the barren privilege of returning to work. Afterward, Arnold emphatically forbade union meetings in Crossett. Subsequently, only three or four meetings of the union were held and the payment of dues was suspended. Union inactivity was recommended by a number of the Executive Board of the United Brotherhood of Carpenters and Joiners of America because of the espionage and likelihood of discharge.

When in November the National Labor Relations Board got into the case, the union was virtually dead. No evidence was introduced at the hearing relative to the petition for certification because of the previous hostile attitude and acts of the company. The board decided that a lapse of time would be necessary to overcome the effects of the unfair labor practices.

Labor troubles were not settled at Warren, Arkansas. On July 6, 1937, the National Labor Relations Board filed a complaint against the Southern Lumber Company, growing out of a charge made by the A.F. of L. local, charging company officers with distributing literature and making speeches hostile to membership of its employees in the union, and that the company had engaged espionage agents.

A hearing was held on July 19, 1937, in New Orleans at which it was decided to hold an election.[12]

In July, 1937, the A.F. of L. local filed a petition seeking certification at the Bradley Lumber Company. The company denied that there was any dispute whatever with respect to the organization selected for collective bargaining purposes, alleging that about 85 per cent of all the production employees were members of the Bradley County Employees Association. A hearing was held in mid-August at New Orleans. This ended in stipulations by and between Bradley Lumber Company, Bradley County Employees Association, and the United Brotherhood of Carpenters local, in which the first two, while denying the jurisdiction of the board, agreed to waive their respective pleas and consent to an election. The balloting was conducted on September 27, 1937. Of 943 counted ballots, the Bradley County Employees Association received 699 and the Carpenter local 244. The association was certified. Within a year, however, the National Labor Relations Board, in a new case, declared the Bradley County Employees Association was illegal and bona fide unionism was allowed a chance to re-establish itself.[13]

These disputes in the southern lumber industry are isolated and few in number. Yet they do reveal a strong opposition to organized labor. In a broad sense, however, they are not typical of the whole industry; for unionism has not spread far enough to reveal conclusively just what the general attitude is. Organizers have continued to work in the South, but they have established only a few local unions. In the southern lumber industry labor organization is still spotty and relatively insignificant. The reasons for the failure of unionism to spread are to be found, perhaps, as much in the economic and social condition of the workers as in employer opposition.

Of more significance to labor in the southern lumber industry than unionism has been the enactment of federal wage and hour legislation. The NIRA brought the first federal legislation which had important implications for southern lumber industry labor. It changed, ever so slightly, the notoriously poor wages and hours conditions. The wage increases under the NIRA were large when considered on a percentage basis. Yet the minimum of 22.5 cents per hour could hardly be justified on humane or on economic grounds. It was no fault of the workers that the southern lumber industry contained so many marginal and submarginal operations whose competition was always an acute factor in the unenlightened "cost-reducing" struggle for survival. The fact that the whole industry grew up on the basis of lower living standards cannot justify the perpetuation of the status quo. While the industry has been in a vicious circle of cost reduction, either to enable producers to compete with each other for a restricted total market or to meet the problems of increasing costs as more inferior timber had to be cut, the workers have been forced to pay for this in terms of depressed living conditions and poor working conditions.

Without some program of control within, or control from without, the industry and its workers would be doomed to continued impoverishment. An improved market gives only temporary relief. This is shown by the rapidity with which small portable mills go in and out of production.

To improve the health of the industry and the status of the worker in the Southern Pine region will involve efforts from many directions. To establish standards for the ultimate good of all, however, and to force otherwise unattainable adjustments are within the province of democratic government. The wage regulations, beginning with the NIRA and continuing in the form of the Fair Labor Standards Act (the Wage and Hour Law), are of this type. Wage and hour regulation has affected the southern lumber industry more than the western industry, and the long-run effect will be wholesome. Forest management in the South cannot be complete until ruthless and unintelligibly wasteful cutting of trees is controlled. Under proper circumstances, individuals will voluntarily follow good practices, but when caught in the grip of uncontrolled competition, and struggling for survival against numerous marginal and even submarginal producers, lumber operators are not truly free agents.

It is noteworthy that a strong element in the industry favored the wage regulation under the code, and that it was the lack of enforcement which changed the feeling toward the code. At the same time, the strong, almost universal opposition to the Wage and Hour Law is explainable in part by the fear that wage regulation could not be enforced and that the law threatened to change the cost level in Southern Pine without touching that in the West, because wages in the West were already well above the minimum level. Southern opposition then grew out of the fear of losing markets in the inter-regional competition.

It was inevitable that the application of the Wage and Hour Law would force some marginal firms out of business. However, even if their only reason for existing was the low wage level, it would be hard to justify their continued life. Also, some short-run unemployment was inevitable. Otherwise there would be simply preservation of an unwholesome situation that inevitably had to be faced. To escape from the low-price, low-wage cycle, help from the outside is needed. There is no moral or economic justification for poor returns to an industry whose competition is determined at its base by firms operating at unduly low wage schedules, which makes it possible to cut trees otherwise uneconomical. Trees under sixteen inches in diameter generally ought not to be cut. Unit costs increase rapidly with smaller diameter logs. To keep wages above minimum levels by law may be an important force in making it unprofitable, in the short run as it always is in the long run, to cut trees of small size. It might materially improve forest management practices. Under such circumstances, those operations which have access to truly merchantable logs might find their costs lower in proportion, or more so, than the increase in wages paid.

The initial, almost universal, opposition to the Wage and Hour Law moderated considerably after 1940 when the first enforcement drive was put into effect. The Wage and Hour Law field inspectors found rather poor compliance but it was not long until persistent efforts at enforcement began to bring forth fruit. The more responsible operators then changed their attitude about the law because they could see its beneficial long-run aspects coming into play. Of course, the improved market for lumber, due at first to the defense effort and then to the war, made it easier for the lumber producers to pay the wages required. The war has obscured some basic conditions but afterward it can reasonably be expected that proper administration of the Wage and Hour Law will assist materially in improving the workingman's position in the lumber industry as it will the position of the lumberman who can, and will, meet reasonable standards.

The continued success in collective bargaining in the West and the successful termination of the strike in Minnesota in January, 1937, aroused interest among Wisconsin and Michigan lumber industry workers. As organization was undertaken, a strike movement developed in mid-May, 1937. For several weeks lumberjacks working for the Cleveland Cliffs Iron Company at its camps near Munising had discussed the matter of a strike as a protest against low wages being paid, and against the filthy bunkhouses, bedbugs and lice, lack of bathing facilities, and the presence of pigs about the camps and under the bunkhouses. On May 24 the lumberjacks voted to strike, established strike headquarters at Munising, and rented a hall. Earlier in the month about half the men at one of the camps near Marenisco walked out in protest against bad food. Within a week the strike movement began to spread, and before long strike headquarters were established in Marenisco.[14] Other headquarters were established at many places throughout northern Michigan at Munising, Ironwood, North Ironwood, Bessemer, Iron River, L'Anse, Covington, and Marquette.

The strikers demanded 55 cents an hour, a forty-hour week, single beds, bathing facilities, recognition of the union, and recognition of camp committees.[15] Almost immediately, several small operators signed temporary agreements pending settlement of the strike, but the union met intense opposition in almost every center. The plight of the men was precarious because of the meager preliminary organization, their dire impoverishment, and the lack of experience in the conduct of such activities.

At Newberry a tragic event occurred. The strike had begun at one of the company camps on May 24 and at another on May 28. On June 3 about one hundred union members and sympathizers—the majority being strikers from the two logging camps—gathered in Newberry to attend a strike benefit dance to be held that night in the Workers Hall. On the same day several of the employees at the company's plant in Newberry requested that the chairman of the strike committee visit the plant to discuss with other employees the possibility of a strike. It was agreed that on the following morning the committee should visit the plant for this purpose.

About 6:00 A.M. the same group of about one hundred men left the Workers Hall and marched unarmed to the plant two abreast in peaceable fashion. The plant manager learned of the plans of the strike committee and informed the local sheriff. Both the manager and the plant superintendent arrived at the plant early. As the strikers came upon the company property the fire whistle blew, although ordinarily it was blown only in case of fire. The day previous there had been talk in the plant that the blowing of the fire whistle would be the signal to assemble to drive the strikers away. At this time, a foreman came into the casthouse where night-shift employees were still working and exhorted the men: "Come on, gang, let's chase the strikers out." Within a few minutes after the whistle had sounded, a crowd of 300 persons, including the sheriff, the plant manager, and the superintendent, had assembled outside the mill. Members of the crowd were armed with clubs, iron bars, rubber hose, and similar weapons. The sheriff halted the marching strikers, informed them that they were on private property, and warned them to leave or trouble would ensue. The leader of the strikers explained that they only desired an opportunity to speak to the men to see if they wanted to strike. The leader and the sheriff then agreed that the men should withdraw and send a committee back to talk with the employees. Thereupon, the sheriff took the strike leader by the arm and led the group down the road. After they had gone about fifty feet the sheriff dropped the strike leader's arm and stepped aside. A foreman immediately shouted, "Let's go," and swung his club in the air. The marching strikers were then set upon and brutally attacked. Many of the strikers were beaten mercilessly. One died soon after. The coroner attributed his death "to heart failure doubtless caused by unusual exertion,"—a peculiarly ironic verdict—because the victim was exerting himself trying to escape the wrath of mob fury.[16]

The one-sided battle strung along the highway for three or four miles as the strikers were driven out of town. Some of the men took refuge in the Workers Hall, only to be pursued by a group led in part by some of the company's foremen. The men were forcibly evicted from the hall, loaded on a truck, and, along with other union members and sympathizers who were rounded up around town, deported. The hall was demolished. The local justice of the peace, whose name was discovered on the union roll when the records were confiscated at the hall, was taken and smeared with grease and dumped in a gravel pit, He was saved from a worse fate by the chemical department foreman, who pointed out the possible fatal effects of an immersion in the company's tar tanks.[17]

On the day following the riot in Newberry on June 5, the people of Munising became highly wrought up over the union activities. Two of the strike leaders were arrested. When Henry Paull, attorney for the union, asked for admittance to the office of the justice of the peace, he was refused. Paull asked the prosecuting attorney what the charges against the two men were. "Murder and riot," was the reply, "and we don't know what the charges are and you better get the hell out of town." As Paull talked with the prosecuting attorney outside the courthouse, a menacing crowd assembled. The sheriff is reported to have asked, "Ain't you the lawyer who defended the Reds down here in Munising four years ago?" Paull replied, "I defended Burman and Immonen here . . . yes." Then somebody is reported to have yelled, "He defended Reds. . . . Drive the bastards out of town." Someone threatened, "If you don't get out of town in fifteen minutes we'll give you another Newberry." Paull, his wife, and the two union men who were with him, including Luke Raik, president of the local, got into Paull's car and drove away.[18]

The same day Joseph Ashmore, deputy state labor commissioner, held negotiations with the employers and a few timber workers in Munising, and announced to the press that the strike was settled. A dispute between the local union leadership and the Brotherhood of Carpenters agent had developed and Ashmore had taken sides against the local leaders because he considered them "left-wingers." Luke Raik called Ashmore twice and asked for a police escort back into Munising, so that he might participate in the negotiations. This was promised but was not provided. Raik asked if it was not a violation of the Wagner Act to conduct negotiations in an atmosphere of terror where the president of the union and the attorney for the union had both just been driven out of town. Ashmore is reported to have told the strikers: "I don't advise you to follow your present leaders. I will gladly open headquarters here tomorrow and help to organize you into a unit of the A.F. of L. Go back to work, appoint a grievance committee, and let it submit your demands in writing. If an agreement isn't reached in 30 days, then the differences will be arbitrated by us." Although Ashmore's proposal was not wholly acceptable, the strike did end at Munising.[19]

Throughout the region strike activity continued. At certain points negotiations were under way, but a reasonable settlement could not be made. The United States Conciliation Service sent a commissioner to investigate the difficulties, but he had little success.[20]

On June 30 Henry Paull, union attorney, went to Ironwood at the request of the union to confer with Nathaniel Clark of the National Labor Relations Board. About eleven o'clock that night, after the conference was over, Paull entered a restaurant with James Rogers, vice-president of the Minnesota local, and Luke Raik, president of the Michigan local. A mob swarmed into the restaurant and roughly hauled the three outside to the street. Paull broke loose, but was caught after a chase. He was severely pummeled, and dragged to a car and driven off. Luke Raik was given similar treatment. Rogers was not harmed. It is said that his Indian blood saved him because the mobsters did not want to become embroiled with federal authorities. Paull and Raik were reported to have been released in Saxon, Wisconsin.[21]

Many protests reached Governor Murphy. The most important came from Congressman J. T. Bernard, who insisted that the vigilantes be prosecuted for kidnaping. Almost immediately afterward

vigilantism broke loose at Bessemer, Michigan, when the union headquarters were raided, windows and furniture broken, and some of
the strikers beaten. After this, either because of some action by the
governor behind the scenes or because the mobsters decided that they
had done enough, the vigilante terror suddenly ended. Strike leaders
walked the streets of Ironwood on July 9 without being molested.
The strike gradually came to an end. By the first week in August
several operators had signed agreements. Most of these were small
jobbers. Many operators did not recognize the union or the demands.
Consequently, there was no clear-cut victory, and afterward many of
the locals lost out.[22] Organization work remained difficult.

In Minnesota the agreement entered into the spring expired on
September 1. In the meantime, the Timber Producers Association
had been formed, claiming to represent 90 per cent of the operators.
Negotiations between the association and the local were undertaken.
On September 8 the operators submitted a proposal which the union
rejected. The operators agreed only to recognize the union "where
the union has a majority of the employees." The following morning
the Timber Producers Association placed an advertisement in the
Duluth *News Tribune* in which they stated that the "union officials
having refused to negotiate under the provisions of the Wagner Act,.
we have called for the services of a Federal Mediator." [23]

A new wage and piecework schedule, approximately 15 per cent
higher than that agreed on in January, was offered by the operators
and was published in Duluth papers on September 9 and 13. It represented an increase of 33 per cent above the going wages paid by the
industry seven months before. It was rejected by the union officials,
who insisted upon a minimum wage of 50 cents per hour for general
woods work and comparative increases in piecework jobs, together
with a closed shop and union hiring halls.[24]

Intermittent sessions covering about forty days preceded the submission of an agreement to a general meeting of the Timber Producers Association by its negotiating committee on October 15, 1937.
This proposed agreement called for an increase of monthly wages
from $70.00 to $83.20, and increased rates for pieceworkers. The
operators had cut down their offer on wages, claiming changed market
conditions forced them to do so. After debate and revision the entire
agreement was adopted by a unanimous vote of the employers. It was
returned to the union officials on Saturday, October 16; they refused
to accept the proposal of the operators and recommended a strike to
the members.[25]

At this stage, Governor Benson intervened and called a meeting to discuss terms of arbitration. Committees representing the workers and the farmers were there, but the operators' committee did not appear. The governor again tried to persuade the groups to get together, and finally, he, together with Frank E. Wenig, commissioner of conciliation of the United States Department of Labor, and A. E. Smith, chief of the Division of Accident Prevention of the Minnesota Industrial Commission, brought the producers and workers together. After a sixty-three-hour conference, an agreement was reached which was to remain in effect until September 1, 1938, covering all operators with five or more men. The agreement provided for a union shop, no fees for employment, grievance committees at each camp, arbitration of disputes, camp conditions to conform to regulations of the State Board of Health and Industrial Commission, wages to be paid at the camp in cash or negotiable check when due—but in no event were wages to be paid more than twice a month except on termination of employment, seniority to begin each season, a pieceworker to be charged at the rate of one dollar per month for tools, and a fee of one dollar a month for filing service. Varying pay increases for pieceworkers were granted, plus a guarantee of ten days' pay per month.[26]

Progress in unionization has been slow in the Lake States lumber industry, and the opposition to unions has continued strong. Yet by persistent efforts applied through the economic field and through the legal field by means of appeal to the National Labor Relations Act, many locals have been established, even in places where unionism was most vigorously fought. Notable victories have been won at the Ford and other lumber camps because aid was given by other union workers interested in seeing the Ford workers organized. Labor organization has improved somewhat the labor conditions in the cut-over area, but a substantial lift in living standards can probably be achieved only through solution of the basic forestry problems.

From 1935 to mid-1937 unionism was extended and strengthened in the West. It was established fairly solidly in Minnesota. In upper Michigan and in the South the few courageous attempts to organize workers produced bitter and ruthless opposition. Without a doubt, progress and experience in collective bargaining were gained in the West and in Minnesota. Unnecessary disputes were common but, under the circumstances of new unionism, a few controversies were perhaps inevitable. The absence of collective bargaining experience was notable. The tragedies in Michigan and the heartbreaking attempts to improve the low level of working conditions in the South may, in the long run, make their contribution in the future to a more reasonable approach to labor relations.

NOTES TO CHAPTER

[1] L. T. Smythe, "Organization of Timberworkers on Vancouver Island." Unpublished Master's Thesis, University of Washington, Seattle, Wash., 1937, p. 6.

[2] Letter Columbia Basin Loggers Association to Columbia River District Council, May 12, 1936; *Oregon Labor Press*, May 22, 1936; Portland *Oregonian*, May 13, 1936.

[3] V. H. Jensen, "Labor Relations in the Douglas Fir Lumber Industry." Unpublished Ph.D. Thesis, University of California, 1939, pp. 277-279; *Four L Lumber News*, June 15, 1936.

[4] Portland *Oregonian*, March 5, 13, 14, 18, 20, 22, 26, 27, 30, April 2, 3, 12, 13, 22, 23, 24, May 3, 6, 7, 8, 1937; *Timberworker*, March 5, 12, 19, April 9, May 7, 1937; *Labor News Bulletin*, No. 33, March 4, 1937, No. 35, March 5, 1937, No. 37, April 7, 1937, No. 38, April 12, 1937, No. 44, May 10, 1937.

[5] Father Thompson, "Arbitration Award and Working Agreement," pp. 2, 3.

[6] "Minutes of Meeting of State Relief Officials and State Representatives," Memorial Hall, Court House, Duluth, Minn., 9:30 A.M., January 21, 1937 (typewritten); *Midwest Labor*, March 18, 1938.

[7] Minneapolis *Tribune*, January 28, 1937.

[8] Duluth *Herald*, April 17, 1937; Duluth *Timber Worker*, April 23, 1937; E. A. Benson, "Conservation and the Lumberjack," *American Forests*, XLIII, No. 8 (August, 1937), 381.

[9] National Labor Relations Board, *Decisions and Orders*. Washington: Government Printing Office, begun 1936, printed periodically, VIII: 416.

[10] National Labor Relations Board, *op. cit.*, I: 629-638.

[11] National Labor Relations Board, *op. cit.*, VIII: 411-453.

[12] National Labor Relations Board, *op. cit.*, III: 445-449.

[13] National Labor Relations Board, *op. cit.*, III: 768-773.

[14] National Labor Relations Board, *News Release*, R-4350, April 14, 1941; Duluth *Timber Worker*, May 21, 1937.

[15] Duluth *Timber Worker*, May 28, 1937.

[16] National Labor Relations Board, *Decisions and Orders*, XVII: 798-800; Duluth *Timber Worker*, June 11, 18, 1937; Milwaukee *Journal*, June 6, 1937.

[17] National Labor Relations Board, *op. cit.*, XVII: 800-801; cf. Milwaukee *Journal*, June 6, 1937.

[18] Duluth *Timber Worker*, June 11, 1937.

[19] *Ibid.*; cf. National Labor Relations Board, *News Release*, R-4350, April 14, 1941.

[20] Duluth *Timber Worker*, June 18, 25, 1937.

[21] Duluth *Timber Worker*, July 9, 1937.

[22] Chicago *Tribune*, July 2, 1937; Duluth *Timber Worker*, August 6, 1937.

[23] *Timber Producers Association Bulletin*, November 1, 1937; Duluth *Timber Worker*, September 10, 1937.

[24] *Timber Producers Association Bulletin*, November 1, 1937.

[25] *Midwest Labor*, October 15, 1937; *Timber Producers Association Bulletin*, November 1, 1937.

[26] *Midwest Labor*, November 11, 1937; Duluth *News-Tribune*, November 22, 1937.

11 *BIRTH OF THE I.W.A.*

A CONFLICT over leadership has plagued unions in the lumber industry almost incessantly from 1935 to the present day. In fact, there has hardly been a time in the history of the western industry when dual unionism has not been a complex problem and source of trouble. This was true all the while the I.W.W. was present in an active way, from 1907 until the early twenties; except that for a part of this time the conflict was a three-cornered one between A.F. of L. unions, the I.W.W., and the 4L. Only from the mid-twenties until the early thirties when the 4L alone functioned in the industry for a minority of the workers was there no dual organization. From the inception of the new unionism, particularly from the 1935 strike on, inter-union and intra-union struggles alternately smoldered and flared into hot disputes with resulting bitterness and confusion.

No sooner had the strike of 1935 closed than a call was issued for a general convention of all Sawmill and Timber Worker Unions to meet on October 12 in Centralia, Washington. The intra-union conflict which was so bitter during the strike was immediately brought back into the open. A week before the convention date, thirteen locals, which had been strongholds of insurgency during the strike, held a preconvention meeting in Olympia to plan an attack on Muir's leadership. As soon as this was discovered, the convention was postponed a week and was transferred to Portland. Those locals which had met at Olympia asserted that they were not even notified of these changes, declaring that the sudden decision to shift the date and place of the meeting was done solely to frustrate the opposition to Muir and to Carpenter control. The outstanding question at the convention was that of central authority, and it was decided to abolish the Northwest Council and to establish district councils. This move, designed to keep the workers in groups amenable to control, was engineered by the Muir faction and had the support of the Carpenters. Under the leadership of the delegates from Grays Harbor, the contention of Muir's group that district organizations would bring closer working harmony among the locals was denied and a vigorous fight for the retention of a council for the whole industry was made.[1]

The formation of the district councils was not accomplished without difficulties. Muir tried to keep the districts, especially where the insurgents had been strong, as small as possible. A Puget Sound District Council and a Columbia River District Council were set up without incident, but a proposal to establish a Southwest Washington District Council was blocked, presumably on the ground that the name itself took in too much territory. That this action was aimed at the insurgents on Grays Harbor is indicated by the fact that the proposed district was much smaller than either the Puget Sound or the Columbia River district in regard to area or the number of locals included. After a sharp controversy the proposed district was whittled down to the Grays-Willapa Harbor District Council. A Longview District Council was set up, and, moving toward "craft" organization, separate district councils were established for the shingle weavers, for the boommen, and for the plywood workers. In addition, district councils were established within the year at Coos Bay, in the Klamath Basin, in British Columbia, and in the Willamette Valley.[2]

The relation of the Sawmill and Timber Worker Unions to the United Brotherhood of Carpenters and Joiners of America spelled friction. Too many workers in the industry were opposed to such leadership from the top. Strong believers in rank-and-file control, they ignored the Brotherhood and, without obtaining its sanction, representatives of all the locals in the ten district councils met in Portland beginning on September 18, 1936, and formed the Federation of Woodworkers, the largest union group on the West Coast. The Federation had no charter and was not officially recognized by the Carpenters, but had sufficient authority from the various locals through the district councils to function. Harold Pritchett, president of the British Columbia District Council, was elected president. Although convened in protest against the Carpenters, the convention voted to stay with the Brotherhood.

That the Federation of Woodworkers was fundamentally incompatible with Carpenter leadership is bluntly revealed in the convention decision to request the Executive Council of the A.F. of L. to withdraw suspension of the national unions connected with the Committee for Industrial Organization and to support the drive to organize the mass production industries. Apart from any other area of conflict this action was enough to damn the Federation in the eyes of the Carpenter officials who were then engaged in leading a vigorous fight to keep the C.I.O. and industrial unionism from developing in the American labor movement. Supporters of industrial unionism had won a paper victory at the A.F. of L. Convention in 1934 when they secured the adoption of a resolution looking forward to organization of the mass production industries, and then witnessed a practical defeat because nothing was done. And seeing a repetition of the events at the 1935 convention, John L. Lewis and others took the initiative and formed the C.I.O. to do the job they knew the craft-minded leaders of the A.F. of L. could not, or would not, do. For this they were suspended from the A.F. of L. and thus was begun an organization that successfully challenged the A.F. of L. for the leadership of American labor. The lumber industry workers, being in a mass production industry, were naturally interested in the program of the C.I.O., which was to organize the unskilled workers of America.

The deep resentment with which sawmill and timber workers everywhere looked upon Carpenter leadership was increased when the Carpenters' Executive Board decided that representatives of the S.T.W.U. were to attend the convention to be held in Lakeland, Florida, during the week of December 7 to 15, 1936, as "non-beneficial" delegates. This decision was based upon the fact that the S.T.W.U. was paying only 25 cents a month per capita tax to the Brotherhood, while carpenters' unions in the construction industry paid 75 cents. The smaller per capita tax denied the lumber industry workers such benefits as pension rights and the Brotherhood home. Numerous protests were sent asking the Executive Board to reverse its decision, but without success. Those among the S.T.W.U. who resented the Carpenters control used the designation "non-beneficial" delegates, to place the existing relationship with the Brotherhood under fire. This opposition always emphasized the autocratic domination which gave them no voice in shaping their destinies. The Carpenters executives justified their position on the ground that their Convention By-Laws provided that no one except a journeyman carpenter, working at or depending on the trade for a livelihood, was eligible to be a delegate. The S.T.W.U. retaliated by pointing out that there was nothing in the By-Laws or Constitution about "beneficial" or "non-beneficial" delegates,[3] and continued to assail the Carpenter officials bitterly.

Nevertheless, thirty-four S.T.W.U. representatives were sent to the convention, officially instructed to seek peace and harmony with the Brotherhood. The question of their status as "non-beneficial" delegates came up immediately following the report of the Credentials Committee when a Carpenter delegate from Longview, Washington, moved to seat the delegates with a full voice and vote on all problems directly affecting them. Frank Duffy, secretary of the Carpenters and Joiners, immediately rose to support the Credentials Committee and belligerently blasted the S.T.W.U. delegates by accusing them of being "more interested in the C.I.O. than in the Brotherhood." To prove his point Duffy read excerpts from the Federation of Woodworkers' Convention reports, which supported industrial unionism. He made it plain that "this is a craft organization" (notwithstanding the fact that the Timber Workers were all organized on an industrial basis when the Carpenters eagerly took jurisdiction over them in 1935), and dared them to leave the Brotherhood. "Do you want to stay or do you want to go? This is not a threat; get out of the Brotherhood and if you do you'll get the swellest fight you ever had." [4]

The treatment at the convention led the S.T.W.U. delegates to Washington, D.C., where they laid their troubles before officials of the C.I.O. They saw both John L. Lewis and John Brophy, who were sympathetic to their plight but informed them that the C.I.O. was set up only to organize the unorganized and not to take in A.F. of L. groups.[5]

As soon as the delegates returned and reported their experiences, the Executive Board of the Federation of Woodworkers called for a convention to be held at Longview beginning February 20. Surprisingly enough, instead of blasting the Carpenters, the Executive Board —in the face of strong opposition, especially from leaders in the Columbia River District—issued a general recommendation that all Timber Worker groups "remain in the organized labor movement. . . .by retaining our affiliation with our International Union." This decision may have been tactical but apparently it was designed to make it possible to take advantage of the organizing assistance promised by the Brotherhood; and there was no other group to turn to.[6]

In spite of the action taken at the convention in February, sentiment among timber workers to affiliate with the C.I.O. gained momentum during the spring. The C.I.O. had been forced, in the meantime, to establish itself independently of the A.F. of L., and was then taking in any groups that desired to affiliate with it. More important than the facts that the timber workers were industrially organized, industrial-union minded, and possessed of an almost inbred opposition to the craft principle was the lumberjack's intensely strong insistence on rank-and-file control. They resented rule by Carpenters who were outsiders, who failed to understand the psychology of the lumberjack, and who knew all too little about the problems of the industry. Revolt was bound to follow.

The first formal move to change affiliation occurred in May, 1937. At a convention of the Grays-Willapa Harbor District, a resolution requesting "the Executive Board of the Federation of Woodworkers to consider ways and means of affiliating with the C.I.O., and to call a special convention of all affiliates in the immediate future for the purpose of considering formal affiliation," was passed. Immediately, the Executive Board of the Federation of Woodworkers called a conference of the executive boards of all district councils to consider the matter.[7]

Meanwhile, high Carpenter officials, including President William Hutcheson, were in the Northwest looking over the situation. Concurrently, John Brophy of the C.I.O. was in the Northwest making an open bid to the timber worker and maritime groups. Both Hutcheson and Brophy were invited to address the conference in Portland. Brophy immediately accepted and was heard on the first day it met, June 7. Harry Bridges, too, was there. Both lauded the C.I.O. highly and strongly encouraged affiliation. Brophy described the existing S.T.W.U. relationship to the Carpenters as "class B" and promised the timber workers their own international in the C.I.O.[8] No word had been received from Hutcheson, and at Harry Bridges's suggestion a second "invitation" was sent. This time Hutcheson replied from Seattle, emphasizing that the Federation of Woodworkers was not a part of the Brotherhood, but that he had no objections to arranging a meeting with representatives of the district councils. Abe Muir, however, appeared before the conference in the afternoon and "filled in" for his chief. Through attempting to defend the Brotherhood of Carpenters, he was kept continually in "hot water" because many lumberjacks were itching to get a crack at him. When he asserted that John L. Lewis and his organization was "getting the damndest lacing any outfit ever got" and, with utter shortsightedness, declared that the Federation of Woodworkers had the "stigma of communist connections," a burst of laughter broke forth. "Don't tell me," he replied, "the communist party is not trying to put something across or I'll show you." A chorus of "Show us!" went unanswered. Muir's contention that "a plan can be easily evolved that will handle any problems confronting you" fell largely on deaf ears.[9]

On the second day of the conference a resolution was introduced calling upon the Federation of Woodworkers to "go on record to immediately conduct a referendum ballot of the entire membership on the question of affiliation with the C.I.O." As certain delegates maintained that the conference was assembled only to consider the question of calling a convention to discuss ways and means of affiliating with the C.I.O., the arguments became sharp. Militant members were for immediate action, taking the position that hesitation would benefit only the enemies of the Federation. Those opposed to the adoption of the resolution, such as Al Hartung and Don Helmick of the Columbia River District Council—who had been so anxious to break away from the A.F. of L., Kenny Davis, John Stanioch, and Homer Haney of the Puget Sound District Council, insisted that a referendum vote was premature. Actually, the controversy was not on the question of the value of industrial, as opposed to craft, unionism. To a certain extent, it was not a question of affiliation with the C.I.O. The opposition group did not want to be "railroaded," and there was evidence that "machine" pressure was being exerted. Many of the men did not like the leadership of the faction which stood for immediate action and the issue was the fundamental one of who was going to lead the organized timber workers.

Besides derogatory references to Muir and Hutcheson and vindictive accusations against other individuals, which helped increase the tension of the gathering, still another source of contention lay in the failure to inform the opposition group in advance of the "real" purpose of the conference or the possibility that direct action would be taken on the C.I.O. question. This explains why the larger district councils, Puget Sound and Columbia River, were not fully represented. The Columbia River District Council had met at Seaside, Oregon, as late as June 5 and 6 and had considered the whole question of C.I.O. affiliation, but had not authorized its representatives to take specific action, and no one could realistically expect timber workers to exceed their authority as representatives of men who were as strong on rank-and-file control as the Columbia River District men. Behind everything, however, the question of leadership was dominant. When a vote resulted in forty-eight in favor and eight opposed, with twenty-six not voting and five absent, Pritchett regretfully announced that the resolution was defeated because it had not received a two-thirds majority. Immediately someone contended that a roll-call vote did not require a two-thirds majority, and the decision was quickly reversed. Members from five district councils, Puget Sound, Columbia River, Shingle Weavers, Longview, and Willamette Valley, then walked out of the meeting. Those who remained created machinery for conducting the referendum vote, with July 10 as the date for all ballots to be in, and set a date in July for a convention in Tacoma.[10]

Upon the heels of the Woodworkers' action to carry on the referendum vote, the C.I.O. made a "$5,000 payment" as a "first installment" of a contribution promised for immediate organization use "to fight the I.E.U." This gesture was calculated to convince the men in the mills and camps that the C.I.O. was giving substantial support. On the other hand, it occasioned sharp rebukes from those who felt it unpolitic to accept such a check before affiliation was voted upon.[11] In accepting the money it was taken for granted that there would be no A.F. of L. unions in the lumber industry, and so the only opponent would be the newly created Industrial Employees Union (I.E.U.) which had grown out of the 4L.

In April, 1937, when the Supreme Court had upheld the constitutionality of the National Labor Relations Act, the Executive Council of the 4L, after obtaining an opinion on the legal status of the 4L, had called the board of directors together in a special session. An attorney made it plain to the board that the lumber industry could not escape being classed as an interstate industry and hence employer contributions and participation in the 4L was illegal. In consequence, the employers withdrew from the organization, and all contracts were terminated as of April 30, 1937. W. C. Ruegnitz resigned as president, giving as his reason the fact that he formerly had been representing both employers and employees, and it would, therefore, not be proper to continue as president when the organization was exclusively a workers' organization. The I.E.U., with A. D. Chisholm as president, was formed on May 1, and a special membership meeting was held in Portland on May 17. About seventy members from twenty-three locals drew up a constitution and by-laws along the lines of the old 4L Constitution. A new departure, however, was the provision for resort to the strike once "all machinery of the I.E.U. organization has been used." [12]

To work up opposition to the move of the Woodworkers to affiliate with the C.I.O., Hutcheson issued a call for all district council officials to meet in Longview on June 19. Most district councils were represented in some fashion, although some of the delegates to the conference attended on their own initiative. The leaders of the Columbia River District Council had never wavered in their opposition to Muir and the Brotherhood even when Pritchett and other high Federation officials had advised collaboration with the Carpenters as late as February. Following the Portland Conference, the Columbia

River District Council decided that affiliation with the C.I.O. was necessary in spite of their opposition to the leadership of those who were engineering the movement. On the other hand, many Puget Sound District Council leaders were uncompromising in their opposition to Pritchett and his supporters, and, although they favored industrial unionism and perhaps affiliation with the C.I.O., they chose, under the existing circumstances, to remain in the A.F. of L. Consequently, some Puget Sound leaders were willing to work with Hutcheson. Little was done at the Longview conference apart from discussion of the situation. But it was decided to continue publication of the *Union Register,* with Hutcheson's financial support, to offset the propaganda of the *Timberworker.*[13]

Battle lines were drawn up and bitter accusations were made during the month previous to the meeting of the Federation of Woodworkers in Tacoma on July 15 for the purpose of finally determining the question of affiliation. At this convention each of the district councils was fully represented and everything except giving up leadership was done by the Pritchett following in order to avoid a split in the ranks. Four clearly defined groups were there: those who were for immediate affiliation with the C.I.O. under Pritchett's leadership, that is, those following the incumbent leadership of the Federation of Woodworkers; those who were for immediate affiliation with the C.I.O. but resisted Pritchitt's leadership, that is, the group led by the Columbia River District Council leaders; those who were probably in favor of affiliation with the C.I.O. but were unalterably opposed to Pritchett's leadership, that is, certain leaders in the Puget Sound District Council; and those who were opposed to C.I.O. affiliation, that is, Shingle Weaver representatives and various individuals.

The Puget Sound District Council and the Columbia River District Council, with such support as they would have received from representatives of other district councils, probably could have controlled the Convention, but they were not brought together on a common program. The Puget Sound District Council representatives who were opposed to the immediate shift in affiliation under Pritchett's leadership would not compromise. On the other hand, as it has already been pointed out, the Columbia River District Council leaders preferred to take their chances in the new organization rather than to remain with the Carpenters.

The referendum vote taken prior to the convention was "for affiliation, 16,754" and "against affiliation, 5,306." Certain district councils and many locals, the Tabulating Committee revealed, had "either refused to vote or voted against putting the question of affiliation with the C.I.O. to a referendum." The opposition group made a point of the fact that the Federation had a membership of "approximately ninety or one hundred thousand," and many delegates wanted to know what right the convention had to accept a ballot for 70,000 of the 100,000 members without their voice and vote, when only 22,000 votes were cast. Pritchett, however, interpreted the vote as being decisive and reported that if they went into the C.I.O. they would have their own international union, having "complete autonomy and jurisdiction" with "full voice and vote." [14]

The convention moved into the third day still lacking harmony, and when Pritchett called for the report of the Executive Board in which was presented a resolution calling for application for a C.I.O. charter, the opposition group objected. It was claimed that the Executive Board was divided on the question of giving this resolution a special dispensation and, because Pritchett had cast the deciding vote, the resolution should not be considered. Bitterness continued to develop. Pritchett, however, was upheld by the convention in giving the resolution a special dispensation.[15] A protracted debate followed and the convention ran far beyond the days allotted. Finally it was deemed necessary to limit the length of speeches and the number who would be allowed to speak. Although the addresses were repetitious and the delegates became restive, Pritchett wanted to avoid the charge that he was not allowing the opposition to have its say. Nevertheless, time and again the "chair" was accused of railroading and undemocratic procedure. Finally, in the afternoon session of the fifth day, July 19, a roll call and tabulation of the 525 votes resulted in 365 in favor of requesting a C.I.O. charter, 75 opposed, 26 absent, and 59 uninstructed. The Shingle Weavers District Council was the only one which voted overwhelmingly against the resolution. The Puget Sound District Council voted 71 to 31 in favor, although there were thirteen absent and 41 uninstructed delegates from that district who did not vote. Most of the delegates who voted against C.I.O. affiliation left the convention, saying "we can no longer sit in the rebel body." [16]

Immediately following, a delegate asked, "When will this organization become officially a C.I.O. organization?" Pritchett replied, "This has now become an official C.I.O. organization." Very quickly the name "International Wood Workers of America" was decided upon, and a delegate suggested, amid humorous cheers, that this was the I.W.W. of America. However, it was ruled that "Wood Workers" appear as one word, and the official name was made "International

Woodworkers of America" (I.W.A.). At the A.F. of L. convention in Denver shortly afterward, Frank Duffy, Carpenter secretary, in the battle to oust Charles Howard, president of the Typographical Union, for his activity in the C.I.O., referred to the issuance of the I.W.A. charter, saying, "They call it the 'International Woodworkers of America!' It is a wonder they didn't call it the I.W.W. It is the I.W.W. anyhow." [17] Duffy's statement was remote from the truth, even though an "I.W.W." tradition and even a few old-time Wobblies are still alive among the lumberjacks.

On July 20 the I.W.A. called its first convention to order and received congratulations from John L. Lewis, who announced that a charter had been granted and was being mailed. This charter nullified in a sense Lewis's earlier action, when, as a vice-president on the Executive Council of the A.F. of L., he made the motion which served to give the Carpenters jurisdiction over these same men. The new International embarked on stormy waters. Factional friction had not been eliminated when the A.F. of L. sympathizers withdrew. The Columbia River District Council vigorously challenged the Pritchett group on a number of issues and thus marked the beginning of a fued that was bitterly fought for four years. They accused Pritchett of openly violating the principle of rank-and-file control by his peremptory action in taking an "expensive airplane" trip to Washington without getting official clearance from the Executive Board members of the Federation.[18] Then they voiced other grievances and resentments. They had had little influence in the selection of the leaders of the I.W.A. and resented the fact that the new officers were handpicked. Evidence that the officers of the I.W.A. were hand-picked is found in the fact that the "Certificate of Affiliation" sent by the C.I.O. had Pritchett's name printed upon it as president. This document was dated July 20, 1937, but the officers were not formally elected until three days later. As a concession to the Columbia River delegates the convention voted 226 to 124 to establish Portland as the headquarters of the I.W.A. The Columbia River delegates chafed, however, when the Executive Board shortly reversed the action of the convention by choosing Seattle as the "temporary" headquarters.[19]

The Carpenters went into immediate action against the refractory group, declaring that they would boycott all C.I.O. lumber. The struggle, of course, was a part of the nation-wide dispute between the A.F. of L. and the C.I.O. and it was through the various building trades councils and central labor bodies that the Carpenters exerted their pressure. This fact is symptomatic of the overwhelming way in which the lumber workers shifted to the I.W.A. The only major points where the Carpenters retained nuclei of strength were in Longview, in the small mills in Tacoma, in Seattle, and at other points in the Puget Sound region. The I.W.A. had support everywhere, completely dominating the Columbia River area, including Portland, the Grays-Willapa Harbor operations, and many units throughout northern Washington. Without a doubt, for the industry as a whole, the I.W.A. had a decided majority of the men.

The first test of strength came at Tacoma. Two days after the convention, carpenters at the St. Regis Kraft Company plant, a pulp mill, laid down their tools and refused to handle a shipment of lumber delivered from the St. Paul and Tacoma Lumber Company mill, where the workers were known to be sympathetic to the C.I.O. This stand later was abandoned on the ground that the rank and file had not yet approved the action of the convention. But within a week the controversy grew more intense. The Tacoma Building Trades Council ordered all affiliated unionists to leave their posts at the St. Paul and Tacoma Lumber Company mill. On August 11 the mill was closed by a Building Trades Council picket line. A few days later a large group of I.W.A. mill workers moved in a body upon the picket line and took control of the situation. The mill, however, did not reopen until the National Labor Relations Board made an "unofficial audit" by comparing the company's payroll with the membership rolls of the I.W.A. local. Seventy per cent, 761 out of 1,092, of the crew were I.W.A. The plant opened on August 23, and stimulated great enthusiasm among the I.W.A. members.[20] Although not yet sure of its life the I.W.A. was breathing.

For the new infant the most serious crisis was ahead. Those who would strangle and choke off its breath of life centered their efforts in Portland in the hope that they could kill its spirit and its will to live. In early August the Portland Central Labor Council, at an executive board meeting, entertained a recommendation to suspend all C.I.O. locals, as well as to oust them from the Labor Temple. Although action was postponed temporarily to give the affected groups time to "think it over," on August 14 the S.T.W.U. officially affiliated with the I.W.A. and was suspended. This meant that no A.F. of L. timber worker union was functioning in Portland, but the struggle was continued by the Building Trades Council, which promptly set picket lines around seven of the city's major sawmills, presumably forcing them to close down. Three explanations of the shutdown were current. The I.W.A. local asserted that the operators

were guilty of a lockout and that they were playing the game for the
A.F. of L. This the employers denied, maintaining that they were
neutral, but that they could not operate until they were assured that
it could be done on a "peaceful, uninterrupted basis." Finally, it was
also claimed that the market was bad and that there was no profit
in operating. The operators were clearly unsympathetic to the C.I.O.,
and it is doubtful whether the picket lines were responsible for closing
the mills. In any event, even if the latter was not intentionally done
to weaken the movement to the C.I.O., it is clear that the lumber
market situation fortuitously operated to aid the A.F. of L.[21]

Hutcheson was not a man to take defeat lying down. Wherever
loyal supporters could be found locals were maintained. The Carpenter Constitution stated that a local union could not withdraw or
dissolve "so long as ten members in good standing objected thereto."
Moreover, any ten members who would stay with the Carpenters
could control all union funds even though all other members went
I.W.A. This was affirmed in the courts in both Oregon and Washington. With the financial backing of the powerful Carpenter organization, it was not difficult to hold the few loyal locals intact, many
of which could claim only the minimum nucleus to retain a charter.
All such groups that remained with the Carpenters were called together in a conference at Longview on August 20 and 21 and organized the "Oregon-Washington Council of Lumber and Sawmill Workers." This organization was given a charter by Hutcheson and became
a permanent legal body, a status which the old Federation of Woodworkers had never enjoyed.[22]

Portland became the battleground upon which was fought one of
the most bitter and involved controversies over jurisdiction that the
labor movement has ever experienced. Without doubt, the C.I.O.-
A.F. of L. jurisdictional dispute developed in its greatest fury and
intensity, during 1937, in the fight between the Carpenters and the
I.W.A. From the beginning the dispute was exceedingly complicated.
Every sort of strategy was utilized. Many labor groups were drawn
into the fray, directly and indirectly: employers, some voluntarily,
some unwittingly, took part in the struggle; government agencies and
public officials played both active and passive roles. In some respects
the fight was a slugfest, in others, a battle of cunning and shrewdness;
also a battle of attrition.

The framers of the National Labor Relations Act had not anticipated a split in the ranks of labor and had made no provision for
resolving jurisdictional disputes, except that the election machinery

was usable for that purpose. And when the Portland I.W.A. local, on August 16, asserting that it had a majority representation, filed charges of a lockout against employers, Charles Hope, regional director, undertook to obtain a consent election. The I.W.A. consented and offered to submit membership cards to be checked against employers' payrolls. The Carpenter officials, knowing that they could not win, and soured by the action in the St. Paul and Tacoma mill case, defiantly told the board to keep its hands off, an attitude which they consistently maintained for months. They insisted that the board had no legal right to interfere because the dispute was one between unions and contended that the Portland mill owners could not legally break their contracts with the A.F. of L. unions.[23] Failing to obtain consent for an election, Hope attempted to use the mediatory prerogatives, which board agents could employ to settle labor disputes, and held a series of conferences with the parties involved with an eye to mediating the dispute. In doing so he was pulled into the fight between the unions and was caught in the cross fire among A.F. of L., certain employers, and certain local public officials.

Hope drew up a settlement memorandum which provided for the reopening of the mills on August 30, under conditions existing on July 1. The Portland mill operators appreciated Hope's work and so informed him. The Policy Committee of the Central Labor Council countered, however, with the proposal that if the workers would return to work under the same conditions as existed on July 1 in so far as their union affiliation was concerned, they would have the boycott lifted "so long as the men retain that affiliation." On the other hand, the I.W.A. was willing to allow its members to return to work under conditions of July 1, with the understanding that no new demands would be made on employers involved "until such time as the question of representation has been determined by the National Labor Relations Board." It was apparent that the A.F. of L. groups were the only ones objecting to the temporary truce. They insisted that no compromise would be made,[24] and continued their bitter and relentless attack on Hope and the NLRB which colored the dispute for months. It was claimed that Hope's proposal was deceptive in that in fact it would have constituted recognition of the I.W.A., and it was admitted that "the provision that the mills reopen under the status quo could mean nothing else than that they reopen as C.I.O. operations." [25]

In spite of the position taken by the A.F. of L. groups, the mills did open, at first without picketing. On September 1 the I.W.A. local withdrew its previous charges against the operators and filed petitions for certification at each of the seven mills. When A.F. of L. pickets appeared their banners were seized and some pickets were beaten. A period of intense struggle followed. The International Brotherhood of Teamsters, Chauffeurs, Stablemen and Helpers of America entered the dispute on the ground that C.I.O. drivers were infringing their jurisdiction. "Goon" squads roamed the city and the I.W.A. drivers had to take along extra men to protect themselves. Wives even organized and carried baseball bats to protect their men, because the local police seemed to be doing nothing to stop the terrorism. Violence was rife, and the I.W.A. appealed for protection to the governor, who refused to act unless asked by the local authorities. Mayor Carson, who had stood aloof, was forced into the situation. The City Council began an "investigation" and demanded a truce while the parties were being heard. Both parties reiterated their earlier stand: the I.W.A. sought peace through the National Labor Relations Board, and the A.F. of L. spokesmen continued their noncompromising position.[26]

At this stage, in line with action being taken throughout the nation in the ever-intensifying struggle between the A.F. of L. and the C.I.O., the Oregon and Washington State Federations ousted all C.I.O. unions. Also, the local A.F. of L. leaders succeeded in reaching W. F. Wedel, financial secretary of the I.W.A. local. He walked out from an I.W.A. meeting, inviting the men to follow him back into the Carpenters' fold. Although only four men followed him, this was the beginning of a new A.F. of L. Sawmill and Timber Worker Union in Portland,[27] but it made little headway.

Varied attempts were made to reopen the mills a second time. Mostly they were attempts to open with A.F. of L. men. The West Oregon Lumber Company alone opened with an I.W.A. crew. As a cargo mill with an outlet for its product through its own retail yard in the California market, it opened in spite of intensely active A.F. of L. picketing.[28] On the other side of the dispute ledger was the opening of the Plylock Corporation plant at St. Johns, a suburb of Portland. This company had a closed-shop agreement at the time when its employees, by a close vote of 210 to 203, decided to affiliate with the I.W.A. Following this action the mill closed. Shortly afterward a Carpenter local was revived and the mill opened on September 6 under police protection, as seventy-two men passed through an I.W.A. picket line. Nevertheless, the I.W.A. succeeded in closing the plant until the Central Labor Council, by threatening to call a "general holiday" of all A.F. of L. workers in Portland unless the "intimidation" was stopped, forced the mayor to call a meeting in his office with mill owners, where plans for reopening the Plylock plant were laid. Again the plant was reopened under police protection, but this time it succeeded in keeping open by securing a restraining order against I.W.A. picketing.[29] At the same time it appeared as if a general move to break the dispute was afoot. The I.W.A. contended that six operators were trying to help the A.F. of L. when they sent out personal letters to their employees to get them to come back individually.[30] When the Inman-Poulson Company appeared to be attempting to reopen with preference for A.F. of L. men, the I.W.A. placed pickets around the mill. The company then peremptorily announced that it was going to hold a plant election of its own "in the very near future. . . . We have plans to open with our own men whichever way they may choose to vote." The I.W.A. local would have nothing to do with the proposed Inman-Poulson Company election, and continued to rely on the NLRB machinery.

The NLRB could not get the A.F. of L. group to agree to a consent election but did get it to participate in a formal three-day hearing held in Portland. Upon the basis of the findings at this hearing, the board, on October 21, formally certified the I.W.A. local as the collective bargaining agency at the seven mills involved. Through comparison of union application cards with payroll records, it was disclosed that I.W.A. strength in the various mills ranged from 68 to 92 per cent. Petitions submitted at the hearing also listed a majority desiring the I.W.A. at each mill. As soon as the board's decision was made public the Central Labor Council Policy Committee reiterated its declaration that the boycott would not be removed, claiming that the decision, "without an election is a high-handed act, indicating that the Board's policy is to usurp powers not given it in the National Labor Relations Act. . . . It further establishes the Board as a subservient ally of the C.I.O." This was highly inconsistent because of the fact that the A.F. of L. group had uncompromisingly refused to consent to an election.[31]

In view of the NLRB certification, which should have clarified the air for the operators, it may seem surprising that most of the mills were to remain closed for another two and one-half months or more. The probability that the operators were delaying in favor of the A.F. of L. is borne out by the fact that other mills in the area were running without difficulty, and the boycott never seemed effective. On the other hand, the operators could not afford to start up unless they were reasonably sure of continuous operation, and the Carpenters had not officially applied the boycott everywhere. In any event, the delay in opening played into the hands of the A.F. of L. leaders.

Because the A.F. of L. representatives had so vehemently blasted the NLRB certification, determined without an election, as a high-handed act, the I.W.A. proposed that a formal vote be taken, suggesting that the NLRB, a joint committee of the unions, or a joint committee of civic and religious groups, supervise it. The A.F. of L. representatives assailed the proposal as mere propaganda and reiterated their statement that the boycott would continue. Likewise, a proposed truce, offered by the Portland Council of Churches following an investigation of the dispute, was rejected by the A.F. of L. as "fine C.I.O. propaganda." A direct challenge, however, by an I.W.A. official to A.F. of L. representatives to sit across the table and try to come to an agreement could not be publicly ignored. David Robinson, a Portland attorney, offered to act as conciliator and met with three representatives from each side. An agreement was worked out, but was so loosely drawn that it would have been meaningless had it been accepted.[32]

Governor Martin of Oregon entered the dispute in a direct way at this juncture. Before this he had scored the NLRB for not settling the dispute. Now he became more vociferous and announced that he would conduct an election of his own as requested by the Inman-Poulson Lumber Company. The governor's election was conducted by notable state and civic leaders and resulted in a victory for the I.W.A. by a vote of 376 to 183. The election corroborated the decision of the NLRB and required the governor morally to give assistance in assuring continued operation. The situation, however, was technically unchanged, as A.F. of L. officials and the Oregon-Washington Council were careful to point out. When the Inman-Poulson mill finally opened on December 13, in the face of heavy picketing, the governor denounced the A.F. of L., urged Mayor Carson to get rid of the pickets, and threatened to suspend the license of any boat pilot who refused to handle any ship in Oregon because of the jurisdictional dispute.[33]

The governor's action did not break the deadlock. On the contrary, the A.F. of L. boycott was intensified. The I.W.A., however, was losing some strength in Portland. The workers had stood fairly solid behind the local but, after more than three months without work and depletion of all their resources, they were in a desperate position. Their morale had been seriously shaken in November by two incidents of a similar nature which were symptomatic of the basic struggle for leadership within the I.W.A., and there is no doubt but that the intra-union struggle somewhat weakened the organization. At the dock in Portland, I.W.A. men were picketing lumber manufactured at an A.F. of L. mill at Forest Grove. The local longshoremen, who were on the most friendly terms with the I.W.A., as was true throughout the whole region because they had commonly given each other mutual assistance, refused to go through the picket lines to load the lumber. Ship operators viewed this a violation of the existing agreement, which stipulated that "hot cargo" boycotts would be ended and that jurisdictional picket lines would not be observed. The Waterfront Employers Association at Portland declared that the port would be immediately closed unless the lumber was loaded. Harry Bridges could not afford to have the Longshoremen's contract violated and a coastwise tie-up on his hands. The obvious escape for Bridges, because the local longshoremen would not have disregarded the picket line, Bridges or no Bridges, was to have the picket line removed. Pritchett, at Bridges's behest, came in and ordered the picket line removed, justifying such action on the ground that the port had to be kept open and the A.F. of L.-C.I.O. struggle "localized." The Portland I.W.A. members bitterly denounced this interference by outsiders for sacrificing them when, as they claimed, united Longshore and Woodworker pressure readily would have brought the whole situation to a head. The other incident involved the removal of the pickets at Toledo, Oregon, in opposition to the will of officials of the Columbia River District Council, who were likewise again keenly incensed at the International officers for stepping into their fight simply because an injunction against picketing had been granted, and in an arbitrary way stopping the picketing.[34]

Additional fuel was added to the blaze of internal dissension within the I.W.A. at the convention held in Portland early in December. When Pritchett and Orton added insult in the form of charges of "rank amateurism," with respect to the conduct of the Portland dispute, to the injury of forced withdrawal of pickets, the Columbia River District Council workers were fighting mad. Whereas before, tongues had been held somewhat in check, now they were loosened. Don Helmick, a Columbia River leader, once friendly but now bitterly hostile to Pritchett, accused the International officers themselves of creating the desperate situation at Portland, and even charged that within the I.W.A. there was "a Communistically controlled machine." Helmick was no "red-baiter" and had always been foremost in fighting anti-Communist organizations. To Helmick the leadership of the

International seemed to be destroying what he had been fighting for, and he pleaded with the organization to get rid of the stigma that was so damaging to it publicly. Others from the Columbia River region were just as strong in their condemnation of the leaders of the International. The president of the Portland local claimed that he had been offered a chance to get on the inside, but refused. "Now I think we had better eliminate this thing," he urged, "and get rid of a machine and build a real democratic organization and have a trade union movement and not play politics." [35]

While these events were transpiring, the operators decided that the time was propitious for opening the plants, which had then been closed for four months. During November, J. B. Fitzgerald, of the Lumbermen's Industrial Relations Committee, Inc., spent considerable time with M. H. Jones in Portland, advising him that working relations should be re-established with the men regardless of affiliation. The L.I.R.C. had evolved from an unofficial labor bureau supported by members of the West Coast Lumbermen's Association, and became active about the time of the 1935 strike. Fitzgerald kept the members informed, extended advice whenever requested, and actually assisted in negotiations. Later, the "bureau" enlarged and formalized its organization and incorporated in 1937 under the above name. Fitzgerald suggested plant autonomy for the crews, which would function through plant committees. Whether the latter suggestion was decisive is not clear. Nevertheless, it was not long until the mills reopened, and, when recognition was extended later to the A.F. of L. locals at some of the mills, it was on a plant basis.

During January the mills which were not running began, one after another, to operate to various degrees, but without agreements with the I.W.A. By the end of the month all the mills, except the Eastern and Western Lumber Company and the Portland Lumber Company, had started. The operators simply had posted "Employment and Working Conditions," comprising a set of twelve rules—the first ever posted in a lumber mill in Portland. The Jones Lumber Company operated a few days and then shut down "for want of orders." It started up again after a few days, but work was delayed while the men were signed up in a newly chartered A.F. of L. local. Quickly following this development, an A.F. of L. plant charter was installed for the employees of the Southeast Portland Lumber Company, and the men were signed up at a plant meeting. The I.W.A. immediately challenged the employers on legal grounds, as violators of a NLRB certification, and on moral grounds, because they established a type of company union "worse than the I.E.U." [36]

Although the I.W.A. still had not lost the West Oregon, B. F. Johnson, Clark-Wilson, and the Inman-Poulson mills, it appeared that the A.F. of L. was gaining ground. Plant charters also had been established at the Kingsley and Portland Lumber Company mills, and the contract at the St. Johns Plylock plant had been renewed. Nevertheless, on the same day that an A.F. of L. mill charter was installed for the Eastern and Western Lumber mill, the I.W.A.—in line with the previous NLRB certification—presented closed-shop contracts to all employers. When this proved futile, the I.W.A. filed charges with the NLRB, accusing six companies—Jones Lumber, B. F. Johnson, Clark-Wilson, Portland Lumber, Inman-Poulson, and Eastern and Western —with refusing to bargain in good faith, and two other companies— Kingsley and Southeast Portland—with interference of employees in self-organization. The A.F. of L. tried to establish other plant charters, and on March 26 lifted the boycott at the Inman-Poulson mill, claiming a majority of the men. This claim had no basis in fact, and the I.W.A. was successful in maintaining its control of the mill. [37]

Throughout 1938 and the early part of 1939 the bitter fight between the two union groups continued. The struggles were more and more fought out on the legal field before the NLRB. Hearings were held. Evidence of close relationships between the A.F. of L. leaders and various employers was presented to the board. Orders requiring companies to cease and desist from interference with membership in the I.W.A. were handed down and elections were subsequently held. The final result was that the A.F. of L. locals won the B. F. Johnson, the Kingsley Lumber, and the Southeast Portland Lumber companies and were so certified. With the Portland Lumber, the Eastern and Western Lumber, and the Jones Lumber companies, the first count of the vote was not decisive. In each case the voting was so close that neither contestant had a majority, and so the challenged ballots had to be investigated and the valid ones counted. Upon first counting, the A.F. of L. led at the Portland Lumber Company, but the I.W.A. led at both the other mills. After the valid challenged votes were added, the A.F. of L. locals had won at the Portland Lumber and Jones Lumber companies, and they were certified. But at the Eastern and Western Lumber Company the final vote stood I.W.A. 123, A.F. of L. 121, with two votes for neither. As no majority had been gained by either contestant, the petition was dismissed and no bargaining agency was certified. [38] Concurrently, the A.F. of L. position at the M. and M.

Plylock plant at St. Johns was made impregnable when the Circuit Court of Appeals set aside the NLRB order and held that the A.F. of L. closed-shop contract was valid. As a result, 140 I.W.A. men were laid off and, pledging themselves never to sign an A.F. of L. card, were bitterly disappointed when the board declined to carry the case to the United States Supreme Court. Instead, a new election was held, which resulted in a vote of 237 to 204 in favor of the A.F. of L. local, and all I.W.A. men were forced out of the plant because of the closed-shop agreement.[39] On the other hand, the I.W.A. won its case at the West Oregon mill, and the company was ordered to cease encouraging membership in the A.F. of L. local; and to rehire thirty-seven I.W.A. employees with back pay.[40] Later the I.W.A. obtained an agreement with the Eastern and Western Lumber Company. With these developments, the alignments became more or less stabilized. The I.W.A. had not been pushed out of the picture by any means. If A.F. of L. locals were in control at five mills, the I.W.A. local was in control of six. Furthermore, the I.W.A. membership was double that of the A.F. of L. locals because the I.W.A. was dominant in all but one of the large mills, while the mills which the A.F. of L. locals held were small ones.

NOTES TO CHAPTER

[1] *Washington State Labor News*, September 4, 1935; *Timberworker*, October 25, December 27, 1935, September 7, 1936.

[2] *Washington State Labor News*, September 4, 1936; *Timberworker*, November 29, 1935, January 17, September 7, 1936.

[3] *Constitution and Laws of the United Brotherhood of Carpenters and Joiners of America*, p. 19; cf. *Timberworker*, October 2, 1936.

[4] *Washington State Labor News*, February 19, 1937; *Timberworker*, December 11, 1936; E. Levinson, "Bill Hutcheson's Convention," *Nation*, CXLIV, No. 1 (January 2, 1937), 11, 12.

[5] E. Levinson, *op. cit.*, p. 12; cf. *Timberworker*, December 18, 25, 1936.

[6] *Timberworker*, January 15, 29, 1937; cf. *Proceedings of the Second Semi-Annual Convention of the Federation of Woodworkers*, February 20-22, 1937, p. 4.

[7] *Timberworker*, June 11, 1937.

[8] Portland *Oregonian*, June 1, 3, 7, 1937; cf. *Report of Proceedings of the A.F. of L. Convention, 1937*, p. 468; *Timberworker*, June 4, 1937.

[9] *Timberworker*, June 11, 1937; Portland *Oregonian*, June 8, 1937.

[10] Portland *Oregonian*, June 9, 1937; *Timberworker*, June 11, 18, 1937; *Labor News Bulletin*, No. 47, June 11, 1937.

[11] *Timberworker*, June 25, 1937; *Union Register*, July 9, 1937; *Convention Proceedings of the Woodworkers Federation*, Tacoma, Wash., Morning Session, July 17, 1937, p. 10.

[12] Portland *Oregonian*, May 1, 1937; *Report of the Meeting of the 4L Board of Directors*, April 29 to May 1, 1937, pp. 1-4; *Minutes of Industrial Employees Union, Inc. Board of Directors Meeting*, May 17-20, 1937, pp. 1-10.

[13] *Timberworker*, June 18, 25, 1937; Portland *Oregonian*, June 15, 1937.

[14] *Convention Proceedings of the Woodworkers Federation*, Tacoma, Wash., Morning Session, July 16, 1937, pp. 8, 9-12.

[15] *Union Register*, July 23, 1937; *Convention Proceedings of the Woodworkers Federation*, Tacoma, Wash., Morning Session, July 17, p. 3; Portland *Oregonian*, July 18, 1937; *Timberworker*, July 30, 1937.

[16] *Convention Proceedings of the Woodworkers Federation*, Tacoma, Wash., Morning Session, July 17, 1937, pp. 5, 12; Afternoon Session, July 17, 1937, pp. 2, 3, 4 *et seq.*; *Timberworker*, July 23, 1937; *Union Register*, July 23, 1937; Portland *Oregonian*, July 20, 1937.

[17] *Convention Proceedings of the Woodworkers Federation*, Tacoma, Wash., Afternoon Session, July 19, 1937, pp. 16, 17; *Report of Proceedings of the A.F. of L. Convention, 1937*, p. 465.

[18] *Proceedings of the International Woodworkers of America Convention*, Tacoma, Wash., Morning Session, July 20, 1937, pp. 2, 7, 11; Afternoon Session, July 20, 1937, pp. 2, 7; *Timberworker*, August 6, 1937; Portland *Oregonian*, July 21, 22, 1937.

[19] Portland *Oregonian*, July 23, 25, 27, 31, 1937; *Timberworker*, July 30, 1937; *Union Register*, July 30, 1937, October 8, 1937; *Report of Proceedings A.F. of L. Convention, 1937*, pp. 257-480.

[20] Portland *Oregonian*, July 27, August 4, 12, 20, 21, 1937; *Timberworker*, August 20, 28, 1937; *Union Register*, September 3, 1937.

[21] National Labor Relations Board, *Decisions and Orders*, III: 859-60; cf. Portland *Oregonian*, August 10, 13, 20, 1937; *Proceedings of the First Constitutional Convention of the I.W.A.*, Portland, Ore., December 3 to 8, 1937, pp. 36-37.

[22] *Constitution and Laws of the United Brotherhood of Carpenters and Joiners of America*, p. 22; National Labor Relations Board, *Decisions and Orders*, VI: 380; *Union Register*, July 9, 30, August 6, 20, October 1, 1937; *Minutes of the Oregon-Washington Council of Lumber and Sawmill Workers Convention*, Longview, Wash., December 10 to 12, 1937, pp. 7, 15.

[23] National Labor Relations Board, "Oregon Lumber Situation," Spring, 1938, p. 1 (memorandum); cf. Portland *Oregonian*, August 21-27, 1937; *Timberworker*, August 28, 1937.

[24] National Labor Relations Board, *loc. cit.*; National Labor Relations Board, *Decisions and Orders*, III: 960; Portland *Oregonian*, August 28, 1937.

[25] Portland *Oregonian*, September 9, 1937; *Timberworker*, September 4, 1937.

[26] Portland *Oregonian*, September 1 to 3, 10, 11, 1937; *Timberworker*, September 11, 18, 1937; *Proceedings of the First Constitutional Convention of the I.W.A.*, p. 36.

[27] Portland *Oregonian*, September 8, 10, 12, 13, 1937; *Timberworker*, September 25, 1937; *Union Register*, September 17, 1937; *Proceedings of the First Constitutional Convention of the I.W.A.*, p. 38.

[28] Portland *Oregonian*, September 9, 15, 16, 18, 1937; *Timberworker*, September 18, October 2, 16, 1937.

[29] National Labor Relations Board, *op. cit.*, VI: 372-285; Portland *Oregonian*, September 5, October 5, 14, 17, 20, 1937.

[30] *Timberworker*, October 16, 1937.

[31] National Labor Relations Board, *op. cit.*, III: 855-866; Portland *Oregonian*, September 19, 21, 22, 23, 24, October 24, 1937; *Timberworker*, October 30, 1937.

[32] Portland *Oregonian*, November 5, 7, 8, 20-24, 29, November 30, December 2-6, 1937; *Timberworker*, November 13, 27, December 4, 1937; National Labor Relations Board, "Oregon Lumber Situation," p. 3; *Proceedings of the First Constitutional Convention of the I.W.A.*, pp. 38, 60-76; *Minutes of the Oregon-Washington Council Convention*, Eugene, Ore., December 10 to 12, 1937, p. 7.

[33] Portland *Oregonian*, December 5, 7, 9, 10, 11, 14, 15, 1937; New York *Times*, December 7, 1937; *Timberworker*, December 18, 1937; *Proceedings of the First Constitutional Convention of the I.W.A.*, p. 61; *Minutes of the Oregon-Washington Council Convention*, Eugene, Ore., December 10-12, 1937, pp. 1-5.

[34] Portland *Oregonian*, November 6, 9, 10, 12, 16, 1937; *Timberworker*, November 13, 20, 27, 1937; *Proceedings of the First Constitutional Convention of the I.W.A.*, p. 144.

[35] *Proceedings of the First Constitutional Convention of the I.W.A.*, pp. 69-73, 110, 144-146; Portland *Oregonian*, December 6, 14, 1937; *Timberworker*, December 4, 1937.

[36] *Lumbermen's Industrial Relations Committee Bulletin*, December 3, 1937 (mimeographed); *Timberworker*, January 29, February 12, 19, 1938; *Union Register*, February 4, 1938; Portland *Oregonian*, January 22, 25, February 2, 5, 1937.

[37] Portland *Oregonian*, February 9, 11, 25, March 6, 26, April 12, 1938; *Timberworker*, March 12, April 16, 1938; *Union Register*, April 1, 1938.

[38] National Labor Relations Board, *op. cit.*, II: 1058-1063, XII: 184-204, 212, XIII: 174-185, 791-794, XIV: 1173-1180, XVI: 568-573, 708-710; National Labor Relations Board, *News Release*, R-1664X, April 12, 1939, R-2054, September 11, 1939, Portland *Oregonian*, July 7, 13, 28, August 14, 15, 1938; *Timberworker*, February 19, April 16, August 6, 20, 1938.

[39] *Union Register*, February 24, March 10, 17, 24, June 16, 1939; *Timberworker*, March 25, 1939.

[40] *Timberworker*, September 16, 1939; *Labor News Digest*, September 15, 1939.

12 INTERNAL CONFLICTS AND JURISDICTIONAL DISPUTES

JURISDICTIONAL disputes colored the lumber industry labor scene everywhere. The fight between the A.F. of L. and C.I.O. lumber industry unions was not confined solely to Portland. The more important of the other fights need mention in order to bring out the nature of the struggle which had, and has, such a profound influence on industrial relations in the industry, primarily in the fir region and in the western pine regions of Washington, Oregon, California, Idaho, and Montana, but also in the Lake States, and in the South. Likewise, the important conflicts within the I.W.A. have colored the picture of labor development and they, too, need fitting into the mosaic of labor relations in lumbering. Both the jurisdictional struggles and the intra-union struggles were bitterly fought. The former often transpired to the detriment of both parties and certainly at a cost to the industry. The employers, however, to some extent, as has already been explained, were partly responsible for creation of the situation in which dualism flourished. The intra-union struggles, too, were carried on only at a cost, but one feature of them is heartening. To the extent that they show democracy at work in the labor movement, political struggles for leadership naturally have decided merit. To learn that leaders can be changed through rank-and-file action is a healthful sign. Normally, however, the extremes of bitterness found among the lumber industry workers ought not to be associated with the internal workings of an organization.

At Tacoma, where there had been an early jurisdictional skirmish, the Tacoma District Council, affiliated with the Oregon-Washington Council, made an abortive attempt, during 1939, to recapture the St. Paul and Tacoma mill. The I.W.A. local had experienced considerable difficulty in getting negotiations started and finally, in the middle of May, resorted to strike action. Negotiations then were begun but dragged out for ten weeks. At this juncture, when the I.W.A. local appeared to be in great difficulty because of the prolonged strike, the Tacoma District Council sent a surprising letter to the company,

claiming a majority of the men in the sawmill. Not before October
was a charter installed by the Brotherhood of Carpenters for the
employees of this mill. Nevertheless, as a result of the letter, Mr.
Griggs, president of the company, under a new ruling of the NLRB,
requested an election to determine the proper collective bargaining
agency. Immediately the I.W.A. local charged that a conspiracy
existed. Nevertheless, it knew its own strength and eagerly signified
its willingness to participate in an election. The new A.F. of L.
"local," however, was reluctant to participate. The wonder is, however, that the A.F. of L. local did not do better than it did in view
of a nasty intra-union dispute which developed within the I.W.A.
family in the midst of this situation.

The International officers, led by Pritchett, attempted to direct
affairs at Tacoma without consulting the strike committee or the
executive board of the local, opposed the insistence upon an unquali-
fied consent election, and attempted to foster a back-to-work movement. It is highly significant that the I.W.A. local decisively won the
election held on August 21, by a vote of 738 to 163, and won its strike
in its own way and that, thereafter, the International leaders of the
I.W.A. could not control the Tacoma union, which maintained almost
complete independence.[1]

At Bellingham, Washington, the majority of the membership of
the Timber Worker local voted to affiliate with the I.W.A. and asked
for recognition, but was refused because of the existence of an unexpired contract. Incidentally, the remnants of the Carpenter-chartered
local claimed the contracts and, after a legal battle, successfully recov-
ered the funds taken when the shift to the I.W.A. occurred.[2] Throughout 1938 the market for lumber was poor, employment was intermittent, and at times the mills were wholly shut down. When, in
February, the I.W.A. again pressed for recognition, the Bloedel-
Donovan Lumber Company, in line with an informal agreement
among employers in the industry, broached the subject of wage cuts
and took no action on the issue of recognition. Meanwhile, the I.W.A.
local filed a petition for certification with the NLRB and introduced,
during the subsequent hearings, membership lists disclosing that it
had 1,076 members, a definite majority. The mill was closed in June
and the company again asked for a wage reduction as a basis upon
which it might resume operations. Some of the leaders of the I.W.A.
local favored the wage cut as a basis for increasing employment, but
the majority opposed such a policy. Thereafter, noticeable discord
developed in the I.W.A. ranks when an attempt was made to separate

sawmill and logging employees into separate locals, with the hope that it then would be possible to accept wage cuts at the sawmills and increase employment. When this failed, an independent union of sawmill workers was established and readily recognized by the company when an exclusive bargaining contract was entered into on December 10. At the same time a wage reduction was agreed upon. When operations were resumed on a restricted basis, mass picket lines were established by the I.W.A. An attempt to stop the picketing by injunction failed and, suddenly, on December 31, the independent union dissolved in open meeting in favor of an entirely new Carpenter-chartered local.[3]

This turn of events surprised everyone, even members of the existing Carpenter-chartered local. Other A.F. of L. groups assailed the issuance of the charter as a sell-out and "because we do not believe in wage cuts nor behind the line charters." Soon after its formation the new local, by means of a one-hour strike, secured restoration of all wage cuts. On this the I.W.A. picket line was removed and the members asked for their jobs, but without success. The NLRB held hearings on January 16, 1939, concerning the matter of representation. By agreement with the NLRB the company shut down its mill and rehired all employees on the basis of seniority and without discrimination as to union affiliation, agreeing at the same time to abide fully with the Wagner Act. The board later ordered an election which the new Carpenter-chartered local won by a vote of 538 to 447, and the company immediately granted the victorious local a union shop, which caused a lot of trouble when many workers refused to join the A.F. of L. local. Nevertheless, the union shop provision proved the means of eliminating the I.W.A. as a factor in the sawmills of Bellingham.[4]

The most spectacular struggle for union control in the lumber industry, outside of Oregon and Washington, occurred at Westwood, California, one of the largest lumber towns in the state. Westwood has always been owned and controlled by the Red River Lumber Company. During NIRA days, when union organization was in the air, the company in conformity with practice of other employers in the pine region, set up a 4L local, which in 1937 was forced to dissolve as a result of the Supreme Court ruling that the Wagner Act was constitutional. Some 4L members then considered organizing their own local, intending to affiliate with the C.I.O. The officers of the 4L in Portland, however, had decided to form the I.E.U.[5] To determine the future of the Westwood 4L local a meeting was held on May 12 and, after company executives had withdrawn from the gathering, an

unofficial ballot to discover preferences was conducted, which gave the
C.I.O. 532 votes, the I.E.U. 511, the A.F. of L. 94, and an entirely
independent union 94. On the strength of this vote the C.I.O. supporters formed the United Woodworkers Local Industrial Union (this
was prior to the formation of the I.W.A.) and asked for recognition.
The company refused to grant it and so the United filed a petition
for certification with the NLRB. At the same time, the company
readily entered into negotiations with the I.E.U. and recognized it as
the exclusive bargaining agency before the board had completed its
investigations.[6]

The NLRB discovered that the I.E.U. local's membership was
between 1,600 and 1,800, while that of the United amounted to only
300 or 400. Nevertheless, it was discovered that the workers were
repressed by "fear of incurring the company's displeasure." The board
was not willing to accept the I.E.U. majority in membership, because
it had once been a labor organization dominated and supported by
the company, and recognized that "a substantial number of employees
feared to withdraw from membership in the I.E.U." because of
unlawful company influence. The fact that "the employee membership
of the 4L's was substantially transferred to the I.E.U. local without
the formality of new membership applications" also created a question
in the mind of the board. After waiting until March, 1938, the NLRB
held an election which the I.E.U. won by a vote of 1,153 to 510 for
the I.W.A. local, the United having affiliated with the I.W.A. in
August, 1937. The I.E.U. was certified but the I.W.A. local immediately brought charges of unfair labor practices although nothing
developed from them.[7]

In July, 1938, the Red River Lumber Company announced that it
was compelled to cut wages 17½ cents per hour. The I.E.U. members
voted 532 in favor to 385 against the wage cut while under the false
impression that their home office favored the move. Because the false
impression had been deliberately fostered, the I.E.U. charter was
revoked by the head office in Portland. Meanwhile, the I.W.A. local
had voted overwhelmingly against the wage cut and decided to strike
in protest, the first strike ever to occur in Westwood. Events moved
rapidly thereafter. Representatives of a large faction in the I.E.U.
visited Edward Vandeleur, secretary of the California State Federation
of Labor, regarding possibilities of affiliating with the A.F. of L. At
Westwood the next morning, on the basis of prearranged signals, a
large crowd assembled and vigilantism ruled the community. An
all-day purge of I.W.A. members and sympathizers and their families

was conducted in which officials of the company took conspicuous part.

The next day the mill reopened, the company announcing that all men employed on the day before the strike could return without discrimination. A few I.W.A. men who were bold enough to appear were told to get out of the plant. A few days later A.F. of L. established a local and enrolled some 1,300 employees of the company. After a week away from their homes the men and their families who had been driven out were allowed to return, and the I.W.A. filed charges of unfair labor practices with the NLRB. After an investigation, the board succeeded in getting the parties, on October 21, to enter a stipulation designed to clear the situation and to correct the existing abuses. The board, however, still judged the situation too unsettled to warrant an election. In February, 1940, because the board still was refusing to conduct an election, the A.F. of L. local called a strike and again violence was rife. The strike, in effect, was a strike against the board. Because Governor Olson took a vigorous stand and threatened to send troops to assist the oppressed workers if ruffian tactics were not dropped, and because the A.F. of L. local was getting bad publicity from the use of ruffian tactics, a truce was finally agreed to on April 3.[8] Not until December 3, 1940, was the situation sufficiently settled for the NLRB to order an election. The balloting was conducted on May 28, 1941, and the A.F. of L. local gained 1,059 and the I.W.A. local only 432 votes. The A.F. of L. local was certified and the I.W.A. men began to pack up their belongings so that they might seek jobs elsewhere.

Although it was at Grays Harbor that the formal action was taken starting the move that culminated in the change of affiliation, that area was not spared jurisdictional trouble. The I.W.A. in that area has had bitter internal disputes as well as those with the A.F. of L. The breach which occurred in the union ranks during the 1935 strike was never really closed, although things went along rather smoothly until early in 1937 when the local was split wide open over the trial of "Red" Johnson and Ernie Kosloski, who were charged with Communist party membership and activity. A committee of the local found both men guilty and was sustained by a referendum vote. Shortly afterward, through continued agitation by the left-wing faction, support for reinstatement was organized and at a small meeting of the local the two men were reinstated by a voice vote.

The issue of communism had split the local, but the decision to affiliate with the I.W.A. was decisive without any left-right differences cropping out, so keen was the opposition to the Carpenter control. Even desperate and concentrated efforts to regain a foothold in this important area bore little fruit for a year and a half. Not until internal dissension again broke out after a trying period of depression, which lasted all through 1938, did a Carpenter-affiliated local gain any considerable support.

The dissension in the Aberdeen local was a counterpart of the fight which had developed between the "administration forces" in the I.W.A. and the "opposition bloc" in the Columbia River District. Harry Tucker had been "hand-picked" by the left-wing faction as the acceptable person who could hold the local together and who, at the same time, they thought, was amenable to control. Being an aggressive fighter in the lumber worker union cause on the harbor from the beginning of unionism in 1933, he was well-known and was elected president. As early as December, 1937, however, at the I.W.A. Convention in Portland, he showed that he would not be swerved from holding fast to principle. The Columbia River District Council had called for a complete report on expenditures of organizers. The "administration forces" interpreted this as an attempt to cast aspersions on their characters. A committee was appointed, nevertheless, to look into the matter and Tucker, who was a member of it, supported the minority recommendation, drawn up by Columbia River committeemen, in the face of the power of his main supporters. It must be kept in mind that the left-wing faction on the harbor had strong influence in the leadership of the I.W.A. It is significant that Tucker was afterward re-elected president of the large Aberdeen local in spite of his action, although practically all other I.W.A. locals in the district, except the one at Raymond, supported the administration forces.

Without a doubt the cleavage in the Aberdeen local contributed greatly to the revival of A.F. of L. locals. In addition, as stated before, the poor market for lumber throughout 1938 played into their hands. Grays Harbor is a cargo-producing area and the inactivity in the industry during 1938 was more marked there than elsewhere. Under the circumstances, the A.F. of L. supporters blamed the I.W.A. dissension for the employer unwillingness to resume operations. Six locals in small plants were organized by the Oregon-Washington Council through separating the loggers from the sawmill men. In March the large mill of the Grays Harbor Lumber Company started operations with a crew that was largely A.F. of L. Later, A.F. of L. spokesmen pointed with glee to the fact that only 851 votes were cast in an I.W.A. election in the Aberdeen local which a year before had polled 3,000 votes. This decline was due, in fact, more to economic conditions than anything else, but the internal controversy obviously had some effect.[9]

Throughout the year, although there was a lot of direct action including some ruffian tactics, a prolonged struggle was carried to the NLRB, which held hearings and elections. The I.W.A. retained complete control of the loggers but the Oregon-Washington Council made considerable inroads into the I.W.A. membership in Aberdeen mills. Of all the votes cast in NLRB elections, which carried the Grays Harbor Lumber Company mill and the Anderson Middleton mill into the A.F. of L., but left the Donovan, Bay City, and Shafer mills with the I.W.A., a total of 638, or 32 per cent, were cast for the A.F. of L. A total of 870 votes, or 45 per cent, were cast for the I.W.A., and 394 eligible workers, or 20 per cent, did not vote.[10]

The upsurge of the A.F. of L. in the area diminished the intensity of the internal fight in the I.W.A., but in 1939 it broke out again in even greater fury. Charges that subversive influences working within the I.W.A. were largely responsible for the existing stagnation of the lumber industry in Aberdeen were frequent. The Tucker group in the local sought to "clean house" in order to clear the local of such charges. There was no secret about their opposition to those whom they accused of being "party" men.

During May, 1939, a circumstance likely to aid in the house cleaning seemed to present itself. Bill Anderson, secretary of the Aberdeen local, who had always been intimate with the left-wing faction, had gone to Canada several months before to attend the British Columbia District Council Convention. He was detained by the immigration authorities and was not allowed to re-enter the United States. Because a "party" man had moved at a meeting of the local that a new secretary be elected, it was thought that Anderson was being dropped for some reason. If only he could be persuaded to go along with the Tucker group he could prove helpful. Anderson was visited, but not having broken with his group he slyly suggested a later meeting, instructing his interviewers to have the officials of the local see certain members of the Better Business Builders in Aberdeen, a group of businessmen who had organized to solve the local lumber industry depression if possible, and to persuade them to use their influence in his behalf. This was done. In the meantime, Anderson informed his own group of what was transpiring and Dick Law, I.W.A. Executive Board member, and Ted Doktor, Grays-Willapa Harbor District Council president, both of the administration faction in the I.W.A., set to work to make a case against the Aberdeen officers. When the men met with Anderson again, their conversation was recorded by a machine concealed in an adjoining room.

A week after the meeting, without preliminary announcement, Doktor unexpectedly made charges over the radio against Joe Clark, John Deskins, "Red" Fadling, and Harry Tucker, accusing them of connivance with the Better Business Builders to destroy the local. The June 3 issue of the *Timberworker* was devoted almost entirely to exposing the "union wreckers." A pretty fight was on. The Tucker faction claimed it was unconstitutional to make charges in such a manner and that the *Timberworker* pages could not be used to attack personalities within the organization. Between then and June 10, when the District Council met in convention, Pritchett, sensing the futility of trying to prove the charges or make them stick, tried appeasement by suggesting that he and Tucker appear on the platform together and thus wipe the slate clean. Tucker refused. His group carried the fight to the Centralia convention, where they forced the playing of the records and the establishment of a committee to investigate. The committee, after a prolonged investigation, reported insufficient evidence to support the charges made. Within a month after the convention, Tucker and his supporters were re-elected even though his opponents ran Dick Law against him. Then, not wishing to let the fight drop, Tucker and his associates filed charges against Pritchett, Orton, McCarty, and Law—all board members and leaders of the administration group—just before the I.W.A. Klamath Falls convention.

The Klamath Falls convention was notable, not only because the Aberdeen quarrel was carried there but because the fight within the I.W.A. between the opposition bloc and the administration supporters reached a new high in bitterness. In fact, the wonder is that any organization remained. Leaders from the Columbia River area, Tacoma, and Aberdeen lined up solidly against the administration faction. The nature of this struggle has already been revealed in part but stemmed mainly from the problem of leadership in a new union and to the many shades of thought expressed by individuals who were thrown or maneuvered into leadership. The opposition to the incumbent International leaders was due to the conflict of personalities, disagreement over policy, and resentment against "orders" which independent thinking rank-and-filers did not want forced upon them. By far the commonest explanation of the opposition to the International officers is that the Communists were responsible. It is, however, difficult to prove this. To what extent Communists were active cannot be ascertained with any precision. The average timberworker has normally rejected communism, but, at the same time, he has not been susceptible to "red-baiting."

The opposing forces were fully prepared for the conflict which everyone expected at the convention. The first incident occurred at the Executive Board meeting when certain members walked out in protest against the trial procedure proposed for handling the charges against the International officers made by members of the Aberdeen local. The constitution provided that if officers of the International were charged with wrongdoing they should be tried by the remaining members of the board—which, in this case, left four administration supporters and four of the opposition bloc to try them. Pritchett came out with the novel idea that the accused should be tried one at a time, which would have left the remainder of the accused, or a majority of seven to four, on the board jury. The charges and this incident loomed large in the internal controversy on the floor of the convention.[11]

The first shot on the floor of the convention was fired by delegate Williams, then business agent of the Longview local and an administration supporter. The opposition bloc had held a caucus the previous night with the delegates from the Columbia River District Council, the Boommen and Rafters District Council, and the Aberdeen, Raymond, and Tacoma locals being present. At the first opportunity in the convention meeting, Williams took the floor and proceeded to flay those who had met the previous night, accusing them of engineering "a move . . . to overrun the I.W.A." through the establishment of a machine under the control of Helmick. Bedlam broke loose. Williams was booed; a delegate called him "a God-damned liar" when he accused Helmick of telling those at the caucus to vote as he said or he'd "get them." In spite of this disorder, Williams completed his remarks, which touched upon Helmick's caucus statements on the question of total membership, paper locals, and control from Moscow.[12]

Helmick immediately rose to answer. After explaining that the caucus was open to any who cared to come or go, he declared: "We are definitely opposed, yes, to the present administration of the I.W.A." He then followed with an account of the grievances against the acts of the International officers, accusing them of mismanagement and destruction of the I.W.A. "I am opposed," he said, "to a stronger swing into the Carpenters and Joiners . . . I am opposed to the Communist Party." Helmick charged Pritchett with threatening that, if he did not play ball, "they would run me out of the industry . . .

If we're a bunch of phonies, how does it happen that the biggest local unions in the I.W.A. are aligned to change the present administration?"

Defending himself, Pritchett offered two unity proposals to the convention, but the controversy raged even while the proposals were being discussed. Finally, by arrangement, a spokesman made a speech full of "sweetness and light" designed to sooth everyone and make it appear that everyone was largely right and only a little wrong. Pritchett's proposal to place the issues in the hands of the Executive Board was passed by a vote of 123 to 107. His request that the convention "repudiate the statements made by individuals" against the officers was accepted only after a heated discussion, again by a close vote.

When the financial report was made, the question was asked as to who paid for the special copies of the June 3 issue of the *Timberworker* which were sent to all the locals, containing the great Aberdeen "exposé." This set the controversy off once again. When the quarreling had subsided, a member called for reconsideration of the action of the Pritchett unity proposal by introducing a resolution asking that a committee of seven from the opposition bloc and seven from the administration supporters be elected in caucus to meet with the three regional directors of the C.I.O. to work out recommendations for unity. The resolution was lost when Harry Bridges, supported by Richard Francis and William Dalrymple, the regional directors of the C.I.O. in California, Washington, and Oregon, respectively, refused to meet with any committee if the International officers were not present. Just before the proposal was voted down, however, Orton declared his willingness to meet with the seven from the opposition. In consequence, the opposition bloc had its representatives at the meeting and for two and one-half hours they argued as to whether they were to sit as equals or were to be simply advisory. Pritchett finally ruled that they had no vote. As a matter of fact, had Pritchett allowed them to vote, the opposition forces would have outvoted the administration supporters at the meeting. The seven refused to stay in the meeting and no constructive report was submitted to the convention next day.

An administration supporter then moved that the three regional C.I.O. directors go into session and work out a solution. Bridges pointed out that this would be done only "on the basis of the C.I.O. program . . . adopted at the National C.I.O. Convention," in conformity with the I.W.A. constitution. The three directors worked out a unity proposal which secured vociferous approval.

Immediately afterward, the question of communism was injected into the controversy when a member asked if the C.I.O. directors recommended that the subject be placed on the ballot. Bridges emphatically said, "They did not recommend any such thing." But the argument on the question continued when a constitutional amendment, designed to exclude Communist party members from the union, reputedly modeled on the constitution of the United Mine Workers, came up for consideration. The opposition bloc insisted that the I.W.A. go on record and "definitely repudiate the Communist Party." When Francis, with impatience, said that it was his opinion that the time of the regional directors in working out a unity proposal had been wasted, and Bridges in a lengthy speech also condemned the continual fighting, Pritchett arbitrarily closed the debate and the resolution was defeated on the ground that a person's politics, whether Republican, Democrat, or Communist, should not be a qualification of union membership. After the defeat of a motion to change the district council representation in order to give the larger ones a greater relative weight than they possessed and bring them more in line with their numerical strength, the convention adjourned but the fight continued.[13]

At Aberdeen the intra-union struggle continued after the convention. In local meetings pitched battles occurred Saturday after Saturday. Tucker and his followers, adopting the tactics of their opponents, met every Friday prior to the regular meetings to plan their attack. In spite of this internal battling the local was able to obtain its first formal collective bargaining agreement with the operators—which was accomplished through negotiations of the local rather than district officers.

Even with such a bitter fight being conducted within the I.W.A. at Grays Harbor, the A.F. of L. locals did not continue to make gains. In early 1940 the Brotherhood of Carpenters levied a special assessment to build a defense fund to fight prosecution of the Carpenters under the antitrust laws. This was imposed on the Timber Worker locals without first going through the Oregon-Washington Council for acceptance, although later a special convention was called to give the assessment the stamp of approval. The Grays Harbor District Council did not accept it. Later, a subcommittee of the Executive Board of the Brotherhood was sent out and meetings were held in Seattle where Grays Harbor representatives were told they would have to pay the assessment or there would be no local unions. When the ultimatum was read in the Grays Harbor locals there was great dissension and a notable lack of interest in the locals thereafter. It was later reported that men who had formerly made up picket lines would not even attend meetings and that the membership was very low.[14]

In January, 1940, Pritchett went to Washington, D.C., where he requested that the C.I.O. furnish at least five organizers to work among the timber workers. Michael Widman, assistant director of organizations for the C.I.O., investigated, and while he was in the West the I.W.A. Executive Board was called together. At the meeting a resolution, which had originated in the Columbia River District area, was presented asking Widman to lead personally an organizing drive—the resolution was a product of the internal controversy. The officers of the I.W.A., with the exception of Worth Lowery, talked against the resolution and recommended an amendment to the effect that the Executive Board ask for someone from the national C.I.O. "to assist and advise" in the proposed drive, leaving the International officers in control. Widman made it plain that if the C.I.O. was going to spend money organizing the timber workers, it would insist on control of the organizers.[15] Nevertheless, the I.W.A. officers and the rest of the board, with the exception of Lowery, Cadieu, Covey, and McSorley of the opposition bloc, voted for the amendment.

When the Forest Grove local, which had been largely responsible for the original resolution, was advised of the action of the Executive Board, it passed a resolution appealing to John L. Lewis and Allen Haywood, director of organization, and to the C.I.O. Executive Board to launch an organizing drive under the direction of Widman, or an equally competent representative of the C.I.O., the cost to be equally borne by the national C.I.O. and the I.W.A. The resolution was sent to all locals in the I.W.A. asking that they take like action. Widman returned to Washington and made his report. Pritchett and McCarty then went to Washington and while there agreed to Widman's recommendation that the membership of the I.W.A. be asked to vote on a 50-cent a month assessment for a period of six months which would be matched by the C.I.O. in order to provide for a director of organization from the national C.I.O. and as many organizers as the funds would permit. The director to hire and fire all organizers and to place them where he saw fit. This proposal was subsequently adopted by the membership. A contract was entered into between the I.W.A. and the C.I.O., and Adolph Germer, with many years' experience as an organizer with the United Mine Workers, was appointed director of organization,[16] revealing a determination on the part of the C.I.O. to concern itself with the internal affairs of the I.W.A.

In the establishment of this organizational pact, the factional fight had been strong. In the ensuing months little happened to erase the differences. When the Washington State Industrial Council met in convention at Olympia in September, the right-left dispute which had split the I.W.A. actually precipitated a pitched battle and completely disrupted this state-wide union convention.[17] One consequence of the struggle was John L. Lewis's removal of the secretary of the Council and the appointment of Harry Tucker of the Aberdeen I.W.A. local in his place. Lewis's drastic action is an indication of the intensity of the struggle within the region, and the appointment of Tucker was a forerunner of the way the national C.I.O. officers were siding in with the opposition bloc in the I.W.A. Afterward, the regional C.I.O. directors of Oregon and Washington stood shoulder to shoulder with the opposition bloc in the I.W.A. and assisted them in their fight against the administration forces. As a consequence, they laid themselves open to a verbal lashing from various left-wing papers published within the region.

Germer swung vigorously into the organizational work, taking sides with the opposition bloc, and although he was kept in constant battle with the administration faction, the organizational work bore rich fruit for the I.W.A. at Everett and Longview, and at many other places of lesser importance. Some people have been surprised that any organizing work could be successful with the intense factional fight going on within the I.W.A., but many say that it succeeded because of it, in view of the fact that the leader of the drive supported the opposition bloc. While there is no evidence that this was true at most places, at Longview it was a factor of no little significance. At Everett it was the growing dislike of the Carpenter control that was significant.

Everett, it will be recalled, was a storm center in the 1935 strike and had emerged poorly organized. After the industry-wide shift to the I.W.A., the A.F. of L. locals gained slightly and took at least two mills from the I.W.A.[18] Carpenter spokesmen afterward claimed that "virtually the entire lumber industry in Everett is A.F. of L.," but the big Weyerhaeuser mills had not as yet signed agreements with either the Carpenters or the I.W.A. In the spring of 1940 the I.W.A. obtained an order from the NLRB calling upon the Weyerhaeuser Company to cease discouraging membership in the I.W.A. and to reinstate an I.W.A. leader. Throughout the year both the I.W.A. and the Oregon-Washington Council worked hard to gain control of the Weyerhaeuser mills. On August 27, the Oregon-Washington Council called a strike as a part of its campaign to get an increase in wages at Snoqualmie Falls and Tacoma.[19] The I.W.A. had gained the upper hand, however, and on October 31, while the A.F. of L. strike was still in progress, completed negotiations and signed a contract covering the two large Weyerhaeuser mills, which in effect put the I.W.A. far ahead in Everett.[20]

Longview was one of the few places that the Carpenters had held successfully at the time of the formation of the I.W.A. Nevertheless, organization disintegrated rapidly. In May, 1938, the Carpenter affiliate at the Long-Bell plant, "unable . . . to carry on the fight alone," was formally dissolved by the remnants of the one-time membership of 800, and the remaining members were transferred to the Weyerhaeuser plant local. And it should be noted that the A.F. of L. strength among loggers was never great because, almost to a man, loggers have a bitter hatred of the A.F. of L.

The I.W.A. came into the scene in a definite way when a Boom-men and Rafters local was organized in July, 1938, which succeeded in winning an agreement about a year later. A.F. of L. spokesmen even admitted the I.W.A. victory and their own "very badly organized condition existing in Longview," although they claimed they had "been fairly well organized two or three times." [21] The I.W.A. then made headway among the loggers. The large Long-Bell camp at Ryderwood was won through an NLRB election.[22]

By the spring of 1940, the Carpenter affiliates were largely demoralized at both Long-Bell and Weyerhaeuser units. A.F. of L. admission of this came in the form of a protest against the organizing techniques employed by certain Brotherhood organizers, who thought the best way to build strength was to organize many locals in the various departments of the large mill units instead of relying upon the industrial form of organization. This procedure was allowed by the Oregon-Washington Council officials under protest because they could not show that any "other form of organization had been successful." A loud protest brought a committee representing the General Executive Board of the Brotherhood of Carpenters to investigate, and Hutcheson promised that if this approach was not successful after a few months' trial the local would again be consolidated.[23] The results were disappointing.

The impotence of the A.F. of L. locals is only a part of the picture. A destructive schism developed within the I.W.A. local and it is surprising that any organized group now functions in Longview. Organizers sent into the locality by Germer were threatened by officers of the I.W.A. local who were administration supporters. The organizers struggled on without receiving any co-operation from the leaders of the local, yet finally built a numerous following. Then on January 10, 1941, the president of the I.W.A. local, K. Deckert, attempted to adjourn a meeting of the local when he realized that his opposition was too powerful for him. Upon declaring that the meeting was adjourned, he laid the gavel down and walked out. Immediately the vice-president, C. Kumler, picked up the gavel and continued the meeting. The office of business agent was abolished and, as a result, one of the stanchest of the administration supporters, R. D. Williams, was without a job in the local. Subsequently Deckert and Williams, with possession of the charter and records, continued to act as if they were still in office. The opposition carried the matter to the courts, and it was held that Kumler acted legally in continuing the meeting of January 10. It was also ruled that Deckert and Williams were illegally in possession of the local's property and that all meetings which had been held by them in Kelso, Washington, were illegal. An injunction was granted to the opposition bloc supporters which restrained the deposed officers and agents, and the International officers, from interfering with the government and administration of the Longview local.[24]

The thing that is most significant is that while this internal struggle was going on, the opposition bloc under Germer's leadership in organizing was signing up the majority of the sawmill workers in Longview. Early in March a decisive victory was won in four separate NLRB elections. The board lumped all the A.F. of L. locals together, and the results were:[25]

	I.W.A.	A.F. of L.	No Union
Weyerhaeuser mill employees	687	484	133
Weyerhaeuser wood employees	332	147	72
Long-Bell mill employees	1,031	391	260
Boommen and Rafters	44	—	—

Following this decisive victory, the internal struggle in the I.W.A. local and the jurisdictional dispute with the A.F. of L. locals subsided at Longview.

The internal struggle within the I.W.A., however, was by no means subsiding. In fact, events at the Aberdeen convention in the fall of 1940 revealed that the internal conflict had reached a more advanced stage than was portrayed by events at the Klamath Falls convention the year before. To the old issues was added the question of who was to conduct the organization drive thereafter. Germer was thoroughly disliked by the administration forces, and they sought to remove him as director. Meanwhile, Pritchett had been denied re-entrance into the

United States from Canada. Resigning as president of the I.W.A., he appointed Orton, who was first vice-president, to fill his unexpired term, and Ilmar Koivunen, a young leader from Minnesota, vice-president to fill the place left vacant by Orton's promotion.

From the very opening of the convention the fight was sharp. The opposition bloc, because of its majority control of the membership, felt optimistic about the results. Worth Lowery, second vice-president and a leader of the opposition bloc, brought the issues into the open in his report. He recommended an increase of the per capita tax to 50 cents, with the additional 25 cents being placed in a special fund for organizing work. He also recommended, as the only "method by which we can secure the wholehearted support of the rank and file" and as the only way of being assured "that the organizational drive will not be used as a political football," that Germer be retained as director of organization. In referring to the recommendations of the three regional C.I.O. directors at the previous convention, he lashed the *Timberworker* because it had come out with "a vicious attack . . . upon one of our most responsible and able leaders in the I.W.A. —Brother Don Helmick . . . knowingly made in violation of the mandate of the Convention." In addition, he accused the Communists of interfering with the organizational drive under Germer, recommending that the convention "go on record as serving notice on the Communist Party to refrain from interfering in any way with the affairs of the I.W.A." [26]

Communism had become so important as an issue that the regional C.I.O. directors for both Oregon and Washington came out strongly against it. Dalrymple spoke at some length and condemned the left-wing papers for their attacks on him, as did Germer. The Communist question was injected bodily into the convention controversies through the presentation of a resolution by Ralph Peoples, secretary of the Oregon State Industrial Council and a timber worker from Toledo, in which it was alleged that certain activities detrimental to the I.W.A. were being fostered by them. The resolution was designed to give support to the regional C.I.O. directors and to Adolph Germer, and, at the same time, to have the I.W.A. "go on record demanding in no uncertain terms that the Communist Party cease at once its interference in the affairs of the I.W.A." Orton declared that Peoples was out of order and referred the resolution to the resolutions committee. After a violent dispute, it was so ordered.

The resolutions committee was divided. The majority returned a different resolution—with no reference to the regional directors—

which was designed to put all political parties on the same basis. The minority returned the original resolution, claiming that "we want a definite clear-cut decision as to whether or not we are going to support our representatives of the C.I.O. in their stand on Communism." By a very close vote, 129 to 127, it was decided to consider the minority report. Accusations became bitter and, after a day-long controversy, in desperation it was decided to refer the subject matter back to the resolutions committee because there were two separate questions involved.

Still the dispute continued. Questions of constitutional changes were all considered along factional lines, with about twenty votes being the margin in each case. The opposition bloc, while representing a majority of the membership, did not have control of the convention because there were many small locals which stood behind the administration faction, giving it a majority of the delegates. Later, however, when the resolutions committee came back with two resolutions in the place of the one which had been so controversial—one supporting the national C.I.O. policy and the other an appeasement resolution on the Communist question—they were both carried. Nevertheless, until Orton summarily closed the debate in the midst of the discussion of the minority report on organization, the controversy continued.

After the convention a "rump" session, claiming to represent 70 per cent of the dues-paying members, was called by the opposition bloc and petitioned John L. Lewis to take over the I.W.A. until such time as the difficulties within the organization were settled. A resolution was adopted charging the officers of the I.W.A. with creating and nurturing factionalism and dissension within the organization; attempting to purge those opposing the theory of communism and showing rank discrimination against subordinate bodies which refused to vote in accord with the dictates of the administration machine; and using the *Timberworker* to promote the "party" program and for other purposes detrimental to the welfare of the organization. The resolution concluded:

Whereas, it is the sole desire of the delegates signing this petition to promote and extend the C.I.O. in the woodworking industry.

Therefore we petition the Congress of Industrial Organizations and J. L. Lewis to take action as deemed necessary to correct the internal strife created by the destructive activities of the above named officers, activities which not only endanger the future success of effective organization but the very existence of the I.W.A.

On the other hand, the Orton-McCarty group, represented by the majority of the Executive Board, also met after the convention and wired John L. Lewis, asking him to remove his personal representative, Germer, from his position as director of organization among the timber workers. When the entire Executive Board met on October 14, Orton requested that he be sent to Washington, D.C., to demand in person Germer's removal. The board, except for the opposition members, voted approval, and the *Timberworker* headline "Board Orders Germer Ousted" was circulated throughout the industry. Orton's personal request in Washington was not granted, but upon his return to the Northwest he tried to break the contract between the C.I.O. and the I.W.A. by advising the organizers that they were under the exclusive direction of the I.W.A. officers and that they were to send all reports and communications to him. Germer had flatly refused to hire Dick Law, a board member, and other administration supporters as organizers. This led the majority of the Executive Board to instruct McCarty, on December 5, to send a letter to Germer telling him he was through with the I.W.A. As soon as this action was revealed, Ed McSorley, board member from the Columbia River District Council, secured a restraining order to prevent the I.W.A. officers from hiring or firing organizers or administering the organization fund. The restraining order was not made permanent, but at the hearing Orton and McCarty admitted that they had had no authority to abrogate the contract with the C.I.O. and agreed to abide by it. Nevertheless, the scathing attack on Germer and the two regional C.I.O. directors was continued in the *Timberworker*.[27]

As an immediate outgrowth of these events, Philip Murray appointed a three-man committee consisting of J. C. Lewis, Reid Robinson, and S. Dalrymple to make an investigation. The administration forces announced that this committee had been created to investigate Germer's activities, but, as a matter of fact, it had been instructed to look into all matters pertaining to the "internal dissension within the I.W.A." The committee held hearings and took testimony. The accusations made were milder than they had ever been before. The hearings were never made public, and what sort of report was made, if any, is not clearly revealed. The opposition bloc claimed that "a stamp of unanimous approval" had been placed upon the work of Germer. In any case, Germer was not removed.

A special authorization by the majority members of the Executive Board of the I.W.A. to Orton, Koivunen, and McCarty to confer with the national C.I.O. officers to work out a mutually satisfactory program upon the expiration of the existing contract did not result in an agreement. Subsequently, the contract was terminated by action of the Executive Board because "we are compelled to protect the welfare of our membership and the autonomous rights of our International Union . . .," and Koivunen sent a letter to Murray informing him of this action.[28]

Worth Lowery immediately challenged the action of his fellow officers in the I.W.A. and asked each local to notify immediately the International that it "does not and will not approve this abrogation and slap in the face of our benefactor." Accusing the administration officers of sabotaging the organizing drive from the beginning and asserting that great progress had been made in spite of their actions, he said, "I am asking each Local Union to rally to the banner of the C.I.O. in turning down the dastardly conduct of self-styled, non-elected Vice-President [Koivunen]."[29]

The controversy continued through the ensuing months. Germer stayed in the region to direct organization, and the administration officers carried on their organizing activities independently. The culmination of the fight came during the course of the year but is better observed in the light of events associated with the collective bargaining difficulties during the year 1941. Our attention now should be turned to the matter of employer-union relations in recent years.

The history of jurisdictional disputes and intra-union conflict in the lumber industry is essential background for an understanding of labor-employer relations in that industry in recent years. Moreover, it throws into relief some of the difficult problems of union leadership. From the story of unwitting blunders, fundamental and honest differences of opinion, hotheaded actions and political motivation and manipulation, as well as solid and substantial accomplishments, certain clear-cut conclusions emerge. For a union leader to lose touch with the rank and file is an unforgivable sin in the minds of most timber workers. He who would shoulder the responsibility of leadership among timber workers, "had," in the words of a lumber worker, "better be pretty damned honest and open or he will find himself on the 'skids.'" Philosophical and tactical differences threw men and groups at variance with each other. Painful lessons have had to be learned, and competent leaders should profit in the future from the errors of the past.

NOTES TO CHAPTER

[1] *Timberworker*, August 5, 12, 26, October 14, 1939; *Union Register*, October 6, 1939; *Proceedings of the Third Constitutional Convention of the I.W.A.*, Klamath Falls, Ore., October 18-22, 1939, pp. 86-89, 101.

[2] National Labor Relations Board, *Decisions and Orders*, VIII: 231-235; *Timberworker*, March 11, 1939.

[3] National Labor Relations Board, *op. cit.*, XI: 258-269; *Timberworker*, March 11, 1939; *Union Register*, January 6, 1939.

[4] *Timberworker*, January 21, February 4, 25, March 11, 1939; *Union Register*, January 6, 13, 20, March 17, April 21, November 3, 10, 1937.

[6] National Labor Relations Board, *op. cit.*, V: 664-673, X: 595.

[7] National Labor Relations Board, *op. cit.*, V: 669-670, 676; IX: 594.

[8] National Labor Relations Board, *op. cit.*, X: 594-611; National Labor Relations Board, *News Release*, R-2069, September 15, 1939; San Francisco *Chronicle*, July 14, 15, October 15 to 22, 1938, February 10, 1939; *Timberworker*, July 16, 23, 30, August 6, 1938, February 25, March 11, 18, 1939; *Labor Herald*, September 21, 1939.

[9] *Lumbermen's Industrial Relations Committee Bulletin*, August 14, December 17, 1937, March 24, July 14, 1938; National Labor Relations Board, *Decisions and Orders*, X: 642-645; *Union Register*, August 20, 1937, February 18, March 25, May 6, July 8, 22, 1938.

[10] National Labor Relations Board, *op. cit.*, X: 638-643, XI: 725-730; *Lumbermen's Industrial Relations Committee Bulletin*, September 13, 1938; *Union Register*, January 27, 1939; *Timberworker*, December 24, 1938, January 28, 1939.

[11] *Timberworker*, June 3, 17, 1939; *Proceedings of the Third Constitutional Convention of the I.W.A.*, 1939, pp. 91, 95, 96.

[12] *Proceedings of the Third Constitutional Convention of the I.W.A.*, pp. 76-78, material in the following paragraphs comes primarily from this source, pp. 78-86, 105-107, 139, 168, 185-201, 205-206, 289, 294-304; cf. *Timberworker*, October 28, 1939.

[13] Portland *Oregonian*, January 8, 9, 10, 1940; *Timberworker*, January 20, 1940.

[14] *Proceedings of the Special Convention of the Oregon-Washington Council*, Portland, Ore., July 19-20, 1940, pp. 1, 13; *Proceedings of the Fourth Annual Convention of the Oregon-Washington Council*, Portland, Ore., January 16-19, 1941, p. 19.

[15] *Woodworker*, January 22, 1941.

[16] *Ibid.; Proceedings of the Fourth Constitutional Convention of the I.W.A.*, Aberdeen, Wash., October 7-12, 1940; *Timberworker*, July 13, August 10, 1940.

[17] *Union Register*, September 27, 1940.

[18] *Proceedings of the Second Annual Convention of the Oregon-Washington Council, 1938*, p. 4; *Proceedings of the Third Annual Convention of the Oregon-Washington Council, 1939*, p. 5; National Labor Relations Board, *Decisions and Orders*, XIV: 931-936, XV: 765; *Union Register*, July 1, 1938, September 15, 1939; *Timberworker*, February 17, July 6, 13, 1940.

[19] See below, p. 251.

[20] *Timberworker*, September 7, November 2, 16, 30, 1940; *Union Register*, August 30, September 20, November 1, 1940.

[21] National Labor Relations Board, *op. cit.*, XVI: 908; *Lumbermen's Industrial Relations Committee Bulletin*, September 13, 1939; *Timberworker*, September 9, 16, 1939; *Proceedings of the Third Annual Convention of the Oregon-Washington Council*, 1939, p. 7.

[22] *Timberworker*, November 25, 1939; National Labor Relations Board, *News Release*, R-2369, December 4, 1939; National Labor Relations Board, *Decisions and Orders*, XVIII: 40-42.

[23] *Proceedings of the Fourth Annual Convention of the Oregon-Washington Council*, 1941, pp. 15-16; cf. *Timberworker*, February 22, 1941.

24 "In the Superior Court of the State of Washington, for Cowlitz County, Local No. 36 of the Columbia River District No. 5, of the I.W.A. vs. I.W.A., et al., Case No. 13515, March 25, 1941" (typewritten).

25 National Labor Relations Board, *News Release,* R-4363 and R-4364, April 16, 1941; *Timberworker,* April 20, 1941.

26 *Proceedings of the Fourth Constitutional Convention of the I.W.A.,* 1940, pp. 13-15, material in following paragraph is found in this same source, pp. 23-35, 39-47, 58-116, 147-148, 285-286; cf. Portland *Oregonian,* October 8, 10, 1940.

27 *Timberworker,* October 19, December 7, 14, 21, 28, 1940; *Woodworker,* January 22, 1941; *Union Register,* October 25, 1940.

28 *Timberworker,* January 25, February 1, March 1, 1941; *Woodworker,* January 22, February 26, 1941.

29 *Woodworker,* February 26, 1941.

MPLOYER-UNION relations in the Douglas fir lumber industry in recent years have been decisively affected by the multiplicity of union groups and the points of difference and friction among them. Intra- and inter-union struggles, together with the depressed condition of the lumber market and heavy unemployment from late 1937 to early 1939, prevented many major employer-employee struggles from taking place. Some did occur during this period, however, and these provide a basis for understanding the important developments of 1940 and 1941 and, therefore, merit attention.

Early in 1938, the I.W.A. "International Policy Committee," created by the convention of the preceding year, joined with delegates from the various district councils to work out a plan for achieving uniformity in contracts throughout the industry. The various employer groups in the Douglas fir region—the West Coast Lumbermen's Association, the Lumbermen's Industrial Relations Committee, the Columbia Basin Loggers, the Columbia Basin Sawmills, the Willamette Valley Lumbermen's Association, and the Pacific Northwest Loggers Association—were informed of its purpose. Representatives from the Lumbermen's Industrial Relations Committee, subsequently meeting with representatives of the I.W.A. to consider the possibility of industry-wide agreements, took the position that such a program was not practical because of the current A.F. of L.-C.I.O. conflict. The Lumbermen's Industrial Relations Committee representatives made clear their desire for greater autonomy for the local crews, which had grown out of the difficulties operators had experienced in dealing with large locals in Seattle, Grays Harbor, Portland, and elsewhere. In view of existing conditions, it is obvious that none of the parties was really prepared for more than district negotiations, and some not even that. Most employers, lacking experience, did not understand how to negotiate with a labor union or its representatives. Previous experiences of many operators had been costly and irritating. The unionists, flushed with the newly acquired sense of power, were militant, and in some cases made intransigent enemies of many operators. The Lumbermen's Industrial Relations Committee, nevertheless, held a number of meetings with the I.W.A. group as well as with the A.F. of L., which were essentially "educational" in character.[1]

Because of the continued depressed conditions in the industry, the unionists did not press any demands and were glad to maintain their existing wage scales. Taking advantage of market conditions which inhibited the unions from voicing new demands, the employers, however, instituted a movement to establish lower wages. To "bring the industry more in line with its competition," the operators decided to undertake negotiations for a wage reduction of $12\frac{1}{2}$ cents per hour "across the board," or for each classification of work. Were it not for the fact that many mills were closed, more wage reductions than actually occurred in the spring and summer of 1938 would have taken place. There was no point in cutting the wage of workers who were not employed. Many of the attempts to depress wages were unsuccessful because the unions found the strength to resist even in the face of acute unemployment. At the same time, however, the Lumbermen's Industrial Relations Committee publication *Where Do We Go from Here?*, distributed throughout the industry in June, 1938, carried sufficient factual weight to defeat the unionists. The latter denied its implications, but lacked data of their own to refute its contentions, even though they insisted that wage cuts were not a solution to the problems of the industry. An I.W.A. proposal of a joint fact-finding committee was rejected by the Lumbermen's Industrial Relations Committee, which asserted that the relevant facts were already found in *Where Do We Go from Here?*[2]

In the Columbia Basin area an early summer proposal of the Columbia Basin Loggers for joint negotiations on the matter of a wage reduction was ignored by the Columbia River District Council. The employers' request to open the agreement arrived one day too late to meet the requirements of the joint contract. The union then legally contended "that neither party to the Father Thompson-Hope award is at liberty to vary its terms."[3] Wage reductions were, however, effected in the Willamette Valley and the Oregon Coast areas and in some of the interior mills and small logging camps.

Demands from the unions for increased wages were numerous throughout 1940. The industry had pulled out of the slump of 1938 with the revival of housing construction on a larger scale during 1939. During 1940 the defense program, which began to be pushed following the spectacular successes of the German army in the Low Countries and in France, added materially to the demand for practically all types of lumber and timber products. Government demand, direct and indirect, for materials for cantonments, defense factories, and shipbuilding came to be the most important factor in the market situation, and full production was rapidly realized.

The first wage increase occurred in connection with the plywood industry in western Washington. Plywood is a relatively new, but rapidly developing member of the lumber industry family. Because of its wide use in new types of housing construction, and its manifold other uses, the demand for plywood was great. Two joint wage negotiations were begun in March and were conducted simultaneously, one involving A.F. of L. and the other I.W.A. workers. During June a 2½-cent per hour temporary wage increase, to run for three months and then to be considered by a joint board, was accepted by the I.W.A. plywood locals. In addition, a modified union shop was granted and a standard form of agreement was established. At the same time, certain A.F. of L. plywood locals, not affiliated with the Oregon-Washington Council, also accepted the 2½-cent increase. In Tacoma, an important sector of the plywood industry, the A.F. of L. locals, affiliated with the Oregon-Washington Council, branded the I.W.A. settlement as a "sellout," and broke off their own negotiations when offered the same terms. In an effort to secure 7½ cents they conducted a strike which lasted only a few days, largely because other A.F. of L. locals had already settled. These Tacoma A.F. of L. plywood locals finally also settled for a 2½-cent increase, and they obtained the union shop as well.[4]

In early 1940 the Hope-Thompson argeement of 1937, which was still in existence in the Columbia River area, was more than due for a modification. On December 11, 1939, the Columbia Basin Loggers notified the Columbia River District Council of its desire to change the terms of the agreement. A month later, probably realizing that a movement to increase wages was developing, the employers indicated a willingness to let the existing agreement stand. If this was not acceptable to the union, then they wanted to negotiate an entirely new one. The union desired certain changes, and negotiations began on March 17, 1940, and continued rather regularly through the month. Bitterness was beginning to affect the negotiations, which, however, continued through April. Suddenly, on April 30, Al Hartung surprised the operators by informing them that the Columbia River District Council was shortly to vote on the question of industry-wide negotiations. This meant a postponement of negotiations between the two groups.

Industry-wide negotiations again had been proposed. During the first week of February, the operators, through the Lumbermen's Industrial Relations Committee, had been requested to enter into such negotiations by the I.W.A. On March 22 the first of several meetings of representatives of the Lumbermen's Industrial Relations Committee and representatives of the Northern Washington and Grays-Willapa Harbors District Councils resulted from this request. Meanwhile, the I.W.A. had been working hard to bring the whole industry into one negotiation. The I.W.A. International Policy Committee had selected a large committee composed of two members each from the Northern Washington, Grays-Willapa Harbors, Columbia River, Plywood and Veneer, and Boommen and Rafters District Council, plus the C.I.O. regional directors from Oregon and Washington and the International officers to meet with the employers. Plans for the broadest negotiations ever undertaken in the industry were under way. It was hoped that the long-looked-for "master contract" covering the competitive fir belt could now be drawn up.[5]

On May 20 the joint committee met at Tacoma. Three days later they recessed by mutual consent, when it was discovered that the Lumbermen's Industrial Relations Committee could only negotiate but not conclude a contract for the individual companies represented. The individual members retained the right to accept or reject the negotiated contract. Too many individuals were still unwilling to tie themselves down legally to any industry-wide agreement. Another reason why the employers insisted on individual contracts was that the Lumbermen's Industrial Relations Committee maintained that under the Wagner Act the committee would become liable for any violation of the agreement by an employer for whom it negotiated and signed. It was not willing to shoulder the task of policing the industry. This interpretation, however, was seriously questioned by the lawyers of the I.W.A. The committee of the latter, on the other hand, had entered into the negotiations with full power to negotiate, conclude, and enforce any contract which the membership of the five participating districts voted by referendum to accept. If approved by a majority of the local unions of the participating district council, the agreement would be binding on all the locals. Because of this stumblingblock, negotiations reverted to either a district or an interdistrict basis.[6]

The Columbia River District Council and the Columbia Basin Loggers then continued their previous negotiations. Many issues still remained to be settled—seniority, "busheling," or piece rates in falling and bucking, preferential hiring, base wage rates, and standards for "gyppo" crews who worked under contract with larger logging companies. The employers held that they could not agree to eliminate busheling or to increase wages. The union insisted on wage increases, but gave up its demand to do away with piece rates in falling and bucking. A tentative agreement was reached on June 14, but later the operators and the union asked for revisions, and it was not until September 10, 1940, that a contract was finally ratified and signed.

Following the breakup of the "industry-wide" meeting on a standard agreement, the Northern Washington and Grays-Willapa Harbors districts, commonly referred to as the "Twin Districts," entered into negotiations with certain employers within the area to arrive at a uniform contract. Approximately sixty companies were involved, and an agreement was reached on September 18, which was later ratified by most of the companies represented.[7] The "Standard Form of Contract," so called by the Lumbermen's Industrial Relations Committee, did not include the union shop which had hardly penetrated the industry anywhere. But it did provide for a wage increase of 4 per cent in the minimum and 5 per cent in all other wage brackets, creating at the same time a base rate of 65 cents per hour.

Two members of the union negotiating committee among those from the Grays-Willapa Harbors District Council returned to their constituents in Aberdeen and Raymond and advised against acceptance of the contract. As a result, the two big locals withdrew their authority from the union committee and so notified their employers. This surprise action, an outgrowth of the intra-union struggle within the I.W.A., angered the employers because no indication of such an eventuality had been revealed during the course of the negotiations. It had, however, been previously understood that any participating local or company might refuse to ratify any agreement arrived at in the joint negotiations. As a result of these developments and the intense opposition to the leaders who were conducting the negotiations, the local in Raymond and the large local in Aberdeen drew away from the influence of the Twin Districts negotiations and finally arrived at separate contracts. Their terms, interestingly enough, including the percentage wage increases, were substantially the same.

The wage increases granted to the Twin Districts I.W.A. locals came somewhat as a surprise to the Carpenter locals, because they thought a base wage of 62½ cents an hour was about as high as wages could go. Union rivalry, already acute, became more intense and even more bitter. The employers were accused by the A.F. of L. spokesmen of favoring the C.I.O.

While the I.W.A. Standard Form of Contract was being negotiated, Tacoma lumber mill employers were negotiating with the Carpenter-chartered locals. The plywood or combination plywood plants which had already agreed to a new contract were not included. In the first part of September, 1940, an agreement was reached; this was approved by the operators but rejected by the crews because of certain working conditions which it permitted. The employers, in subsequent negotiations, gave in on these points, and on September 24 the parties came to a tentative final agreement. But the Twin District I.W.A. had just received wage increases a few days before. A.F. of L. representatives submitted a less favorable agreement to their constituents, and then returned with an ultimatum demanding a wage increase of 7½ cents and a week's vacation with pay, insisting upon an answer before Monday, September 30, or the membership would strike. In reply, the employer committee made two proposals: that the matter of a temporary wage increase be left to immediate negotiations between committees representing all the A.F. of L. mills in the Douglas fir area, or as many as cared to participate; or that a temporary increase in wages of 4 per cent in the lowest bracket and 5 per cent in the other brackets be accepted, subject to review in case of adverse conditions in the lumber market. The employers also expressed a willingness to negotiate the subject of a week's vacation with pay.[8] The unionists might have taken the wage offer if it had been accompanied by a week's vacation with pay. But, without the vacation, the A.F. of L. unionists, in order to keep ahead of their rivals, which is important to note, stood on their demand for an increase in wages of 7½ cents. The operators were beginning to discover that their initial elation over the split in the ranks of labor was a boomerang. Instead of the two groups exterminating each other, they were now fighting to outdo each other to build prestige in the eyes of the workers.

Inevitably a strike resulted. From the beginning it took on industry-wide importance. If the wage demands had been fully acceded to, a move would have been in order for wage increases elsewhere. The employers' committee knew that the wage question was to be reopened in the Twin Districts in December and they cared not to feed the spiraling wage demands. Because of the significance of this local dispute, and the great likelihood that it might spread, E. P. Marsh, federal conciliator, immediately stepped in. On October 8, during the second week of the strike, union representatives proposed a settlement on the basis of a 5-cent per hour increase in all job classifications, with all additional wages and a vacation with pay to be subject to industry-wide A.F. of L. negotiations.[9] On the following day, the employers countered with a written statement that they could not accept the union proposal and insisted on the same wage increase as negotiated in the Twin Districts settlement. In addition, the employers stated that they were willing to join with other employers in the Puget Sound area, or in a larger district, in negotiations with A.F. of L. unions on temporary wage adjustments and vacations with pay. Broader negotiations at the time were hardly feasible. On October 10, in meeting with Marsh, the union representatives withdrew their offer and returned to their original demand of 7½ cents per hour increase in wages and a week's vacation with pay. The negotiators then recessed.

Concurrently, the executive committee of the Puget Sound District Council, after meeting in Seattle on October 12, announced that the Tacoma strikers were to be supported by all other unions in the Council and that they were going to ask for district negotiations in an effort to secure the Tacoma demands for all. On October 14 the Snoqualmie Falls Lumber Company, without negotiating with the A.F. of L. crew which had been certified by the National Labor Relations Board, issued a notice to its employees that the temporary wage increase of 4 per cent in the lowest bracket and 5 per cent in the other brackets was granted to them.[10]

A committee representing a majority of the employers in the Puget Sound area with A.F. of L. sawmill crews began meetings on October 21 with representatives of the Puget Sound District Council in an effort to work out an acceptable regional settlement of the wage issue. The unionists were persistent in pressing for the demands made in the Tacoma dispute. On October 22 they modified them slightly, proposing a permanent increase of 2½ cents to raise the base rate to 65 cents an hour, a week's vacation with pay, and, on top of this, a temporary wage increase of 2½ cents per hour to be subject to reconsideration through joint negotiations on the basis of some agreeable procedure. These terms were not acceptable to the employers and the negotiations failed. Two days later a demand was made on the Snoqualmie Falls Lumber Company for a 7½-cent increase in wages, a week's vacation with pay, and the union shop. The company was unwilling to agree, and a strike followed.[11]

After the failure of the joint district negotiations, representatives of the Seattle locals broke away from the district negotiations and entered into independent conferences with their employers. At the same time, several hundred men, chiefly members of the struck crews of Tacoma and Snoqualmie mills, intent upon spreading the strike and fighting the I.W.A., moved in upon Everett and by means of mass picketing closed the Weyerhaeuser mills "B" and "C," which employed about 1,275 men. At Everett an intense I.W.A. organizing drive had been under way for some months. Aided by an unpopular attempt on the part of the A.F. of L. pickets to close the mills in the late summer, it had resulted in an increase in the I.W.A. local. The Weyerhaeuser Timber Company, engaged in negotiations for some time, entered into an agreement with the I.W.A. while the A.F. of L. pickets were around the mills. Shortly afterward, another Weyerhaeuser affiliate, the White River Lumber Company at Enumclaw, signed the Standard Form of I.W.A. contract. Meanwhile, A.F. of L. negotiations in Seattle were terminating in an agreement providing for a straight 5 cents per hour increase in wages. At the same time, the Tacoma strike leaders took the position that the local employers would accede to their demands if the power of the Weyerhaeuser Timber Company did not stand in the way, and the unionists, therefore, tried desperately to spread the strike further.

While it is frequently true that where the Weyerhaeuser Timber Company leads, the industry has to follow, in this instance the organized employers were working hard to keep all groups on the same wage level. The wage provisions of the Standard Form of the I.W.A. contract had been widely accepted in the region. They had just been installed at three large Weyerhaeuser mills, and they had been applied throughout the Puget Sound area in almost all places where the I.W.A. had control. In addition, the same wage increases had been installed at the Bloedell-Donovan Lumber Company mills in Bellingham, at the Grays Harbor Lumber Company mill at Hoquiam, and at the Shafer Brothers Lumber and Shingle Mill, No. 4, at Aberdeen, all A.F. of L. mills. Also, the same increases had been put into effect in Longview, although without union agreements. It is claimed that more than 15,000 workers had accepted the 4 per cent and 5 per cent wage increases.[12] The employers were not willing to give more to the Tacoma group than they had given elsewhere. It seems obvious that the greatest difficulty at Tacoma was that the A.F. of L. leaders were not willing to take only what their rivals had accepted. The former were, of course, insisting that the industry could well afford the demands they were making.

Nor were the I.W.A. Columbia River District unionists willing to accept the Twin District wage settlement negotiated by their rival leaders in the I.W.A. Strange as it may seem, the officials of the Oregon-Washington Council and the Puget Sound District Council met with I.W.A. leaders from the Columbia River District Council and Grays Harbor in order to take a united stand on the wage question. It seemed impossible to get united action among the A.F. of L. groups in the industry and help was needed if the Tacoma A.F. of L. group was to succeed with its wage demand. The Columbia River District Council officials interpreted the Tacoma stalemate as the spearhead of an industry attack on wages. At the same time, it must be remembered that they, too, were chagrined because the Twin District I.W.A. leaders had surprised them with wage increases. Consequently, they were willing to co-operate with the A.F. of L. group. Out of the collaboration meeting came a criticism both of the wage terms of the Twin District contracts and the 5-cent an hour increase just previously accepted at Seattle. In addition, the parties agreed to send delegates to each other's meetings to bring about further co-operation. A.F. of L. leaders attended a Columbia River District Council meeting on November 9, and I.W.A. leaders from the Columbia River area attended the Puget Sound District Council meeting at Enumclaw on the 10th. The Lumbermen's Industrial Relations Committee appeared to take these developments lightly. "This might be all right," it announced to its members, "if all the parties were free to act jointly, but the Columbia River District Council has an agreement with the Columbia Basin Loggers, [and] while this group is asking the employers to join with them in advancing wages, the matter is optional with the employers and they may not act." [13]

In view of these developments, and the possible prolongation and spread of the strike, Secretary of Labor Perkins, on November 8, called the parties to the dispute to Washington, D.C., for a joint conference with officials of the Department of Labor and the National Defense Commission. She stipulated that "all lumber and lumber products finished for government orders be immediately handled, [and] that pending the conferences . . . all plants not now closed by the present dispute continue to operate uninterrupted." On November 11 the big Weyerhaeuser mills in Everett opened with full I.W.A. crews after a restraining order allowing only five A.F. of L. pickets was obtained. [14]

At Washington, A.F. of L. union representatives and the employers held a preliminary meeting with the Secretary of Labor and representatives of the Defense Commission on November 15. This was the only meeting at which the employers and union people were together. Later the same afternoon, separate discussions started which lasted for seven days. All the discussions were on the facts of the case regarding the industry, its markets, its competition, and its ability to pay wages. The employers declared that there were approximately 27,500 employees in western Washington logging camps and sawmills, and that of these at least 18,000 were, on November 15, receiving the 4 and 5 per cent wage increases, and that some were under A.F. of L. contracts. They also asserted that there were over 1,000 men in Seattle receiving a 5-cent an hour increase, and that the struck mills in Tacoma and Snoqualmie Falls had a total employment not exceeding 1,800. Finally, they pointed out that the employment in logging and sawmilling in the Douglas fir area in Oregon totaled around 22,500, and the maximum base wage was 62½ cents per hour, with several thousand men working for less. These figures embarrassed the A.F. of L. unionists who wanted to show a widespread demand for such a wage increase as they were asking. The facts left them, as they saw it, with only two alternatives—to give up or to spread the strike and make the operators' statements fallacious.[15]

The A.F. of L. leaders were bitter and chagrined that they did not have an agreement with the Weyerhaeuser Timber Company anywhere in the fir belt, whereas the I.W.A. did. Looking upon the strategic position of the Weyerhaeuser interests, the A.F. of L. was determined to win the Snoqualmie dispute. Related to this, and equally important to them, was the wage demand insisted upon for both Snoqualmie and Tacoma. They returned from Washington and extended their collaboration with the antiadministration faction in the I.W.A. A joint meeting was held at Centralia on December 1, at which the group voted to "effect as broad a tie-up as possible . . . as quickly as possible," and appointed a committee of ten to co-ordinate the strike program. The employers attempted to broaden the acceptance of the 4 to 5 per cent wage increases, but in spite of their offers five mills at Everett were closed, and I.W.A. locals at Aberdeen and Portland refused to accept the wage increases. On December 6 pickets moved into Seattle, chiefly from Everett and Tacoma, and closed eight mills because the unionists there were not co-operating and had accepted a lesser settlement of 5 cents per hour. Negotiations, however, had been under way in Portland with both A.F. of L. and I.W.A. groups, but when A.F. of L. "observers" appeared at the I.W.A. meeting the operators became confused. The employers took counsel of each other to discuss the matter of negotiating with strangers in the room and then proceeded. To prove their willingness to collaborate with the A.F. of L. group, the I.W.A. struck two mills. The employers then made a temporary offer of 5 cents per hour. At the same time, the pickets were removed from Seattle and the mills were allowed to open after Hutcheson wired that he did "not believe that this is proper or helpful to the cause of those on strike." Besides, the employers had obtained a restraining order. Then the I.W.A. sawmill workers at Portland voted to accept the 5-cent wage increase with a week's vacation with pay. Later, the loggers got 5 cents, but without reference to a vacation. The Tacoma strike was settled when the men voted to accept the 5-cent per hour increase, plus a week's vacation with pay.[16] The Snoqualmie dispute, however, was not settled for four months.[17]

In early December, 1940, the committee representing the employers and the employees in the Twin Districts negotiations met to consider the question of wages as provided for in the agreement. Within a few days it was agreed that the 4 and 5 per cent wage increases should be continued from January 1 to March 31, 1941, and that an additional 2½ cents per hour would be paid during the same period. At the same time, provision was made for the joint committee to meet on March 5 to reconsider wage adjustments.[18] It is doubtful whether this again put this group ahead on wages. The others, in many cases, had obtained vacations with pay.

In the early part of 1941 negotiations were opened in many places. It is not necessary to consider all these, for the important ones stand out boldly and give an adequate picture of what was going on. Because of defense orders and stimulated economic activities, the lumber industry was prospering. The labor groups all were anxious to participate in sharing the increased revenue accruing to the industry. Likewise, they saw a strategic opportunity to wrest other concessions from the employers. Consequently, hardly had the ink dried on the agreements effected during December—which had carried the basic wage to 67½ cents in most instances—than plans for further increases were made. Of course, this was anticipated inasmuch as the wage adjustments were temporary and in some instances the wage question was to be opened automatically according to agreement.

In the course of the settlement of the Tacoma strike, and to provide factual material to settle and prevent the spread of further labor troubles, the Council of National Defense had given assurance that a study of the Douglas fir lumber industry would be undertaken. Dr. Dexter Keezer, president of Reed College, was selected to direct it. The A.F. of L. wage settlement in December had provided for a temporary increase in wages to run for three months and then wages were to be reconsidered. Hence, in March the A.F. of L. locals were waiting upon the Keezer report. Likewise, other negotiations involving the Columbia River District Council sawmill and logging units and the Twin Districts also were waiting for it, and other independent negotiations were following closely in line with one or the other of these negotiations in most instances. The I.W.A. groups looked askance at the forthcoming Keezer report because it was occasioned by an A.F. of L. dispute and was undertaken largely as a result of A.F. of L. insistence. The A.F. of L. unions, it should be noted, had realized their great handicap in not having authoritative industry facts on costs and other conditions.

In February, 1941, before the publication of the report, the Lumbermen's Industrial Relations Committee unsuccessfully attempted to get all employers who had agreements with A.F. of L. locals and all such locals to deal on wages as a unit. Employers and local unions outside the Puget Sound area wanted to do their own bargaining at home. It has already been indicated that the A.F. of L. locals, whether members of the Northwest Council (formerly the Oregon-Washington Council) [19] or not, exercised considerable autonomy and generally acted rather independently of each other. The employers, on the other hand, were simply taking their traditional position, because they wanted to be free to act in accordance with their "interests."

Although the I.W.A. Policy Committee held meetings in early January to formulate union demands with representatives of six district councils participating, including the Columbia River District Council in some meetings, it should not be assumed that the internal breach was being closed. The antiadministration factions would not deal jointly with their "enemies." Formalities for opening I.W.A. negotiations in the Twin Districts and in the Columbia River District had been carried out in January and February, and specific provisions in the agreements, other than wages, were opened for consideration. [20]

Negotiations with the I.W.A. representatives and sawmill employers in the Portland area began on February 27, 1941. Wages and proposed changes in the working agreement were considered. An interesting sidelight connected with this situation was revealed when the employers questioned the union representatives on the matter of industry-wide negotiations, only to discover a lack of response. This might have been due to the failure the year before, but most likely union disinterest was a product of bad feeling between the opposition bloc and the administration faction. The employers had, in the identification clause in the proposed agreement, specified "Local 3, I.W.A." In place of this the union representatives proposed that there be inserted: "Local 3, presently chartered by I.W.A., its successors or assigns [sic]." It seems clear that the local was preparing for a possible break or change in affiliation.

Negotiations involving the logging operations had also begun, with the employers as well as the employees proposing changes in the working agreement. The union asked for a 15-cent an hour increase in wages, two regular paydays each month, elimination of all piecework, the union shop and exclusive union hiring, two weeks' vacation with pay, and sick leave based on two hours allowance for every forty hours worked. The operators rejected all the demands in a preliminary meeting on March 10, 1941, and then made an offer to leave the existing agreement unchanged.[21] This was not acceptable to the union, and when formal negotiations began the employers requested that the wage question be settled immediately because of the pressure of defense orders and the presence of penalty clauses in the defense contracts. Union spokesmen, however, insisted on a consideration of other issues.

Most involved, and in many respects most significant, of the disputes was the one growing out of the Twin Districts negotiations.[22] The existing contracts continued legally in force, but were open for consideration of union demands for a 7½-cent per hour wage increase, for the elimination of all piecework, for the union shop, and for a vacation with pay. Lengthy arguments on the four issues failed to induce the employers to grant the union's requests. The union negotiators contended that the system of busheling—disliked by the men—resulted in discrimination as to earnings, in increased hazard due to speed-up, and in increased waste in the woods. These assertions were flatly denied by the employers but neither side could produce sufficient factual evidence to establish its point. When it became apparent that the operators would make no concessions on piecework elimination, the union negotiators proposed that a daily guaranteed minimum wage be established, but without success.

Vacations with pay were strongly opposed by the operators on the ground that it was primarily a means for securing extra pay which would increase labor costs by 2 per cent. Consequently, they concluded "that the thing we are talking about in this particular industry actually is a question of a wage increase." The employers held—in the face of strenuous contradictions by unionists—that in making the 2½-cent wage adjustment in December, they were granting as much as other groups in the industry were getting who had been given vacations with pay.

The union negotiators regarded the granting of the union shop as imperative because it had been conceded to A.F. of L. locals in various parts of the industry. They felt that the existing situation—wherein A.F. of L. locals had union shops and they had none—was designed "for the purpose of eliminating our organization." The employers refused to concede the union shop because they had not found "where union shop agreements have contributed to satisfactory relationships between employers and employees." They also contended "that it is the inalienable right of each individual to decide for himself as to whether or not he desires to become a member of any labor organization. . . ." One union spokesman said, "I can't see your consistency. We have requested things in these negotiations that you have already granted to other groups. . . ." Another one said, "You cannot convince us that you are not tied up with the operators that are granting the A.F. of L. a closed-shop contract."

The Keezer report [23] was made public at Olympia, Washington, on March 11, 1941. About that time, the Columbia River District Council I.W.A., the Twin Districts I.W.A., and A.F. of L. negotiations were on the point of considering wages and were actually waiting upon the report. Soon after the report was made public, the A.F. of L. representatives of the Northwest Council and a committee of employers representing chiefly Puget Sound mills met in Tacoma to negotiate on wages. At the same time, the wage question was taken up in the Twin Districts negotiations. The employers were trying to work it so that all three major union groups, the two I.W.A. factions and the A.F. of L., would be held together on the same wage basis. In fact, the employer groups met the A.F. of L. and Twin Districts I.W.A. groups in Tacoma at the same time and in the same building so that neither group could surprise the other on wages.

Before these negotiations were concluded, the Snoqualmie dispute —which had not been settled and which was submitted by mutual agreement in March to the newly created National Defense Mediation Board—was terminated when the board drew up an agreement that was approved by both parties. Notable in the settlement was the "union maintenance agreement" which the company offered the A.F. of L. in place of the union shop. By this the company agreed to require all present and future members of the union to maintain membership in good standing. Shortly after, the A.F. of L. group in negotiations in Tacoma prevailed upon the employers to increase their 5-cent per hour wage offer to $7\frac{1}{2}$ cents. At the same time, a wage board composed of union and employer representatives was established and charged with the responsibility of meeting every four months during the emergency to consider wage adjustments. A basic wage of 62½ cents was agreed upon. This rate was to be permanent, and wages in excess of it were to be the subject for consideration by the wage board. At the same time, the temporary wage on top of the basic minimum was 12½ cents at the lowest level, making a minimum wage of 75 cents. This was a 12½-cent increase over that of September, 1940.[24]

Whereas the A.F. of L. group readily settled the terms of its agreement, the two major I.W.A. groups and their respective employers were not able to come to terms. The I.W.A. sawmill negotiations at Portland, however, were concluded with the acceptance of a wage increase of 7½ cents per hour and a vacation with pay. The plywood workers, both I.W.A. and A.F. of L., also came to terms on the 7½-cent increase in the first part of May.

In mid-April the Twin Districts I.W.A. representatives called G. Simpson of the Pacific Coast Labor Bureau to represent them in their controversy over the meaning of the Keezer report. When the union realized that no headway was being made they requested the employers to submit a definite statement in answer to all the union demands. On April 16 the employers submitted their answer, refusing to eliminate busheling and to grant the union shop or the vacation with pay. As for wages, an offer of 5 cents per hour on top of the temporary increase as of September and the supplemental increase in December was made, to become effective as of April 1, providing acceptance was made by April 22, 1941. This was designed to establish a uniformity in wage adjustments; for it would have given the Twin Districts the same wage increases as of September, 1940, that the A.F. of L. group had—12½ cents. But the union immediately rejected the offer because of employer refusal of all other union demands, and the meetings were recessed. Immediately, representatives of the locals under the Twin Districts agreement met in a conference and decided to take a strike vote.[25]

At this point the U.S. Conciliation Service became interested in the dispute and E. S. Jackson, federal conciliator, began to work on the case. When no headway was made, Jackson was advised that the union was preparing for immediate strike action. The union shop had become the chief issue and union representatives charged the employers with bad faith because many A.F. of L. locals had been granted this demand by employers who refused it to the I.W.A. Finally, the dispute was certified by the U.S. Department of Labor and was turned over to the National Defense Mediation Board.

C. A. Dykstra, chairman of the board, requested both parties to continue negotiations in an effort to reach a settlement or a narrowing of the issues prior to the hearing.[26]

The strike started the next morning as threatened, with fifty-two plants involved,[27] but because of Dykstra's request, negotiations were continued under the direction of E. S. Jackson. On May 9, the employers offered the "Snoqualmie Falls Settlement" in place of the union shop, but withdrew their offer the next day. The union negotiators interpreted this action as an "attempt to stymie or lengthen negotiations." The employers maintained that they were compelled to do this because the full committee was not willing to grant even that much on the "union shop" question.

At a subsequent meeting on May 13, Jackson proposed arbitration, which was followed by "a rather strange silence." After this suggestion was considered, the union spokesman declared: "We cannot accept the belief that the operators have been negotiating in good faith; and in the absence of that good faith, we do not believe that the matters are properly subject to arbitration at this time." The employers were not willing to recommend the subjects of the union shop or elimination of busheling to arbitration, but were willing to arbitrate the question of wages and vacations. Jackson concluded that the dispute was a hopeless deadlock, and the meetings were adjourned.[28]

Because a settlement was not reached, the parties were requested to appear before the National Defense Mediation Board in Washington. In leaving for the East, the union representatives announced that the strike would not be won in Washington but on the picket lines. Before the board in Washington the combatants stood firm. Again the greatest obstacle was the union shop. On May 22, Mr. Dykstra informed the two groups that, because of the failure to reach an agreement, it would be necessary for the panel of the board to consider a reasonable proposal.[29] At the same time the Columbia River District logging dispute had been certified to the board, other disputes seemed headed that way, and a proposal for settlement in the Twin Districts dispute was to serve as a basis for settling all others which might come to it. On May 23, therefore, the board made a report and gave its recommendations.

Properly assessing the nature of the controversy on the four issues (wages, vacations, union shop, and piecework) and the inadequate available factual information useful for the present as well as for future disputes, the board proposed that an impartial commission be appointed. This commission was to make a study of union-management relations, wage practices, the general condition of the industry, influence of seasonal and climatic conditions, problems of hazard, piecework practices, vacation practices, possibilities for the stabilization of the entire industry for the period of the emergency, and other relevant issues. Pending the factual findings of the commission, the board proposed:

A. THAT THE REPRESENTATIVES OF THE I.W.A. UNIONS ACCEPT:

1. The Union Maintenance Agreement here offered and the proffer of the employers' representatives to recommend union membership to all new employees pending any further recommendations of the Board.

2. The basic wage increase amounting to 7½ cents together with the schedule which gives a 12½ cents increase "across the board" as of last September.

3. The revised vacation suggestion which reduces the 1600 hour proposal for the mills to 1400 hours and the 2 cent suggestion for logging camps.

4. The proposal for a study by joint committees of the relation of piece work to hazard.

B. That work be resumed pending the findings of the investigating commission and the final recommendation of the Board with the understanding that any final proposal on wage rates or increases shall be retroactive to the time of resumption of work and any findings on vacation which affect payments of any kind shall also be retroactive as of the same time.

If this proposal is accepted by the parties now in dispute the Board is hopeful that within a comparatively short time a recommendation from this Board will be found useful to the whole Fir belt in establishing a pattern which will bring stability and unity to an industry of unique importance to our national defense. The time is here when the maximum of intelligence and good will must be applied in an industry which has lacked cohesion and unity and which is perhaps ready just now for a constructive plan of organization and operation. This undertaking cannot be piecemeal and sporadic in a time of emergency. It must be as inclusive and comprehensive as joint effort can make it.

This set of recommendations was immediately accepted by the employers' committee and was recommended to the employers for acceptance.[30] The union representatives did not commit themselves, but immediately left Washington for the West Coast to put the matter before the locals. A meeting was held in Olympia on Monday, May 26, at which the board's proposals were rejected because the union held that they were "almost a verbatim copy of the employers' position [which] would completely neutralize the effectiveness of the I.WA.." Specifically attacked was the employer "proffer"—the five points of the Snoqualmie settlement—which provided for "maintenance of membership" of all present union members, maintenance of membership of all who subsequently joined the union, settlement of disputes as to membership by the U.S. Conciliation Service, discipline to be a responsibility and duty of both the employer and the union, and the acceptance of the provisions during the period of the National Defense program as defined by the National Defense Mediation Board. Action was then taken to spread and intensify the strike, while the Long-Bell and Weyerhaeuser companies were accused of interfering with legitimate settlement. "Our problems," maintained the union representatives, ". . . will be solved only through the action of the membership and not through the intervention of federal agencies." [31] As a result, a significant struggle with the board ensued.

The board was notified of the action, and replied that its proposal was only for a temporary settlement and that, pending the findings of the impartial commission, it was essential to national defense that work be resumed. The union officials were asked to reconsider the recommendations and to bring the board's request and telegram "to the personal attention of everyone with power to vote upon the acceptance or rejection of the Board's recommendations." Replying immediately, O. M. Orton and Ilmar Koivunen told Chairman Dykstra that "following conference at which delegated representatives unanimously rejected Mediation Board's recommendations, said recommendations were referred to strike membership who in special meetings considered them and rejected them by an overwhelming vote," and placed the responsibility for the situation "squarely with the employer." Dykstra replied sharply, "It does not appear from your reply that you have complied with the request made in the Board's wire of May 29," requesting that its telegram be brought to the personal attention of all workers with the right to vote. Orton assured Dykstra that the membership had been given an opportunity to vote. Because of the controversy, Orton was called a second time to Washington at the request of Dykstra and Philip Murray.[32]

With this turn of events the Employers Negotiating Committee, which had advised its members to start logging and sawmilling operations on June 2, asked them to defer any initiation of activity at their operations.[33]

At the second conference in Washington, D.C., Orton, supported by Karly Larsen, Northern Washington District Council president, held adamantly to his position. Following one of the conference sessions, Orton released a sensational statement to the press in which he accused the board of being "an all-out labor busting and strike breaking device," and declared that the strike would continue until the workers "obtain a decent living . . . [which] is real national defense Mr. Dykstra's phoney propaganda and bulldozing to the contrary notwithstanding." Orton further complained that upon both visits to Washington at the request of Mr. Dykstra, the union representatives were "confronted with the same edict, namely, that we must accept the proposal offered by him for the Mediation Board, which is in no way different from the proposals previously offered by the Weyerhaeuser Timber Company. . . . This is a very peculiar situation when a government agency receives a proposition from the employer, adopts it as its own, and then, by cajolery, threats and tricky propaganda, advises the workers to take it or leave it, saying 'if you don't take it, you're not patriotic.' " [34]

The International officers of the I.W.A. who were leading the Twin Districts strike were fighting desperately to maintain their leadership and to nullify any advantage that the A.F. of L. groups had gained. Unfortunately for them, they supported an antiwar philosophy at odds with the government program and with the leaders of the C.I.O. Orton's sensational statement in Washington backfired when Philip Murray condemned him and notified all members of the I.W.A. that it was the panel of the board and not just Mr. Dykstra that had issued the recommendations for temporary settlement until an impartial commission could discover the facts for a later final settlement. He also explained that it was understood by the board that in the event of disagreement over the final settlement that the issue would be brought back to it for further recommendations. Murray said:

I have personally recommended the acceptance of the board's proposals to the officers of the I.W.A. . . . Unfortunately the officers of the I.W.A. who have met with Mr. Brophy and me . . . have refused to accept these recommendations which are those not only of the board but also of the president of the Congress of Industrial Organizations. In so doing, they have indulged in a campaign of misrepresentation, slander, and abuse. . . .

Murray held that the refusal to recommend acceptance "indicates the lack of understanding displayed by the international officers of the I.W.A." Murray, commenting on Orton's picture of the board as a labor-busting organiztaion, said, "This is, of course, a most reprehensible, lying defamation."

At this time, while Orton was gaining national notoriety, his bitter opponents in the Columbia River District took advantage of his plight and that of his fellow International officers. They made capital of the situation by peaceably settling their dispute through the office of the board in accord with the May 23 recommendations. Subsequently, the membership voted overwhelmingly to accept the settlement. However, the Twin Districts officials made a point of the fact that the Columbia River dispute was purposely not settled until after the second Washington appearance of the Twin Districts representatives. They claimed that it was so handled to keep the groups divided and thus break the strike and destroy the leadership of the Twin Districts organizations.[35]

The Twin Districts I.W.A. called a conference at Olympia to build support for Orton and his position. The meeting was held on June 9, and it was decided to inform Murray that the I.W.A. locals supported their leader and that the I.W.A. was going to try to spread the strike by getting the Columbia River District workers to reject the settlement approved in Washington. At the same time, the operators, to throw more blame on the union leaders, informed the National Defense Mediation Board that if an honest referendum were taken the vast majority of the employees would return to work under the board's recommendations.

At this juncture, the antiadministration forces in the I.W.A. were literally going to "skid" Orton out of his position. Orton and his followers had been placed in a bad light. Developments in internal politics were rapid. Orton's predicament was appreciated by friends outside the I.W.A., and they came to his rescue. It was said that Bridges called upon his friend Mike Curran, who was also Orton's friend, and that together, working through John L. Lewis, they brought pressure to bear on Murray. In any case, Orton was again summoned to Washington, D.C., where he conferred with Murray, Brophy, Curran, and others.[36] Subsequently the National Defense Mediation Board, on June 13, issued another statement designed to bring the parties together. Actually it increased the confusion and complexity of the situation. The board asked that the parties get together in collective bargaining with the understanding that the employees return to work and "that temporary recommendations one, two, three, and four of the National Defense Mediation Board shall be immediately effective upon resumption of work." The board then re-enumerated the four points which the union was to accept, with an explanation of the first one, having reference to "union maintenance" which it held meant "that every present employee who belongs to the Union and every future employee who joins the Union shall as a condition of employment maintain union membership in good standing and requires further that new employees shall join the Union within forty days after being employed." [37]

The employers refused to accept the June 13 recommendations. They asserted that there had been a "back-to-work movement" and that the men were on the job. Whether the men had returned to work prior to the union's acceptance of the board's June 13 statement or afterward with the union's approval is not clear in many cases. It is clear, however, that following the publication of the board's May 23 recommendations, the employers had prepared to reopen the mills and camps. They claimed they had delayed doing so until about June 8 when certain groups, and some locals, indicated a willingness to return to work on the basis of the May 23 recommendations. Moreover, the Columbia River District Council and some locals in the Grays Harbor area, not parties to the Twin Districts negotiations, had accepted the recommendations. In addition, the employers had been immediately informed by union spokesmen that the June 13 statement constituted a reinterpretation of the May 23 recommendations, and in fact constituted a second set of recommendations—notwithstanding that the employers were not parties to the meeting in Washington. The union claim that "the Board was prevailed upon to issue" the new recommendations at the request of Orton and Murray [38] also led the employers to insist on the May 23 recommendations.

It is obvious that both the employers' committee and the union's representatives were in agreement, whether warranted or not, as to the substance of the May 23 recommendations. The I.W.A. officials had complained, upon the third trip to Washington, that the employers' union maintenance offer could not be accepted by them as it stood. At this time, it is said, Dykstra claimed he knew nothing of those provisions. The union representatives accusingly pointed to this as a simple attempt to make it appear that the union had misrepresented the board's proposal.[39] Whatever understandings or misunderstandings, the board did drop all reference to the three objectional points in the employers' union maintenance offer. This was the thing which placed the employers in opposition to the board; they held that the change had been made in spite of the common understanding of the two contending parties, and that the change had been made without consultation with the employers.

Because of the conflicts in views, commissioners from the United States Conciliation Service attempted to get the parties together and asked the National Defense Mediation Board to clarify its recommendations. On June 24 the board repeated its June 13 statement on the union maintenance proposal. By way of interpretation, the board said that it had recommended nothing with regard to the employers' union maintenance proposal. The employer representatives answered this with a lengthy statement, explaining their position on the whole affair. Finally, they agreed to recommend to the employers the removal of paragraphs four and five of their proposal, provided the union would be willing to accept paragraph three, which in substance would give the United States Conciliation Service the final word in deciding whether an employee belonged to the union or not. At the same time, the employers were willing to accept the National Defense Mediation Board's recommendations on wages, vacations, and busheling. The United States Conciliation Service, however, did not successfully terminate the dispute.[40]

Because the men were at work, the whole situation cleared considerably. But also important was the changed world scene. Russia had entered the war, and many who had opposed the war effort changed their minds about "all-out defense." Certain it is that the approach of the *Timberworker* was changed overnight. Now, it seemed desirable to keep the industry going.

Much to the chagrin and disappointment of the Columbia River District Council officials, Murray, who earlier had so bitingly denounced the I.W.A. officials, now seemed to have mellowed toward Orton and his followers. More likely, however, it was not to uphold Orton but to denounce scandalmongers who were spreading reports of "splits, purges, and red-hunts in the C.I.O." [41]

Although the men were back to work, the dispute was not settled. The employers claimed the men had returned in accord with the May 23 recommendations, while the union spokesmen claimed that the return to work was under the June 13 recommendations. Both groups stood by their interpretations. Accordingly, the National Defense Mediation Board took action by appointing an impartial commission to intervene, composed of Dr. Dexter Keezer, Dean Wayne Morse, Oregon School of Law, and Professor Paul Eliel, Graduate School of Business, Stanford University. The commission brought the parties together under a temporary "face-saving" settlement concerning wages and union status, and proceeded to study the issues involved through joint discussions with the parties, through investigations, and through holding public hearings.[42] Besides gathering information on the specific issues in dispute, the commission concerned itself with many other problems of the industry. Among the most interesting aspects of its work was the exploration of the feasibility of establishing an industry-wide board for the Douglas fir industry in order to formulate a program of stabilization. This question was considered at public hearings in Seattle and in Portland, and with the respective groups in the industry. The testimony constantly revealed that the establishment of an industry board would be desirable, if it could be done, which most persons doubted because of the heterogeneity of the industry and the lack of unity in the ranks of labor. The diversified structural units and the widespread geographical differences within the Douglas fir region were emphasized. Furthermore, could the Douglas fir industry be stabilized without reference to "western" pine and "southern" pine? The employers, moreover, were convinced, and logically so, that the union groups could not be brought together harmoniously.

Meanwhile, the A.F. of L. locals, whose contracts provided for a reconsideration of wages on August 1, 1941, were anxious to open the wage question, but were chagrined when they met with representatives of the employers to find that there were no data at hand with which the question of wages could be settled. Because of this fact and the desire of the "Keezer Commission" to secure more information about the industry, it was decided that the Keezer study of the Douglas fir lumber industry should be brought up to date. Until the study was completed and published on November 1, 1941, the A.F. of L. locals marked time.

Within the I.W.A. significant events were transpiring. The internal fight continued unabated. Late in July the national officers of the C.I.O. had decided to take a hand in the matter. Adolph Germer, the C.I.O. director of I.W.A. organization, was called to Washington by Allan Haywood, director of organization within the C.I.O. A week later, O. M. Orton and Al Hartung, leaders of the opposing factions within the I.W.A., were summoned.[43] Subsequently, Haywood made some recommendations concerning the inner union problems, and with these as a starting point, a unity committee was established by Haywood composed of O. M. Orton, acting I.W.A. president, and Bertel McCarty, I.W.A. secretary, from the administration faction, and Al Hartung, Columbia River District Council president, and Ed McSorley, I.W.A. board member from the Columbia River District Council, from the opposition bloc. Under the guidance of national

C.I.O. officials the committee met and drew up a mutually acceptable unity proposal for the October convention.

The Unity Committee's chief proposals concerned the basis of voting at the convention and the voting in meetings of the Executive Board. Delegates to the convention were to be elected with the right to cast one vote for one hundred members, plus one additional vote for the next hundred; but no delegate could cast more than two votes, and there was to be no proxy voting. Locals with less than one hundred members could join with other locals near-by and elect a joint delegate. The Executive Board was to be permitted to vote as a unit. If a roll-call vote was requested, each member would cast one vote for each one hundred represented members or fraction thereof, the number of votes being computed on the basis of the average monthly per capita tax through the preceding twelve months' period. The International officers were to have equal votes equivalent to the greatest number cast by any one member of the Executive Board.[44]

The watchword before the convention was "unity," even if the two factions had not yet reconciled their differences. It was apparent that the opposition bloc had increased its convention strength through the terms of the unity proposal and was confident that it would dominate the course of the convention.

Trade union democracy at work is revealed in the convention which was assembled in Everett, Washington, from October 8 to 13, 1941. Punches were not pulled, but the convention was orderly in contrast to the previous conventions of the I.W.A. Grievances and complaints were fully aired and the rank and file was in the saddle. Of greatest significance were the nominations for offices. O. M. Orton was not nominated for president, although he was nominated for vice-president. Ilmar Koivunen was not nominated for any office. Worth Lowery, incumbent vice-president, and Harold Evans, member of the Olympia local, were both nominated for president. In addition to Orton, James Fadling, Carl Winn, and N. E. Mason were running for the two vice-presidencies. The incumbent Bertel McCarty was opposed by Ed Benedict for the office of secretary-treasurer.[45]

Seeing their inability to control the referendum election, the administration faction proposed, with great fanfare in the *Timberworker*, a "Unity Slate" composed of two of the administration group and two of the opposition group. Lowery was proposed as the president with Orton and Fadling as vice-presidents and McCarty as secretary-treasurer. As a part of the plan of the administration faction to share the offices, N. E. Mason withdrew from the race for vice-president and called upon Winn and Benedict also to withdraw.[46] The opposition bloc immediately branded the whole movement as a "cheap political trick," and both Lowery and Fadling announced that they had nothing to do with the Unity Slate proposal and that they would not go contrary to the wishes of the convention delegates but would give the rank and file a chance to vote for all nominees.[47]

In the referendum election a completely new slate of officers was carried to the head of the I.W.A. Worth Lowery became president. James Fadling and Carl Winn became the new vice-presidents, and Ed Benedict became the new secretary-treasurer. Culminating a struggle lasting more than five years, the rank-and-file action changed the leadership of the I.W.A. by using democratic procedures. There is no doubt, however, that it was fortunate that such a person as Worth Lowery was available as the leader because he commanded respect from timber workers everywhere. It was fortunate too that he could rise above the bitterness which had developed during the long struggle and the bitter convention arguments. Under his leadership the organization achieved a unity that it never experienced before. The strength and importance of the I.W.A. in the industry has been noticeably increased.

The events and crosscurrents of the years 1940 and 1941 in the western lumber industry reveal the chaotic conditions present in the lumber industry as a whole. Toward the end of the year it appeared that perhaps some order would be established. The operators had succeeded in keeping base rates more or less uniform in the face of a constantly shifting barrage from the three major groups, the two factions within the I.W.A., and the S.T.W.U., which were seeking to outdo the other. The internal situation in the I.W.A. was undoubtedly more wholesome after the referendum election in which the rank and file expressed themselves in a definite fashion. It was even logical, on the surface, to speculate that perhaps the I.W.A. and the S.T.W.U. could be brought together because of the close co-operation of the S.T.W.U. and the leadership which had just come to the fore in the I.W.A. This, however, was destined not to be for reasons that will develop later. The Keezer Commission was still studying the lumber industry. Its scope was extended to the pine region of the West and it was greatly hoped that its reports and recommendations might set the basis for a program of co-operation and united action in stabilizing the industry.

Some signs were favorable, although admittedly the turbulence of the industry was only calmed at the time, but forces without were to interfere with any real effort to achieve stabilization. On December 7, 1941, the attack on Pearl Harbor occurred, causing industrial changes of great magnitude, which had only partly been appreciated in the defense preparation period, to take place in the country as a whole. The demand for lumber increased more than ever, but apart from the lumber industry great changes were taking place. Shipbuilding and airplane construction created problems of gigantic import for the Pacific Northwest. The whole economy of the Northwest was completely unstabilized at the manpower level. The lumber industry stood in the center of the complex problems which faced the area.

NOTES TO CHAPTER

[1] *Timberworker*, January 15, 22, 1938; *Lumbermen's Industrial Relations Committee Bulletin*, January 18, March 15, April 20, June 28, August 23, 1938.

[2] *Union Register*, July 7, 1938; *Lumbermen's Industrial Relations Committee Bulletin*, May 20, July 23, 1938.

[3] *Labor News Digest*, July 15, 1938.

[4] *Lumbermen's Industrial Relations Committee Bulletin*, September 30, 1940; *Proceedings of the Fourth Annual Convention of the Oregon-Washington Council*, p. 13; *Union Register*, July 26, 1940.

[5] *Timberworker*, April 6, 13, May 11, 1940; Portland *Oregonian*, March 1, 1940.

[6] *Timberworker*, May 25, June 1, 1940.

[7] *Report(s) of Two District Negotiations on A Proposed Standard Form of Working Agreement, July 10 to September 18, 1940.* Lumbermen's Industrial Relations Committee, Seattle, Wash.

[8] *The Lumbermen's Industrial Relations Committee Bulletin*, September 30, 1940.

[9] Tacoma *Times*, October 3, 1940; *Lumbermen's Industrial Relations Committee Bulletin*, October 15, 1940.

[10] *Lumbermen's Industrial Relations Committee Bulletin*, October 15, 1940; Seattle *Post-Intelligencer*, October 13, 1940.

[11] *Lumbermen's Industrial Relations Committee Bulletin*, October 23, 1940; Tacoma *Times*, October 24, 1940; National Labor Relations Board, *Decisions and Orders*, X: 398-406.

[12] *Lumbermen's Industrial Relations Committee Bulletin*, September 4, October 4, November 7, 14, 1940; *Proceedings of the Fourth Annual Convention of the Oregon-Washington Council*, pp. 12, 13.

[13] *Lumbermen's Industrial Relations Committee Bulletin*, November 4, 12, 1940; Seattle *Post-Intelligencer*, November 4, 1940; Portland *Oregonian*, November 5, 11, 1940; *Union Register*, November 8, 1940.

[14] *Lumbermen's Industrial Relations Committee Bulletin*, November 12, 1940; *Union Register*, November 15, 1940.

[15] *Lumbermen's Industrial Relations Committee Bulletin*, November 29, 1940; *Union Register*, November 22, 1940; *Proceedings of the Fourth Annual Convention of the Oregon-Washington Council*, p. 12.

[16] Seattle *Post-Intelligencer*, December 2, 14, 1940; Portland *Oregonian*, December 2, 11, 1940; Tacoma *News-Tribune*, December 9, 1940; Seattle *Times*, December 9, 1940; *Lumbermen's Industrial Relations Committee Bulletin*, December 3, 7, 13, 17, 1940, January 13, 1941; *Union Register*, December 13, 1940.

[17] See above, p. 256.

[18] *Report(s) of Negotiations on the Temporary Adjustment of Wages Clause in the I.W.A. Standard Form of Working Agreement, December 5 and December 10, 1940.* Lumbermen's Industrial Relations Committee, Seattle, Wash.

[19] *Proceedings of the Fourth Annual Convention of the Oregon-Washington Council,* p. 16.

[20] *Timberworker,* January 11, February 15, 1941; *Lumbermen's Industrial Relations Committee Bulletin,* January 31, 1941; Letter of Columbia Basin Sawmills to Columbia River District Council, February 22, 1941; Letter of Columbia River District Council to Columbia Basin Loggers, January 23, 1941.

[21] Letter Columbia River District Council to Columbia Basin Loggers, April 1, 1941; Letter W. R. Ruegnitz to Columbia River District Council, March 13, 1941.

[22] *Report(s) of Negotiations on Reopening of the I.W.A. Standard Form of Working Agreement, May 13, 1941.* Lumbermen's Industrial Relations Committee, Seattle, Wash.

[23] Advisory Commission to the Council of National Defense, Bureau of Research and Statistics, *The Douglas Fir Lumber Industry,* by D. M. Keezer, Washington, D.C., 1941, *passim.*

[24] *Lumbermen's Industrial Relations Committee Bulletin,* April 25, 1941; *Union Register,* March 28, May 25, 1941.

[25] *Timberworker,* April 17, 24, 1941.

[26] *Lumbermen's Industrial Relations Committee Bulletin,* May 12, 1941.

[27] *Timberworker,* May 15, 1941.

[28] *Report(s) of Negotiations on Reopening of the I.W.A. Standard Form of Working Agreement,* May 9, 10, 1941.

[29] *Timberworker,* May 22, 1941; *Lumbermen's Industrial Relations Committee Bulletin,* May 22, 1941.

[30] *Lumbermen's Industrial Relations Committee Bulletin,* May 23, 1941.

[31] *Timberworker,* May 29, 1941.

[32] *Timberworker,* June 5, 1941; *Lumbermen's Industrial Relations Committee Bulletin,* May 29, June 2, 1941; Portland *Oregonian,* May 31, June 1, 1941.

[33] *Lumbermen's Industrial Relations Committee Bulletin,* June 2, 1941.

[34] Portland *Oregonian,* June 5, 1941; *Timberworker,* June 12, 1941.

[35] The Washington *Post,* June 6, 1941; *Lumbermen's Industrial Relations Committee Bulletin,* June 4, 1941; Portland *Oregonian,* June 4, 11, 16, 1941; *Timberworker,* June 12, 1941.

[36] *Timberworker,* June 19, 1941.

[37] *Lumbermen's Industrial Relations Committee Bulletin,* June 17, 1941.

[38] *Lumbermen's Industrial Relations Committee Bulletin,* June 17, 1941; *Timberworker,* June 19, 1941.

[39] *Timberworker,* June 12, 1941.

[40] Telegram, R. T. Seward, executive secretary of the National Defense Mediation Board, to E. S. Jackson, commissioner, United States Conciliation Service, June 24, 1941; Letter Employers Negotiating Committee to E. S. Jackson, June 27, 1941, p. 7.

[41] Portland *Oregonian,* June 12, 17, 1941.

[42] *Report of Meeting Between Representatives of the I.W.A and Committee of Employers, Before a Committee Appointed by the National Defense Mediation Board,* July 30, 1941 and August 19, 1941 (mimeographed); *Public Hearings on the Douglas Fir Industry,* Seattle, Wash., September 8, 1941, Portland, Ore., September 10, 1941 (mimeographed); cf. *Timberworker,* August 14, September 4, 1941.

[43] Seattle *Times,* July 23, 28, 1941.

[44] *Timberworker,* September 11, 1941.

[45] *Proceedings of the Fifth Constitutional Convention of the I.W.A.,* Everett, Washington, October 8 to 13, 1941, *passim;* cf. *Timberworker,* October 23, 1941.

[46] *Timberworker,* October 30, 1941.

[47] *Woodworker,* November 12, 1941.

14 *WAR YEARS AND PROSPECTS*

IT was inevitable that the lumber industry would be of critical importance in the war effort. It had been so during World War I and, although metal had displaced spruce in airplane construction, the needs for lumber in World War II were manifold and the volume of lumber required was staggering. The war economy's appetite for lumber seemed limitless. The gigantic building program, including both military installations and production facilities, the huge requirements for lumber in shipbuilding, and the need for creating materials in shipment of war goods overseas stimulated the greatest demand for lumber and timber products in many decades.

To a large extent the industry failed to produce a sufficient volume of the strategic lumber materials as needed. Many were the factors which contributed to the difficulties encountered in organizing lumber production for war. Although labor relations problems were not of least importance, and certainly were inextricably tied to the whole, it was the utter absence of any industry program of co-ordination of efforts within regions and from region to region that was as great a drag on production as anything else. Governmental agencies too, whose functions carried them into lumber industry problems, failed to co-ordinate their efforts, and each acting alone could contribute little toward a constructive program.

This highly competitive industry with extremely individualistic operators, who have always been abnormally suspicious and independent of each other, could make no more than an opportunistic approach to the problems at hand. Lacking effective leadership, the industry was plunged into the war economy without guidance. Faced by the uncertainties of war, and with an eye to the postwar period as well as to the present, and being cognizant of unsolved problems and their ramifications for the future of the industry, it is little wonder that there was hesitance and reluctance in getting the job of producing lumber for war adequately under way. Of course, no one tried soon enough—but no one had the power—to formulate a constructive plan to offset or avoid the development of a maze of problems and highly unstable conditions. At best, in "normal" times it will take patient effort over many years to achieve stability in the industry and the capacity to operate in a dynamic economy without serious fluctuations and uncertainty. Consequently, a well-ordered industry should hardly have been expected to emerge from uncertain and unstable conditions accompanying war.

Each of the regions, the West, the Lake States, and the Southern Pine, faced its own particular difficulties. Naturally in the field of labor problems, each region had unique ones which stemmed from its basic characteristics. Each of the regions requires some special attention but, without a doubt, the most serious labor and production situation developed in the West.

Hopes for stability in labor relations in western lumbering were not immediately destroyed by the outbreak of war. In spite of the jurisdictional rivalry, negotiations offered some promise that balance might be attained. The most important basis for optimism was that negotiations were substantially industry-wide, for both the I.W.A. and the Northwest Council of L.S.W.U.; that is, industry-wide in the Douglas fir region. The scope of the bargaining is evidence of the new unity within the I.W.A. The breach had been filled, making it possible to achieve the broadest negotiations ever undertaken in the lumber industry. Upward of 180 companies were brought together through the auspices of the L.I.R.C. and bargained as a unit with the I.W.A. Negotiating Committee. The Northwest Council, too, had arranged for its broadest industry-wide negotiations, although the workers represented constituted only about one-third as many as were involved in the I.W.A. negotiations. The industy-wide bargaining was indicative, too, of a new spirit among the operators, since they were now willing to act as a unit. To be sure, however, there were important exceptions to the industry-wide breadth of the negotiations, notably in the traditional aloofness of the Willamette Valley units; and the western pine areas were still on the lumber labor relations periphery, with the operators effectively maintaining an independence of the bargaining in fir. Labor did not have the strength to bring either the Willamette Valley operators or the western pine operators together with the major fir operators for joint negotiations.

Bargaining had not proceeded far when the operators realized that the two labor groups were still vying for advantage. The time element was in favor of the Northwest Council inasmuch as it was first able to open its contracts on the question of a wage increase. It asked for an increase of 30 cents per hour. The I.W.A., on the other hand, asked only for a 12½-cent per hour increase, but in addition it was asking for special adjustments in certain classifications and new standard vacation and hours clauses. The I.W.A. demands were designed to bring uniformity into all I.W.A. contracts. The rivalry of the two union groups became an unwholesome factor in the negotiations in so far as the operators were concerned. And the two separate negotiations presented them with serious problems. There is no doubt that most of them were much interested in standardized conditions for the industry, but found themselves struggling hard to keep the two union groups together on a basis of wage equality. For that reason alone, as much as for anything else, the employers could not accede to any wage increase until they were sure that increases would be uniform for each group. Feeling that an impartial government agency would strive to keep the industry in balance, the operators were willing, if not anxious, that the wage negotiations of the Northwest Council and the I.W.A. be stalemated and then certified to the National War Labor Board at the same time. The National Defense Mediation Board, which had had its hands full with the dispute the year before, had lost its standing in the settlement of the coal industry dispute in the fall of 1941. After Pearl Harbor, the National War Labor Board had been created as a tripartite agency to settle all labor disputes which threatened to interfere with war production.

The NWLB received the two lumber industry dispute cases among the first which crowded the agenda of this busy agency, and the method of handling them was to secure the partys' acceptance of arbitration. Pendleton Howard, dean of the University of Idaho Law School, was named arbitrator in the Northwest Council dispute and hearings were held during the first week in April. The author, then professor of economics at the University of Colorado, was named arbitrator in the I.W.A. case. The NWLB provided for review of the Jensen award and later requested Howard to submit his award to Washington for release. The Howard award, which involved only wages, was submitted late in April but was not immediately released because the board was hopeful that a simultaneous release could be made of the awards in the two disputes so that neither group could claim favor with the workers in the area. The Northwest Council was angry at the delay and the insistence on getting an early release of the award in its case was part and parcel of the jurisdictional rivalry. The Howard award was released only a few days before the Jensen award and both provided for the same increase in wages, 7½ cents "across the board." The wage increase, in each instance, ,was based primarily on the increased demand for lumber and the consequent ability of the industry to pay. Also considered, although it was not deemed decisive in either arbitration, was the fact that workers were leaving the industry for jobs in shipbuilding and other war industries. In the I.W.A. case it was pointed out that it was hardly expedient to attempt to solve the recognizable manpower problem through wage policy alone.[1]

The NWLB unmistakably was trying to establish a stable condition in the lumber industry and it was hoped that the settlement in the two major cases would provide the basis for stabilization for the duration of the war. To some extent the hope was momentarily realized when other pending disputes were settled in accord with the two arbitration awards, but under the circumstances it was impossible to achieve lasting stability. Diversity of interests in the Douglas fir region between the Willamette Valley employers and those in the rest of the area, between the Douglas fir region and the western pine region, the immaturity of labor relations and the sparsity of unionization in some areas, to say nothing of the pervading inter-union conflict, all led to continued unbalance. Wage stabilization alone, of course, was not enough and even it was not actually achieved.

Although it was generally expected that wages had reached their upper limit, the wage question soon afterward was thrown open again because of the inter-union rivalry and the unsettling war conditions. As a matter of fact, the rivalry between the two union groups became more intense, but lest the inter-union struggle be overemphasized—it certainly was not the most decisive factor—it is necessary to point out that one of the greatest unstabilizing factors was the failure to establish a workable national manpower policy and, specifically, to solve the manpower problem on the West Coast and in the lumber industry. Likewise, the fact that a national wage policy and national wage stabilization had not then been achieved by the NWLB was of great significance in the situation. The growing acuteness of the manpower problem, discernible in the latter part of 1941, but which grew progressively worse thereafter, made the lumber industry labor problem one of the most critical in the nation by midsummer of 1942.

Because of the grave shortage of lumber and timber products and the menace of impending problems, Donald Nelson, head of the War Production Board, on June 18, formally asked the lumber operators to do everything within their power to maintain maximum production of lumber and timber products. Then, early in July, Nelson appointed F. H. Brundage of the United States Forest Service to serve as western log and lumber administrator, with the understanding that some sort of joint council would be established to consider and solve production problems. The NWLB, however, was to retain jurisdiction over all labor disputes. Representatives of the various groups were brought together in an Advisory Board. Unfortunately this gesture at solving the problems of lumber production was quite fruitless, and later the labor groups became antagonistic toward Brundage.[2]

The manpower problem grew more acute and production not only was not stepped up to full capacity but declined late in the summer. Lumber industry workers could get better-paying jobs in other industries near-by, and the tradition and fact of movement of individuals from job to job within the lumber industry—the knowledge that workers were not losing long-established rights by moving away from the lumber industry—continued to aggravate the situation. Besides, it is apparent that many lumber operators, for whatever reasons, were not co-operating. Perhaps they were caught in a hopeless spiral of uncertainty and should not be blamed. Although the most direct way of holding workers is to pay higher wages, a program of promiscuous wage increases was bad. Many employers refused to increase wages for the purpose of holding workers in the industry. At the same time, there were some lumber operators, thinking in terms of individual self-survival, who voluntarily increased wages and threw the whole competitive wage structure out of line; and were severely castigated by their fellow employers. Then there were those lumber operators, whether in resentment of government and union policy requiring pay at rate and one-half for overtime work, or for lack of equipment, or shortage of key workers, who actually would not work more than forty hours a week in spite of the acute shortage of many kinds of lumber and the pressing need of the government war program. Superficial inspection of the situation indicates that if employers everywhere had been willing to work a full forty-eight-hour week, even with their smaller crews, production could have been noticeably increased. But the complexity of the factors must be fully analyzed before a sound judgment is possible. And it should be kept in mind that logging camps had experienced the greatest drain of manpower. Loggers were "naturals" for many shipbuilding jobs. Without logs sawmills could not operate and many mills were short on logs—some having less than enough for two weeks, and facing uncertainty as to future supplies.

The decline in production was so alarming that several governmental agencies took action to increase output of lumber. Paul V. McNutt, chairman of the War Manpower Commission, on September 7, issued an order "freezing" lumber industry workers to their jobs. Shortly after, Donald Nelson, on September 12, issued an order requiring forty-eight-hour operations wherever possible. Even the Selective Service agencies were directed by Lewis B. Hershey, on October 15, to give the most serious consideration to deferment of men giving the full measure of their time and energy to the production and manufacture of essential lumber and timber products.[3]

While these orders were being considered, the NWLB, too, was contemplating special action with respect to the labor relations situation, which was deteriorating perceptibly. New cases were being certified to the board so fast that it was proving impossible to keep the different parts of the industry in line with each other. It was not feasible to settle cases on the basis of the previous industry settlements because fundamental conditions had changed. The board, however, had made one major contribution to broaden industry stabilization in its final action on the Willamette Valley dispute case which was sent to arbitration early in the summer. The arbitration award created quite a furor. It was poorly worded and the arbitrator was challenged by the union with respect to his authority for dealing with certain questions. The union carried its case back to the NWLB and, because of the confused statement of terms of the arbitration and the actual unstabilizing effect of the award, the board referred the case back to a panel headed by N. P. Feinsinger. The dispute was finally settled under a stipulation signed by both parties which, in effect, brought wages in the Willamette Valley in line with those in the fir region as a whole. Long before the Willamette Valley case was settled, the principals in the two previous major disputes carried new wage issues to the board and it was apparent that nothing was added to stabilization of wages through attempting to settle each case on its individual merits. Altogether, the board had seventeen lumber industry cases before it and, realizing that some uniformity in settlement was imperative, worked feverishly to develop a solution to the problem.

To Wayne Morse, outstanding public member on the NWLB, because of his experience with labor in the West—including the lumber industry—fell the task of formulating for the board the approach to the lumber industry labor problems. Most of the worry about the lumber industry situation during these trying times fell on him. The board actions were based primarily on his suggestions. At first it was decided to appoint a five-man panel, including one I.W.A.

and one Northwest Council representative and two employer representatives, and one public representative to hear all cases and to make simultaneous recommendations for the settlement of each. Although the members of such a panel were named, it was almost immediately dissolved in favor of a permanent West Coast Lumber Commission, which was established by directive order of the NWLB on September 17. The commission was composed of five members with the specific requirement that the men be not directly connected with the lumber industry. The NWLB was anxious to have an excellent commission and succeeded in securing the services of Ben H. Kizer, Spokane attorney, to take over the chairmanship. The two employer members of the commission were E. B. McNaughton, Portland banker, and Dean Ballard, of the Seattle Chamber of Commerce. The two labor members were James Landye, Portland attorney, and William Guerts, director of migratory labor camps of the Farm Security Administration in the Northwest.[4]

The commission was established out of a recognition of the critical importance of the lumber industry and the serious problem of labor scarcity and industrial unrest, and was specifically directed to settle the disputes then pending. It was given wide latitude and authority to determine its proper realm of jurisdiction over such labor disputes as might interrupt lumber production in the states of Washington, Oregon, California, Idaho, and Montana.

On October 14, the commission issued a statement of jurisdiction which was accepted by the NWLB, and then decided to hear the fir and pine cases separately. After almost a month of continuous hearings in the fir cases on the vigorously contested issue of wage increases, in which "every argument that ingenuity could have devised" was offered on each side and "every repetition that astute minds could make possible" had been indulged in, the commission made its first "industry-wide" decision on December 17, 1942. It recognized the grave exodus of workers from the industry and commented on the fact that so alarming had this exodus become that "for the first time in American history the war powers of the Chief Executive, delegated by him to the War Manpower Commission for that purpose, were used to 'freeze' the men to their jobs" in the industry. It was pointed out that implicit in the freeze was the need to compensate in part, at least, these workers for this unprecedented curtailment of their liberty, one resting unequally upon them, since it was fixed upon no other group of workers, except those in the nonferrous mining and smelting industry who were covered by the same WMC order. Likewise, the commission pointed to the action of Donald M. Nelson, director of the WPB in requiring the forty-eight-hour week and to the investigation by the Truman Committee of the U.S. Senate, which had become alarmed at the disparity between lumber production and the demand. Frankly predicating its decision on manpower considerations, the commission established a 90-cent minimum wage. This involved a 7½-cent increase, which was applied uniformly "across the board" to all other classifications. This minimum wage was designed to approach but not equal the basic minimum of 95 cents prevailing in the Northwest shipyards and to restore the historical differential in favor of lumber over smelter workers whose basic rate had recently been set at 88 cents by a decision of the NWLB.[5]

At the same time, the commission recognized that measures taken to bring lumber workers back into the industry would not prove sufficient to satisfy the war demand for forest products, and stated that other measures would have to be taken. It recognized its own limitations and urged that the NWLB and the WMC join in seeking to obtain, as they had done for nonferrous miners, the furloughing of loggers from the army.

The pine cases were more seriously contested, if possible, than the fir cases. Both union groups were insisting on the same base rate in pine as in fir, but a study by Dr. A. L. Morgan on the western pine lumber industry,[6] was given considerable weight by the majority of the commission. While the majority concluded that the same sort of adjustment as made in the fir cases should be ordered, it fell back on the Morgan report which recognized "eight fairly homogeneous districts" and set up a series of basic rates ranging from 80 cents to 87.5 cents. This position was based on the statement in the report "that districts of lowest wage scales are the districts of lowest price realization due largely to the greater percentage of the lower paid fir and larch, and that they are likewise the districts of narrowest profit margins." The commission further justified its position by reference to the NWLB statement that "wage differentials which are established and stabilized are normal to American industry and will not be disturbed by the Board."[7] Again the chronic problem of intra-industry competition had raised its head.

In a dissenting opinion the two labor members on the commission vigorously challenged the position of the majority, first, on procedural grounds and, second, on substantive factors. With respect to the former it was claimed that the majority decision was not based upon the evidence in the records established by the parties. This question is not of great importance, but the substantive factors throw into broad relief one of the most difficult of industry problems. For years wage competition has been a chronic problem in the industry and has been the cause of much hardship and uncertainty to operators and workers alike. Labor is interested in elimination of wage competition and the maintenance of standard conditions. Of course, differences in wages cannot be said to result in wage competition without regard to other competitive factors. Undue competition of any sort is disastrous for the industry and in normal times can be approached adequately only if there is a planned control of output and forest utilization. Under the impact of war and the demand for all the lumber that possibly could be produced, ability to pay, from the employers' standpoint, and protection of adequate working standards, from the labor standpoint, involve a neat problem in balancing. Whether the commission in the face of the war situation could approach the wage question in the pine cases with the intent to accomplish real wage equalization is open to conjecture. Whether it did or not, industry and wage stabilization must, by and large, wait for time of peace to be effectively considered, if at all.

The minority of the commission pointed out that the operators were not pleading inability to pay and claimed that the majority was in error in basing its conclusions upon the existence of "historical and traditional" wage differentials. It was pointed out that the differences in wages is to be explained only on the bases of the history of labor relations, because the pine region was the last stronghold of the 4L and later to be organized than the fir region. It was further pointed out that under the 4L, till 1925, the period for which there are records, wages were the same (this was true only of basic minimum),[8] that wages were the same in both regions under the NIRA code, that the differences are not traditional and emerged after 1935 because of the failure or difficulty in organizing in pine. Furthermore, it was contended that the action of the majority undid the stabilizing effect of the NWLB action in the Willamette Valley case.[9]

The NWLB upheld the majority of the commission when the unions appealed the cases, but Wayne Morse, standing steadfastly to principle, dissented vigorously on one point. He probably personally felt that wages should be standardized but he did not challenge the majority of the commission or the board on this point. He challenged the manner in which the rates were finally reached. He admitted that the majority and minority opinions were primarily differences in judgment and differences of opinion as to the weight that should be given to various items of evidence in the record, and that the two groups of commission members had reached an honest difference of opinion as to the interpretation and weight to be given the evidence. The record shows that the majority offered an additional 2½ cents per hour if the minority of the commission would join in a unanimous decision. Morse insisted that if the workers could have had an extra 2½ cents if the minority had gone along with the majority, "then those workers are entitled to the same 2.5 cents increase irrespective of whether or not the minority joined with the majority." [10]

The Lake States lumber industry, too, became highly unsettled during this period. It is true that the war gave a commercial lift to the sickly, marginal sector of the industry, and the hardwoods of Michigan and Wisconsin were of exceptional importance. Newly developed war industries in the area, however, almost immediately began to lure workers to them. Many employees of lumber companies went after higher wages. This seemed, to many, like an opportunity to escape from the shackles of submarginal living, which has been a characteristic of the cut-over area. [11] Many others had to remain and dissatisfaction increased everywhere.

The organized groups reacted in a natural manner and requested higher wages. On a smaller scale, we find a replica of the pattern of labor relations prevailing in the West. Only in Minnesota were employers organized for bargaining and, speaking relatively, labor relations have been markedly better there than in Michigan or Wisconsin, where employers not only resisted labor bitterly but refused to work with one another. The inter-union jurisdictional fight between the L.S.W.U. and the I.W.A. groups also colored the picture.

The Michigan and Wisconsin area, the center of hardwood production in the North, was the scene of greatest difficulty. The operators refused to grant wage increases and one by one disputes were certified to the NWLB until in February, 1943, there were thirty separate cases, twenty-six involving I.W.A. locals and 2,575 workers and four involving L.S.W.U. locals and 435 workers. Many issues other than wages were pressed in these cases, including demands for union security.

Indicative of the pervading unwholesomeness in the situation is the fact that each company was adamant in presenting its own case and each urged that decisions be made case by case rather than that there be one decision which would encompass all companies. On the other hand, the I.W.A. and the L.S.W.U. did not make joint demands or present a uniform stand. Rather, the I.W.A. stated its arguments and then, without making any attempt to create a link with what had preceded, the parties involved in the L.S.W.U. cases stated their position. The operators were firm in their contention that only if price relief were granted could any wage increase be met, and insisted that the solution to the production problem was not increased wages since the greatest part of the turnover could be accounted for by the draft and by migration to such centers as Detroit, where wages were higher than any wages that could conceivably be ordered for the lumber industry. They also contended that an increase in wages would decrease production, "since it will encourage an increase in drunkenness and hence an increase in absenteeism."

The panel decided that the wage structure was "obsolete" and that it was interfering with the prosecution of the war. While it did not recommend as much as the unions were demanding, substantial adjustments were proposed. The board accepted the findings of the panel and directed that the minimum hourly rate for logging operations be increased from 45 to 57½ cents and for sawmills from 50 to 62½ cents. The wage increases were substantially approved by Judge Vinson, director of Economic Stabilization, who had to consider them because of the price relief question.

On the question of union security it was clear to the panel that neither the companies nor the unions had fulfilled the responsibilities which go with satisfactory collective bargaining. Yet, despite the immaturity of approach on all sides, it was the panel's opinion that the interests of production would best be served by giving the union the stability and security necessary for it to function in a co-operative and productive manner. Consequently, it recommended continuance of the union shop agreements wherever they existed and maintenance of membership at the other plants.[12]

Unionization of lumber industry workers in the Southern Pine region was not stimulated under the impact of war as might have been expected by casual observers. Even though a tremendous industrialization took place in the South, much of it accompanied by unionization of workers, it altered labor relations in the southern pine industry but slightly. It cannot be said, however, that the war and industrialization did not affect lumber production. It increased the demand for lumber and stimulated output. In certain respects it helped the industry by making it commercially feasible to operate more continuously. It also had the effect of increasing the number of small portable mills that were operating. Whether the stimulus to increase production was wholly salutary can only be answered in light of circumstances and cannot be considered apart from the war effort. Certainly the industry's problems [13] were not made lighter and they will appear in their stark reality whenever demand for lumber falls off. The only compensation during the period of war is that the output of the industry is of critical importance to the military effort.

One noteworthy incident in the labor relations fields, although it was not a product of the war, was the wholesale engulfment of the organized lumber industry workers in Alabama by District 50 of the United Mine Workers of America. This fact was a development of the internal breach in the C.I.O. which occurred when John L. Lewis became embittered toward President Roosevelt and, losing his fight, withdrew from the C.I.O. taking his followers with him. This development is not significant of itself but is another evidence of the highly unstable condition of labor in the industry.

As stated before, labor organization was not increased to any marked extent. This is explicable in light of conditions which have been peculiar to the South.[14] Small groups of workers, scattered, lacking leadership—the fact that it was more profitable from the standpoint of labor organization to expend the limited services of organizers elsewhere—in an environment which has not been conducive to organization, has left the Southern Pine region practically free of unionism. No force is found to maintain minimum conditions except governmental legislation.

It was in the West that conditions continued to be most unstable. The settlement of the fir and pine cases hardly gave more than a temporary respite. Wages could not immediately be brought to the forefront although they continued to be a serious problem. The question of vacations was one of the chief issues confronting the industry. This issue is significant because, in the language of Wayne Morse, "there have been few cases coming before the War Labor Board in which the parties have been more guilty of dealing at arms length with each other and relying upon strained and technical interpretations than the instant one." He also pointed out that each side presented contentions and demands which seemed to be devised to take maximum advantage of each other. This reveals one of the basic weaknesses of the practice of collective bargaining in the industry.

The vacation issue harks back to the Jensen award, which provided a plan whereby vacations would be earned upon the basis of the number of hours worked.[15] As soon as the award was issued the parties met together and decided that they were in agreement as to the meaning and application of the clause and formally signified this understanding. The vacation period was to begin in May, 1943, but in February the I.W.A. carried questions of interpretation to the WCLC. The commission thereafter received briefs from the parties in order to clarify positions and later issued its interpretation in June. It held, contrary to the employers' contention, that an employee accrued a right to a vacation and that he need not be employed at the end of the vacation year or at the time allotted for him to take a vacation in order to be qualified for vacation pay, but to so qualify he must merely have worked the requisite number of hours.

The employers requested a rehearing. It was granted and was held on August 12, in Portland, and the commission immediately reaffirmed its interpretation. Thereupon the L.I.R.C. filed for the employers a petition for review of the commission's directive on the grounds that the order was contrary to board policy in that it set aside a valid contract and that the commission had exceeded its jurisdiction. The NWLB recognized the petition and decided that a division of the board should hold a hearing on the matter, and one was held in Portland on September 21. When the matter finally came back to the board it was considered at some length. Finally, after considering the voluminous records accumulated in the case, the language of the award and intent of the arbitrator, and the memorandum of agreement signed by the parties shortly after the arbitration award had originally been issued, the board decided that the commission had exceeded its authority. Acccordingly, the commission's directive was set aside and, in order to clarify the situation which the parties themselves had made complex, the board issued a directive in which it outlined the conditions under which vacations were to be considered earned and to be taken. It was pointed out that the arbitrator had apparently struck a compromise between the positions which the parties had held at the time of the arbitration hearing, taking the view that vacations are of value to both employer and employee: to the employer if continuity of employment results; and to the employee because he obtains a right to time off for which he is paid and thus can obtain needed relaxation free of anxieties which accompany idleness resulting from forced unemployment. The board then excoriated the parties, calling to their attention "the desirability, at least during these war times, of adopting less of a litigious attitude in their industrial relations and more of a manifestation of a willingness on both sides to lay all the facts on the table" to the end that they might through collective bargaining work out among themselves the problems which hinge on technical knowledge of industry operations;

saying also that it was unwise in principle and not in the interest of sound labor relations to get into the habit of substituting government boards or officials for the collective bargaining table.[16]

While the vacation issue was being hotly contested, the WCLC received a host of fir and pine cases, seventy-seven in all, which formed the so-called "second round" of wage demands in the northwestern lumber industry. The fir disputes were certified in May and the pine disputes in September. The wage demands were based almost purely and simply on manpower considerations. As a matter of fact, the previous increase ordered by the commission was predicated on manpower grounds. The Northwest Council asked for a basic minimum of $1.05 per hour, a bonus of $1.00 per day for all regular employees who remained on the payroll ninety days, and a guarantee of forty-eight hours of pay each week. The I.W.A. asked for a basic minimum of $1.025 per hour, a guaranteed weekly wage for the duration of the emergency equal to six and one-half days' pay, night-shift differentials of 10 and 15 cents for second and third shifts, and a number of other things.

The WCLC, on March 4, made its final decision on all issues except wages, and retained jurisdiction over it in order to give representatives of the War Production Board and the War Manpower Commission an opportunity to amplify certifications made by these agencies. The WCLC had concluded that a general wage increase could not be justified by the application of any of the normal principles of wage stabilization and that the record as it stood did not demonstrate that the cases were "rare and unusual" ones calling for special upward wage adjustments to meet "critical needs of war production." Hearings on the certifications of the WPB and the WMC were held in Portland, Oregon, on March 22 and 23. Two days before, however, the NWLB, sensing the importance of the wage issue in these cases, notified the commission that it was assuming jurisdiction "with respect to the wage issues raised as a result of the communications of the War Production Board and the War Manpower Commission." The WCLC, however, was to act as a fact-finding panel "to hear all parties and to report to the National War Labor Board without recommendations the facts involved." Later the commission, upon invitation, discussed the findings with the board. On May 17 the board issued a directive denying the increase, with labor dissenting. The unions petitioned for reconsideration, but so wrought up were the workers that many spontaneous walkouts occurred. Only with great difficulty could the International officers persuade the men to return to their jobs. So critical was the situation that the board seriously considered requesting the President to issue a directive taking over the lumber industry. The men, however, gradually returned to work, and within a few days the electrifying news of the invasion of the continent of Europe was received. This had the effect of sobering the workers and settling the situation, at least temporarily.

On June 12 the board conducted an all-day hearing at which it heard representatives of the parties. Thereafter it held an extended conference with representatives of the WPB, the WMC, and the War and Navy Departments at which it sought any new light they could throw on the issue. On June 16 the board affirmed its decision, with labor again dessenting.[17]

The WPB and the WMC made a strong presentation and their arguments failed on only one of the five points which the board set out for determining a "rare and unusual" case. The product was of critical importance to the war effort, there was a convincing demonstration of a serious manpower problem which could not be solved by nonwage measures, evidence was conclusive that the existing wage structure was inadequate to hold and attract the necessary supply of labor, and concerted effort had been made on the part of the various war agencies concerned to devise a program to remedy the production and manpower problems and which necessitated a wage adjustment as an indispensable part of the combined plan. Only on the fifth point, that there must be substantial evidence to demonstrate that a wage increase would accomplish the desired result and that the advantage of the wage increase would not be offset by undue disruption of the wage structure of the industry or region, did the case weaken. Even the WMC could not say with any assurance that the wage adjustments requested would solve the manpower problem. As a matter of fact, its representatives expressed considerable doubt about this. On the other hand, they were not particularly concerned about unstabilizing the local labor market. The fact that it was obvious that men would be drawn back from the shipyards, if they were to be obtained at all, did not perturb the WMC, because it was pointed out that it was relatively easy to recruit and train people for shipyard work, whereas only trained people could be sent to the woods and mills.

The board was obviously concerned more with its national wage stabilization program than with the impact that an increase of wages in the lumber industry might have on the local area. There is little doubt that it considered the national situation of greater importance than relief of the lumber industry manpower problem. The board had logical support for its denial of wage increases, but much of its argument appears based on technicalities. A considerable portion of the truth of the matter is found in a statement in the dissenting opinion written by the labor members of the board. They pointed out that early in its history the board had sufficient confidence in itself, and its power to hold the wage line, to direct an increase to nonferrous miners, based on manpower considerations; but that now it was afraid of the "serious repercussions on the national stabilization program" and that it refused to give an increase to this major war industry for fear it would have to grant wage increases all along the line. Obviously the board could not lose sight of the steel industry case, nor the attacks of organized labor then being directed at the wage stabilization program. On the other hand, the lumber industry workers were not trying to destroy the wage stabilization principles as then constituted, and whether the board was correct in its judgment only the future can tell.

The wartime labor disputes in the lumber industry, although to a certain extent colored by the dynamic changes which took place in the economy, reveal in bold outlines some of the most difficult of industry problems; problems which for many years have been chronic and at some times and in various places acute. Wage competition, although it was in the form of resistance to wage increases—at the risk of losing essential workers—rather than in the more common form of wage cutting, whether inspired by reference to interregional relationships or to interindustry considerations such as the ability to stand up in the market against substitutes, shows the basically unstable and insecure position of the industry. There naturally exists a fear that the cost structure of the industry will make it impossible to meet competition successfully in the postwar period. This, of course, is not a new problem, and is a consequence of lack of planning and organization within industry and on the part of the government.

The future welfare of the lumber industry is inextricably tied, of course, to that of the economy as a whole. It is essential that a reasonably high level of production and consumption be maintained in the postwar period. Without it conditions will be chaotic in lumber production, for lumbering is highly sensitive to changes in the economy. Lumber industry problems will require great effort and endless patience if they are to be solved, even in times of full employment. They will be impossible of satisfactory solution if the economy as a whole is not reasonably healthy.

Even if a high level of production and employment is maintained in the economy, the competition of plastics, metals, and other wood

substitutes undoubtedly will increase after the war to plague the industry. Of course, the higher the level of production the less decisive will
be this competition. In any event, it must be faced inasmuch as it is
part and parcel of an enterprise economy. At the same time, a well-
ordered industry that is not suffering the ravages of cutthroat competition, which fundamentally grows out of unplanned and uncontrolled use of forest resources, will be better able to face it.

To meet its opportunities and responsibilities successfully will require organization, planning, and co-operation such as the industry
has never known; such as it has never tolerated. The crying need of
the industry is effective organization with leaders of vision. Independent action will be as futile in the future as it has been fruitless
and disastrous in the past. Reckless and wasteful use of forest and
human resources has not paid dividends. The credits recorded in the
ledger are heavily offset by the debits, both private and social. To have
a profitable private and social investment in the lumber industry requires a planned use of the forest resource. To achieve this will require
governmental assistance, by means of modification of tax policy and a
program of forest acquisition and utilization. On its part, capital can
best serve its own welfare by organized application of enlightened
self-interest, which involves concerted action in planning the industry's
proper place in the economy and in applying the program worked
out. The welfare of the workers probably cannot be achieved or maintained unless they, too, have a part in planning the industry's future,
particularly with respect to the conditions under which labor services
may be used. Organized workers can effectively police the industry
and stop cutthroat competition at the wage level, which is so disastrous
to labor and industry alike. Cutthroat competition in the realm of
prices also must be eliminated. This undoubtedly will require industry
and government co-operation. Although economic obstacles to control
of production and prices always have been a greater deterrent than
legal restrictions, it may be that legal restraints should be modified.
Any production and price policy should be carefully worked out and
integrated with the over-all plan of industry organization. The struggle to achieve industry stabilization will have to be carried out simultaneously on several fronts.

Labor relations in the lumber industry will surely continue strained
so long as the war lasts, because it is practically impossible now to
solve the basic problems which are keeping them unsettled. No one
can predict possible occurrences while the economy is in a state of
wartime flux. Neither can it be predicted with any certainty just what
the postwar era will bring. The past decade has been one of turmoil

and strife. Much of the trouble dates back to the strike of 1935 and to the factors which made it a long and drawn-out test of strength. Anti-union attitudes and the unpreparedness of most employers to grant the right of labor to organize, although some were ready and willing to concede it, and the failure to prepare an employer collective bargaining agency at the time, resulted in confusion, prolonged the strike, and made for a nonuniform settlement of the dispute. The fact that the strike was prolonged gave rise to a schism within labor's ranks which then proved, and has since proved, costly to workers as well as to others directly and indirectly involved. It was unfortunate that the Carpenters were given jurisdiction over the Timber Workers because the superimposition of this leadership was widely resented. Knowing neither the mentality of the lumber industry workers nor their problems, this leadership only injected confusion into the situation.

The period since 1935 has been marked by intra- and inter-union strife, which has reacted against the prestige of the unions. It has made both public and employers wary of the ability of the unions to function in a responsible manner. At first, the struggle was against outside leaders, coupled with the dispute over conservative versus militant tactics. The latter aspect of the struggle would have settled itself through time. The question was present because it was a product of belligerent anti-unionism. Militant leaders were thrown to the front, but leaders are always sobered by responsibility. Questions of disciplined leadership and violent tactics, therefore, normally tend to be settled when unionism is given a chance to function. However, the dispute over the imposition of outside leadership upon the Timber Workers has been almost an outright loss to the cause of unionism. The struggle between A.F. of L. and C.I.O. unions has, to be sure, been a phase of a broader struggle which has gripped the whole country. But it is especially unfortunate that it became so intense in the Northwest, where the new unions were struggling to maintain respect and prove their worth.

Employers, who at first inwardly gloated over the struggle, have learned through sad experience that the disputants would not exterminate themselves and thereby eliminate a vigorous unionism from the industry. They have discovered, rather, that they have been caught in a cross fire of rival unionism and have borne the brunt of attacks designed to build the prestige of the contending groups. They have come to realize that a united unionism would be a good thing for the industry.

Complicating the whole picture was the rivalry within the I.W.A. and the controversy over communism, which at one time seemed to threaten the very existence of the I.W.A. itself. Finally, the left-wing leaders were shelved, and the I.W.A. emerged a strong fighting union with respected and trusted leaders; although late in 1944 there are signs which indicate that the old dispute might rise again. Without a doubt, however, the I.W.A. controls the majority of organized lumber industry workers.

The future of unionism is not entirely certain. It is to be hoped that the struggle between the C.I.O. and A.F. of L. groups can be worked out to the mutual satisfaction of both parties. The absence of unionism in broad areas of the industry is, of course, a dangerous weakness. Unionism's future in the Lake States seems somewhat more assured than in the South. Whether the southern workers can be effectively organized remains to be seen. In each region fundamental economic and social problems remain to be solved. The days of continuous migration must be made a thing of the past. Permanent and stable communities must replace the transitory, shifting communities where normal lives cannot be lived, and which have always been breeders of discontent.

NOTES TO CHAPTER

[1] Bureau of National Affairs, Inc., *War Labor Reports*, Vol. I, p. 151, *passim*, Vol. II, pp. 1-19, Washington, 1943; *Timberworker* and *Union Register*, all issues during period.

[2] *International Woodworker*, July 8, 1942.

[3] *International Woodworker*, September 16, 1942; *Union Register*, September 11, 1942.

[4] *International Woodworker*, August 26, September 16, 23, 1942; *Union Register*, September 18, 25, 1942; N.W.L.B., *News Release*, September 17, 1942.

[5] N.W.L.B. before the West Coast Lumber Commission, *Decision*, L-13, December 17, 1942 (mimeographed); N.W.L.B., "Report on Wage Stabilization Activities of the West Coast Lumber Commission," prepared by J. C. Hill and H. D. Bloch, March 28, 1944 (mimeographed); *International Woodworker*, December 23, 1944; *Union Register*, December 25, 1944.

[6] A. L. Morgan, "Report of the Western Pine Lumber Industry for the National War Labor Board." Portland, Ore., November, 1942 (mimeographed).

[7] N.W.L.B. before the West Coast Lumber Commission, *Decision*, L-37, March 15, 1943 (mimeographed).

[8] See above, p. 136.

[9] N.W.L.B. before the West Coast Lumber Commission, *Decision*, L-37, March 15, 1943 (mimeographed).

[10] N.W.L.B., *News Release* B-586, April 18, 1943.

[11] See above, p. 63.

[12] Bureau of National Affairs, Inc., *War Labor Reports*, Vol. IX, pp. 492-510. Washington, 1943.

[13] See above, pp. 71-72.

[14] See above, p. 85.

[15] Bureau of National Affairs, Inc., *War Labor Reports*, Vol. II, pp. 1-19.

[16] N.W.L.B., *News Release* B-1123, November 19, 1943.

[17] N.W.L.B., *News Release* B-1600, June 23, 1944.

BIBLIOGRAPHICAL NOTE

Relatively little has been written about labor relations in the lumber industry, and for large sectors of the industry only piecemeal information is available. Prior to this study, the only attempt to portray the history of labor in the lumber industry as a whole was made in Charlotte Todes, *Labor in Lumber* (New York: International Publishers, 1931). This is a partisan, left-wing, sketchy and unbalanced treatment. Although it cannot be called a history of labor in the lumber industry, the I.W.W. publication *The Lumber Industry and Its Workers,* I.W.W. Publishing Company (not dated, about 1920), is interesting and worth consulting. Certain phases of the industry for particular periods have been treated in studies of special merit and contain material on labor. These include: Richard G. Wood, *History of Lumbering in Maine, 1820-1861* (Orono, Maine: University of Maine Studies, 1935, XXXVII, No. 7); U.S. Department of Agriculture, Bureau of Forestry, *A History of the Lumber Industry in the State of New York,* by William F. Fox, Bulletin No. 34 (Washington: Government Printing Office,* 1902); and Robert F. Fries, "A History of the Lumber Industry in Wisconsin" (Unpublished Ph.D. Thesis, University of Wisconsin, 1939). Two studies which cover employer and labor relations in the western lumber industry, one up to and the other through World War I period, must be noted: John H. Cox, "Organizations of the Lumber Industry in the Pacific Northwest, 1889-1914" (Unpublished Ph.D. Thesis, University of California, 1937); and U.S. Department of Labor, Bureau of Labor Statistics, *Industrial Relations in the West Coast Lumber Industry,* by Cloice R. Howd, Bulletin No. 349, 1924. The author's recent study of labor relations in the western industry offers a full account and fresh interpretation of the functions of the Loyal Legion of Loggers and Lumbermen: "Labor Relations in the Douglas Fir Lumber Industry," by Vernon H. Jensen (Unpublished Ph.D. Thesis, University of Cali-

---

* All federal government publications, unless otherwise noted, are published so: Washington: Government Printing Office. Only the date will be shown hereafter.

fornia, 1939). A popular history of some aspects of labor in the lumber industry, running to the romantic and overplaying the sensational, is found in Stewart Holbrook's, *Holy Old Mackinaw—A Natural History of the American Lumberjack* (New York: The Macmillan Company, 1939).

For a good description of the forest regions of the United States there is the publication of the U.S. Department of Agriculture, *Forest Trees and Forest Regions of the United States,* Miscellaneous Publication No. 217, 1936. The most comprehensive early treatise on the lumber industry, but which makes only slight reference to labor, is the two-volume work by James E. Defebaugh, *History of the Lumber Industry in America* (Chicago: American Lumberman, 1907). A later book-length work on the lumber industry with an historical perspective is Wilson Compton's, *The Organization of the Lumber Industry* (Chicago: American Lumberman, 1916). A significant early study of the economic problems of the lumber industry is the U.S. Department of Agriculture publication, *Some Problems and Economic Aspects of the Lumber Industry,* by William B. Greeley, 1917. The Copeland Report, in two volumes, U.S. Department of Agriculture, *A National Plan for American Forestry,* 73rd Congress, 1st Session, Senate Document No. 12, 1933, gives a comprehensive survey of the characteristics and recent problems of the lumber industry regionally and as a whole. A publication of the National Recovery Administration, Division of Review, *Economic Problems of the Lumber and Timber Products Industry,* Work Materials No. 79, Industries Studies Section, March 1936 (mimeographed), contains a general picture of the industry and its problems. A more recent and more objective investigation of the industry's raw material problems is found in the National Resources Board, *Forest Land Resources, Requirements, Problems and Policy,* 1935. Wilson Compton deals succinctly with the industry's depression problems in "Recent Developments in the Lumber Industry," *Journal of Forestry,* XXX, No. 4 (April, 1932). One of the most difficult economic problems in the industry is well surveyed by C. H. Cheney, *New Competition in the Lumber Industry,* Report before the Annual Convention of the National Association of Manufacturers, Chicago, Ill., April 28, 1927 (circular); and by Wilson Compton, "Lumber: An Old Industry and the New Competition," *Harvard Business Review,* X, No. 26 (January, 1932). An earlier examination of the economic problems of the industry, which shows that many of them are of old standing, is found in a publication of the National Lumber Manufacturers Association, *Before the Federal Trade Commission,*

Brief on Behalf of the National Lumber Manufacturers Association,
Vol. I, "Problems of the Industry" (Washington: National Lumber
Manufacturers Association, 1916). Other publications of the same
organization, such as *Lumber Industry Facts* (Washington: National
Lumber Manufacturers Association, 1939), throw light on the indus-
try's problems.

Regional lumber trade association statements which deserve attention include L. C. Boyle, *Argument Before the Federal Trade Com-
mission* (New Orleans: Southern Pine Association, 1916); Charles S.
Kieth, *Conditions in the Lumber Industry,* address before a special
meeting of the Southern Pine Association, December 15, 1921 (New
Orleans: Southern Pine Association, 1921); Southern Pine Association,
Economic Conditions in the Southern Pine Industry, statement and
brief in behalf of the Southern Pine Association before the National
Recovery Administration, February 2, 1935 (New Orleans: Southern
Pine Association, 1935); West Coast Lumbermen's Association, *West
Coast Lumber Facts* (Seattle, Wash.: West Coast Lumbermen's Asso-
ciation, 1937); David T. Mason, *Timber Ownership and Lumber
Production in the Inland Empire* (Portland, Ore.: The Western Pine
Association, 1920).

A useful recent study of the Douglas fir lumber industry has been
made under the direction of Dexter M. Keezer, *The Douglas Fir
Lumber Industry* (Washington: Advisory Commission to the Council
of National Defense, March, 1941). A companion study covering
western pine under the direction of A. L. Morgan has been made:
"Report of the Western Pine Lumber Industry for the National War
Labor Board" (Portland, Ore., November, 1942 [mimeographed]).

Current lumber industry trade journals which contain helpful
information about the industry, and occasionally about labor problems, are the *American Lumberman,* published in Chicago; the *Southern Lumber Journal,* published in Jacksonville, Fla.; the *Southern
Lumberman,* published in Nashville, Tenn.; the *Mississippi Valley
Lumberman,* published in Minneapolis, Minn.; the *West Coast Lumberman,* published in Seattle, Wash.; and the *Timberman,* published
in Portland, Ore. Two other trade journals, which are no longer
published, should be consulted for the early part of the century:
the *Lumber Trade Journal,* published in New York; and the *Pacific
Lumber Trade Journal,* published in Seattle, and in 1913 merged with
the *West Coast Lumberman.*

A useful account of processes in lumbering of forty years ago is
found in the Twelfth Census of the United States, 1900, Vol. IX,

Manufactures, Part 3. Quite recently industrial processes and a comparison of practices in the West and in the South have been covered in Work Projects Administration, *Mechanization in the Lumber Industry,* by Alfred J. Van Tassell and David W. Bluestone, National Research Project Report No. M-5 (Philadelphia: Work Projects Administration, 1940). An excellent analysis of logging practices in the Douglas fir region, showing how highly mechanized logging can be, is Axel J. F. Brandstrom, *Analysis of Logging Costs and Operating Methods in the Douglas Fir Region* (Seattle, Wash.: Charles Lathrop Pack Forestry Foundation, 1933).

Full descriptions of the jobs in the industry have been undertaken in two government studies: Federal Board for Vocational Education, in co-operation with others, *The Lumber Industry—Logging, Sawmilling,* Opportunity Monograph, Vocational Rehabilitation Series No. 19, 1919; and U.S. Department of Labor, Bureau of Labor Statistics, *Job Descriptions for the Lumber and Timber Products Industries,* Job Analysis and Information Service, Division of Standards and Research, 1939. These are complete in scope but suffer from some inaccuracies. Recent studies of job classifications and relative wage rates were prepared for the West Coast Lumber Commission by the Pacific Northwest Forest and Range Experiment Station: *Job Classification Study of the Sawmill Industry—Douglas Fir Region* (Portland, Ore., 1943), and *Job Classification Study of the Logging Industry—Douglas Fir Region* (Portland, Ore., 1943).

The growth, changes, and composition of the labor force are best measured in the U.S. Census reports. In addition, the Census reports reveal the number of establishments, the size of establishments, and, since 1919, the degree of concentration of production within particular sized units. The Immigration Commission also has provided information about the composition of the working force: Reports of Immigration Commission, *Immigrants in Industry,* 61st Congress, 2nd Session, Senate Document No. 633, 1911.

Only scattered and piecemeal information exists on wages in the lumber industry. The U.S. Department of Labor, Bureau of Labor Statistics, supplies the most trustworthy data in a series of bulletins: *Wages and Hours of Labor in the Lumber Millwork, and Furniture Industries, 1890 to 1912,* Bulletin No. 129, 1913; *Wages and Hours of Labor in the Lumber, Millwork, and Furniture Industries, 1915,* Bulletin No. 225, 1916; *Wages and Hours of Labor in Lumber Manufacturing, 1921,* Bulletin No. 317, 1923; *Wages and Hours of Labor in the Lumber Industry in the United States, 1928,* Bulletin No. 497,

1929; *Wages and Hours of Labor in the Lumber Industry in the United States, 1930,* Bulletin No. 560, 1932; *Wages and Hours of Labor in the Lumber Industry of the United States, 1932,* Bulletin No. 586, 1933.

Although accidents in the lumber industry are so great in number and frenquency that the industry must be classified as one of the most hazardous, information about the frequency and severity of accidents is fragmentary. However, two good studies by Max D. Kossoris and Swen Kjaer demonstrate the hazardous nature of the industry: "Industrial Injuries in the United States During 1939," *Monthly Labor Review,* LI, No. 1 (July, 1940) and "Causes and Prevention of Accidents in Lumber Manufacturing, 1939," *Monthly Labor Review,* LI, No. 3 (September, 1940).

The manner of acquisition of timber lands has had a profound influence upon the development and problems of the lumber industry which bear upon the history of the working force in it. The *Annual Report(s) of the Commissioner of the General Land Office,* over the period of years when timber lands were being disposed of by the government, must be consulted. *The Public Domain,* 47th Congress, 2nd Session, House of Representatives, Miscellaneous Document 45, Part 4, by Thomas Donaldson, 1884, also provides an insight into some of the ways in which forest lands were acquired. The most significant government study covering the lumber industry was made by the U.S. Department of Commerce and Labor, Bureau of Corporations, *The Lumber Industry,* 1913. This study threw light on the methods of timber acquisition, and for the first time revealed the exact extent of concentration of timber ownership as well as other problems incident to management of forest lands. Another solid treatment of the subject of timber acquisition and forest ownership problems is John Ise, *The United States Forest Policy* (New Haven: Yale University Press, 1920). Of special significance in showing the pattern of land acquisition in the Lake States is the study of Matthias N. Orfield, *Federal Land Grants to the States With Specific Reference to Minnesota* (Minneapolis, Minn.: University of Minnesota Press, 1915). A more popular but fairly accurate account of timber acquisition is found in the article by Charles E. Russell, "The Mysterious Octopus," *World Today,* XXI, Nos. 8, 9, 10 (February, March, April, 1912). For a picture of forest land acquisition in the South, there is an excellent work in Paul W. Gates, "Federal Land Policy in the South, 1866-1888," *Journal of Southern History,* VI, No. 3 (August, 1940). For the West, besides the Bureau of Corporation's report cited above, a helpful account of land acquisition is Stephen A. D. Puter, *Looters of the Public Domain* (Portland, Ore.: Portland Printing House, 1908).

A close relationship exists between forestry practice and living conditions in the lumber industry. These aspects are well-considered in a number of studies. U.S. Department of Agriculture, *Forestry and Community Development*, Bulletin No. 638, 1918, presents the general problems of forest destruction and the impact on community organization. Carter L. Goodrich and Others, *Migration and Economic Opportunity* (Philadelphia: University of Pennsylvania Press, 1936), shows some of the consequences of cutting out the forests. Most revealing of all, however, is the U.S. Department of Agriculture publication, *The Economic Aspects of Forest Destruction in Northern Michigan,* by William N. Sparhawk and Warren D. Brush, Technical Bulletin No. 92, 1929. What has occurred in the South is presented in T. Lynn Smith and Martha R. Fry, *The Population of a Selected "Cut-Over" Area in Louisiana,* (Louisiana State University and Agricultural and Mechanical College Bulletin No. 268, January, 1936). What happens when the timber has been unwisely cut is traced in a collection of typewritten reports, U.S. Department of Agriculture, Forest Service, Southern Forest Experiment Station, "Reports on Abandoned Sawmill Towns and Sustained Yield Forest Communities in the South." The effects of unwise forest devastation in the West is covered in a report of the U.S. Department of Agriculture, Forest Service, North Pacific Region, *Industrial Development of Olympic Peninsula Counties* (Portland, Ore., 1937).

Of similar import, but pointed more directly to conditions in the West where migratory laborers have been common in the past, are the following interesting publications: Ferdinand A. Silcox, "Forestry and Labor," *Journal of Forestry,* XVIII, No. 4 (April, 1920); Burt P. Kirkland, "Effects of Destructive Lumbering on Labor," *Journal of Forestry,* XVIII, No. 4 (April, 1920). Also of value on these and related problems are the report of the U.S. Commission on Industrial Relations, *Final Report and Testimony on Industrial Relations,* Vol. V, 1916; the well-known work of Carlton Parker, *The Casual Laborer and Other Essays* (New York: Harcourt, Brace and Howe, 1920); and the unpublished Master's Thesis of the Reverend J. Herbert Geohegen, "Exploitation of the Migratory Worker" (University of Washington, Seattle, Wash., 1923).

The nature and problems of the early lumber industry in the Northeast are treated in a number of specialized works. Early lumbering in Maine is succinctly portrayed in Richard G. Wood, *History of Lumbering in Maine, 1820-1861,* previously cited. Three more specialized studies carry the story closer to the present: Alfred G. Hempstead, *The Penobscot Boom* (Orono, Maine: University of Maine Studies, 1931, XXXIII, No. 11); *Thirteenth Annual Report of the Bureau of Industrial and Labor Statistics for the State of Maine, 1899,* "The Lumber Industry" (Waterville, Maine, 1900); *First Biennial Report of the Department of Labor and Industry of the State of Maine, 1911-1912,* "Industrial Conditions in the Maine Woods," by James P. Flanagan (Waterville, Maine, 1913). For a vivid description of early logging camps and conditions, Henry D. Thoreau, *The Maine Woods* (New York: Thomas Y. Crowell and Company, 1906) is indispensable. For New York a useful early study is William F. Fox, *A History of the Lumber Industry in the State of New York,* cited above. An article, "The Spectator in an Adirondack Lumber Camp," *Outlook,* LXX, No. 1 (January 4, 1902), also gives a vivid account of conditions in early logging camps. A complete history of lumbering in Pennsylvania for any period has never been published but the following are of considerable value and interest: D. F. Magee, "Rafting on the Susquehanna," *Papers Read Before the Lancaster County Historical Society,* XXIV, No. 9 (1920); George W. Huntley, Jr., *A Story of the Sinnamahone* (Williamsport, Pa.: Williamsport Printing and Binding Company, 1936); J. Herbert Walker (ed.), *Rafting Days in Pennsylvania* (Altoona, Pa.: Times-Tribune Company, 1922).

No general history of lumbering for the Lake States exists, and much of the published material overemphasizes the romantic aspects of the industry. The best and most comprehensive treatment for a particular state is Richard F. Fries, "A History of the Lumber Industry of Wisconsin" (Unpublished Ph.D. Thesis, University of Wisconsin, 1939). The most objective treatment of labor conditions within the area is found in a study conducted by William M. Leiserson and published under the auspices of the Industrial Commission of Wisconsin, *Labor Camps in Wisconsin* (Madison, Wis., 1913). A revealing biography, although it places too great emphasis on the glamorous side, is Isaac Stephenson, *Recollections of a Long Life 1827-1915* (Chicago: Privately Printed, 1915). Specialized, realistic accounts which deserve notice include A. S. Draper, "Reminiscences of the Lumber Camp," *Michigan Historical Review,* XIV, No. 2 (July, 1930), one of the best; La Crosse County Historical Society, *La Crosse County Historical Sketches,* Series 3, "The Lumber Industry" (La Crosse, Wis., 1937), which contains a number of articles of particular significance; Wright

T. Orcutt, "Minnesota Lumberjacks," *Minnesota History*, VI, No. 1 (March, 1925), is particularly good; Frank D. Bohn, "This Was The Forest Primeval," *Michigan History Magazine*, XX (Spring, 1937); Louise Davenport, "Logging Camps in the Northern Woods," *World Today*, IX, No. 5 (November, 1905); Agnes M. Larson, "On the Trail of the Woodman in Minnesota," *Minnesota History*, XIII, No. 4 (December, 1932); A. W. Miles, "End of the Drive," *Michigan History Magazine*, XX (Spring and Summer, 1936); and William F. Raney, "Pine Lumbering in Wisconsin," *Wisconsin Magazine of History*, XIX, No. 1 (September, 1935).

Ballads revealing important aspects of lumberjack life are found in a number of collections: Roland P. Gray (ed.), *Songs and Ballads of the Maine Lumberjacks* (Cambridge, Mass.: Harvard University Press, 1924); Franz L. Rickaby, *Ballads and Songs of the Shanty-boy* (Cambridge, Mass.: Harvard University Press, 1926); J. C. Bowman, "Lumberjack Ballads," *Michigan History Magazine*, XX (April, 1936); and John A. Lomax, *Our Singing Country* (New York: The Macmillan Company, 1941).

For information about early strikes in the Lake States and on hours, wages, and other conditions of work, the *Second (Third, Fifth, and Tenth) Annual Report of the Bureau of Labor and Industrial Statistics, Michigan, 1885 (1886, 1888, and 1893)*, and the *First (Second and Third) Biennial Report of the Bureau of Labor and Industrial Statistics, Wisconsin, 1883-84 (1885-86 and 1887-88)* are essential.

The migratory aspects of the lumber industry are studied in the U.S. Department of Agriculture, *The Economic Aspects of Forest Destruction in Northern Michigan*, previously cited; and R. W. Watson, "Forest Devastation in Michigan," *Journal of Forestry*, XXI, No. 5 (May, 1923). Relief problems in the cut-over region of the Lake States were significant and extensively studied. Particularly valuable are Federal Emergency Relief Administration, *Six Rural Problem Areas*, by P. G. Beck and M. C. Forester, Research Monograph No. 1, 1935; Works Progress Administration, Division of Social Research, *Rural Families on Relief*, by Carle C. Zimmerman and Nathan L. Whetten, Research Monograph XVII, 1935. An objective statement of the whole problem is found in an article by G. S. Wehrwein, "A Social and Economic Program for the Submarginal Areas of the Lake States," *Journal of Forestry*, XXIX, No. 10 (October, 1931). The first-rate statements of the impact of conditions on labor are: Elmer A. Benson, "Conservation and the Lumberjack," *American Forests* (August, 1937); H. Gilbert White, "Forest Conservation and the Working Man," unpublished manuscript, Lake States Forest Experiment Station, St. Paul, Minn., dated October, 1939; and Gordon B. Fox, "Some Economic, Social, and Administrative Aspects of Small Timber Sales of Public Forests in the Lake States," unpublished manuscript in the files of the Lake States Forest Experiment Station, St. Paul, Minn.

Of all industries in the South, lumbering has been the most shamefully neglected by economic historians. One of the most substantial, yet admittedly incomplete, studies is found in the two chapters on lumbering in *Labor In the Industrial South*, the Institute for Research in the Social Sciences, University of Virginia, 1930, by Abraham Berglund, George T. Starnes, and Frank T. DeVyver. A general and inadequate account of the development of lumbering is found in the *Southern Lumberman*, CXLIV (December 15, 1931) and CXLV (January 1, 1932), "Fifty Years in the Southern Pine Industry," by James Boyd. A field survey of the National Research Planning Board, the report of which was obtained from the files of the Atlanta, Ga., office, contains information on some phases of recent labor conditions in a restricted area of the southern lumber industry. Chapter IV, "The Lumber Sub-region of Alabama, Georgia, and South Carolina," of the Works Progress Administration publication *Part-Time Farming in the Southeast*, Research Monograph IX, 1937, reveals many of the conditions of labor peculiar to a broad section of the southern lumber industry. Another useful statement concerning a part of the southern lumber industry is found in U.S. Department of Agriculture, Southern Forest Experiment Station, *Primary Wood-Products Industries in the Lower South*, by H. F. Smith, Forest Survey Release No. 51 (New Orleans: Southern Forest Experiment Station, 1940).

Objective but incomplete information on early living and working conditions in the southern lumber industry, including information on hours, wages, and labor practices, is found in the *First Annual (Second, Third, and Ninth Biennial) Report of the Bureau of Statistics of Labor of the State of Louisiana, 1901 (1902-03, 1904-05, and 1916-17)*; in the *Second Biennial Report of the Bureau of Labor Statistics of the State of Texas, 1911-12*; in George Creel, "Feudal Towns of Texas," *Harpers Weekly*, LX, No. 3031 (January 23, 1915); and in the *Eighth Biennial Report of the Bureau of Labor Statistics of the State of Texas, 1923-24*.

The conditions and problems of Negro workers in the lumber industry are nowhere adequately treated, although the industry provides more employment for Negroes than any other industry in the

South except agriculture. The following studies of Negro labor are of some help: Lorenzo J. Greene and Carter G. Woodson, *The Negro Wage Earner* (Washington: Associated Publishers, Inc., 1930); Carter G. Woodson, *The Rural Negro* (Washington: Associated Publishers, Inc., 1930); Sterling D. Spero and Abram L. Harris, *The Black Worker—The Negro and the Labor Movement* (New York: Columbia University Press, 1931); and Charles S. Johnson, *The Negro in American Civilization* (New York: Henry Holt and Company, 1930).

The conditions of Negro labor are treated in some reports of peonage, such as U.S. Department of Justice, *Annual Report of the Attorney General, 1907;* Mary C. Terrell, "Peonage in the United States," *Nineteenth Century and After,* LXII, 1907; the New York *World,* November 24, 1929; and Monroe N. Work, *Negro Yearbook, 1931-32* (Tuskegee, Ala.: Negro Yearbook Publishing Company, 1933).

A number of publications in recent years by the Southern Pine Association are helpful in understanding the economic characteristics of the industry and the conditions of labor in the South, even though the association was pleading a special case. Southern Pine Association, *Economic Conditions in the Southern Pine Industry,* presented to the U.S. Timber Conservation Board, July 1, 1931 (New Orleans: Southern Pine Association, 1931); C. C. Sheppard, *Wages and Hours of Labor in the South,* statement in behalf of the southern lumber industry before the National Industrial Recovery Administration, July 20, 1933 (New Orleans: Southern Pine Association, 1933); Southern Pine Association, "Labor Conditions in Southern Pine Industry," compiled by Southern Pine Association, March 3, 1934 (mimeographed); P. A. Bloomer, *Economic Conditions in Southern Pine Industry,* statement and brief in behalf of the southern pine industry before the National Industrial Recovery Board (New Orleans: Southern Pine Association, 1935); Southern Pine Association, *Employment Conditions and Living Costs and Conditions in Southern Lumber* (New Orleans: Southern Pine Association, 1937); Southern Pine Association, "Costs, Employment, Wage and Other Operating Data for 50 Southern Pine Manufacturers," compiled by Southern Pine Association, October 20, 1939 (mimeographed). Information on company stores is found in "Company Stores and the Scrip System," in the *Monthly Labor Review,* XLI, No. 1 (July, 1935).

The difficulties faced by labor organizations in the South may be sketched in U.S. Commission on Industrial Relations, *Final Report and Testimony on Industrial Relations,* 1916, V: 4394, 4412); Frederic Myers, "The Knights of Labor in the South," *Southern Economic*

Journal, VI, No. 4 (April, 1940); Industrial Workers of the World, *The Lumber Industry and Its Workers* (Chicago: I.W.W. Publishing Company [third edition, not dated]); Charlotte Todes, *Labor and Lumber,* cited above; William D. Haywood, *Bill Haywood's Book* (New York: International Publishers, 1929); the *Voice of the People,* an I.W.W. weekly issued in New Orleans, La., from October, 1913, to July, 1914, and in Portland, Ore., from July, 1914, to December, 1914; the New Orleans *Times-Democrat,* May, 1911, to November, 1912, various issues; the *Lumber Trade Journal,* various issues in May and June, 1912; the New Orleans *Times-Picayune,* various issues in November, 1919. For the attitude of a leading lumber producer who was bitterly opposed to unionism, John H. Kirby, *The Perils of Democracy* (New Orleans: Southern Pine Association, 1918), should be consulted.

Material on the western lumber industry is far richer than that available for other regions. The *Biennial Reports of the Bureau of Labor, Statistics, and Factory Inspection for the State of Washington,* particularly up to World War I period, gave periodic reports on strikes and labor practices in the lumber industry. A study conducted by the U.S. Department of Agriculture, *Logging in the Douglas Fir Region,* Bulletin No. 711, 1918, has a good account of the nature of the work in the lumber industry of western Washington and Oregon and reveals the circumstances under which workers lived and labored. Of equal importance with respect to the California area are *Sixteenth Biennial Report of the Bureau of Labor of the State of California, 1913-14* (Sacramento: California State Printing Office, 1914); and U.S. Department of Agriculture, *Lumbering in the Sugar and Yellow Pine Region of California,* Bulletin No. 440, 1917. A worth-while discussion of the administration of labor legislation in the three main lumber-producing states of the West, is U.S. Department of Labor, Bureau of Labor Statistics, *Labor Laws and Their Administration in the Pacific States,* Bulletin No. 211, 1917. For conditions in the interior pine region, there are two useful reports: *Eighth Report of the Bureau of Agriculture, Labor and Industry of the State of Montana, 1902,* and *Third Biennial Report of the Department of Labor and Industry of the State of Montana, 1916-18.* A scholarly treatment of both labor and employer organizations down to 1914 is found in John H. Cox, "Organizations of the Lumber Industry in the Pacific Northwest, 1889-1914," cited above. Also useful, although its evaluation of the Loyal Legion of Loggers and Lumbermen is uncritical, is a study published under the auspices of the U.S. Department of Labor, Bureau of Labor

Statistics, *Industrial Relations in the West Coast Lumber Industry,* by Cloice R. Howd, cited above. This covers the period through World War I and deals accurately with the early labor disputes.

Labor disputes in the western lumber industry achieved a peculiar notoriety because of the type of labor and the strength of the I.W.W. Carlton Parker deals with insight with the circumstances which gave rise to the I.W.W. in the western lumber industry in *The Casual Laborer and Other Essays,* cited above, and in his article, "The I.W.W.," in the *Atlantic Monthly,* CXX, No. 5 (November, 1917). The standard treatments of the I.W.W. cover much more than the lumber industry, and are: Paul F. Brissenden's *The I.W.W.,* Columbia University Studies in History, Economics, and Public Law, No. 83, 1919, and John S. Gambs's *The Decline of the I.W.W.,* Columbia University Studies in History, Economics, and Public Law, No. 361, 1932. The convention proceedings of the I.W.W. and pamphlet literature already listed contain some useful information. More important are two weekly newspapers, the *Industrial Worker,* published at Spokane, Washington, from 1909 to 1914, and in Seattle, Washington, from 1916 to 1918 and from 1919 to 1923, and *Solidarity,* published at Chicago from 1909 to 1917, and from 1918 to 1923 under slightly modified names.

A number of sources are worth consulting on the conditions of the early western lumber industry. Rex G. Tugwell, "The Casual of the Woods," *Survey,* XLIV, No. 14 (July 3, 1920); and E. Bigelow Thompson, "The Case of the Lumberjack," *World Outlook* (June, 1920). The *Report of the President's Mediation Commission to the President of the United States—Unrest in the Lumber Industry* (Washington: Government Printing Office, 1918) contains a mine of information and several sections of *History of the Spruce Production Division,* prepared by the U.S. Spruce Production Corporation (Washington: U.S. Army, 1920 [?]) are very useful. Events leading up to the great strike of 1917 are related by Cloice R. Howd, cited above, and in Walker C. Smith, *The Everett Massacre—A History of the Class Struggle in the Lumber Industry* (Chicago: I.W.W. Publishing Company, 1917). A short account by the latter author is "The Voyage of the Verona," *International Socialist Review,* XVII, No. 6 (December, 1916). Also interesting is B. S. Coleman, "The I.W.W. and the Law —The Result of Everett's Bloody Sunday," *Sunset Magazine,* XXXIX, No. 1 (July, 1917). The beginning of the strike of 1917 is covered by C. R. Griffin, "The Short Log Country," *International Socialist Review,* XVII, No. 7 (January, 1917). An interesting series of articles on the role of the I.W.W. in the strike of 1917 was written by Robert Bruere, "Following the Trail of the I.W.W.," New York *Evening Post,* beginning February 16, 1918. Charles Merz's "Tying Up Western Lumber," *New Republic,* XII, No. 152 (September 29, 1917), shows how extensive the strike really was. Out of the strike emerged the Loyal Legion of Loggers and Lumbermen—the 4L, and an objective treatment of its function is Edward B. Mittleman, "Loyal Legion of Loggers and Lumbermen—An Experiment in Industrial Relations," *Journal of Political Economy,* XXXI (June, 1923). The most complete study of the structure and functions of the 4L is found in the author's doctoral dissertation, cited above. The role of the War Department in establishing and directing the 4L can be followed in U.S. Department of War, *A Report of the Activities of the War Department in the Field of Industrial Relations During the War,* 1919. Also essential for a study of the 4L is its Constitution and By-Laws, as amended in 1921 and 1936, and *Semi-Annual Reports for the 4L Board of Directors* and convention reports. The *Monthly Bulletin·* was published by the 4L from March, 1918, to February, 1919. It was succeeded by the *Four L Bulletin,* which was published monthly from March, 1919, to February, 1926. Thereafter, until the 4L was disbanded in favor of the Industrial Employees Union at the time the National Labor Relations Act was declared constitutional, the 4L published *Four L Lumber News* twice monthly.

The "Centralia Massacre" has been extensively written about. The I.W.W. version is by Ralph Chaplin, *The Centralia Conspiracy* (Chicago: I.W.W. Publishing Company, 1920). The American Legion version of the tragedy was written by Ben H. Lampman, *The Centralia Tragedy and Trial* (published by the American Legion, 1920). The most objective and unbiased account of the events is found in the report of the investigation made by the Federal Council of Churches of Christ in America, and Others, *The Centralia Case—A Joint Report on the Armistice Day Tragedy at Centralia, Washington, November 11, 1919* (New York: Department of Research and Education, Federal Council of Churches of Christ in America, 1930). Useful articles dealing with the tragedy are: Theresa S. McMahon, "Centralia and the I.W.W.," *Survey,* XLIII, No. 6 (November 29, 1919); Anna L. Strong, "Centralia, An Unfinished Story," *Nation,* CX, No. 2859 (April 17, 1920); *Nation,* CX, No. 2859 (April 17, 1920); *Survey,* XLIII, No. 20 (March 13, 1920), and XLIV, No. 3 (April 17, 1920); J. W. Lockhart, "The I.W.W. Raid at Centralia," *Current History,* XVII, No. 1 (October, 1922); C. E. Payne, "Captain Coll—Legionnaire," *Nation,*

CXXIX, No. 3340 (July 10, 1929); E. Barnett, "From A Centralia Prisoner," *Christian Century,* XLVI, No. 18 (May 8, 1928).

The strike at Klamath Falls, Oregon, in 1922, which marked the end of the International Brotherhood of Sawmill and Timber Workers, is well-reported by the Oregon State Board of Conciliation, "Findings of the State Board of Conciliation—In the Matter of a Controversy Between Big Lakes Box Company, et al. . . . and Their Employees," dated April 26, 1922 (typewritten).

An interesting study which bears on the history of labor in the lumber industry during and following World War I is Eldridge F. Dowell, *A History of Criminal Syndicalism Legislation in the United States,* The Johns Hopkins University Studies in Historical and Political Science, Series LVII, No. 1 (Baltimore: The Johns Hopkins Press, 1939).

The National Industrial Recovery Act had a decisive effect upon the lumber industry. The NRA lumber industry code of fair competition was just what many operators had prayed for years to obtain. For their attitude consult Wilson Compton in *The Lumber Industry and the Anti-Trust Laws,* a speech before the National Conference on the Relations of Law and Business at New York University, October 26, 1931 (leaflet). The most complete statement of the experience under the code is National Recovery Administration, Division of Research and Planning, "History of the Code of Fair Competition for the Lumber and Timber Products Industries" (typewritten, not dated). Useful in following the course of developments under code administration are the *Lumber Code Authority Bulletins,* in two volumes, published at Washington during the life of the code authority throughout 1933 to 1935. Another statement by one of the code administrators is David T. Mason, *The Lumber Code,* Yale University, School of Forestry, Lumber Industry Series XI (New Haven, 1935). Two good articles are Franklin Reed, "The National Lumber Code," *Journal of Forestry,* XXXI, No. 10 (October, 1933), and C. W. Bahr, "A Brief Survey of the Provisions of the Lumber and Timber Products Code," *Journal of Forestry,* XXXIII, No. 3 (March, 1935).

The Southern Pine Association published a guide to code administration which gives an insight into certain features of code administration in the southern section of the lumber industry, *Administration of the Lumber Code in the Southern Pine Division* (New Orleans: Southern Pine Association, 1934). Two other articles worthy of note are: John B. Woods, "The Lumber Code Situation," *Journal of*

Forestry, XXXIII, No. 6 (June, 1935), and Constant Southworth, "Planning in the Lumber Industry," *Plan Age,* I, No. 5 (May, 1935).

For the period since World War I, information is available from several different types of sources. The *Four L Lumber News* and the *Semi-Annual Reports for the 4L Board of Directors* are indispensable for the labor problems of the late twenties and early thirties. For the "New Deal" era, local newspapers in the West are rich in information. Particularly useful are the Portland *Oregonian,* Portland *News-Telegram,* Seattle *Post-Intelligencer,* Seattle *Star,* Tacoma *Times,* Tacoma *News,* and Everett *News.* Two periodicals which present the employer point of view are *Crow's Pacific Coast Lumber Digest,* and the *Oregon Voter,* both published in Portland, Ore. A number of local and regional labor papers also contain news about the lumber industry. They include the *Oregon Labor Press,* the Seattle *Union Record,* and the *Washington State Labor News.* Since 1935, the *Oregon State Federation of Labor Yearbook* has given an occasional brief accounting of the year's developments in the lumber industry. From 1934 to 1936, a left-wing weekly newspaper, the *Voice of Action,* published in Seattle, Wash., contained running accounts, and its own interpretations, of organizing activities.

After the establishment of unions following the strike of 1935, the *Timberworker* was published at Aberdeen, Wash., first by the Aberdeen local and then by the Grays Harbor District Council, until August, 1937, when it was taken over by the International Woodworkers of America. The *Timberworker* has been a continuous source of information since its inception, but it must be read with caution because of elements of bias. A second union weekly newspaper, the *Union Register,* was established by the Carpenter International sympathizers, following the formal split in the ranks of the Sawmill and Timber Workers Unions. During 1941, a third paper, the *Woodworker,* was established by the "opposition bloc" within the I.W.A. in order to counter the propaganda of the *Timberworker.* When the breach in the I.W.A. was healed early in 1942, the *Timberworker* and *Woodworker* were merged into the *International Woodworker.* Another labor newspaper, the Duluth *Timber Worker,* succeeded by *Midwest Labor,* published in Duluth, Minn., contains a running account of events in the lumber industry of the Lake States region.

The most complete coverage of the 1935 strike and the events which followed through the first year of the fight between the A.F. of L. and C.I.O. unions is found in the author's study cited above. An interesting, but extremely biased, account of the 1935 strike is the article by N. Sparks, "The Northwest General Lumber Strike," *Communist*, XIV (September, 1935). A solid and authoritative account of the development of timberworker unions among the workers on Vancouver Island, Canada, is L. T. Smythe, "Organization of Timberworkers on Vancouver Island," unpublished Master's Thesis, University of Washington, Seattle, Wash., 1937.

The records of the various union groups in the industry also contain a wealth of information written from different viewpoints. The *Minutes of the Board of Directors of the Industrial Employees Union, Inc.*, the successor to the 4L, offers one interpretation. The convention proceedings of the Federation of Woodworkers are particularly rich in information about the split with the Carpenter's International: *Proceedings of the Second Semi-Annual Convention of the Federation of Woodworkers, February 20 to 22, 1937*, and *Convention Proceedings of the Woodworkers Federation, July 15 to 25, 1937*. Internal union problems of the International Woodworkers of America are contained in the proceedings of the annual conventions of the I.W.A.: *Proceedings of the First (Second, Third, Fourth, and Fifth) Constitutional Convention of the International Woodworkers of America, 1937 (1938, 1939, 1940, 1941)*. Internal problems and the struggle with the I.W.A. can be followed in the minutes and proceedings of the conventions of the Oregon-Washington Council of Lumber and Sawmill Workers conventions: *Minutes of the Oregon-Washington Council of Lumber and Sawmill Workers Convention, 1937*, and *Proceedings of the Second (Third, Fourth, and Fifth) Annual Convention of the Oregon-Washington Council, 1938 (1939, 1940, 1941)*. The convention at Lakeland, Fla., in 1936, looms large among events leading to the break with the Carpenters. A lively description of the treatment of the timber worker delegates is found in the article by Edward Levinson, "Bill Hutcheson's Convention," *The Nation*, CXLIV, No. 1 (January 2, 1937). The *Report of Proceedings of the American Federation of Labor Convention, 1937*, contains pertinent material on the circumstances of the split with the Carpenters and the formation with the I.W.A.

One of the richest, authoritative sources of information covering labor relations in the lumber industry is found in the National Labor Relations Board, *Decisions and Orders*, printed currently since 1936. In addition, the News Releases of the National Labor Relations Board are useful. Since the outbreak of war, the decisions and rulings of the War Labor Board have recorded valuable information. Most of these are found in *War Labor Reports,* published by the Bureau of National Affairs, Inc., Washington, D.C.

The most significant employers' organization is the Lumbermen's Industrial Relations Committee, Inc., who has published industry *Letters* and *Bulletins* from time to time. The Columbia Basin *Loggers* and Columbia Basin Sawmills have issued mimeographed summaries of lumber industry labor events in the *Labor News Digest.* A valuable source of information about the progress of collective bargaining negotiations has been established in the verbatim reports of the Lumbermen's Industrial Relations Committee, Inc., of the various negotiations, such as, *Report(s) of Two District Negotiations on a Proposed Standard Form of Working Agreement,* July 10 to September 18, 1940, *Report(s) of Negotiations on the Temporary Adjustment of Wage Clause in the I.W.A. Standard Form of Working Agreement,* December 5 and 10, 1941, and *Report(s) of Negotiations on Reopening of the I.W.A. Standard Form of Working Agreement,* March to May, 1941.

INDEX

Accidents, *see* Injuries
Agencies, employment, 41, 109-110; government, 273
American Civil Liberties Union, 179
American Federation of Labor, 88, 89, 133; internal conflicts, 225-243; leadership challenged, 204-205
American Lumberman, 127
Anderson, Bill, 231, 232
Antitrust laws, effect on industry, 152-153
Appalachian lumber region, extent of, 9
Ashmore, Joseph, 199
Associations, *see* Trade associations

Baker, Newton D., 129
Ballads, 55-56
Ballord, Dean, 279
Barnett, E., 143
Beckman, Victor, 115
Benedict, Ed., 269
Bernard, J. T., 199
Bickford, Frank, 142
Bingham, William, 34
Bjorklund, Jack, 175
Blacksmiths, work of, 56
"Boom man," work of, 14
Borah, Senator, 127, 128
Brands, registered, 34-35
Bridges, Harry, 207, 234, 235
Brophy, John, 206, 207, 265
Brotherhood of Timber Workers, 87-91
Brundage, F. H., 277
"Bucker," work of, 12
Buxton, S. B., 90

Callender, Frank, 175
Carpenters, work of, 56
Census reports, labor supply, Great Lakes region, 50-51; lumber products establishments, 16; monthly earnings, Southern Pine region, 81; wages, Northeastern region, 40
Central Hardwood lumber region, extent of, 9

Centralia massacre, 137-145
Child labor, 51
Chippewa Valley Workingmen's Association, 59
Chisholm, A. D., 209
Clark, Joe, 232
Climatic factors, Northeastern region, 35-36
Code for lumber industry, NIRA, 153-161; enforcement, 155-157; failure of, 158; formulation, 153-154; operators' reactions to, 157; price-fixing provisions, 157-158; provisions, 154-155; strikes under, 159-160; violations, 156-157
Coleman, Norman, 106, 137
Coll, E. P., 143
Collective bargaining, immaturity of, 187-189
Columbia Basin Loggers Association, 188
Committee for Industrial Organization, 204; formation, 205; independence established, 206; internal conflicts, 225-243
Communism, 232-242
"Company store," 38; Southern Pine region, 79-80
Company town, Southern Pine region, 78-80
Competition within lumber industry, 26-27; control, 153
Concentration, lumber industry, 17-18
Connell, J. W., 171
Cooks, authority, 55
Crews, size, Northeastern region, 38
Crow, C. C., 168
Curran, Mike, 265
"Cutter," work of, 12

Dacus, Sol, 92
Dalrymple, 5, 242
Dalrymple, William, 234
Davis, Kenny, 208
Deckert, K., 239

Depletion, Great Lakes region, 63-65; Southern Pine region, 73, 85
Depression, 151-161
Deskins, John, 232
Disque, Bryce P., 129-137
Doktor, Ted, 231, 232
Donkey engine, introduction, 47
Donnels, W. L., 93
Douglas fir region, employer-union relations, 246-268; extent of, 9
Duffy, Frank, 206
Duluth *News Tribune,* 200
Dykstra, C. A., 261, 263, 264, 266

Economic factors effecting lumber industry, 25-31
Eight-hour day, 126-132
Eliel, Paul, 267
Emerson, A. L., 90
Employers, opposition to unionism, 4, 5, 6, 118; trade associations, *see* Trade associations; union relations, 246-271
Employers Association of Washington, 116
Employment, agencies, *see* Agencies, employment; Great Lakes region, 49-50; intermittent, 30; maximum hours, NIRA code, 154; "off-season," 36; part time, 77-78; regional, 9-11; Southern Pine region, 75
Erie Canal, 45
Evans, Harold, 269

Fadling, James, 232, 269, 270
Fair Labor Standards Act, 194-196
"Fallers," work of, 12
"Family" operators, 65-66
Federal Emergency Relief Administration, 165-166
Federal Mediation Board, 181, 183, 184
Federation of Woodworkers, 204, 207, 210
Feinsinger, N. P., 278
Fitzgerald, J. B., 220
Food, camp, 38, 54-55
Foreign-born labor, Great Lakes region, 50-51; West lumber region, 104-105
Francis, Richard, 234
Frankfurter, Felix, 128
Free speech struggle, 120, 122-123

Galloway, M. M., 90
Geographic factors effecting lumber industry, 24-25
Germer, Adolph, 236, 237, 238, 239, 240, 242, 268
Gompers, Samuel, 130
Government agencies, 273

Grading lumber, standards, 115
Gram, C. H., 171
Gram, C. R., 188
"Gram-Marsh Agreement," 189
Great Lakes lumber region, 45-67; depletion, 63-65; development, 45; employment in, 10-11, 49-50; extent of, 8; food, 54-55; forest land acquisition, 28; labor supply, 50-51; living conditions, 51-55; logging operations, types, 65-67; martial status, 51; mechanization, 46-47; migration of industry, 21, 48; mill size variations, 15; ownership, 47-48; production, 48; seasonal activity, 49; speculation, 48; strikes, 58-61; unions, 59-61; wages, 56-58; war problems, 282-283
Green, B. A., 176
Green, William, 174, 180
Griggs, E. C., 115, 175
Grimm, W. O., 142
Guerts, William, 279

Hall, Bert, 171
Hall, Edgar, 164
Hall, E. S., 174
Haney, Homer, 208
Hanna, Mark, 119
Harris, Gerald, 191
Hartung, Al., 208, 248, 268
"Haywire" operators, 65, 66-67
Haywood, Allen, 236, 268, 269
Haywood, Bill, 89
Health conditions, 53-54
Hegge, E. M., 175
Helmick, Don, 208, 233
Hemlock peeling, 36
Hershey, Lewis B., 278
Hope, Charles, 165, 189, 215
Hope-Thompson agreement, 248
Hospitalization, 84
Hours of work, NIRA code, 154; Northeastern region, 40-41; Southern Pine region, 83
Housing, *see* Living conditions
Howard, Charles, 212
Howard, Pendleton, 275
Hubbard, F. B., 138
Hutcheson, William, 91, 174, 207, 209, 214

Individualism of lumber industry, 18, 24
Industrial Employees Union, 209; internal conflicts, 227-228
Industrial Workers of the World, attitudes toward, 6-7; Southern Pine region, 87-

94; West Coast lumber region, 108, 114-115, 119-129, 135, 137-145

Injuries, frequency, 36; Southern Pine region, 83-84; West lumber region, 110-111

Inmon, W. E., 144

International Brotherhood of Woodsmen and Sawmill Workers, 119

International Brotherhood of Teamsters, Chauffeurs, Stablemen and Helpers of America, 216

International Shingle Weavers Union of America, 114, 117

International Timber Workers Union, 91

International Union of Sawmill and Timber Workers, 122, 145-146

International Union of Shingle Weavers, Sawmill Workers and Woodsmen, 122

International Union of Timber Workers, 114, 125, 135

International Woodworkers of America, birth of, 212-222; internal conflicts, 225-243, 268-271

Involuntary servitude, 84-85

Jackson, E. S., 260, 261

James, Sidney, 175

Jensen, Vernon H., 275, 284-285

Johnson, Hugh S., 154

Johnson, P. V., 144

Jones, M. H., 220

Keezer Commission, 267-268, 270

Keezer, Dexter, 256, 259, 267, 268

Kelly, Pat, 177

Kerwin, H. L., 167

Kimsey, W. E., 172

Kirby, John H., 87-88

Kizer, Ben H., 279

Knights of Labor, Great Lakes region, 61, 62, 63; Southern Pine region, 86-87

Koivunen, Ilmar, 263, 269

Labor, child, 51; disputes, see Strikes; foreign-born workers, Northeastern region, 39; hours worked, see Hours of work; sawmill workers, Northeastern region, 39; soldier, 131; strikes, see Strikes

Labor relations, history of, 4; Southern Pine region, 85-86; West Coast lumber industry, 114-147

Labor supply, Great Lakes region, 50; Northeastern region, 38-39; Southern Pine region, 76; Western lumber region, 104-105

Lake State region, see Great Lakes lumber region

Lamb, J., 143

Land speculation, see Speculation in forest land

Landye, James, 279

Lange, Norman, 164, 170

"Larger" operators, 65, 67

Larson, Karly, 264

Lassiter, Tom, 138

Law, Dick, 231, 232, 242

Legislation, antitrust laws, 152-153; employment agencies, regulation, 109-110; employment contract enforcement, 41; federal wage and hour, 5, 194-196; need for, 6; payment of wages, 58; personal injuries, liability limited, 116; ten-hour day, Michigan, 61-63; vagrancy laws, abuse, 85; workmen's compensation laws, see Workmen's compensation laws

Lewis, J. C., 242

Lewis, John L., 205, 206, 212, 236, 237, 241, 242, 284

Living conditions, Great Lakes region, 51-55; Northeastern region, 36-37; Southern Pine region, 78-81; Western lumber region, 106-107

Living standards, 5

Log drive, companies, 34; Great Lakes region, 45-46; Northeastern region, 33, 34, 36

Logging, Great Lakes region, 48-49; types of operations, 65-67; mechanical aids, 47; nature of, 11-13; essential operation, 12-13; primary activity of industry, 7; seasonal aspect, 12, 35; seasonal classification, NIRA code, 155; specialization, 13; techniques, 13

Lowery, Worth, 236, 240, 243, 269, 270

Loyal Legion of Loggers and Lumbermen, 129-137, 161, 175, 187, 227

Lumber Code Authority, 154, 155, 156

Lumber industry, changing conditional forces, 23-24; characteristics of, 7-18; code for, NIRA, 153-161; competition in, 26-27; concentration, 17-18; control, 17; depression and, 151-161; economic factors effecting, 25-31; employment by regions, 9-11; extent of, 7; geographic factors effecting, 24-25; individualism, 18, 24; manpower problem, 277-278; migratory nature, 1, 20-22; nature of, 3; ownership, 18; production by regions, 10; regions of, 8-11, employment by, 9-11, importance, 9; variations in

mill sizes, 15-16; war effect on, 16-17, 273-291; West region, 101-102
Lumber Trade Journal, 89-90
Lumber Workers Industrial Union, 135-136
Lumberjacks, changing conditioning forces, 23-24; characteristics of, 4, 22-23; Great Lakes region, 50-51; intermittent employment, 30; life of, 3; migratory nature, 21-22; nature of work, 23; unionism reappearance among, 189-191
Lumbermen's Protective League, 117, 125, 131
Lumm, Fred, 164

Maine, first lumbering state, 33
Management, forest land, effect on industry, 27-29
Manpower problem, 277-278
Market, waning nature of, 25
Marsh, E. P., 123, 128, 188, 251
Marsh, E. S., 167-168, 170, 177
Martial status, Great Lakes region, 51; Southern Pine region, 77; West lumber region, 106
Mason, N. E., 269
McCarty, Bertel, 268, 269
McNaughton, E. B., 279
McNutt, Paul V., 278
Mechanical equipment, changes brought about by, 23-24; employed in logging, 13; Great Lakes region, 46-47; sawmilling, 13-14; Southern Pine region, 74-75; West region, 102
Medical care, Southern Pine region, 84; West lumber region, 110-111
"Michigan-I-O," 56
Michigan ten-hour law, 61-63
Migratory nature of lumber industry, 1, 20-22; Great Lakes region, 48, 63; Northeastern region, 33; West region, 99-100
Mills, *see* Sawmills
Monopolistic control of forests, lack of, Northeastern region, 34-35
Morgan, A. L., 280
Morse, Wayne, 267, 278, 281-282, 284
Muir, A. W., 164, 166-167, 169, 171, 172, 173, 174, 183
Murray, Philip, 242, 263, 264, 265, 267

National Defense Mediation Board, 261-267, 275
National Industrial Recovery Act, 153-161; constitutionality upheld, 209; effect on organization in South, 190-191, 194-195; invalidation, 172-173
National Labor Relations Board, 165, 166, 192, 193, 194, 215, 216, 221, 226, 227, 228
National Lumber Manufacturers Association, 27, 153
National Union of Forest and Lumber Workers, 121
National War Labor Board, 275-282
Negroes, employment of, 4, 76-77, 89
Nelson, Donald, 276, 278, 280
Northeastern lumber region, 33-42; camp facilities, 36-38; climatic factors, 35-36; crew sizes, 38; employment in, 9-10, 11; extent of, 8; hours, 40-41; labor disputes, 41-42; labor supply, 38-39; lumbering activities, 33-34; migration from, 33; mill size variations, 15; ownership, 34-35; sawmills, 39; speculation, 34; wages, 39-40

O'Brien, Ed., 93
Operators, logging, types of, Great Lakes region, 65-67; *see also* Employers
Oregon Emergency Relief Administration, 168
Organizations, *see* Unions
Orton, O. M., 240, 263-265, 268
Osborne, Ben, 171
Overproduction, problem of, 29
Ownership, lumber industry, 18; effect on industry, 27-29; Great Lakes region, 47-48; Northeastern region, 35; West lumber region, 100-101

Pacific Lumber Manufacturers Association, 115-116
Panama Canal, 100
Parish, Madeline, 189
Part-time work, 77-78
Paternalism of "Old South," 77-79
Paull, Henry, 198-199
Payment of wages, methods, Great Lakes region, 58; Southern Pine region, 80; West lumber region, 109
Peonage, 84-85
Peoples, Ralph, 240
Perkins, Frances, 179-180, 254
Plummer, O. M., 172
Pritchett, Harold, 204, 226, 233, 234, 235, 236
Production, regional, 9-10
Puget Sound Timberman's Association, 115

Rafting, Northeastern region, 34
Raik, Luke, 199
Railroad transportation, Great Lakes region, 35; Northeastern region, 13; Southern Pine region, 71; West region, 100
Ransom, F. H., 180
Recreation, 107
Regions of lumber industry, 8-11; competition between, 26; employment, 9-11; importance, 9; production by, 10
Relief problem, Great Lakes region, 67
"Road monkeys," work of, 56
Robinson, David, 218
Robinson, Reid, 242
Rocky Mountain lumber region, extent of, 9
Rogers, James, 199
Ronkainen, Frank, 190
Royal Loggers, 119
Ruegnitz, W. C., 151, 209
Russell, G. F., 138
Ryan, C. M., 172

St. John, Vincent, 120
Sanitation, logging camp, 53
Sawmills, concentration, 17-18; efficiency, 17; foreign-born workers, Northeastern region, 39; hours worked, Northeastern region, 41; location, 13; Negro labor in, 76-77; Northeastern region, 39; number, 16, Great Lakes region, 49; West lumber region, 103; mechanization, 13-14, Southern Pine region, 74-75; overdevelopment, 29; primary activity of industry, 7; processes, 14-15; Southern Pine region, 73-74; variations in size, 15-16; effect of war on, 16-17; wages, Great Lakes region, 57, Northeastern region, 40; West lumber region, 102-103; workers, 4
Sawyers and Filers Union, 91, 92
Scalers, work of, 56
Scales, William, 138
Script payment of wages, 80
Seasonal activity, Great Lakes region, 49; Southern Pine region, 75; West region, 103-104
Seattle *Union Record,* 138, 140
Sever, Frank, 176
Simpson, G., 260
Sleeman, B. W., 188
Smith, A. E., 201
Smith, Roscoe R., 180
"Snoqualmie Falls Settlement," 261
Social life, 107

Soldier labor, 131
Southern Homestead Act of 1866, 72
Southern Lumber Operators Association, 86, 87-89, 191, 192
Southern Pine Association, 81, 85, 86
Southern Pine lumber region, 71-94; accidents, 83-84; company stores, 79-80; depletion, 73, 85; development, 71, 72-73; employment in, 10-11, 75; extent of, 8; forest land acquisition, 28; hours worked, 83; housing, 80-81; labor relations, 85-86; labor supply, 76; living conditions, 78-81; logging in, 12; martial status, 77; mechanization, 74-75; medical care, 84; migration of industry, 21; mill size variations, 15; part-time work, 77-78; peonage, 84-85; sawmills, 73-74; seasonal aspect of work, 75; speculation, 71-72; strikes, 87-94; trade associations, 86; unions, 86-94; vagrancy laws, abuse, 85; wages, 81-83; war effect on, 16-17, 283-284
Southwest Washington Manufacturers Association, 115
Spangler, J. L., 128
Speculation, in forest land, 28-29; Great Lakes region, 48; Northeastern region, 34; Southern Pine region, 71-72; West region, 99
Spruce Production Corporation, 108
Stanioch, John, 208
Steam power, application, 46
Strikes, Great Lakes region, 58-61; great strike of 1935, 164-185; new period of unionism, 187-202; "riots of 1872" at Williamsport, 41-42; Southern Pine region, 87-94; West lumber region, 118-147
Sullivan, W. H., 91, 92

Tacoma *Times,* 178
Thompson, Father George F., 180, 189
Thoreau, 36
Timber Producers Association, 200
Timberworker, 232, 234, 240, 241, 267, 269
Trade associations, 26, 30, 86; *see also* under name of association
Trautmann, W. E., 120
Trucks and tractors, 102
Tucker, Harry, 230, 232

U. S. Conciliation Service, 260, 267
Unemployment, increase in, 151
Union Register, 210

Unions, conflict over leadership, 203; development of, 5; early organization attempts, 41-42; employer relations, 246-271; Great Lakes region, 59-61; immaturity of collective bargaining, 187-189; internal conflicts, 225-243; jurisdictional disputes, 225-243; opposition to, 4, 5, 6, 30, 87-94; period of new unionism, 187-202; reappearance among lumberjacks, 189-191; Southern Pine region, 86-94; stimulated by NIRA code provisions, 159; weakness of, 30; West Coast lumber region, 117-147; see also under name of union
United Brotherhood of Carpenters and Joiners of America, 91, 164, 187
United Mine Workers of America, 284
United Woodworkers Local Industrial Union, 228

Vagrancy laws, abuse, 85

Wage and hour legislation, 5, 67, 194-196
Wages, 30; cuts in, 152; employer-union relations, 247-268; Great Lakes region, 56-58; NIRA code provisions, 155; Northeastern region, 39-40; payment, Great Lakes region, 58, West lumber region, 109; Southern Pine region, 80-83; West lumber region, 108-109
Walker, J. H., 128
Walsh, J. H., 120
"Wangin," 38, 53, 56
War, effect on lumbering, 16-17; lumber industry in, 273-291
War Department, Loyal Legion of Loggers and Lumbermen, 129-137; Spruce Production Corporation, 108
Washington State Federation of Labor, 133

Wedel, W. F., 176
Wenig, Frank E., 201
West Coast Lumbermen's Association, 116, 133, 154, 166, 168
West Coast Lumber Commission, 279-282
West lumber region, 99-111; accidents, 110-111; development, 99; employment in, 11; extent of, 8-9; forest land acquisition, 28; labor relations, 114-147; labor supply, 104-105; living conditions, 106-107; logging, 12; martial status, 106; mechanization, 102; medical care, 110-111; migration, 21, 99-100; mill size variations, 15-16; organizations, early, 114-147; ownership, 100-101; seasonal activity, 103-104; speculation, 99; transportation, 100; wages, 108-109; war effect on, 16-17, 284-288
Western Operators Association, 109
Western Pine Association, 154
White, G. A., 171
Widman, Michael, 236
Wieland, E. E., 122
Williams, Lum, 92-93
Williams, R. D., 239
Wilson, W. B., 128
Wilson, Woodrow, 128
Winn, Carl, 269, 270
Wood-processing industry, 7-8
Wood-using industry, 7-8; development, Great Lakes region, 64
Workmen's compensation laws, 67; Southern Pine region, 83-84; West lumber region, 111
World War II, lumber industry in, 273-291

Yellow Pine Manufacturers Association, 86
Young, C. C., 180

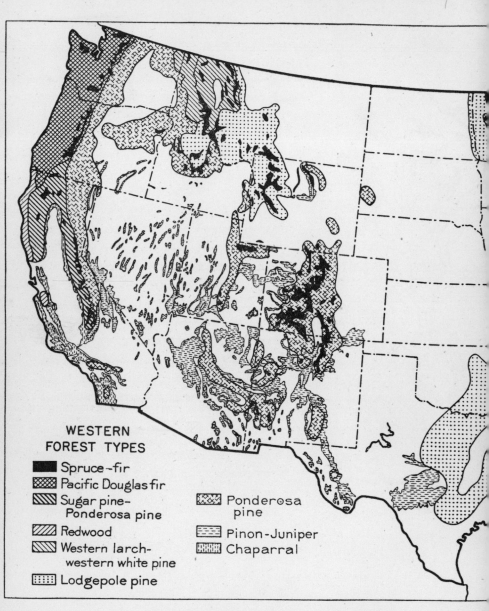

WESTERN
FOREST TYPES

- ■ Spruce-fir
- ▨ Pacific Douglas fir
- ▨ Sugar pine-
  Ponderosa pine
- ▨ Redwood
- ▨ Western larch-
  western white pine
- ▦ Lodgepole pine

- ▨ Ponderosa
  pine
- ▤ Pinon-Juniper
- ▥ Chaparral

PRINCIPAL FOREST TYPE